COMBINED SECOND EDITION

Guided Comprehension
in Grades 3–8

MAUREEN MCLAUGHLIN
MARY BETH ALLEN

INTERNATIONAL
Reading Association
800 BARKSDALE ROAD, PO BOX 8139
NEWARK, DE 19714-8139, USA
www.reading.org

The International Reading Association attempts, through its publications, to provide a forum for a wide spectrum of opinions on reading. This policy permits divergent viewpoints without implying the endorsement of the Association.

Executive Editor, Books   Corinne M. Mooney
Developmental Editor   Charlene M. Nichols
Developmental Editor   Tori Mello Bachman
Developmental Editor   Stacey L. Reid
Editorial Production Manager   Shannon T. Fortner
Design and Composition Manager   Anette Schuetz

Project Editor   Matthew W. Baker

Art   Cover Design: Linda Steere; Cover Photography (from top): Maureen McLaughlin, Sarah Rusnock, Maureen McLaughlin; Interior Photography: Sarah O'Neill (page 1), Maureen McLaughlin (page 75), Alexandria Gibb (page 183)

The publisher would appreciate notification where errors occur so that they may be corrected in subsequent printings and/or editions.

Library of Congress Cataloging-in-Publication Data
McLaughlin, Maureen.
  Guided comprehension in grades 3-8 / Maureen McLaughlin, Mary Beth Allen. -- Combined 2nd ed.
    p. cm.
Includes bibliographical references and index.
  ISBN 978-0-87207-712-6
1. Reading comprehension--Study and teaching (Elementary)--United States. 2. Reading (Elementary)--United States. I. Allen, Mary Beth. II. Title.
  LB1573.7.M375 2009
  372.47--dc22
                                                                                      2009011726

For Matt　　　—MM

For Hannah, Esther, Ruthie, Matthew, and Nicholas　　　—MBA

CONTENTS

Maureen McLaughlin is a professor of reading education at East Stroudsburg University of Pennsylvania in East Stroudsburg, Pennsylvania, USA. She earned her doctorate at Boston University in reading and language development. Prior to her tenure at the university, Maureen spent 15 years as a classroom teacher, reading specialist, and department chair in a public school system.

A member of the Board of Directors of the International Reading Association from 2005–2008, Maureen is the author of numerous publications about the teaching of reading, reading comprehension, and content area literacies. She is the coauthor of *Guided Comprehension: A Teaching Model for Grades 3–8* and *Guided Comprehension in Action: Lessons for Grades 3–8*, and the author of *Guided Comprehension in the Primary Grades*. Her latest book is *Content Area Reading: Teaching and Learning in an Age of Multiple Literacies* (Allyn & Bacon, 2010). A frequent speaker at international, national, and state conferences, Maureen is a consultant to school districts and universities throughout North America.

Mary Beth Allen is a professor of reading education at East Stroudsburg University of Pennsylvania in East Stroudsburg, Pennsylvania, USA. Prior to that, she worked for 18 years in the Baltimore (Maryland) County Public Schools as a classroom teacher, resource teacher, and reading specialist. She consults with school districts supporting teachers as they refine their literacy instruction, specifically in using small groups for guided reading and comprehension, implementing literacy centers, and teaching comprehension strategies.

Mary Beth is the coauthor of two books published by the International Reading Association: *Guided Comprehension: A Teaching Model for Grades 3–8* and *Guided Comprehension in Action: Lessons for Grades 3–8*. She has also created two videos with the Bureau of Education and Research: *Current, Best Strategies for Teaching Reading Comprehension, Grades K–2* and *Strengthening Students' Reading Comprehension, Grades 3–6*.

It doesn't seem long ago that we were writing the Preface to the first Guided Comprehension book. Now we are welcoming you to the second edition—*Guided Comprehension in Grades 3–8*—a book that combines new versions of *Guided Comprehension: A Teaching Model for Grades 3–8* and *Guided Comprehension in Action: Lessons for Grades 3–8* into one comprehensive teaching resource. Writing the second edition has provided us with opportunities to update the research base, integrate 16 new Guided Comprehension lessons, share ideas for differentiating instruction, present all new theme resources, and include new examples of student work. We also revised the appendixes. For example, we have integrated teaching ideas from both books, provided all new teaching examples, updated the forms for organizing and managing centers and routines, and extended the list of literature response prompts to a total of 101.

While we have been busy revising, we have continued to focus on our ultimate goal: helping students become good readers—readers who actively engage with text and naturally use a repertoire of strategies to facilitate the construction of meaning. We know from a variety of research studies that comprehension strategies and the skills that underpin them can be taught. We also know that Guided Comprehension, a context in which students learn comprehension skills and strategies in a variety of settings, has emerged as a successful teaching framework. The Model fosters students' transactions with text by integrating explicit and guided instruction of comprehension strategies; multiple levels and types of text; and varied, scaffolded opportunities for strategy application.

Guided Comprehension is based on the idea that reading is a social-constructivist process. Underpinned by current research and beliefs about best practice, the Model provides a detailed, research-based, classroom-tested process for teaching reading from a comprehension-based perspective. When we use the Model, we teach students to become active, strategic readers by providing explicit strategy instruction, numerous opportunities for engagement, and a variety of texts and instructional settings.

This new edition is divided into two parts. Part One features a detailed description of the Guided Comprehension Model for grades 3–8, including its research base, multiple stages, assessment connections, and use of leveled texts. Sixteen theme-based Guided Comprehension lessons are presented in Part Two. The lessons, which focus on four themes, also include student examples, assessment possibilities, and ideas for differentiating instruction. Resources that underpin the Guided Comprehension Model and facilitate its use are featured in the appendixes.

In Chapter 1 we begin by introducing Guided Comprehension, a context in which students and teachers engage in reading as a strategy-based thinking process. Then we explain the Guided Comprehension Model and the research-based tenets that underpin it.

Chapters 2, 3, and 4 focus on the stages of the Model. In Chapter 2, we describe teacher-directed whole-group instruction. Practicing comprehension strategies is the focus of Chapter 3, in which we discuss the small-group instructional settings, including teacher-guided small groups and student-facilitated comprehension centers and routines. We delineate the final stage of the Model, whole-group reflection and goal setting, in Chapter 4. Throughout these chapters we also make a variety of connections to related information in Appendixes A, B, and C.

In Chapter 5 we discuss the multiple roles of assessment in the Guided Comprehension process. We describe a variety of practical, informative assessments that offer insights into students' thinking and performance. We also make connections to various reproducible assessment forms that are included in Appendix D.

In Chapter 6, we discuss the role of text selection in Guided Comprehension. We also examine the reader and text factors that influence accessibility, and we make connections to Appendix E, which includes leveled book resources.

In Part Two, which includes Chapters 7–10, we present Guided Comprehension lessons focused on four themes:

- Life Stories: Biography, Autobiography
- Identity: Who Are You?
- Poetry: Extraordinary Wonder
- Fantasy: Unbridled Imagination

Each theme includes the following elements:

- Theme description
- Theme-based plan for Guided Comprehension
- Four new Guided Comprehension lessons
- Planning forms
- Teacher commentaries and Think-Alouds
- Samples of student work
- Ideas for differentiating instruction
- Theme-based resources including related texts, websites, performance extensions across the curriculum, and culminating activities

New samples of student work are featured throughout the chapters and in Appendix A, which provides strategy descriptions and graphic organizers. Appendixes B, C, D, E, and F contain forms to facilitate classroom management, prompts to promote literature response, assessment materials, leveled text resources, and Guided Comprehension lesson planning forms.

Because we both have extensive experience in the classroom, we have designed this combined second edition to be a teacher-friendly comprehensive resource. Whether you are a classroom teacher, staff developer, reading specialist, or teacher educator, this is a book that will remain on your desktop and emerge dog-eared and well-used over the years. It contains everything you need to teach Guided Comprehension, from detailed explanations of the stages of the Model and 16 new Guided Comprehension lessons to newly revised resource-filled appendixes.

Acknowledgments

As always, there are many people to thank for making this book possible. We express our appreciation to them now for their insight, their understanding, and their support.

We are particularly grateful to the following people:

- Stephanie Romano
- Alexandria Gibb
- Lisa Jaferis
- Christine Godiska
- Jennifer Reuter
- Christine Newhard
- Mary Ellen Rock
- David Bishop
- Victoria Principe
- Shannon Foschetti
- Our families, colleagues, and friends
- Shannon Fortner, IRA Editorial Production Manager, for her extraordinary knowledge of the publication process
- Matt Baker, Project Manager, for his unparalleled editorial expertise

Finally, we again thank you, our readers, for joining us in our search for greater understanding of reading comprehension. We hope you find this second edition to be a valuable teaching resource, one that you and your colleagues will use to further our common goal of helping students understand what they read.

—MM and MBA

PART ONE

Guided Comprehension: A Teaching Model for Grades 3–8

Guided Comprehension: In Chapter 1, Guided Comprehension, a context in which students and teachers engage in reading as a strategy-based thinking process, is introduced. Then the Guided Comprehension Model is explained, and 10 research-based tenets that support the Model's emergence from research and best practice are presented. Guided Comprehension connections to the tenets are also featured.

Whole-Group Instruction and Comprehension Routines: Chapter 2 focuses on teacher-directed whole-group instruction, including the five-step process for explicit teaching. This is followed by the presentation of comprehension strategies and related teaching ideas. Comprehension routines including Literature Circles, Reciprocal Teaching, and Questioning the Author are also introduced in this chapter.

Teacher-Guided Small Groups and Centers: In Chapter 3, teacher-guided small groups, including the four steps of guided instruction, are featured. Student-facilitated independent practice is explained. A wide variety of ideas for creating centers and related activities are described, and student writing samples are included. Organizing and managing comprehension centers are special emphases in this chapter.

Reflection and Goal Setting: Engaging students in reflection, sharing, and goal setting is the focus of Chapter 4. Practical guides for facilitating these processes are also presented.

Assessments: In Chapter 5, the multiple roles of assessment in Guided Comprehension are discussed, connections are made to state assessments, and a variety of practical measures are described. Guided Comprehension connections are provided for each assessment. Then the Guided Comprehension Profile, an organizational framework for documenting student progress, is introduced.

Leveled Texts: The various roles of leveled text in Guided Comprehension are introduced in Chapter 6. Factors that influence accessibility, including reader and text factors, are discussed. Reader factors include student interest, background knowledge, and social identities. Text factors include type, structure, length, and content. This is followed by descriptions of elements essential for making student–text matches. Finally, methods of leveling and organizing classroom texts are delineated.

CHAPTER 1

Guided Comprehension: Helping Students Transact With Text

When Michael Pressley addressed the 2006 Reading Research Conference at the annual convention of the International Reading Association, his presentation was titled *What the Future of Reading Research Could Be*. Among the ideas he discussed was the importance of continuing to research the teaching of reading comprehension strategies. In a 2001 presentation, P. David Pearson called for similar studies. Noting that much of what we know about teaching reading comprehension strategies is not making its way to classroom teachers, Pearson espoused the need to "curricularize" reading comprehension strategy instruction—to make it part of every school's curriculum so all students will have access to strategy instruction. Today, even though we know that students benefit from using comprehension strategies, the instructional necessities are still not part of many teachers' repertoires.

As literacy professionals, our ultimate goal is to help our students comprehend to their maximum potentials. To accomplish this, we encourage students to expand their background knowledge, deepen their understanding of how language works, develop rich vocabularies, and construct personal meaning. We engage them in reading, writing, and discussion for a variety of purposes. We provide them with different types of text at a variety of levels and explicitly teach them a repertoire of comprehension strategies they can use as needed while reading.

We believe that students should be able to strategically think their way through reading. Durkin (1978/1979) defines reading as *comprehension*, indicating that the focus of reading instruction should be on the strategies readers use in order to make sense of text. Smith (2005) extends this idea by defining reading as a thinking process. These ideas about comprehension and cognition suggest that the focus of instruction should not be on the print but rather on how readers connect with the print. Hiebert, Pearson, Taylor, Richardson, and Paris (1998) endorse this idea, noting, "Teachers support their students' strategic reading through lessons that attend explicitly to how to think while reading" (p. 4).

Describing reading as a thinking process seems quite logical and natural if we examine readers' strategic interactions with text. To begin, students contemplate text selection and *make connections* between background knowledge and the text. They *preview* the text by activating background knowledge, making predictions about the content, and setting purposes for reading. Students *self-question, make connections, visualize, think about how words work, monitor, summarize,* and *evaluate* as they read. After reading, students may *make further connections, summarize* the text, and *evaluate* the author's message or intent, all the while engaging in cognitive processes. To be successful, strategic readers, students need to think. To effectively think through the reading process and transact with a variety of texts, students need to know and use a variety of comprehension strategies.

In this chapter, we begin by introducing Guided Comprehension, a context in which students and teachers engage in reading as a strategy-based thinking process. Next, we present the Guided Comprehension Model, a framework designed to help teachers and students engage in reading as a thinking process. Finally, we discuss the 10 tenets of reading comprehension and describe their connections to the Model.

What Is Guided Comprehension?

Guided Comprehension is a context in which students learn comprehension strategies in a variety of settings using multiple levels and types of text. It is a three-stage process focused on explicit instruction, application, and reflection. In Stage One, teachers explicitly instruct students in a whole-group setting using a five-step process. In Stage Two, students apply the strategies in three settings: teacher-guided small groups, student-facilitated comprehension centers, and student-facilitated comprehension routines. Students' placement in the small groups is dynamic and evolves as their reading abilities increase. Students also have access to a variety of leveled texts in the centers and routines. In Stage Three, teachers and students engage in reflection and goal setting.

The Guided Comprehension Model

The Guided Comprehension Model is a framework designed to help teachers and students think through reading as a strategy-based process. Designed for use in grades 3–8, the Model is based on what we have learned from existing research, knowledge of best practice, and personal experience. It integrates the following:

- Explicit instruction of comprehension strategies
- Leveled independent, instructional, and challenging texts
- Dynamic assessment
- Scaffolded instruction (varying levels of teacher support, with gradual release of responsibility to students)
- Various genres and text types
- Reading, writing, and discussion
- Strategy instruction and application in a variety of settings
- Guided practice, independent practice, and transfer of learning in multiple settings
- Reflection and goal setting

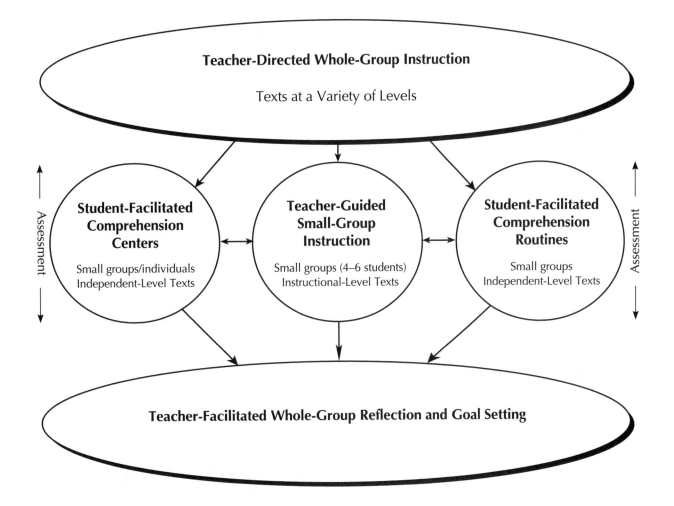

Structurally, the Model has three stages that progress in the following sequence:

Stage One: Teacher-directed whole-group instruction

Stage Two: Teacher-guided small-group instruction and student-facilitated independent practice

Stage Three: Teacher-facilitated whole-group reflection and goal setting

Naturally situated within the context of a balanced approach to literacy, the Guided Comprehension Model is active for both teachers and students. For example, in addition to planning lessons, teachers engage in explicit instruction and select texts and strategies based on student needs, which are frequently assessed. Teachers also participate by facilitating and scaffolding students' engagement in reading, writing, and discussion. Students' active roles in Guided Comprehension include thinking through the reading process, transacting with text in multiple settings, using strategies, and responding in a variety of ways.

The Guided Comprehension Model includes opportunities for whole-group, small-group, paired, and individual reading experiences. Students transact daily with texts at a variety of levels. Teachers direct whole-group instruction, explicitly teach strategies and skills, and work daily with Guided Comprehension small groups. Teachers also observe and assess students as they engage in their independent comprehension activities and encourage reflection and goal setting.

Figure 1. Overview of Guided Comprehension Instruction

STAGE ONE

Teacher-Directed Whole-Group Instruction—Teaching a comprehension strategy using easy, instructional, or challenging text.

Explain the current strategy and how it relates to the class goal.

Demonstrate the strategy using a Think-Aloud and a read-aloud.

Guide students by reading additional sections of text aloud and inviting students to work with partners to apply the strategy with support. Monitor students' applications.

Practice by encouraging students to apply the strategy to another section of text you have read, providing minimal support.

Reflect by inviting students to think about how they can use this strategy with texts they are reading on their own.

STAGE TWO

Students apply the comprehension strategies in teacher-guided small groups and student-facilitated comprehension centers and routines. In these settings, students work with varying levels of support and use appropriate instructional- and independent-level texts.

Teacher-Guided Small-Group Instruction—Applying comprehension strategies with teacher guidance using instructional-level texts and dynamic grouping (4 to 6 students).

Review previously taught strategies and focus on the current strategy. Introduce the text, provide an overview of the text structure, and focus on essential vocabulary.

Guide the students to apply the current strategy as well as previously taught strategies as they read a section of the instructional-level text. Prompt the students to construct personal meanings. Scaffold as necessary, gradually releasing support as students become more proficient. Encourage discussion and repeat with other sections of text.

Practice by encouraging students to continue reading and applying strategies. Ask students to record their thinking in their Guided Comprehension Journals or on graphic organizers.

Reflect by inviting students to share their strategy applications from Stage Two and think about ways in which the strategy helped them to understand the text. Talk about ways in which students can apply the strategy in the comprehension centers and routines.

Student-Facilitated Comprehension Centers and Routines—Applying comprehension strategies individually, in pairs, or in small groups with independent-level texts.

Comprehension centers are independent opportunities to practice strategy application and extend understandings.

Comprehension routines are procedures that foster habits of thinking that promote comprehension of text.

STAGE THREE

Teacher-Facilitated Whole-Group Reflection and Goal Setting—Reflecting on performance, sharing experiences, and setting new goals.

ASSESSMENT OPTIONS

Use authentic measures in all stages.

The Model progresses from explicit teaching to independent practice and transfer (see Figure 1). All stages of the Model are necessary to ensure that students can independently apply comprehension strategies in multiple settings. Assessment permeates every aspect of the Model, facilitating our gathering of information about student progress, which continually informs teaching and learning.

In the next section we describe Guided Comprehension's natural emergence from current research on best practice. To illustrate this, we discuss 10 research-based comprehension tenets and describe how they relate to the Model.

Tenets of Reading Comprehension

Studies have shown that multiple factors affect successful reading comprehension. The following research-based tenets delineate those we believe to be the most influential:

- Comprehension is a social constructivist process.
- Excellent reading teachers influence students' learning.
- Good readers are strategic and take active roles in the reading process.
- Reading should occur in meaningful contexts.
- Students benefit from transacting with a variety of texts at multiple levels.
- Vocabulary development and instruction affect reading comprehension.
- Engagement is a key factor in the comprehension process.
- Comprehension strategies and skills can be taught.
- Differentiated reading instruction accommodates students' needs, including those of English learners and struggling readers.
- Dynamic assessment informs comprehension instruction.

Although the tenets have strong research underpinnings, they are also designed to inform instruction. In the section that follows, we make connections between theory and practice.

Comprehension Is a Social Constructivist Process

To understand comprehension as a social constructivist process, we must first understand constructivism as a theory about knowledge and learning. From a constructivist perspective, learning is understood as "a self-regulated process of resolving inner cognitive conflicts that often become apparent through concrete experience, collaborative discourse, and reflection" (Brooks & Brooks, 1993, p. vii). Constructivists believe that students construct knowledge by linking what is new to what is already known. They construct meaning through these connections when educators pose relevant problems, structure learning around primary concepts, seek and value students' ideas, and assess student learning in context (Brooks & Brooks, 1993).

Cambourne (2002) suggests that instructional principles emerge from constructivist theory. They include the following:

- Creating a classroom culture that encourages deep engagement with effective reading
- Using strategies that are a blend of explicitness, systematicity, mindfulness, and contextualization

- Creating continuous opportunities to develop intellectual unrest
- Encouraging students to develop their conscious awareness of how text functions and how we create meaning
- Designing and using tasks that will support the authentic use of the processes and understandings implicit in reading behavior

Short and Burke (1996) note that constructivism frees students of fact-driven curricula and (1) encourages them to focus on larger ideas, (2) allows them to reach unique conclusions and reformulate ideas, (3) encourages them to see the world as a complex place with multiple perspectives, and (4) emphasizes that they are responsible for their own learning and should attempt to connect the information they learn to the world around them through inquiry.

Constructivism is manifested in classrooms that are characterized by student-generated ideas, self-selection, creativity, interaction, critical thinking, and personal construction of meaning (McLaughlin, 2000). In such contexts, authentic literacy tasks assimilate real-world experiences, provide a purpose for learning, and encourage students to take ownership of learning (Hiebert, 1994; Newmann & Wehlage, 1993).

In reading, constructivism is reflected in schema-based learning development, which purports that learning takes place when new information is integrated with what is already known. The more experience learners have with a particular topic, the easier it is for them to make connections between what they know and what they are learning (Anderson, 1994; Anderson & Pearson, 1984). Constructivists view comprehension as

> the construction of meaning of a written or spoken communication through a reciprocal, holistic interchange of ideas between the interpreter and the message in a particular communicative context. Note: The presumption here is that meaning resides in the intentional problem-solving, thinking processes of the interpreter during such an interchange, that the content of meaning is influenced by that person's prior knowledge and experience, and that the message so constructed by the receiver may or may not be congruent with the message sent. (Harris & Hodges, 1995, p. 39)

Vygotsky's principles enhance the constructivist perspective by addressing the social context of learning (Dixon-Krauss, 1996). According to Vygotsky, students should be taught within their zone of proximal development (Forman & Cazden, 1994; Vygotsky, 1978). The zone of proximal development is the level at which students can learn with the support of a more knowledgeable other. As students' understanding increases, the support from the more knowledgeable other decreases and the students take on more responsibility. This gradual release of responsibility is known as scaffolding.

Instruction within the zone should incorporate both scaffolding and social mediation. As Dixon-Krauss (1996) notes when explaining this Vygotskian principle, "It is through social dialogue with adults and/or more capable peers that language concepts are learned" (p. 155). Such social interaction encourages students to think and share their ideas.

Guided Comprehension Connection The Guided Comprehension Model is based on the view of comprehension as a social constructivist process. This is shown in the Model in numerous ways, including the ultimate goal of students' transaction with text, the importance of discussion, and the value placed on learning in a variety of social settings.

Excellent Reading Teachers Influence Students' Learning

Excellent reading teachers are valued participants in the learning process. As the National Commission on Teaching and America's Future (1997) has reported, the single most important strategy for achieving U.S. education goals is to recruit, prepare, and support excellent teachers for every school.

A knowledgeable teacher is aware of what is working well and what each student needs to be successful. A knowledgeable teacher knows the importance of every student having successful literacy experiences, and it is the teacher's knowledge that makes a difference in student success (International Reading Association, 1999).

The teacher's role in the reading process is to create experiences and environments that introduce, nurture, or extend students' abilities to engage with text. This requires that teachers engage in explicit instruction, modeling, scaffolding, facilitating, and participating (Au & Raphael, 1998).

Reading researchers and professional organizations have delineated the characteristics of excellent reading teachers (Fountas & Pinnell, 1996; International Reading Association, 2000; Ruddell, 1995, 2004). The following characterization of such reading teachers integrates their ideas.

Excellent reading teachers believe that all children can learn. They base their teaching on the needs of the individual learner. They know that motivation and multiple kinds of text are essential elements of teaching and learning. They understand that reading is a social constructivist process that functions best in authentic situations. They teach in print-rich, concept-rich environments.

Such teachers have in-depth knowledge of various aspects of literacy, including reading and writing. They teach for a variety of purposes, using diverse methods, materials, and grouping patterns to focus on individual needs, interests, and learning styles. They continually monitor student learning and adjust teaching as needed to ensure the success of all learners. They also know the strategies good readers use, and they can teach students how to use them.

Excellent reading teachers view their teaching as multifaceted and view themselves as participants in the learning process. They integrate their knowledge of the learning cycle, learning styles, and multiple intelligences into their teaching.

These teachers understand the natural relationship between assessment and instruction, and they assess in multiple ways for a variety of purposes. They use instructional strategies that provide formative feedback to monitor the effectiveness of teaching and student performance. They know that assessment informs both teaching and learning.

Guided Comprehension Connection Teachers who engage in Guided Comprehension are knowledgeable not only about reading but also about their students. They know that students read at different levels, and they know how to use the Model to accommodate each reader's needs. These educators are active participants in the reading process. They are strategic thinkers who know how to use a variety of materials in a variety of ways, within a variety of settings. Guided Comprehension provides a context for such teaching.

Good Readers Are Strategic and Take Active Roles in the Reading Process

Reading researchers have reported that much of what we know about comprehension is based on studies of good readers (Block, Schaller, Joy, & Gaine, 2002; Duke & Pearson, 2002; Pearson, 2001; Pressley, 2000). They describe good readers as active participants in the reading process, who have clear goals and constantly monitor the relation between the goals they have set and the text they are reading. Good readers use a repertoire of comprehension strategies to facilitate the construction of meaning. These strategies include previewing, self-questioning, making connections, visualizing, knowing how words work, monitoring, summarizing, and evaluating. Our students need to know how to use these strategies so they can use them during the reading process. Researchers believe that using such strategies helps students become metacognitive readers (Palincsar & Brown, 1984; Roehler & Duffy, 1984)—readers who can think about and monitor their own thinking while reading.

Good readers read from aesthetic or efferent stances and have an awareness of the author's style and purpose. Reading from an aesthetic stance is for the emotional, lived-through experience; reading from an efferent stance is for extracting factual information (Rosenblatt, 1978, 2002). Good readers read both narrative and expository texts and have ideas about how to figure out unfamiliar words. They use their knowledge of text structure to efficiently and strategically process text. This knowledge develops from experiences with different genres and is correlated with age or time in school (Goldman & Rakestraw, 2000).

Good readers spontaneously generate questions at different points in the reading process for a variety of reasons. They know that they use questioning in their everyday lives and that it increases their comprehension. These readers are problem solvers who have the ability to discover new information for themselves.

Good readers read widely, which provides exposure to various genres and text formats, affords opportunities for strategy use, increases understanding of how words work, provides bases for discussion and meaning negotiation, and accommodates students' interests.

These readers monitor their comprehension and know when they are constructing meaning, and when they are not. When comprehension breaks down due to lack of background information, difficulty of words, or unfamiliar text structure, good readers know a variety of "fix-up" strategies to use. These include rereading, changing the pace of reading, using context clues, cross-checking cueing systems, and asking for help. Most important, good readers are able to select the appropriate strategies and to consistently focus on making sense of text and gaining new understandings.

Guided Comprehension Connection Creating successful, strategic readers is the ultimate goal of Guided Comprehension, and students fully participate in the process. Students' roles are extensive and include engaging in comprehension as a thinking process and transacting with various levels of text in multiple settings.

Reading Should Occur in Meaningful Contexts

Duke (2001) has delineated an expanded understanding of context for present-day learners. She suggests that context should be viewed as curriculum, activity, classroom environment, teachers and teaching, text, and society.

One of the interesting aspects of this expanded notion of context is the number of influences that impact student learning. As Cambourne (2002) reminds us, "what is learned cannot be separated from the context in which it is learned" (p. 26).

Lipson and Wixson (2009) suggest that the instructional context encompasses settings, practices, and resources. The instructional settings include teacher beliefs and literate environment, classroom interaction, classroom organization, and grouping. Instructional goals, methods, activities, and assessment practices are part of instructional practice. Commercial programs, trade materials, and technology are viewed as instructional resources.

More specific, literacy-based descriptions of context include ideas offered by Gambrell (1996), Hiebert (1994), and Pearson (2001). They suggest that the classroom context is characterized by multiple factors including classroom organization and authentic opportunities to read, write, and discuss. They further note that the instruction of skills and strategies, integration of concept-driven vocabulary, use of multiple genres, and knowledge of various text structures are other contextual components.

Guided Comprehension Connection   Guided Comprehension is a context for teaching and learning comprehension strategies. It incorporates a variety of settings, practices, and resources. Students have numerous opportunities to read, write, and discuss using multiple genres and levels of text.

Students Benefit From Transacting With a Variety of Texts at Multiple Levels

Students need to engage daily with texts at multiple levels. When such levels of text are being used, teachers scaffold learning experiences, and students receive varying levels of support, depending on the purpose and instructional setting. For example, when text is challenging, teachers can use a read-aloud to provide full support for students. When the text is just right for instruction, students have support as needed, with the teacher prompting or responding as necessary. Finally, when the text is just right for independent reading, little or no teacher support is needed. (For a more detailed discussion of leveled text, see Chapter 6.)

Transacting with a wide variety of genres enhances students' motivation and understanding. Experience in reading multiple genres provides students with knowledge of numerous text structures and improves their text-driven processing (Goldman & Rakestraw, 2000). Gambrell (2001) notes that transacting with a wide variety of genres—including biography, historical fiction, legends, poetry, and brochures—increases students' reading performance.

Guided Comprehension Connection   In Guided Comprehension, students have opportunities to engage with a wide variety of texts at students' independent, instructional, and challenging levels on a daily basis.

Vocabulary Development and Instruction Affect Reading Comprehension

Vocabulary development and instruction have strong ties to reading comprehension. As the National Reading Panel (National Institute of Child Health and Human Development, 2000) notes, "Reading comprehension is a complex, cognitive process that cannot be understood without a clear description of the role that vocabulary development and vocabulary instruction play in the understanding of what has been read" (p. 13). Snow, Burns, and Griffin (1998) support this view, observing, "Learning new concepts and words that encode them is essential to comprehension development" (p. 217).

Harris and Hodges (1995) describe students' ever-growing knowledge of words and their meanings as *vocabulary development.* They note that vocabulary development also refers to the teaching–learning processes that lead to such growth. Vocabulary development is also influenced by the amount and variety of text students read (Baumann & Kame'enui, 1991; Beck & McKeown, 1991; Snow et al., 1998). Teacher read-alouds, which offer students access to a variety of levels of text, contribute to this process (Hiebert et al., 1998).

Blachowicz, Fisher, Ogle, and Watts-Taffe (2006) suggest that effective vocabulary instruction is characterized by the following:

- An environment that fosters word consciousness—"the awareness of and interest in learning and using new words and becoming more skillful and precise in word usage" (Graves & Watts-Taffe, 2002, p. 144)
- Students who actively participate in the process
- Instruction that integrates vocabulary with the curriculum and word learning throughout the day and across subject areas
- Instruction that provides both definitional and contextual information
- Teachers who provide multiple exposures to words
- Teachers who provide numerous, ongoing opportunities to use the words

Baumann and Kame'enui (1991) suggest that direct instruction of vocabulary and learning from context should be balanced. The instruction should be meaningful to students, include words from students' reading, and focus on a variety of strategies for determining the meanings of unfamiliar words (Blachowicz & Lee, 1991). Another important aspect of such teaching is making connections between the vocabulary and students' background knowledge.

 In Guided Comprehension, students are immersed in words. They engage daily with texts at multiple levels in a variety of settings, and they learn words through both direct instruction and use of context. They also learn vocabulary strategies in scaffolded settings that provide numerous opportunities for practice and application, paired and group reading, and teacher read-alouds.

Engagement Is a Key Factor in the Comprehension Process

The engagement perspective on reading integrates cognitive, motivational, and social aspects of reading (Baker, Afflerbach, & Reinking, 1996; Baker & Wigfield, 1999; Guthrie & Alvermann, 1999). Engaged learners achieve because they want to understand, they possess intrinsic motivations for interacting with text, they use cognitive skills to understand, and they share knowledge by talking with teachers and peers (Guthrie & Wigfield, 1997). Engaged readers read widely for enjoyment and have positive attitudes about reading.

Engaged readers transact with print and construct understandings based on connections between prior knowledge and new information. Baker and Wigfield (1999) note that "engaged readers are motivated to read for different purposes, utilize knowledge gained from previous experience to generate new understandings, and participate in meaningful social interactions around reading" (p. 453).

Gambrell (1996) suggests that "classroom cultures that foster reading motivation are characterized by a teacher who is a reading model, a book-rich classroom environment, opportunities for choice, familiarity with books, and literacy-related incentives that reflect the value of reading" (p. 20). Gambrell, Palmer, Codling, and Mazzoni (1996) note that highly motivated readers read for a wide variety of reasons including curiosity, involvement, social interchange, and emotional satisfaction.

Motivation is described in terms of competence and efficacy beliefs, goals for reading, and social purposes of reading (Baker & Wigfield, 1999). Motivated readers believe they can be successful and are willing to take on the challenge of difficult reading material. They also exhibit intrinsic reasons for reading, such as gaining new knowledge about a topic or enjoying the reading experience. Motivated readers enjoy the social aspects of sharing with others new meanings gained from their reading.

Guided Comprehension Connection The Guided Comprehension Model is based on students' active engagement. Guided Comprehension is a cognitive experience because students think through the reading process, it is motivational because students' interests and opportunities for success are embedded in the Model, and it is social because students negotiate meaning with teachers and peers on a daily basis.

Comprehension Strategies and Skills Can Be Taught

Durkin's research in the late 1970s reported that little if any comprehension instruction occurred in classrooms. Instead, comprehension questions, often at the literal level, were assigned and then corrected; comprehension was assessed but not taught. Current studies demonstrate that when students experience explicit instruction of comprehension strategies, it improves their comprehension of new texts and topics (Duke & Pearson, 2002). Comprehension strategies generally include

- *Previewing*: Activating background knowledge, predicting, and setting a purpose
- *Self-questioning*: Generating questions to guide reading
- *Making connections*: Relating reading to self, text, and others
- *Visualizing*: Creating mental pictures while reading
- *Knowing how words work*: Understanding words through strategic vocabulary development, including the use of graphophonic, syntactic, and semantic cueing systems to figure out unknown words
- *Monitoring*: Asking, "Does this make sense?" and adapting strategic processes to accommodate the response
- *Summarizing*: Synthesizing important ideas
- *Evaluating*: Making judgments about text content and author's craft

Fielding and Pearson (1994) recommend a framework for comprehension instruction that encourages the gradual release of responsibility from teacher to student. This four-step approach includes teacher modeling, guided practice, independent practice, and application of the strategy in authentic reading situations. This framework is supported by Vygotsky's (1978) work on instruction within the zone of proximal development, and scaffolding, the gradual relinquishing of support as students become more competent in using the strategy.

Linking skills and strategies can facilitate comprehension. Comprehension strategies are generally more complex than comprehension skills and often require the orchestration of several skills. Effective instruction links comprehension skills and strategies to promote strategic reading. For example, the comprehension skills of sequencing, making judgments, noting details, making generalizations, and using text structure can be linked to summarizing, which is a comprehension strategy (Lipson, 2001). These and other skills—including generating questions, making inferences, distinguishing between important and less important details, and drawing conclusions—facilitate students' use of one or more comprehension strategies. Generating questions is an example of a skill that permeates all the Guided Comprehension strategies. Figure 2 features narrative and informational text examples of how generating questions underpins each strategy.

After explaining and modeling skills and strategies, teachers scaffold instruction to provide the support necessary as students attempt new tasks. As they observe students gaining competence in using the strategies, teachers gradually release responsibility for learning to the students, who apply the strategies independently after practicing them in a variety of settings.

 This tenet is a core underpinning of Guided Comprehension because the Model is designed to promote comprehension as a strategy-based thinking process. It incorporates the explicit teaching of comprehension strategies and the skills that enable their use. The Model also provides multiple opportunities for practice and transfer of learning.

Differentiated Reading Instruction Accommodates Students' Needs, Including Those of English Learners and Struggling Readers

Duke and Pearson's (2002) work reminds us that learners need different kinds and amounts of reading comprehension instruction. As teachers, we understand this. We know that we have students of differing capabilities in our classes and we strive to help them to comprehend to the best of their abilities.

Differentiated instruction enables us to accommodate the diversity of students' needs (Gibson & Hasbrouck, 2008; Tyner & Green, 2005). To develop environments that promote differentiated instruction, Gibson and Hasbrouck (2008) suggest that we do the following:

- Embrace collaborative teaching and learning
- Use whole-class and small-group explicit strategy instruction
- Establish consistent routines and procedures
- Scaffold student learning
- Increase student engagement
- Teach students how to learn, as well as what to learn
- Change the way teaching occurs

Figure 2. Generating Questions: A Skill That Supports Comprehension Strategies

Comprehension Strategy	Narrative Text (*Dog Breath* by Dav Pilkey)	Informational Text (*Wolves* by Seymour Simon)
Previewing	What is this story about? What might happen in this story?	What do I already know about wolves?
Self-Questioning	How will they solve the dog's problem?	Why do people fear wolves?
Making Connections	What are some other dog stories I know?	How do the photographs of the wolves compare or contrast with the documentary we watched? To the article we read?
Visualizing	How did my mental picture of Hally Tosis change from the start of the story?	How are my mental pictures of the Mexican wolf and the Rocky Mountain wolf different? How are they the same?
Knowing How Words Work	Does the word make sense in the sentence?	What clues in the text can I use to figure out the word *hierarchy*?
Monitoring	Does what I am reading make sense? If not, what can I do to clarify?	Does what I am reading make sense? If not, what can I do to clarify? What other sources can I check?
Summarizing	What has happened so far?	What is the most important information in this section?
Evaluating	In what other ways could Hally have been saved?	Will wolves become extinct? What can we do to prevent this?

We can differentiate a number of instructional components to support students as they gain competence and confidence in learning. These include *content*—the information being taught, *process*—the way in which the information is taught, and *product*—how the students demonstrate their learning (Tomlinson, 1999).

When we differentiate instruction we create multiple pathways to learning. This supports our goal of helping students to perform to their maximum potentials.

Guided Comprehension Connection Differentiated instruction is embedded in the Guided Comprehension Model. Flexible small-group instruction, multiple levels of text, and differentiated tasks are three examples of how we can accommodate individual students' needs when teaching Guided Comprehension. Examples of ideas for differentiating instruction are presented at the start of each theme in Chapters 7–10.

Dynamic Assessment Informs Comprehension Instruction

Dynamic assessment captures students' performance as they engage in the process of learning. It is continuous and has the ability to afford insights into students' understandings at any given point in the learning experience. Dynamic assessment reflects constructivist theory and is viewed not as an add-on, but rather as a natural component of teaching and learning (Brooks & Brooks, 1993).

Dynamic assessments, which are usually informal in nature, can be used in a variety of instructional settings. This includes scaffolded learning experiences in which students have varying degrees of teacher support. Assessing in this context captures the students' emerging abilities and provides insights that may not be gleaned from independent settings (Minick, 1987). Dynamic assessment is also prevalent in portfolios because it provides an ongoing view of student growth. (For a more detailed discussion of the role of assessment in Guided Comprehension, see Chapter 5.)

Guided Comprehension Connection Assessment permeates the Guided Comprehension Model. It occurs for multiple purposes in a variety of settings. Dynamic assessment provides insights into students' thinking as they engage in all stages of the Model. This, in turn, informs future teaching and learning.

The Guided Comprehension Model is dynamic in nature. It accommodates students' individual needs, employs a variety of texts and settings, and utilizes active, ongoing assessment. In Chapters 2, 3, and 4 we detail the stages of the Model: teacher-directed whole-group instruction, teacher-guided small groups and student-facilitated independent practice, and teacher-facilitated whole-group reflection and goal setting.

Making Connections to Theory and Practice

To learn more about current developments in reading instruction, read the following:

Duffy, G.G. (2009). *Explaining reading: A resource for teaching concepts, skills, and strategies* (2nd ed.). New York: Guilford.

Gambrell, L.B., Morrow, L.M., & Pressley, M. (Eds.). (2006). *Best practices in literacy instruction* (3rd ed.). New York: Guilford.

Kamil, M.L., Pearson, P.D., Moje, E.B., Afflerbach, P., Mosenthal, P.B., & Barr, R. (Eds.). (2010). *Handbook of reading research* (Vol. 4). New York: Routledge.

CHAPTER 2

Teacher-Directed Whole-Group Instruction

The first stage of the Guided Comprehension Model, teacher-directed whole-group instruction, is the focus of this chapter. The purposes of Stage One include the following:

- To provide a meaningful, comfortable context for a community of learners
- To afford students access to multiple levels of authentic text, including those that may otherwise be viewed as challenging
- To teach comprehension strategies through explicit instruction

Organizing for Stage One

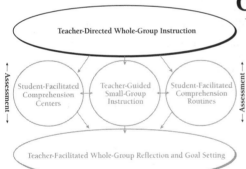

Guided Comprehension is a context that includes a variety of instructional settings, resources, and teaching methods. In Stage One of the Model, we use whole-group instruction to provide students with a positive sense of belonging to a community of learners. Student opportunities to interact with peers of mixed abilities afford additional advantages in this form of grouping. The sense of community also is fostered by student–teacher and student–peer interaction, print-rich environments, numerous opportunities to engage with authentic texts from a variety of genres, students who are active learners, and teachers who are knowledgeable about current best practice.

Because the instruction in Stage One is teacher-directed and allows us to fully support student learning, we can choose to teach from books that range in level from easy to challenging. For example, if we choose a text that is interesting to the students and works well when teaching a particular strategy but is challenging in nature, we can share it with students through a read-aloud. We may also select an easier text as the focus of the lesson because it may be the best choice for teaching a particular strategy within a particular timeframe. Because the teacher is doing the reading in Stage One, text level is not usually a factor when choosing a text. Instead, we think about text usefulness for teaching a particular strategy or set of strategies, student interests, and connections to literacy themes.

Engaging in Explicit Instruction

In working with a wide variety of literacy professionals, we have heard many comment that reading educators often describe teaching comprehension strategies as "going over" the strategies with students. "Going over" or "covering" a strategy is equivalent to mentioning it or assigning it without teaching it. Effectively teaching comprehension strategies requires more than "going over" these ideas; it requires explicit instruction: explaining, demonstrating, guiding, practicing, and reflecting.

We use authentic text to explicitly teach comprehension strategies in Stage One. Assessment is a natural part of this process. The strategies associated with the Model are previewing (activating prior knowledge, predicting, and setting a purpose), self-questioning, making connections, visualizing, knowing how words work, monitoring, summarizing, and evaluating. Regardless of the strategy being taught, the process of explicit instruction remains the same. It includes the following steps.

1. *Explain the strategy*: We begin by explaining the strategy. We focus on how the strategy works and how it contributes to comprehension. Then we invite students to make connections to their background knowledge. For example, when introducing self-questioning, we explain the strategy, describe the process, and provide an example. Next, we ask students how they use questioning in their lives to help them make connections to their background knowledge. This creates a contextual framework for the strategy. During this step, we also explain to the students the teaching idea we will be implementing to help them learn how to use the strategy. For example, if we are using Question–Answer Relationships (QAR; Raphael, Highfield, & Au, 2006) to teach the students how to ask questions while they read, we would explain that teaching idea at this point.

2. *Demonstrate the strategy*: We demonstrate strategies by reading a selection aloud and using a Think-Aloud and a visual to share ideas with students. As we think aloud, we orally explain precisely what is triggering our thoughts and how it is affecting our understanding. (For a description of the Think-Aloud strategy, see Appendix A, page 222.) This can lead to the development of personal connections, questions for clarification, and refined predictions. When using the Think-Aloud process to demonstrate strategies, we need to explain our thinking so students have a clear idea of the cognitively active process readers experience as they transact with text. For example, when demonstrating self-questioning, we read a text selection and think aloud about the questions we generate to guide our reading by stating the questions, why they occurred to us, and what responses we expect. If the strategy requires a written or sketched response, we also model that during this step. For example, if students need to write Question–Answer Relationships on a blackline, we demonstrate how to do that during this time.

3. *Guide the students to apply the strategy*: We read the next section of the text aloud, and ask the students to work with a partner to apply the strategy just taught. For example, if we explained and demonstrated self-questioning, we would then read aloud a portion of the text and ask the students to create, orally or in writing, Question–Answer Relationships about the text. Then we would discuss the questions the paired students created and read aloud another section of text.

4. *Practice the strategy*: We monitor as students work independently within the whole-group setting. We either continue reading segments of the text with reduced teacher support or invite the students to read independent-level text on their own. In either case, the students independently use the strategy, in this case self-questioning, to generate and respond to Question–Answer Relationships. During this stage, we differentiate our instruction by providing scaffolding for those students who need more support, and by releasing the task to those students who are ready to use it. The goal is to ensure that students know the strategy and the process for using it. Ultimately, the students develop a repertoire of strategies that they can use as needed when they are reading on their own.

5. *Reflect on the strategy*: We encourage students to reflect on how using the strategy helped them to understand the text. Invite students to share their reflections in small groups or with the whole class. Discuss how they can use the strategy when they are reading on their own.

We also use multiple authentic assessments in Stage One. These include observation, discussion, sketching, and informal writing.

Throughout Stage One, we scaffold students' learning. When students learn how the strategy works, they have our total support. When they engage in guided practice, they have our support as necessary. When they apply the strategy independently, our support is diminished and the students are in control.

Comprehension Strategies

During Stage One of the Guided Comprehension Model, we use a number of teaching ideas to clarify and reinforce students' understanding and application of the comprehension strategies. Although we initially use these ideas as frameworks for teaching, our goal is for students to eventually use them on their own. In this section, we explain each comprehension strategy and link it to a list of teaching ideas. These lists are not exhaustive, but they do include the ideas we use most frequently. In Appendix A, we examine each idea by describing its purposes and procedures, as well as its links to reading stages, comprehension strategies, and types of text.

Previewing

Previewing is activating background knowledge, predicting, and setting purposes for reading. The following teaching ideas support previewing:

- Anticipation/Reaction Guide
- Predict-o-Gram
- Prereading Plan (PreP)
- Probable Passages
- Questioning the Text
- Semantic Map
- Story Impressions
- Text Introductions

Self-Questioning

Self-questioning is generating queries to guide our thinking while reading. We read to answer the questions we create. The ability to generate questions is a skill that underpins not only this strategy, but also many of the dimensions of transacting with text. For this reason we always use explicit instruction to teach our students how to generate and respond to questions.

When teaching students about questioning, we explain what questions are, discuss their purposes, and delineate their multiple levels. For example, we explain that there are many reasons for generating questions, including information-seeking, connected understanding, psychological and moral reconstruction, historical speculation, imagination, and research. We also immerse students in topics from multiple perspectives by reading, writing, speaking, listening, and viewing to foster their questioning abilities (Busching & Slesinger, 1995).

We teach students how to generate questions at four levels: memory, convergent, divergent, and evaluative. Ciardiello (1998, 2007) suggests the following signal words and cognitive operations for each category:

Memory Questions

Signal words: *who, what, where, when?*

Cognitive operations: naming, defining, identifying, designating

Convergent Thinking Questions

Signal words: *why, how, in what ways?*

Cognitive operations: explaining, stating relationships, comparing and contrasting

Divergent Thinking Questions

Signal words: *imagine, suppose, predict, if/then*

Cognitive operations: predicting, hypothesizing, inferring, reconstructing

Evaluative Thinking Questions

Signal words: *defend, judge, justify/what do you think?*

Cognitive operations: valuing, judging, defending, justifying

When students become proficient in generating and responding to questions, they apply their knowledge to comprehension strategies, including self-questioning. The following teaching ideas support self-questioning:

- "I Wonder" Statements
- K–W–L and K–W–L–S
- Paired Questioning
- Question–Answer Relationships (QAR)
- Thick and Thin Questions

Making Connections

Making connections is thinking about the text in relation to ourselves, other texts, and the world (Keene & Zimmermann, 2007). The ability to make connections provides the basis for learning, as students connect new information with their own experiences. This, therefore, is necessary for understanding. The following teaching ideas support making connections:

- Coding the Text: Text–Self (T–S), Text–Text (T–T), Text–World (T–W)
- Connection Stems: That reminds me of..., I remember when...
- Double-Entry Journal
- Drawing Connections
- Save the Last Word for Me

Visualizing

Visualizing is creating pictures in our minds based on what is happening in the text. The following teaching ideas support visualizing:

- Gallery Images
- Graphic Organizers/Visual Organizers
- Guided Imagery
- Open-Mind Portrait
- Photographs of the Mind
- Sketch to Stretch

Knowing How Words Work

Knowing how words work is understanding words through strategic vocabulary development, including using graphophonic, syntactic, and semantic cueing systems to figure out unknown words. The graphophonic cueing system involves creating grapheme (written letter)–phoneme (sound) matches. The syntactic cueing system deals with the structure of the language. The semantic cueing system focuses on meaning. Readers use all three of these cueing systems, along with other knowledge of words, to effectively engage with text. The following teaching ideas support knowing how words work:

- Concept of Definition Map
- Context Clues
- Decoding by Analogy
- List–Group–Label
- Possible Sentences
- RIVET
- Semantic Feature Analysis
- Vocabulary by Analogy
- Vocabulary Self-Collection Strategy

Monitoring

Monitoring involves asking, "Does this make sense?" and clarifying by adapting strategic processes to accommodate the response. Monitoring is knowing if meaning is being constructed and what to do if it is not. When readers monitor, they are actively engaged in thinking while reading. The following teaching ideas support monitoring:

- Bookmark Technique
- INSERT
- Patterned Partner Reading
- Say Something
- Think-Alouds

Summarizing

Summarizing is extracting essential information—including the main idea and supporting details—from text. The following teaching ideas support summarizing:

- Bio-Pyramid
- Lyric Retelling/Lyric Summary
- Narrative Pyramid
- Paired Summarizing
- QuIP (Questions Into Paragraphs)
- Retelling
- Summary Cubes

Evaluating

Evaluating is making judgments about text. The following teaching ideas support evaluating:

- Contrast Chart
- Discussion Web
- Evaluative Questioning
- Journal Responses
- Meeting of the Minds
- Mind and Alternative Mind Portraits
- Persuasive Writing

These strategies and teaching ideas provide the foundation for instruction in Guided Comprehension. It is important to note that although we have organized the teaching ideas by strategy, many of them can be used for more than one purpose. Additionally, once we teach a particular strategy, we encourage students to add it to their repertoire so they can integrate the strategies to engage authentically and deeply with the text. We also often contextualize the strategies in larger teaching routines, which we describe in the next section.

Comprehension Routines

Duke and Pearson (2002) define *routines* as integrated sets of practices that students can use with multiple texts in various settings. They are designed to help students gain deeper understanding of the text and to equip them with strategies they can use when reading other texts on their own. In Guided Comprehension, these include comprehension routines such as Literature Circles, Reciprocal Teaching, and Questioning the Author. We teach these routines to the students through direct instruction in Stage One, and when they become proficient they use them independently in Stage Two.

Literature Circles, Reciprocal Teaching, and Questioning the Author are described in this section. These routines, along with Directed Reading–Thinking Activity and Directed Reading–Listening Activity, are presented in a step-by-step teaching process in Appendix A.

Literature Circles

The basic goal of Literature Circles is to help students converse about texts in meaningful, personal, and thoughtful ways (Brabham & Villaume, 2000). Ketch (2005) notes, "Conversation helps individuals make sense of their world. It helps to build empathy, understanding, respect for different opinions, and ownership of the learning process" (p. 8). Researchers also report that small-group conversations motivate students, foster higher order thinking, and promote comprehension (Berne & Clark, 2008; Gambrell, 2004; Ketch, 2005; Kucan & Beck, 2003). Blanton, Pilonieta, and Wood (2007) further note that students of diverse linguistic and cultural backgrounds benefit from participating in such discussions.

Implementing Literature Circles. To facilitate students' use of Literature Circles, we need to explicitly teach the concept and actively demonstrate how to engage with text (Stien & Beed, 2004). Brabham and Villaume (2000) caution against a "cookie-cutter" approach to implementing Literature Circles and instead recommend designing and using them in ways that emerge from students' needs and challenges. These circles may not all have the same format, but they all encourage the implementation of grand conversations about the texts (Peterson & Eeds, 1990). Although the procedural decisions about the implementation of Literature Circles need to emerge from specific classrooms, there are some guidelines that do facilitate their use.

It is important to remember that the students' personal interpretations drive the discussion. There is not a list of questions to be answered, but rather a focus on students' inquiries, connections, and interpretations. The teacher may need to model how to converse in critical ways by doing some class demonstrations or using Think-Alouds.

Daniels (2002) and Tompkins (2006) suggest guiding principles for using Literature Circles. We have incorporated their ideas into our process for explicit instruction, which includes the following steps:

1. *Explain*: Begin by explaining that Literature Circles are discussion formats for sharing meaningful ideas about books that group members have selected to read. Note that groups are formed based on book selections and meet on a regular basis according to predetermined schedules. Explain that when we first begin using Literature Circles, each person will have a particular role, such as discussion director, passage master, connector, illustrator, or word finder. Note that everyone in the group will need to know every role, because the roles rotate every time the Circle meets. Share the Guided Comprehension Literature Circle Bookmarks (see Appendix B, page 284) with the students and explain how they can be used to record information that will later be shared within the Literature Circles.

2. *Demonstrate*: Model how Literature Circles work by gathering a preselected group of students and engaging in a Literature Circle. You and the students will have read the same segment of text in preparation for the demonstration. It is helpful if the text is one the rest of the students have already read because this will help the students who are observing to focus on the process. All circle participants should think aloud about their roles as they complete them. Then use an overhead projector to share responses from the perspective of the roles used in Literature Circles. Think aloud about how the information students recorded contributed to the discussion.

3. *Guide*: Encourage students to engage in Literature Circles by forming roles and choosing roles. Read aloud another brief text and encourage students to jot or sketch notes or reactions they have on their Literature Circle Bookmarks or in their Guided Comprehension Journals. Then guide students to use the information they recorded to facilitate their discussions. Monitor students' abilities to engage in meaningful discussion. Support or prompt as needed. Discuss the process with the whole group.

4. *Practice*: Invite students to self-select brief texts and engage in Literature Circles. Remind them to use their Literature Circle Bookmarks to record ideas they want to contribute to the discussion. Also remind them to rotate the roles.

5. *Reflect*: Think about how Literature Circles help us comprehend by providing opportunities for strategy use and discussion of text. Encourage students to complete the Literature Circle Group or Self-Assessment (see Appendix B, pages 285–286). This will lead to further goal setting.

Once students are comfortable engaging in Literature Circles, explain how they can integrate the use of comprehension strategies in the process.

There are several factors related to Literature Circles that we need to consider when preparing to implement them. In the next section, we begin by describing some of the choices students can make concerning Literature Circles and the types of text that may be used. Then we examine schedules, talk, and roles. Finally, we discuss student response and assessment.

Student choice in Literature Circles. Students make many choices within the framework of Literature Circles: They choose the books they will read, the group they will join, the schedule of their reading, and the direction of the conversation. We can set the parameters for students to make these choices by providing a variety of texts for student selection, setting minimum daily or weekly reading requirements, and prompting ideas for conversations. However, the ultimate responsibility for the group rests with the students.

Selecting texts for Literature Circles. Although students traditionally read authentic literature while participating in these circles, they may also read high-quality informational text (McLaughlin, 2010; Stien & Beed, 2004). Text choices should relate to students' experiences, help them make personal connections, contain relevant themes and rich language, and prompt critical reflection (Brabham & Villaume, 2000; Noe & Johnson, 1999; Samway & Wang, 1996). These books should also be engaging, meaningful, interesting, and accessible for students. Including theme-based leveled texts ensures that students will be able to engage in the circles independently— without teacher assistance. Although students in Literature Circles usually read the same text, they can also read similar texts about the same theme or a variety of theme-related genres on multiple levels. The texts that are selected will need to accommodate a wide range of student interests and abilities.

There are several ways to select texts for Literature Circles. One way is to choose books that relate to a theme, topic, genre, or author (Noe & Johnson, 1999). When using this method, we choose several texts on varying levels and the students make reading choices based on interest and ability. Another way to select text is to create collections of text sets related to a theme or topic (Short, Harste, & Burke, 1996). Texts within each set are related but can vary in levels of difficulty. Students select the theme or topic and then choose the reading material from within that set. For example, text sets might focus on the theme of survival, include a variety of versions of a fairy tale, or be comprised of a group of biographies. A third way to choose reading material is to allow students to self-select from a predetermined list of titles.

After selecting the texts to be used in Literature Circles, we introduce the books to readers. Although there are various methods for doing this, we have found these two to be especially effective:

1. *Book talks*: This is a short oral overview of the book, focusing on the genre, the main characters, and the plot.
2. *Book pass*: Several books are passed among students. Each peruses a book for a few minutes, noting the title, reading the book cover, and leafing through the opening chapter. If the students find a book appealing, they jot the title in their notebook and pass the book to the next person. After previewing several titles, students make choices. To make sure that there are an appropriate number of students in each group, we often ask them to list their top two or three choices; that way, we can create groups of a reasonable size and still make sure the students get one of their top selections. Groups are formed on the basis of book selections.

It is important to remember that we may need to guide some students in making appropriate text choices. If text sets are used, we will want to introduce the theme of the set and the kinds of texts that are in it. If selections are used from an anthology, we can use them as the basis for book talks.

Schedules, talk, and roles in Literature Circles. Once the groups are formed, students meet and develop a schedule to determine how much they will read and to create meeting deadlines. At first, we can provide the schedule as a way to model how to set these goals. After reading goals have been set, students read independently or with a buddy. At the designated group meeting time, the students gather to discuss the texts. Notes from their reading that have been recorded in their Guided Comprehension Journals inform this discussion. Prior to this point we model how to respond to text and how to use these responses to get the group conversations started.

The time spent in Literature Circles varies by length of text, but a maximum of 20 minutes is usually sufficient. We can use a mini-lesson to demonstrate a particular literary element—such as plot, theme, or characterization—on which the students may focus their discussion. It is important, though, that we allow each group's conversation to evolve on its own.

Gilles (1998) has identified four types of talk that often occur during Literature Circles: (1) talk about the book, (2) talk about the reading process, (3) talk about connections, and (4) talk about group process and social issues. Teachers can encourage all types of talk with demonstrations and gentle prompts during the Literature Circle conversations.

Some teachers prefer to use assigned roles and responsibilities as a way to guide the conversations. Daniels (2002) has found that the following roles, which students rotate, provide a wide level of conversation within the Literature Circle:

- *Discussion director*: Takes on the leadership of the group and guides the discussion. Responsibilities include choosing topics for discussion, generating questions, convening the meeting, and facilitating contributions from all members.

- *Passage master*: Helps students revisit the text. Responsibilities include selecting memorable or important sections of the text and reading them aloud expressively.

- *Connector*: Guides the students to make connections with the text. Responsibilities include sharing text–self, text–text, and text–world connections and encouraging others to do the same.

- *Illustrator/artful artist*: Creates a drawing or other symbolic response to text. Responsibilities include making the visual response and using it to encourage others to contribute to the conversation.

- *Vocabulary enricher/word finder*: Locates an interesting word or two to share with the group. Responsibilities include finding the word(s), noting the page and paragraph in which it is located, and sharing the word and its meaning based on its use in context.

- *Summarizer*: Restates the essential ideas discussed in Literature Circles at the conclusion of the Circle or as requested by group members.

The advantage of using these roles is that they represent response in a variety of learning modes. The disadvantage is that continuing to use roles over long periods of time may stifle responses. We have found that starting with clearly defined roles and then relaxing or relinquishing them as the students gain competence in Literature Circles is effective. Daniels (2002) concurs, noting that role-free discussions are the ultimate goal.

Student response in Literature Circles. After reading, students gather in their small group to share understandings from the text and make personal connections. This sharing, in the form of a conversation, helps students broaden their interpretations and gain new perspectives from the other group members. After the sharing has concluded, groups often engage in projects to extend their thinking about the text. (For a list of literature response prompts, see Appendix C.)

Assessing students in Literature Circles. There are several ways to assess the students' comprehension, contributions, and cooperation within Literature Circles. Options include informal assessments such as self-reflection, observation, and response sheets or journal entries.

- Students may self-reflect on their contributions to the group and the group's ability to function. To record this information, we can provide forms for students to complete (see Appendix B, page 286). The group can also reflect (see Appendix B, page 285).

- We may assess individual students or the group as a whole through observation. Although the students meet independently, we can observe their conversations and make anecdotal notes about individual contributions to discussions. We can also keep a checklist about the content and depth of discussions. If the students are focused on basic recall of story events, we can choose to do a mini-lesson on making meaningful connections with texts.

- Students' response sheets or book journals provide another opportunity for assessment. In this format, students take notes about the text, document understandings, and make personal connections to bring to the discussion.

Each of these assessments provides insights into students' thinking. We should use the results of these informal measures to inform future instructional decisions.

Reciprocal Teaching

Reciprocal Teaching is a routine designed to promote students' comprehension of text. It involves four comprehension strategies—predicting, questioning, clarifying, and summarizing—and takes the form of reciprocal interactions between group members regarding segments of text. The teacher demonstrates the "role of the teacher" in leading a strategy-based discussion about the text. Then the teacher engages in a gradual release of responsibility and students take turns engaging in that role (Palincsar & Brown, 1984).

Reciprocal Teaching has three purposes:

1. To help students participate in a group effort to bring meaning to a text
2. To teach students that the reading process requires continual use of the four strategies (predicting, questioning, clarifying, summarizing) for effective comprehension
3. To provide students with the opportunity to monitor their own thinking and learning

Implementing Reciprocal Teaching. In order to successfully implement the Reciprocal Teaching procedure, we teach it explicitly. The following steps facilitate this process:

1. *Explain:* Begin by explaining that Reciprocal Teaching is a routine that involves four comprehension strategies and reciprocal discussion among group members. Explain each strategy—predicting, questioning, clarifying, and summarizing—and how it is used as students silently read a segment of text. Remind the students that they have already

learned how to use these strategies individually and now they will be using them together in Reciprocal Teaching.

2. *Demonstrate*: Begin by introducing the text. Next, read aloud a small section of text and demonstrate each of the strategies using verbal prompts, such as those suggested by Mowery (1995). Think aloud as you demonstrate the four strategies.

Predicting

I think _____

I bet _____

I imagine _____

I predict _____

Questioning

I wonder _____

I am curious about _____

What connections can I make?

How does this support my thinking?

Clarifying

I did not understand the part where _____

I need to know more about _____

Summarizing

The important ideas in what I read are _____

In my own words, this is about _____

Then engage in Reciprocal Teaching with a preselected demonstration group of students. Think aloud as you and the participating students prepare to read a segment of text silently and discuss it using the four comprehension strategies. Think aloud about the "role of the teacher" and how students will eventually assume that role. Give one of the four strategies and suggested prompts to each group member. Read a section of text silently. Invite students to explain how they used the strategies. Rotate strategies and repeat this process with at least three segments of text.

3. *Guide*: Read aloud another section of text and invite groups of four students to participate in Reciprocal Teaching using the process modeled. Provide the students with Reciprocal Teaching Bookmarks (see Appendix B, pages 297–298) to support their strategy use. Continue the process of reading aloud a section of text and guiding students to use the four Reciprocal Teaching strategies with at least two segments of text. Observe students as they engage in Reciprocal Teaching and assist as needed. Then discuss the text and Reciprocal Teaching with the students.

4. *Practice*: Continue the process of reading aloud a section of text, as students independently use the Bookmarks as they engage in Reciprocal Teaching with at least two sections of text. Reduce support as students demonstrate increased ability to successfully use this routine.

Invite the groups to use Reciprocal Teaching as they finish reading the selection. Engage the students in discussion of the text and Reciprocal Teaching.

5. *Reflect*: Provide opportunities for the students to reflect on their Reciprocal Teaching experiences. Encourage them to share their ideas in small groups and to record their thoughts on a Reciprocal Teaching Self-Assessment form (see Appendix B, page 299). This will lead to further goal setting.

This process provides students with opportunities to share their thinking in a reciprocal fashion. While students are participating in their groups, we can monitor their activity and scaffold the dialogue when appropriate. Once the students are skilled at using Reciprocal Teaching, they can use it as an independent comprehension routine.

Studies by Palincsar and Brown (1984) demonstrate that students with a wide variety of abilities can use Reciprocal Teaching successfully. Although originally designed to help students who could decode well but had weak comprehension skills, Reciprocal Teaching benefits all students because it encourages students to read, effectively use the strategies, and understand more challenging texts.

Selecting texts for Reciprocal Teaching. Text selection is influenced by students' abilities and interests, as well as the instructional setting in which Reciprocal Teaching is being used. Narrative texts should have complex story lines that require critical thinking. Informational texts should have complex organizations and enough information for students to distinguish essential from nonessential content.

Assessing students in Reciprocal Teaching. We can assess students in Reciprocal Teaching groups by observing their conversations and documenting their ability to successfully execute the strategies. (An observation checklist for Reciprocal Teaching is included in Appendix D, page 328.) Students may use a form to self-reflect on their contributions (see Appendix B, page 299) or they may keep notes of the ideas they contributed on their Reciprocal Teaching Bookmarks or in their Guided Comprehension Journals. Guided Comprehension Journals are used for recording students' ideas. They can be any kind of notebook. Students use the journals in all stages of the Model. For example, when engaging in Reciprocal Teaching, students can use their journals to record ideas, to respond to prompts, or to reflect on new insights. This information promotes discussion and informs future instruction.

Questioning the Author

Questioning the Author (QtA; Beck & McKeown, 2006; McKeown, Beck, & Worthy, 1993) is a text-based instructional format that helps students engage in deeper understanding of texts by learning to query the author. This process helps readers engage with text by considering text ideas in-depth and using a "reviser's eye." QtA can be used with both narrative and informational texts (Beck, McKeown, Hamilton, & Kucan, 1997).

QtA empowers the reader to actively make something understandable. Students learn to construct personal meanings and therefore make texts understandable—something mature readers do when reading (McKeown et al., 1993). When using QtA, students learn that building understanding involves determining what information means, not just extracting it from the text (Beck et al., 1997). In other words, QtA strongly supports the view of reading as a thinking process.

Implementing Questioning the Author. Before students can use QtA, we need to explicitly teach it. The Guided Comprehension Model provides opportunities not only for this explicit teaching, but also for students' transfer and application. To teach students QtA, we follow these steps:

1. *Explain*: Begin by explaining that Questioning the Author (QtA) helps us to understand text when authors leave out important details or parts of the text. Using QtA helps readers determine what information is missing, implied, and/or needed in order to engage meaningfully with the text. Explain that we use questions, known as queries, as general probes to initiate discussion. Queries are essential components of QtA and include the following (Beck et al., 1997):

   - What is the author trying to tell us?
   - What is meant by that?
   - Why is the author telling us that?
   - Did the author say it clearly?
   - How could the author have said it better?

2. *Demonstrate*: Introduce the text. Throughout the demonstration, read aloud a portion of the text and, using Think-Alouds, verbalize queries that could be posed to discern what the author really means. Begin with a query related to the big idea of the section, such as "What is the author telling us?" Then follow up with more specific queries such as, "Why is the author telling us that?" and "How could the author have said it better?" Think aloud so students can observe this thinking process. Guide students to respond to the queries, noting that ideas can later be refuted, revised, or challenged by other others in the class. Engage the students in discussion about the text. (See Appendix A, page 222, for details about Think-Alouds.)

3. *Guide*: Then read another section of text aloud and guide students to work with partners to respond to similar queries, beginning with the big idea of the section and then analyzing what the author is saying. Engage the students in discussion to build an understanding of the text.

4. *Practice*: Continue to read aloud sections of text and gradually reduce the amount of support as the students demonstrate their ability to independently use QtA to make meaning from the text. Discuss students' query responses and encourage students to use QtA as they read texts on their own.

5. *Reflect*: Encourage students to reflect on how QtA helps them to comprehend and how they can use it in other settings.

After we demonstrate QtA with the whole class, we ask students to practice the process in small groups. An effective way to guide this practice is to provide groups with the same text and guide them through the process of reading, querying, discussing responses in groups, and sharing answers with the class. We scaffold this process until students grasp how to generate the queries. Then we can turn over the responsibility to the students in the group, providing assistance as needed. As the students engage in this process, we observe and probe, helping them move through the text. Once the students understand how to question the author, they can engage in the process independently during comprehension routines.

QtA helps students learn to use queries as a way to interact with text for the purpose of understanding. In other words, they are constructing meaning by interacting with the text from their perspective and the author's, not just reading and recalling what is on the page (Allen & Mohr, 2008). Students can work in pairs or small groups to talk about the ideas the author is trying to convey. This cognitively active process helps students assume a responsible role in understanding text. When students become proficient in using QtA, they can use it with peers as a comprehension routine in Stage Two of the Guided Comprehension Model.

Selecting texts for Questioning the Author. Text choices for using QtA can be based on a number of factors. When demonstrating QtA for the class, the text should be one that poses some challenges, encourages critical thinking, and leaves questions to be answered. The following examples suggest ideas for selecting narrative and informational text:

- For a narrative text, a good choice would be one in which certain aspects of story elements are given, but others are implied. This may be related to plot structure, characterization, or theme. The goal is to use QtA to help students work through a complex text, "reading between the lines" and creating understandings based on what message they think the author is trying to convey.
- With informational text, a good choice would be one that provides some of the information but assumes additional reader knowledge. When students use QtA, they can learn to determine what information is missing, discounted, implied, or needed in order to comprehend text.

Another factor to consider when choosing a book to demonstrate QtA is students' background knowledge. It is important to be able to guide students through the process of generating questions for the author. To successfully create questions, students must have some knowledge of content, understanding of the type and purpose of the text, and familiarity with levels of questioning. (For ideas about teaching students how to generate questions, see the discussion of self-questioning earlier in this chapter.)

Assessing students in Questioning the Author. Because assessment in QtA is based on the questions students ask and the conclusions they draw, observation is often the most effective method. We make notes about what the students say and do, which provides the impetus for more demonstrations about the process. (An observation checklist to facilitate this process is included in Appendix D.) We also ask students to reflect on their questions and subsequent understandings as a way to assess comprehension of the text. We use a self-assessment form to facilitate documentation and provide data for later lessons and demonstrations (see Appendix B, page 296).

Using teaching routines such as Literature Circles, Reciprocal Teaching, and Questioning the Author not only provides us with frameworks for teaching, but also helps students to comprehend. This supports Duke and Pearson's (2002) belief that students can use an integrated set of strategies with any text to help build deeper understandings while they read. When students become proficient, they can use Literature Circles, Reciprocal Teaching, or Questioning the Author as independent comprehension routines in Stage Two of the Model.

When reviewing the components of the Guided Comprehension Model, it is important to acknowledge that in addition to the whole-group instruction that occurs in Stage One, all students participate in teacher-guided small groups and experience small-group, paired, and independent practice and transfer on a daily basis. This assures that students transact with multiple types and levels of text in a variety of settings.

Once Stage One of the Model is completed, the class progresses to Stage Two, which is the focus of the next chapter. This stage is comprised of three different instructional settings: teacher-directed small groups, student-facilitated comprehension centers, and student-facilitated comprehension routines.

Making Connections to Theory and Practice

To learn more about Literature Circles, Reciprocal Teaching, and Questioning the Author, read the following:

Beck, I.L., & McKeown, M.G. (2006). *Improving comprehension with Questioning the Author.* New York: Scholastic.

Blanton, W.E., Pilonieta, P., & Wood, K.D. (2007). Promoting meaningful adolescent reading instruction through integrated literacy circles. In J. Lewis & G. Moorman (Eds.), *Adolescent literacy instruction: Policies and promising practices* (pp. 212–237). Newark, DE: International Reading Association.

Palincsar, A.S., & Brown, A.L. (1986). Interactive teaching to promote independent learning from text. *The Reading Teacher, 39,* 771–777.

CHAPTER 3

Teacher-Guided Small Groups and Student-Facilitated Independent Practice

I n this chapter we delineate Stage Two of the Guided Comprehension Model. In Stage One, students learn in a whole-class setting. In Stage Two, they learn in teacher-guided small groups and a variety of independent settings. We have designed this chapter to address the multiple purposes of Stage Two:

- To provide meaningful, comfortable settings for a community of learners
- To afford students a variety of opportunities to apply strategies
- To provide students with occasions to work with teacher support, with peer support, and on their own

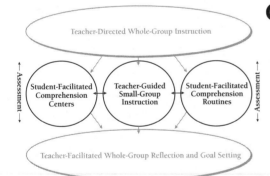

Organizing for Stage Two

In Stage Two of Guided Comprehension, students participate in three different instructional settings: teacher-guided small groups, student-facilitated comprehension centers, and student-facilitated comprehension routines. In this stage we provide students with opportunities to apply the comprehension strategies in a variety of settings with varying levels of support. Texts in this stage vary from the instructional-level texts used in the teacher-guided small groups to the independent-level texts used when students work independently in comprehension centers and routines.

Because students are working in three different settings in this stage, having an organizational plan is essential. One way to manage this time is to use a chart that illustrates the settings in which students should be at given times (see Figure 3). Other organizational plans can be found in Appendix B. A visual display noting where students should be at specific times eliminates students' needing to ask, "Where should I be now?" It also keeps students from interrupting the teacher, who is engaging in guided reading with a small group of students.

Figure 3. Organizing for Stage Two

Centers	Session 1	Session 2
Partner Reading	▭ ▭ ▭ ▭	▭ ▭ ▭ ▭
Mystery	▭ ▭ ▭	▭ ▭ ▭
Poetry	▭ ▭ ▭	▭ ▭ ▭
Making and Writing Words	▭ ▭	▭ ▭
Writing	▭ ▭ ▭	▭ ▭ ▭

Routines	Session 1	Session 2
Literature Circles	▭ ▭ ▭ ▭	▭ ▭ ▭ ▭
Reciprocal Teaching	▭ ▭ ▭	▭ ▭ ▭
Questioning the Author	▭ ▭ ▭	▭ ▭ ▭

Teacher-Guided Small Groups	▭ ▭ ▭ ▭ ▭ ▭	▭ ▭ ▭ ▭ ▭ ▭

Teacher-Guided Small-Group Instruction

Although Stage Two of Guided Comprehension is characterized by three different settings, only one is teacher-guided. In this small-group setting, students of similar abilities apply their knowledge of strategies to leveled texts to become active, engaged readers. Students are dynamically grouped and progress at individual rates, changing groups as they become prepared to transact with increasingly challenging levels of text.

When organizing for teacher-guided small-group instruction, we need to consider the following factors:

- All students in the group need to have similar instructional levels; this means that all students in this Guided Comprehension setting should be able to read the same texts with some teacher support.

- What we are teaching is determined by students' needs, interests, and use of strategies while constructing meaning.

- While teaching in this setting, we also need to monitor students who are working independently.

Once the small groups are formed and the appropriate texts are matched to students' abilities (see Chapter 5 for assessments to facilitate grouping; see Chapter 6 for text leveling processes), we meet with one or more guided small groups every day. During our time with the students, we use the Guided Comprehension small-group lesson format, which progresses in the following manner:

1. *Review* previously taught strategies and focus on the strategy that was taught in Stage One. Introduce the text.

2. *Guide* the students to work on their own to apply the current strategy, as well as previously taught strategies, as they read a section of the instructional-level text. Prompt the students to construct personal meanings. Scaffold as necessary, gradually releasing support as students become more proficient. Encourage discussion. Include written documentation, such as ideas recorded on graphic organizers, if appropriate. Repeat this process with other sections of text.

3. *Practice* by asking students to continue to apply the strategies. Ask students to record their applications in their Guided Comprehension Journals or on blacklines and share them in either small group or whole group during Stage Three.

4. *Reflect* by inviting students to share ways in which the strategy helped them to understand the text. Discuss ways in which students can apply the strategy in the comprehension centers and routines.

Review the Strategies

Each guided small group begins with the teacher reminding students about strategies that have been taught previously. It is helpful to have all the strategies posted on a chart in the classroom or to have them listed on a bookmark or other quick reference for the students. This review reminds students about the strategies and prepares students to apply them as they read; our goal is for students to build a repertoire of strategies they will use to facilitate their construction of meaning. After this quick review, our focus shifts to revisiting the strategy most recently taught in the whole-group setting.

Guide Students to Apply the Strategies

We begin by introducing the text and helping students preview. Then students read a designated portion of the text silently or in whisper tones. We sometimes ask the students to read in whisper tones so we can check for fluency and observe strategy use. During reading we guide students to use all appropriate comprehension strategies and briefly discuss the text. After reading, we guide the students to discuss their understandings. To facilitate this, we may revisit predictions, verbalize connections, or share visualizations. We may ask, "What does this remind you of?" "Have you ever had an experience like this?" "How is this character like...?" We can also revisit students' original predictions and ask students to determine why their thinking has changed or remained the same. After this, the students read another predetermined section of the text and stop for more guided discussion. Sometimes we also have students document their thinking on a graphic organizer or sticky note. This serves as a quick visual documentation of thinking and helps the students remember their ideas.

Practice the Strategies

When we believe the students are actively engaging with the text and constructing meaning, we invite them to practice. For example, we may have them finish reading the text independently and then discuss it with members of the small group. If the text appears challenging for the students, we may continue guiding their comprehension until they are more successful.

Reflect on the Strategies

After the students have finished reading the text, the group discusses the text as a whole. Students may make personal responses, retell portions of the text, share new information or insights, or reread favorite or interesting parts. This is also when we guide students to make broader connections to other texts and extend their understandings. These may be documented through writing, drawing, dramatization, or oral discourse. This is a good time for us to observe student responses and connections; this information will inform dynamic grouping, future student–text matches, and instructional planning. During discussion, it is important to encourage students to reflect on their reading and review the strategies they used to make sense of the text. This will remind students to transfer what they have learned in whole-group instruction and in their Guided Comprehension small groups to their reading of other texts. The Guided Comprehension Model provides students with two settings for such independent practice: comprehension centers and comprehension routines. These components are detailed in the next two sections of this chapter.

Student-Facilitated Comprehension Centers

Comprehension centers provide purposeful, authentic opportunities to apply strategies individually, with a partner, or in small groups. Activities in these centers emerge from a strategy-based perspective of literacy that promotes the integration of reading, writing, and discussion. The centers are related to themes students have been reading about and the strategies and skills that have been taught in whole-group settings.

The centers offer a variety of ways for students to practice various aspects of comprehension. The centers are usually located around the perimeter of the classroom and away from the teacher-guided small-group area. They vary in appearance from a table-top display to file folders, pizza boxes, or gift bags. It is important to remember that the content of the center is more important than its physical appearance.

When creating Guided Comprehension Centers, we recommend that clear, concise directions be provided for students. These should appear on the center and copies should also be available, so students who choose to work at their seats can take a copy of the directions with them (see Figure 4).

Students can move from center to center in a variety of ways, depending on the structure of the literacy schedule and the independence of the students. One way to organize the center time is to use a chart that provides a visual organizational system of the day (see Figure 3, page 34). This chart shows where each student is during Stage Two. Center options are included on the chart and student names can be placed in the spaces provided. The number of students who may work at a given center or at a given activity is designated. For example, there are three designated spaces provided on the chart for the poetry center; therefore, three students may choose that

Figure 4. Sample Directions for a Guided Comprehension Theme Center

1. <u>Choose</u> a partner.

2. <u>Select</u> a book from the theme center that you will both enjoy reading.

3. <u>Take</u> two "I Wonder" Bookmarks from the green folder.

4. <u>Think</u> about the title and the cover of the book. <u>Discuss</u> with your partner.

5. <u>Wonder</u> before you begin reading and <u>write</u> your wonders and your reasoning on the bookmark. <u>Discuss</u> with your partner. As you continue reading, <u>think</u> about the information the text may provide about your wonder.

6. <u>Decide</u> with your partner how much you will read silently. <u>Wonder</u> while you are reading the book and <u>write</u> your wonders and your reasoning on your bookmark. <u>Discuss</u> with your partner. <u>Think</u> about the information the text may provide about your wonders.

7. <u>Wonder</u> after you have read the book and <u>write</u> your wonder and your reasoning on your bookmark. <u>Discuss</u> with your partner. <u>Think</u> about how you can verify your wonder.

8. <u>Take</u> a center self-assessment from the blue folder and <u>reflect</u> on your work.

9. <u>Put</u> your completed "I Wonder" Bookmark and your center self-assessment in your Guided Comprehension folder.

center. When students complete their work at the poetry center, they may move on. For example, a student may write a poem at the poetry center and then choose to work on a project at the research center. This assures that student choice is being accommodated on multiple levels: They can choose what goals they are trying to achieve that day, which centers to visit, how long to stay, and how to manage their time. We can also provide students with a framework for required and optional centers (see Appendix B, page 300). Sometimes we may choose to assign students to the centers where they will start and then students can move as they complete their tasks, and when there are openings at other centers.

Some teachers prefer to move the students using a rotational schedule. With this, students move periodically among three or four activities (see Appendix B, page 288). This rotational format provides maximum control by the teacher, but limits students' opportunities to manage their own time.

Student Accountability

It is important to have accountability for the time students spend at the centers, because they are working independently—without teacher monitoring. Record-keeping systems can help teachers keep track of which centers each student visits during the week. For example, we can use a whole-group chart to monitor who visits which centers each week, or we can place charts at individual centers for students to record their visits. Students may also keep track of their work in their Guided Comprehension Journals. We can also keep student work and reflections in a two-pocket folder and review them weekly or biweekly.

Students share their work in Stage Three or during individual conferences. Reflection forms and rubrics facilitate this process. Students can complete center rubrics or use response sheets to reflect on what they have learned at each center and how they have progressed toward their current goal. We do not believe we need to evaluate every task students complete at centers, but students do need to be accountable for the work. (Reproducible center rubrics, reflection forms, and self-assessments can be found in Appendix B, pages 276–278.)

Ideas for Creating Comprehension Centers

Guided Comprehension centers should provide motivational, engaging opportunities for students to apply comprehension strategies. When participating in comprehension centers, students should have access to independent-level text. This is the level at which students can read without any support from the teacher. (See Chapter 6 for more information about leveled text.)

We suggest using several different types of Guided Comprehension Centers. Some centers, such as the independent reading center and the writing center, will be available to students throughout the year with changes in themes and resources. For example, we have an alphabet book center, in which students create their own books. During the course of the year, the topic of the books as well as the resources provided could change from the state in which we live to outer space to the Holocaust, depending on the current theme. Other centers may be specific to a genre or a content area topic. These centers, which feature projects, literature extensions, or research directly related to specific topics, may be available to students only at certain times during the year.

During comprehension center time, students can work on their own, in pairs, or in small groups to complete comprehension-based activities, projects, research, or extensions related to the topics they are studying or the books they are reading. We like to provide structure for these projects, but we make sure that they are open-ended to provide students with opportunities to make choices and apply their thinking and personal interpretations. Suggestions for centers and accompanying activities, open-ended projects, extensions, and research follow.

Drama center. Students use drama to demonstrate understandings of stories and content area topics. While students are working at this center, they can be creating, planning, and rehearsing for the dramatic performance. Following are some ideas for implementing drama in the classroom.

Dinner Party (Vogt, 2000): Students choose people—such as characters from novels or short stories, scientists, presidents, military leaders, artists, explorers, or authors—from content areas of study. They then have a dinner party and act out the conversation that the guests would be having. Dialogue must relate to information gained in their studies.

You Are There (Vogt, 2000): Students select a content area event that they will research. After they gather information, they select a character that was important in the event. They then create interview questions and responses related to that person. Pairs of students reenact the event through this interviewer–interviewee format.

Readers Theatre: Students either transcribe a story or other text into a play format or use an existing one to dramatize stories. Then they rehearse the dramatization using voice, facial expressions, and movement to portray characterizations. They use scripts during the performance. There are several websites that provide scripts for Readers Theatre. The following are among our favorites:

- www.aaronshep.com

   Author Aaron Shepherd's website on Readers Theatre contains resources, stories, scripts, and more.

- www.proteacher.com/070173.shtml

   This site provides a listing of websites that offer suggestions for writing scripts, ideas for using Readers Theatre, and scripts for classroom use.

- www.teachingheart.net/readerstheater.htm

   Extensive listing of scripts and other tips for using Readers Theatre in your classroom.

- www.readingonline.org/electronic/carrick/

   Internet Resources for Conducting Readers Theatre—This article discusses how to implement Readers Theatre and suggests Internet sites to help.

Genre center. We maintain a genre center that changes as the year progresses. Examples of topics include science fiction, biography, folk tales, mythology, historical or realistic fiction, legends, fantasy, mysteries, or poetry. For examples of how to create a genre center, see the mystery center and poetry center sections.

Mystery center. Students use the mystery center to engage in inquiry-based learning and problem solving. When using this center, students question, read, write, solve, and dramatize to extend their understandings. The following are descriptions of our favorite ways to engage students in the Mystery Center.

Create-a-Mystery: Label bags or boxes with the major components of a mystery (i.e., suspects, clues, victims, detectives, criminals, motives, crimes, and crime scenes). The students will record on index cards examples of each from mystery novels they have read. Then they will place the index cards in the appropriate bag or box. Other students will select one index card from each box and use that information to create another mystery. After writing their mystery, they can illustrate it and share it with the class. The students can extend this activity by participating in a mystery theater.

Suspicious Suspects: The students will organize their thoughts of the suspects in a novel by completing the Mystery Suspect Organizer (see Appendix B, page 290). Based on the clues, the students can easily come to a conclusion about who committed the crime. This organizer also can be completed before writing a mystery.

Write Your Own Mystery: The students will use the Write Your Own Mystery graphic organizer to help create a new mystery story (see Appendix B, page 302). On the organizer, they will draw, describe, or explain the crime scene. They will write four clues and describe a main character. They will also write a brief description of how the mystery is solved. The students may also use this activity to retell mysteries they have read. As an alternative writing activity, students can read the introduction to *The Mysteries of Harris Burdick* (Van Allsburg, 1984) and choose a picture and story starter from the book. Then they can either write a solution to what happened to Harris Burdick or write a story based on the picture they selected. Figure 5 contains a mystery that Connor Watkins, a sixth-grade student, wrote based on a Harris Burdick picture and story starter.

Mystery Poems: Using different poetry formats such as acrostic, cinquain, diamante, bio-poem, and definition poem, have students write about various aspects of a mystery novel (see Appendix B, pages 294–295, for poetry forms). Students can then use their poems for a poetry theater

Figure 5. Mystery Center Sixth-Grade Writing Sample

The House on Maple Street

It was a perfect lift-off. I had no idea what had happened. I was watching television, while my parents were visiting friends next door. Suddenly, I felt as if I were being launched into space.

When I ran to the window, I saw that it was true! My house had lifted off its foundation and was now heading into outer space! I didn't know what to do, but I found myself grabbing a chair and sitting near the front window. It was as if I were in a planetarium. The stars were so close I felt as if I could touch them. I couldn't take my eyes off them. Then I would see different planets as my house raced by them.

After that my house seemed to lose much of its speed and began drifting through space as if it were a tour bus. It passed Mars—the red planet. Then suddenly camera flashes were blinding me! As I tried to focus, I could see martians continuing to take my picture.

All of a sudden my house started falling through the stars and I could see Earth again. I was certain my house was going to crash and I wondered where in the world it would land. After what seemed like an endless amount of time, it settled right back down on its very own foundation. I was amazed and struggled to catch my breath. When I was finally breathing normally again, my parents walked through the back door. Then suddenly cameras started flashing again.

presentation. For example, students can write an acrostic about one of the suspects in a mystery novel. The name can be written vertically. The letters in the suspect's name can be starters for the clues related to this suspect.

Mystery Pyramid: Students can summarize or manipulate language by trying to fit all the elements of a mystery into a Mystery Pyramid (see Appendix B, page 289).

Mystery Theater: The students can script and practice a scene from a mystery to perform to the class. The students will try to guess what mystery the scene is from and the characters involved.

Word Detective: Using the Sequential Roundtable Organizer, the students can create a master list or word wall of mystery words from novels read (see Appendix B, page 301). This can then serve as a writing tool or be used for word sorts.

Independent reading center. Students choose to read leveled text from a variety of genres on their own. While reading, students use appropriate Guided Comprehension strategies. They also use a variety of formats to record their thinking. These may include bookmarks, sticky notes, graphic organizers, or journals.

Making books center. Students can retell key events from stories, gather data and create reports on content area topics, or write creative pieces that can be published. These pieces may be self-created or follow a familiar structure, such as alphabet books or biographies. The following is a list of books and suggestions for using them (see Appendix B, page 281, for directions for making books):

- *Accordion books*: retellings, content area facts, creative stories with illustrations
- *Origami books*: retellings, facts, short stories, story elements
- *Flip/flap books*: word work (parts of speech, antonyms, synonyms, rhymes, story elements, prefixes/suffixes), story elements, character traits
- *Slotted books*: journals, reading response, word books, alphabet books
- *Dos à dos books*: dialogue or buddy journals, research and report, compare/contrast
- *Stair-step books*: riddle books, sequence story events, timelines

Pattern book center. Students use a pattern from a familiar book and retell their story or share information using the pattern. Examples of books that have effective patterns include *The Important Book* (1990) by Margaret Wise Brown, *Animal Fact/Animal Fable* (1979) by Seymour Simon, question-and-answer books by Melvin and Gilda Berger, or alphabet books. We have found it helpful to provide specific organizers to help students plan these books (see Appendix B, pages 291–293).

Poetry center. We keep a large supply of poetry books and poetry cards at this center. We also provide lots of copies of poems that students can read, act out, or illustrate. Following is a list of activities our students have enjoyed completing at the poetry center.

Form Poems: Students create their own poems using structured formats. Poems can be written about stories, informational texts, or other topics about which the students are reading.

(Reproducible forms for bio-poems, cinquains, diamantes, definition poems, and others can be found in Appendix B, pages 294–295.)

Poetry Frames: Students create their own versions of published poems. We create frames in which students can write their own words, keeping the structure but changing the content of the original poem. (A poetry frame for "If I Were in Charge of the World" is included in Appendix B, page 283.)

Poem Impressions: Students write story poems based on a series of clues provided from an existing story poem. Then students share their poems. Finally, the original poem is read and discussion focuses on comparison or contrast of the impressions and the original poem.

Poetry Theater: In small groups, students plan and practice dramatizing a poem. These dramatizations include minimal theatrics and props, and maximum expression through voice and actions. Students practice for an appropriate amount of time and then perform the poems for their classmates. We encourage students to respond to each poem performance by praising their peers and offering one suggestion.

Project center. Students work on specific extensions or projects related to literature or the content area of study. These may include multiple modes of response including reading, writing, illustrating, dramatizing, or other modes of investigation. Here are some projects our students have enjoyed the most:

Bookmarks: Students create bookmarks about the book they read. We can set the criteria or give students a choice about what to include on the bookmark. Some suggestions for narrative texts are title, author, main characters, critique, and illustrations of characters or events. For informational texts, students can include title, author, and key ideas they learned and their reactions or reflections.

Literature Response Projects: Students may self-select a project from an extensive list of literature response ideas (see Appendix C). They may work on these projects over time and may choose whether to work individually or with a partner. We add literature response ideas throughout the year.

Open-Mind Portraits: Students draw two or more portraits of one of the characters in the story. One is a regular face of the character; the others are one or more pages that represent the mind of the character at important points in the story. The mind pages include words and drawings representing the character's thoughts and feelings (Tompkins, 2006). For longer texts, we encourage students to keep track of a character's thoughts and feelings throughout the text—organized chapter by chapter or by beginning, middle, and end.

Choose Your Own Project: Students make selections from the project chart to design their own product or performance related to a theme or text. The teacher has demonstrated all choices in previous lessons. A chart listing students' options facilitates this process (see Appendix B, page 279).

Research center. Students work on research specific to content literacy studies. Various reference materials, from encyclopedias to books to the Internet, are readily available. Our students' favorite research center activities include the following.

PowerPoint Presentations: Students gather information about a topic and then create a series of PowerPoint slides to share the information. We show students how to synthesize key points, use transitions, and select appropriate templates, slide layouts, and graphics. We also teach them how to find and import photos and clip art to support the text. When the presentations are completed, students share them with their classmates. This adds to students' content knowledge and also provides opportunities to practice communicating with an audience.

Press Conference (McLaughlin, 2010): This is an inquiry-based activity that promotes oral communication. Students choose a topic to investigate, and then peruse newspapers, magazines, or the Internet to find at least two sources of information about the topic. After reading the articles, focusing on essential points, raising questions, and reflecting on personal insights, the student presents an informal summary of his or her research to a group of classmates or the entire class. Members of the audience raise questions that can lead to "I Wonder" Statements that they can record in their investigative journals.

Questions Into Paragraphs (QuIP) (McLaughlin, 1987): Students ask questions related to a chosen topic and use two or more sources to find answers to each question. The information is recorded on a QuIP Research Grid and then used to write a summary paragraph or to organize research for a Press Conference (see Appendix A, pages 226–227 and 268).

The Rest of the Story (McLaughlin, 2010): This inquiry-based investigation encourages the researcher to go beyond the basic facts generally known about a person, discovery, invention, or event in content area study. For example, students could choose a famous inventor such as Alexander Graham Bell and use The Rest of the Story to learn about his life. Students use numerous resources to locate information, including the Internet. Technology also plays a role in the way students choose to format their investigations to share them with the class; they may elect to design a webpage or create software. CDs or DVDs are other popular formatting selections. When using DVDs, students may report their research as a news story or choose to dramatize the results of their investigation.

ReWrite (Bean, 2000): In this activity, students write songs before and after content area study. For example, students write a song based on what they think they know about bats. Then they read to learn about bats and rewrite their lyrics based on the new information. ReWrite represents how students' knowledge, perceptions, and feelings have changed after studying the topic. Tunes may include familiar songs or instrumental tapes.

The Electronic Class Newspaper: Students use class computers to write a variety of newspaper articles related to the topic being studied and publish them in an electronic newspaper format. They can also create "period" newspapers (e.g., the setting of a novel).

Theme center. Students work on their own or with a partner and apply Guided Comprehension strategies while reading theme-related texts. The theme could be a favorite author, such as Shel Silverstein (see Figure 6). A variety of theme-related books at multiple levels are provided at this center. Copies of related blackline response sheets are also available.

Transmediation center. When creating transmediations, students choose ideas in an existing medium and change it to another. For example, students might choose to take a poem and turn it into a picture book or they might choose song lyrics and turn them into a work of art. Several examples of published transmediations are provided at this center. Examples include *Life Doesn't Frighten Me* (1993), a poem by Maya Angelou that has been turned into a picture book illustrated

Figure 6. Theme Center

with the paintings of Jean-Michel Basquiat, and *New York State of Mind* (2005), song lyrics by Billy Joel that have been turned into a picture book that is illustrated by Izak Zenou.

Vocabulary center. This center might have a word wall or other display of words that can be the focus of study. These words may be structurally similar (rhymes, prefix, suffix, roots) or may be theme related. This may also include interesting word books (such as *The Weighty Word Book* [1990] by Paul Levitt, *Animalia* [1996] by Graeme Base, or books by Fred Gwynne, Ruth Heller, or Marvin Terban) that can provide the impetus for word study. Students work on learning, using, and making connections to these new vocabulary words. Following is a list of activities students can complete at the vocabulary center.

Acrostics: Students write the name of a topic or character vertically and then write words or phrases to describe the topic, each description starting with one of the letters in the name. The focus can include characters, places, people, or any other topic related to areas of study. In the first example, students created an acrostic about Brian, the main character from Gary Paulsen's *Hatchet* (1987).

B rave enough to land a plane

R adio used to call for help

I n the wilderness he used his hatchet

A nimal attacks, hunger, and extreme weather

N ever gave up

In the next example, students used the acrostic format to retell the story of *Cinderella*.

C inderella lived in a far away land

I n a home with her stepmother and stepsisters

N ot allowed to attend the ball

D ear Cinderella sobbed

E vening brought Cinderella's fairy Godmother

R iding in a horse-drawn carriage

E legantly dressed Cinderella arrived at the castle

L aughing and twirling Cinderella danced until midnight

L eaving her glass slipper behind

A determined prince found Cinderella and they lived happily ever after

When writing acrostics, students can also use descriptive vocabulary to provide details about an informational topic they are studying. The following acrostic was written by a fifth-grade student after studying her home state of Maryland.

M id-Atlantic state

A nnapolis is the capital

R avens are the football team

Y achts are everywhere in the Chesapeake Bay

L argest city is Baltimore

A n oriole is the state bird and black-eyed susan is the state flower

N aval Academy is in Annapolis

D uring the bombardment of Fort McHenry, Francis Scott Key wrote "The Star Spangled Banner"

Invent a Word: Students use their knowledge of prefixes, suffixes, and roots to create new words and their meanings. They sketch a picture of the new word to demonstrate its meaning based on the word parts, and then write a sentence explaining their drawing.

Making and writing words center. For making and writing words (Rasinski, 1999), we use a mystery word related to the theme we are studying and provide the letters in random order on a chart or on a sheet for recording words. Students use the letters to make as many words as they can. Younger students may need to manipulate letter cards or tiles as they begin to make words; older student can write them as they think of them. We can provide clues to specific words or just let the students create as many as they can (see Appendix B, page 287). For example, if we are studying life cycles, we might use the word *caterpillar* as the mystery word. Then we would ask the students to make and write as many words as they can using the letters in that word. These words can be recorded for future use.

- Two-letter words: *at, it*
- Three-letter words: *cat, rat, pat, pit, lit, car, par, tar, all, ill, lip, tip, rip, air, act, ape, are, arc, art*
- Four-letter words: *rate, late, care, rare, pare, pear, pair, tall, call, clip, trip, pill, pact, cape, ripe, cart, race*
- Five-letter words: *trail, liter, alert, peril, price, alter, plate, trial, pleat, pearl, petal, relic, taper, crate, crept, crier, lilac, alert, later*
- Six-letter words: *pillar, carpet, pirate, taller, triple, parcel, caller, cellar, crater*
- Seven-letter words: *trailer, erratic*

Word Sorts: Students sort vocabulary words into categories provided by the teacher (closed sort) or by self-selected categories (open sort). These might include rhyming words, parts of speech, vowel sound, syllables, synonyms, words that describe particular characters, and specific content subtopics. Sorts may be completed in a hands-on fashion using word cards, and then students can record responses on a word-sort sheet. This activity also may be completed in writing on a web or other organized structure.

Word Storm: A visual display—such as a picture from a book, a piece of art, or a poster—provides the impetus for word brainstorming. Students look at the visual and brainstorm and record words that come to mind. Then they use some or all the words to create a detailed sentence or paragraph about the visual.

Writing center. This is a place for free and structured writing. For example, students can use writing to respond to literature, retell or summarize information, or share personal thoughts and feelings. Students can also take pieces through the various writing stages and publish their work. We can also support student writing by using one or more of the following ideas.

Journals:

- *Free writing*: Students write about self-selected topics. We brainstorm with the students a list of possible things they can write about—family members, friends, pets, vacations, sports, school, hobbies, books—and post this list at the center so students have ideas for their writing.
- *Prompted writing*: Students write in-depth about a variety of topics. We provide a sentence starter or a prompt to help students think about what they are reading in greater depth. (For a list of topics for prompted writing, see Appendix C.)
- *Reader response*: Students respond to texts they are reading in a journal or on a graphic organizer. Sometimes we prompt with specific stems or questions connecting to the strategy lesson that day; other times we encourage a free response.

    Example stem: This text reminds me of _____ because _____.

    Example question: What did you think was most important in the story? Why?

We keep a fresh list of literature response prompts at this center. These can be used at any time for responding to text. Students can then share responses in small groups and during the whole-group reflection time. These responses also may be turned in as documentation of student thinking and making connections.

Patterned Writing: Provide forms based on pattern books, poetry, fractured fairy tales, and nursery rhymes. (See Appendix B, pages 291–295, for pattern books and poetry forms.)

Sticker or Stamp Stories: Use stickers or stamps to create an illustration with action. Write a story to accompany the picture.

Story Bag: Put a variety of items in a bag. Students pull out one item at a time and build a story using these props to stimulate thinking. Students can also create their own Story Bag with artifacts representing key ideas from the text they have read and then they or other students can use the artifacts to summarize the story or information.

Story Collages: Instead of writing a story and then illustrating it, students create textured illustrations first and then develop stories based on them. Because the illustrations are textured (using pine cones, aluminum foil, felt, sand), students can use their tactile modalities (Brown, 1993). Students can write original stories or adapt versions of familiar tales they have read.

Story Impressions: Students write a story based on approximately 10 clues from a story. Each clue is from 1 to 5 words. The clues are placed sequentially and connected with downward arrows. The title of the original story may or may not be shared. When the story is completed and the student shares his or her story, the original author's story is read for comparison or contrast. (See Appendix A, pages 194 and 244, for details about how to teach Story Impressions and a blackline master for students to use.)

Regardless of what the centers include or how they are managed, it is important to remember that these are places for independent exploration by students. Guided Comprehension strategies, processes for documenting thinking, and center assessments should be taught explicitly before students are expected to use them independently at centers. The centers should include clear directions and activities that are familiar to students so they can apply skills and strategies without teacher support.

Student-Facilitated Comprehension Routines

After we teach and model a variety of comprehension strategies, students practice and transfer what they have learned in other settings, including comprehension routines. Comprehension routines are those habits of thinking and organizing that facilitate reading and response in authentic contexts. Students can use routines with multiple texts in various settings. The purpose of routines is to help students gain a deeper understanding of the text and to equip students with a set of strategies they can use with other texts on their own. These are independent settings; this implies that students are knowledgeable about the strategies and routines, they are provided with texts at their independent levels, and they have ample time for practicing and transferring these processes.

Routines are courses of action that are so ingrained that they can be used successfully on a regular basis. As we presented in Chapter 2, the routines we find most effective for promoting comprehension in both whole-group and small-group settings are Literature Circles, Reciprocal Teaching, and Questioning the Author. Before students can use these comprehension routines independently, they need to understand why they are engaging in the routines and how each functions. We accommodate these needs by explicitly teaching the routines. As the learning process progresses, we gradually release control of the routines to the students. Brief overviews of the routines are included here; detailed descriptions and ideas for teaching them can be found in Chapter 2. (For step-by-step processes for teaching these and other comprehension routines, see Appendix A, pages 237–240.)

Literature Circles

Literature Circles are group discussions in which students share meaningful ideas about texts they have read (Brabham & Villaume, 2000). In planning for Literature Circles, we explicitly teach students how to use the comprehension strategies, document their thinking, and work together. We also teach our students how to have a meaningful conversation about a text from different perspectives. Students then use the information they have recorded to guide their discussions with peers.

Reciprocal Teaching

Reciprocal Teaching is a comprehension routine that is strategy based and involves discussion of text. When using it as a comprehension routine, the students take turns assuming the role of "teacher" in leading the discussion (Palincsar & Brown, 1984). The discussion is focused on four comprehension strategies: predicting, questioning, clarifying, and summarizing.

Questioning the Author

Questioning the Author (QtA) is a text-based instructional format that helps students build a deeper understanding of texts by learning to query the author (Beck et al., 1997). Students engage in thinking about the big idea of the selection, and then use questions to probe further to clarify the information the author has presented.

Within each setting of Stage Two, we encourage students to reflect on what they have done and how well they have done it. This facilitates their transition into Stage Three, which is the focus of the next chapter. There we address teachers' and students' roles in the reflection and goal-setting processes.

Making Connections to Theory and Practice

To learn more about teacher-guided small groups and literacy centers, read the following:
Diller, D. (2005). *Practice with purpose: Literacy work stations for grades 3–6*. Portland, ME: Stenhouse.
Diller, D. (2007). *Making the most of small groups: Differentiation for all*. Portland, ME: Stenhouse.
Morrow, L.M. (2002). *The literacy center: Contexts for reading and writing*. Portland, ME: Stenhouse.

CHAPTER 4

Teacher-Facilitated Whole-Group Reflection and Goal Setting

n Stage Three of the Guided Comprehension Model, students engage in reflection, sharing, and goal setting. We have structured this chapter to address the multiple purposes of this stage:

- To provide a meaningful, comfortable setting for students to celebrate their learning
- To afford students opportunities to monitor learning by engaging in self-reflection
- To provide opportunities for students to share their thinking
- To create connections between self-reflection and goal setting

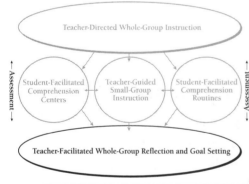

Organizing for Stage Three

In this setting we encourage students to think about what they have accomplished in the first and second stages of the Model. We want students to actualize their learning and be accountable for it. Bringing the class together also provides opportunities for closure and for celebrating new knowledge.

In Stage Three, students actively engage in reflection, sharing, and goal setting. The cyclical process of setting goals, engaging in learning experiences, reflecting on performance, and setting new goals helps students to perceive themselves as empowered, successful learners. It encourages students to think critically, observe progress, and take ownership of their learning. It also helps students to refine their thinking. As Brevig (2006) reminds us, when reflections are shared, students can bounce ideas off others and develop new insights.

It is these active roles in which students engage, not reflection itself, that is new to the educational process. In 1933, Dewey suggested that teachers become reflective practitioners to gain a better understanding of teaching and learning. In 1987, Schon noted that reflection offers us insights into dimensions of teaching and learning that can lead to better understanding. In the

1990s, when reflection became a valued component of evolving assessment practices, students were encouraged to actively engage in the process (Darling-Hammond, Ancess, & Falk, 1995; Hoyt & Ames, 1997; McLaughlin, 1995). In 2002, Douillard observed that "reflective activities in the classroom help make thinking more visible, enabling students to learn from one another and to gain greater insights into their own thinking and learning processes" (p. 93).

Self-reflection focuses on what students have learned and how they feel about their learning (Cooper & Kiger, 2001). It includes both self-assessment, which addresses process and product, and self-evaluation, which makes judgments about performance. Questions raised for self-assessment purposes include "What is confusing me?" and "How did I contribute to the discussion?" Questions that foster self-evaluation include "What did I do well?" and "Did I achieve my goal?"

Self-reflection offers insights into students' thinking. It not only illustrates that they are thinking, but also details *how* they are thinking. According to Hoyt and Ames (1997), "Self-reflection offers students an opportunity to be actively involved in internal conversations while offering teachers an insider's view of the learning and the student's perception of self as learner" (p. 19). This focus on internal conversations parallels Tierney and Pearson's (1994) idea that "literacy learning is an ongoing conversation with oneself.... If we view learning as dynamic in character, as that evolving dialogue with oneself, then even major shifts become little more than the natural, almost inevitable, consequence of human reflection" (p. 514).

Goal setting is a natural outgrowth of reflection. As Hansen (1998) notes, "learning proceeds from the known to the new" (p. 45). What students have learned to a given point influences what they learn next; this is the foundation of goal setting. Students reflect on what they have learned and set future personal goals for continuous improvement. When students actively engage in creating both personal and class goals, they appear to be more motivated and take more responsibility for their learning (Clemmons, Laase, Cooper, Areglado, & Dill, 1993; Hill & Ruptic, 1994).

Reflection and Goal Setting in Guided Comprehension

In Guided Comprehension, we engage in both whole-group and personal goal setting. Because our ultimate goal is to help students use comprehension strategies to transact with text, our whole-group and personal goals often focus on comprehension. Examples of whole-group goals include "We will use a variety of methods to preview text," and "We will use multiple approaches to evaluate text." Students engage in evaluation by sharing their work with peers and discussing everyone's progress. Students and teachers then decide if progress has been made in attaining the goal, if the goal has been achieved, and if a new goal needs to be set.

Because explicit instruction of reflection and goal setting is necessary, we apply the steps we presented in Chapter 2 to this process. We often use nonacademic topics such as hobbies or special interests to introduce strategies or concepts (McLaughlin, 1995). This works especially well in this stage, because students often have not had much experience with reflection; in fact, many may not even be familiar with the concept. The following is an excerpt from the explicit instruction of reflection and goal setting. Although students participated in this process through discussion, the excerpt focuses on our "thinking aloud" during the process.

- *Explain*: We explain to the students what reflection is and how it works.

Today we're going to learn about reflection, a special kind of thinking that allows us to examine something that we did or something that we learned. It can help us to understand how we learned and how well we learned.

- *Demonstrate*: We model reflection in action and use a Think-Aloud to share our reasoning process with students. For example, a teacher might provide a personal example to encourage students to engage in reflection.

I am a runner. I usually run a particular course that is about three miles long. I am going to explain reflection to you by sharing information about my last run. I am going to think about my run and then think about how I can improve it next time. When I started out, I was on a level part of the running path. I was able to keep a good pace for more than two miles. Then the path stretched up a series of hills and my pace slowed because the hills were more difficult than the level path and I wasn't strong enough or experienced enough to run the hills at a better pace. I continued to run and soon I was back on an easier part of the path. Before I knew it, I was at the end of my run. It was a good run except for the hills. When I think about what I can do to improve my run next time, my goal is to practice running just the hills to try to get stronger on that part of the course.

- *Guide*: We guide students to apply reflection to something they have learned. We often use reflection forms to facilitate this process (see Appendix D).

The forms I'm distributing are going to help you create your reflections. Remember how I reflected on my running? Well, now it is your turn to reflect on something you have learned to do. First, you'll need to think of a hobby, sport, or special interest that you have. Now focus on the last time you did it and think about what it was like. Consider these questions: How well did it go? What did you do well? What do you think you could do to improve your performance next time? What will your new goal be?

  Once we know the students understand how reflection works, we demonstrate how to transfer the process to reading. We prompt with questions such as, What did you do well in reading today? What strategies worked for you? Why did you use them? How did they help you? Were any of the ideas confusing? What did you need to do to clarify them?

- *Practice*: When we observe through their oral and written responses that students know how to reflect on their own understandings and performance, we provide opportunities for them to reflect in writing and orally share their insights and goals.

Today we were all engaged in Stage Two of Guided Comprehension. Let's reflect on something we did in Stage Two, how well we did it, what we could do to improve it next time, and what our new goal(s) will be.

We provide a few minutes for students to reflect and write. Then we invite them to share their reflections and new goals with partners, in small groups, or with the whole class. Our goal is for students to naturally engage in reflection as part of the learning process.

When they transferred their abilities to reflect and set goals to Guided Comprehension, students focused either on the process as a whole or on a particular component. The following are examples of new goals created at various grade levels:

- My goal for next time is to retell the story better. (Grade 3)
- I want to ask thicker questions, ones that have longer answers. (Grade 3)

- Next time I want to stay focused on my reading for a longer time and read a longer book. (Grade 4)
- My goal is to write a better summary. (Grade 5)
- My new goal is to say more when I'm in my Literature Circle. (Grade 6)
- My new goal is to use at least three sources when I research. (Grade 7)
- My new goal is to use the Internet to find sources for my research. (Grade 8)

When students become comfortable with reflection and goal setting, they are able to transfer their learning. For example, they can analyze their performance in all stages of Guided Comprehension, which means that they can reflect on their performance as a member of a whole group, small group, or pairs as well as individually. (See Appendix D for reflection forms students can use to document their thinking.)

Because reflection and goal setting are essential components of Guided Comprehension, it is important to motivate students to participate in them. The following are other teaching ideas we use to foster students' engagement in these processes.

Vary the Components

When planning reflection and goal setting, we make selections from the following four categories:

1. *Type of goal*: individual or whole-class, short-term or long-term
2. *Reflection setting*: whole-group, small-group, paired, or individual
3. *Reflection mode*: speaking, writing, illustrating, or dramatizing
4. *Sharing setting*: whole-group, small-group, paired, or individual

Choices can vary according to lesson content, student learning styles, or student interest. For example, students can create new personal goals by working in pairs to reflect on their learning, create sketches to illustrate their thinking, and then share them with a small group. We often encourage students to reflect and then share, first in small groups and then with the class. We cannot always hear everyone's ideas but this provides a larger audience for some students each day and provides us with windows into their thinking. We also gather important data when we read their reflections in their Guided Comprehension Journals.

There are several formats for engaging students in written reflection. Two we find effective are Guided Comprehension Journals and Tickets Out.

Guided Comprehension Journals. Guided Comprehension Journals are provided for students to use during all stages of the Model. For example, students can use them to record notes for Literature Circles, store their word choices from vocabulary self-selection, jot down questions that arise during Guided Comprehension, and engage in reflection. In Stage Three, they can use the journals to record their reflections and set new goals.

Tickets Out. Tickets Out is one of our favorite teaching ideas because it fosters reflection, helps us monitor students' learning, and takes very little time. It is called Tickets Out because students hand their tickets to us as they exit the classroom at the end of the period or the day. To participate in this activity, students use a half sheet of paper. On the first side, they write the most important thing they learned that day. On the other side, they write one question they have about something they learned that day. Whether students put their names on their tickets is the teacher's choice.

Students need only about 5 minutes to complete this activity and hand in the tickets. We should collect the tickets with side one facing up. When students have left the room, we read side one of their tickets first. This is not a time-consuming process, but it does provide valuable information. For example, it offers insight into what students valued about their learning and also gives us an opportunity to monitor and clarify any misconceptions they may have. During this part of Tickets Out, we set aside any tickets that need clarification. Next, we turn over the entire pile of tickets and read the questions students have about their learning. Some days more than one student will raise the same question, and other days not every student will have a question. During this part of Tickets Out, we set aside questions that we think address significant topics. We begin the next day's class by clarifying any information necessary from side one of the tickets. Then we respond to the selected questions, which usually number between four and six. Directly responding to students' thoughts and questions helps students understand that we value their thinking and enhances the continuity from class to class. (A graphic organizer for Tickets Out can be found in Appendix D, page 335.)

Provide Prompts

Providing prompts can assist students when they are engaging in reflection and goal setting in a variety of settings. Prompts help to focus students' thinking on various dimensions of learning.

Questions to Guide Reflection

- What was your goal today? What did you do to make progress toward your goal?
- What did you learn today? How will this learning help you as a reader?
- What did you do today that you have never done before?
- What strategies did you find most helpful? How did they help you?
- What confused you today? How did you figure it out?
- How did your group do? What contributions did you make to your group? What contributions did others make?
- What questions do you have about what you learned today?
- How do you think you will use what you learned today?

Questions to Guide Goal Setting

- What do you need to work on? Why?
- Where will you start next time?
- What do you hope to accomplish?
- What is your new goal? Why?

Reflection Stems

- I was really good at _____.
- The best thing was _____.
- I learned that _____.
- I contributed _____ to our literature discussion.
- I read _____ and found out that _____.
- When I was confused today, I _____.

Goal-Setting Stems

- I need more work on _____.
- Tomorrow I hope to _____.
- My goal for tomorrow is to _____.

Students can think about one or more of these prompts and then share their responses. Sharing can take place with a partner, small group, or the whole class. We often use Think–Pair–Share (McTighe & Lyman, 1988) as a framework for this. Students *think* about their learning, *pair* with a partner to discuss ideas, and then *share* their thoughts with the class. Students can also write their reflections in their Guided Comprehension Journals and then use Think–Pair–Share. This technique also can be adapted for goal setting. First, students think about their performance and new goal(s), then they write the goal(s). Next they pair with a partner to discuss their new goal(s). Finally, they share their goal(s) with the whole class. Sharing with the whole class is beneficial because it shows that everyone values reflection and goal setting and provides good models for the other students.

Assessment is another factor that affects student reflection and goal setting. In the next chapter we take a closer look at the multiple roles assessment plays in Guided Comprehension and examine related issues including connections to state assessments, practical assessment measures, and Guided Comprehension Profiles.

Making Connections to Theory and Practice

To learn more about reflection and goal setting, read the following:

Douillard, K. (2002). Going past done: Creating time for reflection in the classroom. *Language Arts*, *80*(2), 92–99.

Moore, J., & Whitfield, V.F. (2008). Musing: A way to inform and inspire pedagogy through self-reflection. *The Reading Teacher*, *61*(7), 586–588.

Schunk, D.H. (2003). Self-efficacy for reading and writing: Influence of modeling, goal setting, and self-evaluation. *Reading and Writing Quarterly*, *19*(2), 159–172.

CHAPTER 5

Assessment in Guided Comprehension

Assessment is a natural component of teaching and learning. It helps us gain insights into students' abilities, needs, experiences, and interests. We use assessment results to inform our teaching and help students to achieve their maximum potentials.

When we are teaching, we use assessments for a variety of purposes. For example, before teaching we use diagnostic assessments to determine what students know, to learn about their interests, and to identify approximate reading levels. While we are teaching we use formative assessments to document student progress and check for understanding. After we have taught, we use summative assessments to determine what students have learned, to gain insights into how successful our teaching has been, and to make decisions about what to teach next.

In this chapter we present a practical approach to student assessment. We begin by focusing on the dynamic nature of assessment and its multiple roles in Guided Comprehension. Next, we discuss how the Guided Comprehension Model supports student performance on state assessments. Then we describe a number of practical, informative assessments and their connections to Guided Comprehension. Finally, we introduce Guided Comprehension Profiles— tools to organize and manage student progress—and explain how they function. Throughout the chapter we also make connections to Appendix D, which contains a variety of reproducible assessments and assessment forms.

The Multiple Roles of Assessment in Guided Comprehension

Assessment in Guided Comprehension is dynamic in nature. It occurs in an ongoing manner, offers insights into students' thinking, chronicles student development, and is a natural component of teaching and learning (McLaughlin, 2002). This aligns with constructivist thinking about purposeful assessments (Brooks & Brooks, 1993; Tierney, 1998) and supports Vygotsky's belief that assessment should extend to scaffolded experiences to capture students' emerging abilities (Minick, 1987).

Assessment in Guided Comprehension has several purposes, including the following:

- To provide an approximate range of reading levels for students
- To offer insights into student attitudes and interests
- To facilitate student–text matches
- To inform grouping for teacher-guided instruction

- To check for student understanding
- To provide insights into students' thinking
- To document students' performance
- To provide information for evaluative purposes

Assessment permeates every stage of the Guided Comprehension Model and occurs in a variety of forms and settings. For example, we use diagnostic assessments to determine approximate student reading levels and analyze students' use of skills and strategies to decode and comprehend. These assessments provide valuable information for grouping students for small-group instruction in Stage Two and for guiding our decisions about which texts to use and which strategies to teach. We employ formative measures to monitor student learning as we are teaching and guiding. These assessments allow us to check for student understanding in a continuous, ongoing manner, and to adjust our teaching to better meet the needs of our students. We use summative assessments to examine what students have learned over time and to help us make instructional decisions for future lessons.

Connections to State Assessments

Since 2000, U.S. students in grades 3–12 have been required to show annual yearly progress (AYP) on standardized measures as part of the No Child Left Behind Act. This high-stakes testing environment has put pressure on students to do well and on teachers to ensure that students demonstrate proficiency. Although the pressure is great, we should resist the temptation to teach to the test and instead focus on providing excellent reading instruction. We believe that this, coupled with the knowledge that the single most important influence in student learning is the teacher (Gambrell, Malloy, & Mazzoni, 2007), will produce the desired results. Guided Comprehension supports student performance on these measures by focusing on student understanding, explicit strategy instruction, and multiple types and levels of text. It also emphasizes knowledge of text structure and encourages question generation at multiple levels. In addition, Guided Comprehension promotes student writing. When we view reading and writing as inextricable processes, students become more aware of how they think and more adept at sharing their thoughts

In the next section, we describe the assessments we use most frequently in Guided Comprehension.

Practical Assessment Measures

When preparing to teach Guided Comprehension, we assess for a variety of purposes. We gather information to learn about students' reading backgrounds and interests, to determine approximate range of reading levels, and to gain insights into students' knowledge of strategies and their ability to apply them. Results of these assessments inform several aspects of our planning, including lesson content, student–text matches, and grouping students for guided instructional settings.

In this section we present a number of practical, effective assessments. We provide a description of each measure, briefly explain its functions, and note its connection to Guided Comprehension.

Assessments to Learn About Students' Backgrounds and Interests

Some assessments provide insights into students' pasts that enable us to better understand their present attitudes toward and performance in reading. Examples of these measures include attitude surveys, interest inventories, literacy histories, motivation profiles, and reader and writer self-perception scales. (Reproducible copies of these measures are included in Appendix D.)

Attitude surveys. Attitude surveys are designed to illuminate students' feelings about reading and writing and the resulting impact on motivation and effort. The most common formats are question and response, sentence completion, and selected response. Information we can obtain from attitude surveys includes how students feel about various aspects of reading and writing, how they would define reading and writing, and how they would describe successful readers and writers. Information gleaned from these surveys also provides insights into factors that may have contributed to students' current attitudes toward literacy. (Reproducible reading and writing attitude surveys can be found in Appendix D, pages 311–312.)

 The completed attitude surveys provide information about students' perceptions of literacy processes. They also offer information about students' reading preferences that we can use when making student–text matches and selecting texts for Stages One and Two.

Interest inventories. Interest inventories are informal surveys designed to provide information about students' personal interests. They usually include topics such as students' reading preferences, hobbies, and special interests. The most common formats for interest inventories are question and response or incomplete sentences. These surveys are relatively easy to complete, and they provide information about numerous topics including the following: genre and author preferences, what students are currently reading, and whether students choose to read beyond required assignments. (An example of an interest inventory appropriate for grades 3–8 can be found in Appendix D, page 314.)

 Completed interest inventories provide information about students' backgrounds. We can use that knowledge to make decisions related to motivating students and making student–text matches.

Literacy histories. Literacy histories chronicle students' literacy development from earliest memory to present day (McLaughlin & Vogt, 1996). They facilitate students' ability to make connections between their past literacy experiences and their current beliefs.

To create their personal literacy histories, students engage in questioning and reflection. Sources they use to construct their histories range from family memories to early-grade writing samples to copies of favorite books. Students can choose the mode of presentation; we have received everything from time lines to scrapbooks filled with family photos. To model this assessment, we share our own literacy histories and provide students with prompts to guide the process. (Reproducible copies of the literacy history prompts are included in Appendix D, page 315.)

Literacy histories help us learn about the present by examining the past. They provide students' personal insights into their literacy development and contribute to our understanding of students' current attitudes toward literacy.

Motivation to Read Profile. The Motivation to Read Profile (Gambrell et al., 1996) consists of two instruments: the Reading Survey and the Conversational Interview. The cued response survey, which requires 15 to 20 minutes for group administration, assesses the self-concept of a reader and value of reading. The interview, which features open-ended free response questions and requires 15 to 20 minutes for individual administration, assesses the nature of motivation, such as favorite authors and interesting books. The Conversational Interview (included in Appendix D, pages 323–325) has three emphases: narrative text, informational text, and general reading.

Knowledge of what motivates students to read both narrative and informational text enhances our understanding of our students and informs meaningful text selection.

Reader Self-Perception Scale. The Reader Self-Perception Scale (Henk & Melnick, 1995) offers insights into how students think about themselves as readers. When responding, students indicate how strongly they agree or disagree with each of 33 statements. Sample items include "I think I am a good reader" and "Reading is easier for me than it used to be." (A reproducible copy of this measure is available in Appendix D, pages 329–331.)

This scale helps us understand how students perceive themselves as readers. It also provides ideas about how best to increase their self-perceptions and effectively meet their instructional needs.

Writer Self-Perception Scale. The Writer Self-Perception Scale (Bottomley, Henk, & Melnick, 1997/1998) provides information about how students feel about their writing abilities. The students respond to 38 statements, indicating how strongly they agree or disagree. Sample items include "I am getting better at writing" and "I enjoy writing." (A reproducible copy of this measure is available in Appendix D, pages 336–339.)

This scale helps us know how students perceive themselves as writers and guides us in planning effective instruction to meet their needs. It also provides information about what we can do to increase students' self-perceptions related to writing.

Attitude surveys, interest inventories, literacy histories, motivation profiles, and self-perception scales provide background information that informs our understanding of individual students and their literacy needs. These measures contribute vital information as we seek to provide optimum literacy experiences for our students. These assessments are easy to administer, require little time, and provide insights that may not be discerned from other literacy assessments.

Assessments to Learn About Students' Use of Strategies

Some assessments provide insights into how students use reading strategies. The Metacomprehension Strategy Index and the Metacognitive Reading Awareness Inventory are two examples of such measures. (Reproducible copies of these measures are included in Appendix D, pages 316–322.)

Metacomprehension Strategy Index. The Metacomprehension Strategy Index (Schmitt, 1990) is a questionnaire that contains 25 items with selected responses. It is designed to evaluate elementary students' awareness of before-reading, during-reading, and after-reading metacomprehension strategies when reading narrative text.

Guided Comprehension Connection — This measure informs our understanding of elementary students' metacognitive strategy knowledge and application. In Guided Comprehension we can use what we have learned to gain an understanding of what strategies students know and how they use them.

Metacognitive Reading Awareness Inventory. The Metacognitive Reading Awareness Inventory (Miholic, 1994) is designed for students from seventh grade through college. It consists of 10 statements with selected responses. The focus of this measure is how students use strategies to respond to difficulties they encounter while reading. Students select all the responses they think are effective.

Guided Comprehension Connection — In Guided Comprehension, this inventory provides information about how seventh- and eighth-grade students use reading strategies. We can use this as background knowledge about the students and as a starting point for strategy instruction.

Assessments to Learn About Students' Reading Levels

Some measures provide information about how students use cueing systems, and others pair miscue analysis with comprehension assessments. Examples of these measures include oral reading assessment with miscue analysis and published leveled passages kits such as the Qualitative Reading Inventory–4, Developmental Reading Assessment 2—Grades 4–8, and Fountas and Pinnell Benchmark Assessment System: Grades 3–8.

Miscue analysis. Miscue analysis (Goodman, 1997) helps us to assess students' use of the graphophonic, syntactic, and semantic cueing systems. Miscues indicate how a student's oral reading varies from the written text. In miscue analysis, students read aloud, and we record their attempts, self-corrections, and miscues. Recording the students' attempts and analyzing the miscues provides us with valuable information for our teaching.

To analyze miscues, Goodman, Watson, and Burke (1987) suggest we use the following four questions:

1. Does the miscue change the meaning?
2. Does the miscue sound like language?
3. Do the miscue and the text word look and sound alike?
4. Was an attempt made to self-correct the miscue?

To facilitate the use of the miscue analysis, we select some "anchor books"—both fiction and nonfiction at varying levels—and invite students to do an informal oral reading, which we tape record. At this point we code and analyze all their attempts, self-corrections, and miscues. We also ask the students to do a brief retelling based on this text. These two pieces of information provide approximate student reading levels and insights into their strategy use and comprehension. There are some defined accuracy percentages that may influence the determination of a reader's range of levels: below 90%, frustration; 90–95%, instructional; 96–100%, independent. When assessing students' levels, we also need to consider factors such as background knowledge about the content, interest in the text, and supports within the text.

Guided Comprehension Connection Miscue analysis provides approximate reading levels, helps us to make matches between readers and texts, and informs instruction.

Qualitative Reading Inventory–4. The Qualitative Reading Inventory–4 (Leslie & Caldwell, 2005) is a comprehensive assessment that ranges from preprimer to high school. It includes both narrative and informational leveled passages, questions to assess prior knowledge, and word lists. To assess comprehension, students can retell passages or respond to implicit and explicit questions. The leveled passages and word lists enable the teacher to estimate students' reading levels, match students with appropriate texts, and verify suspected reading difficulties. Because there are so many components to this measure, we need to make choices when using it. For example, we may choose to do the miscue analysis and then use either the retelling checklist or the comprehension questions that accompany each leveled passage to determine students' instructional levels. The leveled passages also can be used to assess silent reading comprehension.

Guided Comprehension Connection This assessment provides information necessary to place students in teacher-guided small groups and to create student–text matches.

Developmental Reading Assessment 2—Grades 4–8. The Developmental Reading Assessment 2—Grades 4–8 assessment kit (Beaver & Carter, 2009) includes a variety of fiction and nonfiction texts at levels 4–8. It also includes a set of bridge titles that allows for assessment of students who are below a fourth-grade level. Detailed record-keeping forms help the teacher document student levels, reading behaviors, and comprehension over time.

Guided Comprehension Connection This assessment provides information necessary to determine student placement in teacher-guided small groups and to create student–text matches.

Fountas and Pinnell Benchmark Assessment System: Grades 3–8. The Fountas and Pinnell Benchmark Assessment System: Grades 3–8 assessment kit (Fountas & Pinnell, 2008) provides graded word lists, fiction and nonfiction leveled readers at levels L–Z, and detailed forms for analyzing and recording students' comprehension, writing, and fluency over time.

Guided Comprehension Connection This assessment helps us to determine approximate reading levels for students in teacher-guided small groups. This, in turn, helps us to make student–text matches and plan appropriate instruction.

Assessments to Learn About Students' Everyday Progress

Other assessments are more informal. These measures can be used every day to provide insights into students' progress. Examples of these measures include student writing and teacher observation.

Student writing. Student writing is a flexible assessment. It can be used for numerous purposes including applying strategies, summarizing and synthesizing information, documenting student thinking, recording personal responses, and as a mode of reflection and goal setting. We observe and analyze student writing for multiple purposes including content, focus, organization, language structure, use of vocabulary, and knowledge of sight words and spelling patterns.

Guided Comprehension Connection — Writing is a mode of expression that informs all stages of the Guided Comprehension Model. It documents students' thinking and provides evidence of learning.

Observation. Observation is one of the most flexible assessments because it can offer information about virtually any aspect of literacy in which students engage. For example, we can observe students as they read, write, and discuss. We can also monitor their ability to stay on task when working independently, and use observation to assess their fluency, record ideas about their engagement, or comment on their roles during cooperative learning activities.

Before we begin observing, we need to establish a purpose and determine how we will record the information gleaned from this measure. For example, if we are observing a student who is doing an oral retelling, we can use a checklist that includes information such as the characters, setting, problem, attempts to resolve the problem, resolution, and a section for us to record additional comments. In contrast, if we are observing a student's contribution to a cooperative activity, our checklist might include items such as the student's preparation for the group's work, engagement with peers, and contributions to the group. (Reproducible observation checklists can be found in Appendix D, pages 326–328.)

Guided Comprehension Connection — Observation is an informal technique that can be used in all stages of the Model to gain insights into students' performance and inform our planning of future learning experiences.

What we want to know about our students determines which assessments we use. Therefore, our goal is not to use all these measures to assess each reader, but rather to make choices and use the measures that provide the information we need. The assessments we have described are practical, can be used for multiple purposes, and offer valuable insights into students' backgrounds and abilities.

In addition to the measures described, informal assessment opportunities, including strategy applications, are embedded in all stages of the Guided Comprehension Model. These formative measures are situated in a variety of instructional settings and provide occasions for students to demonstrate what they know through multiple modes of response including reading, writing, discussion, sketching, drama, and singing.

Guided Comprehension Profiles

We use Guided Comprehension Profiles to organize and manage student assessments. These profiles are strategy-based collections of assessments and indicators of student progress. Maintaining the profiles is an active process for both the students and teacher. As our students transact with texts and people in multiple settings in a variety of modes, we collect information to document their progress. Although Guided Comprehension offers numerous opportunities for assessment, there are some measures such as student writing, oral reading fluency, and comprehension that we systematically include. We use the results of these assessments to document student progress, refine guided instruction groups, and inform future instruction.

We store the students' assessments and work samples in pocket folders and we use a Profile Index to organize assessment information. This offers an at-a-glance overview of student progress and facilitates reporting student progress. (A reproducible copy of this organizer is included in Appendix D, page 313.)

In Guided Comprehension, assessment is viewed as a natural part of instruction, a dynamic process in which both students and teacher actively participate. In the next chapter, we use assessments to create student–text matches. We also explore the reader and text factors that influence our selection of leveled texts.

Making Connections to Theory and Practice

To learn more about reading assessment, read the following:

Afflerbach, P. (2007). *Understanding and using reading assessment, K–12*. Newark, DE: International Reading Association.

McAndrews, S.L. (2008). *Diagnostic literacy assessments and instructional strategies: A literacy specialist's resource*. Newark, DE: International Reading Association.

McKenna, M.C., & Stahl, K.A.D. (2009). *Assessment for reading instruction* (2nd ed.). New York: Guilford.

CHAPTER 6

Leveled Text: An Essential Resource for Reading Comprehension

I f we want our students to achieve at their maximum potentials, we need to use leveled, accessible, engaging text. Providing students with text they *can* read and *want* to read promotes achievement. This implies that students should have access to a rich and varied collection of leveled texts in addition to core programs and classroom libraries.

This type of text is a critical component of reading comprehension instruction. If the text is accessible, students can read it. If the text is leveled, students can read it at their instructional level during teacher-guided small groups or at their independent level when they engage in independent practice. For example, when students are participating in Guided Reading, they can read instructional-level texts with some assistance from the teacher. When students are engaged in independent practice, such as centers or routines, they can read independent-level texts with no assistance from the teacher. If the text is of interest, students will choose to read it.

In this chapter, we discuss the role of text selection in reading comprehension instruction. We begin by discussing student reading levels, student interests, and text selection. Next, we examine the reader and text factors that influence accessibility. Then we provide the rationale for using leveled texts, make suggestions for making decisions about the ease or difficulty of text, and present ideas for organizing texts.

Student Reading Levels, Student Interests, and Text Selection

When considering which texts to use during Guided Comprehension, it is important to begin by determining the reading levels and interests of our students. There are a number of informal reading assessments that we can use to help determine students' approximate reading abilities. We also use informal measures to learn about students' interests. Details about these assessments and measures can be found in Chapter 5.

Student Reading Levels

There are general guidelines for determining students' reading levels related to word accuracy, comprehension, and fluency. For *word accuracy*, the text is considered easy if students can read it with 95%–100% accuracy, provided the fluency and comprehension are appropriate. The instructional level is reached when students can read most of the text, but there are some challenges with words or content. This is usually between 90% and 94% accuracy. Students who read a text below 90% accuracy often struggle with fluency and comprehension because they must use so much of their cognitive focus to figure out unknown words. This is considered a frustration level. At this level, key words are often misunderstood and comprehension is compromised.

In addition to word accuracy, *comprehension* must also be assessed. This often involves determining students' background knowledge as well as their ability to retell or summarize what was read, effectively discuss the text, or predict what will happen next. If a student is unable to successfully complete such tasks, the text may be too difficult.

Fluency, the third factor, is directly related to comprehension. In fact, Rasinski (2003) notes that fluency is the ability to read accurately and expressively at a natural rate with good phrasing and good comprehension. Fluency checks, which can easily be completed during Guided Reading, contribute to our understanding when creating appropriate student–text matches. We can complete fluency checks by asking individual students to whisper read during teacher-guided small groups.

When we assess students' word accuracy, comprehension, and fluency, we gain insights into their reading abilities. Although the results of these informal measures are approximations, they do provide a starting point for making appropriate student–text matches for guided and independent practice.

Student Interests

Student interests are essential considerations when making student–text matches. We can easily learn about students' interests by engaging our students in informal conversations or inviting them to complete interest inventories (see Chapter 5 and Appendix D, page 314, for an example). When students are reading texts that interest them, they are more motivated to read and generally have more background knowledge about the topic of the text. This makes reading the text easier and more enjoyable for students.

Text Selection

Once we have determined students' reading levels and interests, we can begin considering texts that will contribute to students' reading success. A common way to do this is to use leveled texts, reading materials that begin at a certain level and become progressively difficult (Brabham & Villaume, 2002). The criteria for leveling text may be standards set by well-respected literacy professionals such as Marie Clay or Fountas and Pinnell, or they may involve the use of readability formulas, such as the Fry Readabilty Graph (1977), which consider length of text, length of sentences, and complexity of vocabulary. Another approach is to level text by considering a variety of text or reader factors. Whichever method is used, leveled text is an essential resource when we create student–text matches.

Students can usually engage with multiple levels of text depending on the setting in which they are reading. For example, when students read on their own, they can read independent-level or "easy" text. At this level, students have familiarity with the genre and content, can read all or most of the words, and can comprehend with no help. When students are reading with the support

Figure 7. Text Levels and the Guided Comprehension Model

Text Level	Teacher Support	Guided Comprehension
Independent	No teacher support needed.	Stage Two: Independent Centers and Routines
	Just right when students are reading on their own and practicing strategy application.	
Instructional	Some teacher support needed.	Stage Two: Teacher-Guided Small Groups
	Just right when guiding small groups.	
Challenging	Full teacher support needed.	Stage One: Teacher-Directed Whole Groups
	Just right when doing teacher read-alouds in whole group.	

of a teacher, they can read instructional-level or "just right" text. At this level, students have some familiarity with the content and genre, know most of the words, and can comprehend with some teacher support. Students can also experience independent, instructional, and challenging texts when the teacher reads texts to them in teacher-directed whole-group instruction or during daily read-alouds. This means that even though students should not read challenging or frustration-level texts on their own, they can experience such texts when we share them through read-alouds or books on CD. Figure 7 illustrates how leveled texts are generally situated in the Guided Comprehension Model. It is important to remember that these text levels are approximations, and that factors beyond the text influence student accessibility.

Factors That Influence Accessibility

There are several factors that influence the accessibility of a text; some reside in the reader, others are determined by the text. Reader factors include interest and motivation, background knowledge, and sociocultural identities (Dzaldov & Peterson, 2005; Pitcher & Fang, 2007). Text factors include text type and structure, text length, content, vocabulary, language, and literary features (Brabham & Villaume, 2002; Dzaldov & Peterson, 2005; Rog & Burton, 2001/2002; Tompkins, 2006). Considering these factors helps us to make good text selections for reading instruction as well as independent practice.

Reader Factors

Reader factors such as interest and motivation, background knowledge, and sociocultural identities influence text selection. Dzaldov and Peterson (2005) suggest that these factors are as important as text features when making text choices for students. Similarly, Pitcher and Fang (2007) report that knowing students' interests, instructional backgrounds, experiential backgrounds, and sociocultural identities is as important or more important than text features and levels when making good matches between readers and texts.

Interest and motivation. Students who read materials on topics of interest tend to read more, can read more difficult materials, and are more motivated to read (Wigfield & Guthrie, 1997). Reading motivation is influenced by several factors, including content goals, student book choice, social structures for learning, teacher involvement, and rewards (Guthrie et al., 2006). When students are interested, they will work harder at constructing meaning. In addition, student self-efficacy, a student's belief about his or her ability to be successful, is a crucial factor in reading motivation that is connected to interest in reading and amount of time spent reading (Bogner, Raphael, & Pressley, 2002). Student motivation is influenced by students' previous experience with texts. Students who have spent years reading textbook chapters and answering the questions at the end can have negative feelings when asked to read for information. This is also true for students who have had stories so segmented for vocabulary study or detail recall that the major themes and meaning have been lost. Students who have had positive, successful experiences with texts have greater motivation to read, and therefore tend to read more, often trying longer or more challenging texts.

Background knowledge. Readers' background knowledge of text content, language, and text type influences accessibility. When students have a great deal of experience with a specific topic or type of text, they have a network of information in their minds that allows them to make connections with the new information. This often helps them to make predictions and inferences while reading. They also have knowledge of specific vocabulary and language patterns that helps them to read with meaning at a good pace. This is true for both narrative and informational texts and is influenced by the amount of time spent reading each type.

Sociocultural identities. Social and cultural identities influence students' interests as well as their ability to read and understand texts. When characters and contexts are familiar, students can make connections to the content or story line, and that makes the text easier to read. Dzaldov and Peterson (2005) report that students who are not familiar with certain versions of fairy tales struggle to read and understand these texts, even if texts were at a lower level than versions more familiar to the students.

Alvermann, Phelps, and Ridgeway (2007) suggest that teachers who consider students' social and cultural backgrounds when planning instruction create learning environments in which students feel engaged and successful. Holmes, Powell, Holmes, and Witt (2007) recommend having classroom libraries that represent a variety of races and people, which will help students build awareness of and greater sensitivity toward one another.

Text Factors

When considering students' abilities and interests, it is important to match those with the supports and challenges present in the text. Text features to consider when deciding on appropriateness of a book for a particular student include text type and structure, text length, language and literary features, complexity of the content, and uniqueness of the vocabulary (Brabham & Villaume, 2002; Dzaldov & Peterson, 2005; Rog & Burton, 2001/2002; Tompkins, 2006).

Text type and structure. Texts are organized in different ways depending on their purpose. Narrative text tells a story and usually includes the basic story elements: characters, setting, problem, attempts to resolve the problem, and resolution. This format is very familiar to students because they have heard and read many stories. This knowledge of the text structure helps students anticipate what might happen next in the story and, consequently, the story is often easier for students to read. On the other hand, informational texts provide facts about a topic. There are five main informational text structures: description, sequence, cause and effect, compare and contrast, and problem and solution (Vacca & Vacca, 2008). These are often less familiar to students and, consequently, may be more challenging to read. Additionally, the syntax and vocabulary in these texts may be more difficult for students.

Goldman and Rakestraw (2000, p. 321) have drawn the following three conclusions from existing research on students' knowledge of text structure:

1. Readers use their knowledge of structure in processing text.
2. Knowledge of structural forms of text develops with experience with different genres, and is correlated with age/time in school.
3. Making readers more aware of genre and text structure improves learning.

Text length. As students become more competent readers, they are able to read longer texts. These stories are more complex and may have many characters and multiple story lines. Longer informational texts often include several subtopics and many more facts. Although a long text is not always a more difficult text, length is one factor to consider when thinking about the appropriateness of text for a particular reader. We also need to consider the setting in which the student will be reading. For example, in Guided Reading, which usually lasts only 20 minutes, shorter texts usually work better.

Text content. Text content is a critical factor in text selection because readers must be able to make connections between what they know and what they are reading. This requires that students either have background knowledge about the topic or gain some knowledge about it before they begin reading. For stories, this may include knowledge of how narrative texts work, such as character and plot development, or conflict and resolution. Additionally, much of the story may be told with dialogue between and among characters, making inferential thinking important to understand the plot. In informational texts, content includes the topic and how it is presented. As such texts get more challenging, the information is presented in more detail, with many more complex and abstract concepts. Also, the number of content-specific words generally increases. We must consider the content and how it is presented in the text when trying to determine text level and student accessibility. The size of print, the number or availability of pictures or other visual cues, the range of punctuation, the layout and organization of print, and the number of words per page are also influential factors in this category.

Vocabulary, language structure, and literary features. To understand and make meaning from a text, students need to be able to understand most of the words they read. If they come to a word they do not know, they need to be reading with enough understanding to infer the meaning of the unknown word. When there are too many unknown words, students lose the meaning of the text and focus more of their working memory on decoding. As texts become more challenging, the vocabulary usually becomes more complex. For example, there are differences in the types of words students encounter in narrative and informational text. In a narrative text, there may be several difficult words, but they often represent other concepts that the students already understand (Hiebert, 2006). That is not usually true with informational text. Many of the difficult words in informational texts are content-specific words that are critical to understanding.

We should also think about the complexity of the language structure when creating student–text matches. Compound and complex sentences may be more challenging for students when reading about particular topics. Other factors we should think about when deciding if a more challenging text is a good match for a student include literary features, such as figurative language, plot twists, dialogue, metaphors, similes, and poetic language (Dzaldov & Peterson, 2005; Rog & Burton, 2001/2002).

Considering all these text features is essential when we choose texts and create student–text matches. Figure 8 features a list of the text features and prompts we can use to determine the appropriateness of text when making these matches.

Choosing Texts to Promote Student Success

Before making student–text matches, we need to assess our students, be aware of their interests, and ensure that we have a wide range of engaging texts at a variety of levels available for student use. We also need to consider how to organize the texts so students can easily access books at the appropriate levels.

Student Information

Before planning meaningful Guided Comprehension instruction, we need to determine each student's independent and instructional level and gather information about his or her interests and background. We use this information for three purposes: to form teacher-guided small groups, to provide appropriate text for students to read when working in the comprehension-based centers and routines, and to inform text selection for teacher-directed whole-group instruction. Miscue analysis (Goodman, 1997), which we can use to assess students' oral reading and comprehension, is a viable source of this information. There are also several commercially prepared assessment tools that allow teachers to assess students' reading levels, fluency, and comprehension. (For further discussion of a variety of these assessments, see Chapter 5.)

Hunt (1996/1997) suggests that students also contribute to determining text accessibility. He recommends that students engage in self-evaluation during independent reading by responding to questions such as the following:

- Did you have a good reading period today?
- Were you able to concentrate as you read independently?

Figure 8. Factors to Consider When Matching Students and Texts

Reader Factors	Questions to Consider
Interest and Motivation	• Is the topic of interest to students? • Will students find the text engaging?
Background Knowledge	• Is the story or topic familiar? • What previous experiences with reading and reading instruction have students had? • How much experience have students had with this genre or type of text? • Do students know the vocabulary necessary to construct meaning from this text?
Sociocultural Identities	• Is the text culturally connected to students? • Is the language simple and direct? • Is the vocabulary familiar to students? • Are there illustrations to help students understand the text?

Text Factors	Questions to Consider
Length of Text	• Do students have the stamina to read this text? • Will students be able to maintain interest in this text?
Text Type and Structure	• Are students familiar with this type of text? • How much experience have students had reading this type of text? • Do students understand the structure of this text? Can they use the structure to help set a purpose or understand what they read?
Page Layout	• Do students know how to use picture and other visual cues to help them read and understand? • Is the text considerate toward the students? Is it appropriate for their developmental and achievement levels?
Text Content	• How much background knowledge do students have about this topic? • How much experience do they have with this content? • How familiar are the students with the language patterns and vocabulary used in this text? • Are students familiar with the format in which the content is presented?
Vocabulary and Literary Features	• Are there many difficult words in this text? • Do students have the background knowledge to infer the meanings of many of the words? • Do students have enough knowledge of language to make inferences and understand the subtle messages in the text? • Do students understand the use of literary devices and how authors use them to tell the story?

- Did the ideas in the book hold your attention?

- Were you bothered by others or outside noises?

- Could you keep the ideas in the book straight in your mind?

- Did you get mixed up in any place? Were you able to fix it?

- Were there words you did not know? How did you figure them out?

- Were you hoping the book would end, or were you hoping it would go on and on?

Although these questions require only yes or no responses, they do provide insights into students' perceptions of their performance. Other ways to gather similar information include holding individual student–teacher conferences and using informal measures such as quick writes and Tickets Out. (For information about Tickets Out, see Appendix D, page 335.)

We also need to gather data about student experiences and interests. As noted earlier, this can be accomplished through interviews, observations, or interest inventories. In addition, students can complete self-perception scales. (See Chapter 5 for a more complete discussion of diagnostic measures.)

Text Information

Once we have the appropriate information about our students, we need to consider what texts we will use. We use the following steps to facilitate this process:

1. *Identify the texts available in the classroom*: These may include but not be limited to core programs, anthologies, trade books, textbooks, magazines, newspapers, online text, poetry books, and picture books.

2. *Organize the texts to facilitate Guided Comprehension*: We use the following questions to accomplish this:

   - Does this text add to existing content area study or knowledge?

   - Can this text be used in a genre study?

   - Does this text exemplify a particular style, structure, language pattern, or literary device? Can this text be used to teach a comprehension strategy?

   - Are there multiple copies of the text available?

   - Does this text match a particular student's interests?

   - Is this a good example of a text structure?

   - Is this text part of a series?

   - Is it written by a favorite author?

   These questions can be used with both narrative and informational texts. This includes individual stories in literature anthologies, as well as individual articles within magazines.

3. *Acquire additional materials to assure ample accessible texts for all readers*: It is important to have some sets of books to use during teacher-guided comprehension small groups, but it is also necessary to have a wide array of texts, varying in type, genre, length, content,

and level. All students must have a multitude of accessible books within the classroom. These books should represent a wide range of readability and genre. It is important to include novels of varying lengths, nonfiction trade books, picture books, poetry books, and magazines. We keep in mind the following ideas when adding to classroom collections:

- Content areas—informational and narrative text to supplement studies in math, science, and social studies
- Student interests—a variety of texts (narrative, informational, poetry) about diverse topics to match students' interests
- Read-aloud—texts that offer examples of a variety of text structures and engaging story lines to be used to demonstrate comprehension processes and fluency
- Anchor books—texts used in whole-group and small-group instruction to demonstrate a specific strategy or routine
- Sets of books—Four to six copies of the same title to be used in Guided Comprehension teacher-guided small groups; these should be based on students' levels and interests, as well as the strategies that can be taught using them
- Text sets—series books, favorite author, genre, topic; several books that have a common characteristic

Once we have accumulated the texts, we need to organize them to accommodate all stages of the Guided Comprehension Model.

Methods for Leveling Texts

All text levels are approximations, and there is no specific rule for determining them. Text ease or difficulty is determined by both text and reader factors. Each text will need to be evaluated with specific readers in mind. Leveling systems, teacher judgment, paralleling books, and using leveled lists developed by others facilitate this process.

Leveling Systems

Several systems exist that will help determine the approximate level of a text. These take into consideration factors such as format, language structure, and content (Weaver, 2000). The following are examples of these formulas: the Fry Readability Index (Fry, 1977), Lexile Framework for Reading Book Database (www.lexile.com), and Scholastic's Teacher Book Wizard (bookwizard .scholastic.com/tbw/homePage.do). The Fry Readability Index takes into consideration sentence length and number of syllables for three random 100-word selections within a text. These two numbers are plotted on a graph and an approximate reading level is provided for each selection. The Lexile Framework for Reading Book Database has thousands of books leveled using the Lexile leveling system. This system takes into consideration word frequency and sentence length. The higher the Lexile score, the more difficult the text is related to those two features. Scholastic's Teacher Book Wizard allows teachers to put in a book and find an approximate level based on their leveling system. In addition, you can put in a book title and find other books that have similar levels.

Leveling systems provide helpful information about the ease or difficulty of a text, and also help to find books that may be similar in levels.

Teacher Judgment

Although these leveling systems provide a starting point for leveling texts, teacher judgment may be the most frequently used method in leveling texts for the upper grades. In grades 3–8, it is important to identify reader factors, such as familiarity with content or genre, as well as motivation to read, when trying to match a text with a reader.

We often use the following processes for leveling texts:

- Separate books into narrative, informational, and poetry.
- For each type of book, divide the books into harder and easier.
- Take each pile of books and sort by hardest to easiest (repeat this process as necessary).
- Label or color-code levels for student access.

Although these methods do not provide exact text levels, they do allow us to organize our books by type and by degree of difficulty. This information is very helpful when teaching students to select texts, or for us to guide students in that selection process.

Paralleling Books

Another way to level texts is to match classroom books with published leveled texts that have similar text features, such as length, font size, number of illustrations, and genre. This process, called paralleling books, provides a format for informally identifying approximate levels of existing classroom materials. In Appendix E, we provide lists of model books that represent approximate levels.

Published Lists and Websites for Leveled Books

Many publishers provide lists of leveled titles that we can use in creating student–text matches and in all stages of Guided Comprehension. We can use these lists as resources for identifying anchor books as well as for assessment purposes. Many of these sets of leveled books, which include narrative and informational texts, are available for purchase. (Information about these sources is provided in Appendix E.)

Classroom Text Organization

Once we have leveled our classroom collections, our goal is to organize the texts efficiently to promote their optimum use. This includes texts for use in whole-group and small-group teaching, as well as texts for students to use during comprehension centers and routines. To facilitate accessing text for our teaching, Harvey and Goudvis (2000) suggest accumulating a master list of titles and organizing them according to what they have to offer as teaching models. Approaches to such organization include listing books by strategy to be modeled, by book title, by genre and level, and by topic and level.

To provide accessible texts for student-facilitated comprehension centers and routines, we use the following methods of organization:

- *Class book baskets*: Creating book baskets by author, series, content, or approximate reading level is one method. With our help, students can then make selections from a whole collection of books in the basket.

- *Individual book baskets*: We can also help students to create individual book baskets in which they keep an ongoing collection of books they want to read. This eliminates any "down time" when students need to select text for independent reading.

- *Individual student booklists*: Students keep these lists in the back of their Guided Comprehension Journals. Titles can be added to the list in an ongoing manner to accommodate student progress. This often happens when students share ideas from their reading in Stage Three of the Guided Comprehension Model or when we share book talks of new and favorite books.

To further facilitate text organization, Szymusiak and Sibberson (2001) recommend that books in classroom collections be placed face out so that readers can easily see the covers and preview the texts and that sections for fiction, nonfiction, and poetry be marked clearly.

The two most important factors in matching students with appropriate texts are students' reading levels and interests. We can determine students' range of approximate reading levels by using informal assessments. Additionally, we can learn much about students' interests through simple inventories. This information helps us to create meaningful matches between students and texts.

Making Connections to Theory and Practice

To learn more about leveling books and using leveled text, read the following:

Mesmer, H.A.E. (2008). *Tools for matching readers to text: Research-based practices*. New York: Guilford.

Pinnell, G.S., & Fountas, I.C. (2009). *The Fountas & Pinnell leveled book list, K–8*. Portsmouth, NH: Heinemann.

Szymusiak, K., Sibberson, F., & Koch, L. (2008). *Beyond leveled books: Supporting early and transitional readers in grades K–5* (2nd ed.). Portland, ME: Stenhouse.

PART TWO

Theme-Based Guided Comprehension Lessons

Focus: Situating Guided Comprehension in a variety of themes.

Theme Overviews: The planning graphic that appears at the start of each theme is based on Wiggins and McTighe's (2008) belief that we should begin the planning process by identifying the desired results. In this case, the desired results are expressed as the theme's goals and resulting connections to state standards. The next step is determining acceptable evidences; these are listed as assessments on the graphic. The final step is planning learning experiences and instruction. These are represented by the texts, comprehension strategies, teaching ideas, and instructional settings such as comprehension centers and routines. Website resources complete the plan.

Themes: Four Guided Comprehension lessons are provided for each theme. The lessons were written and taught by teachers in grades 3–8. You will notice a change in voice as each teacher speaks about his or her classroom teaching experience. The Guided Comprehension Lesson Overviews are plans these teachers wrote for their lessons. The lessons focus on a variety of comprehension strategies and multiple types and levels of theme-related texts. The lessons also include multiple modes of representation, critical and creative thinking, and multiple literacies. Theme-based resources including related texts and websites, suggestions for performance extensions across the curriculum, and a culminating activity follow each set of lessons. The sidebar at right presents an overview of the themes, including the comprehension strategies and teaching ideas that are embedded in each lesson.

Theme Topics, Strategies, and Teaching Ideas

Chapter 7: Life Stories: Biography, Autobiography
Previewing: Bio-Impression
Making Connections: Save the Last Word for Me
Summarizing: Bio-Pyramid
Summarizing: Questions Into Paragraphs (QuIP)

Chapter 8: Identity: Who Are You?
Self-Questioning: Paired Questioning
Visualizing: Draw and Label Visualizations
Summarizing: Narrative Pyramids
Evaluating: Evaluative Questioning

Chapter 9: Poetry: Extraordinary Wonder
Previewing: Anticipation/Reaction Guide
Knowing How Words Work: Concept of Definition Map
Monitoring: Photographs of the Mind
Summarizing: Lyric Retelling

Chapter 10: Fantasy: Unbridled Imagination
Self-Questioning: "I Wonder" Statements
Visualizing: Open-Mind Portraits
Monitoring: Double-Entry Journals
Monitoring: Say Something

CHAPTER 7

Life Stories: Biography, Autobiography

Perhaps because we all have life stories, biographies seem to fascinate us. We read about the goals, successes, and failures of people we know only in a very general way. This often leads to our writing biographies about the lives of others and creating autobiographies about our own experiences. A biography about Barack Obama, Hillary Clinton, Bruce Springsteen, J.K. Rowling, or John Adams may have been the one that drew us to this genre, but it is the biographies and autobiographies that we have yet to read that keep us coming back.

The sample Theme-Based Plan for Guided Comprehension: Life Stories: Biography, Autobiography (see Figure 9) offers an overview of the thinking and resources that support this theme. It presents a sampling of goals, state standards, assessments, texts, website resources, comprehension strategies, teaching ideas, comprehension centers, and comprehension routines. The plan begins by delineating examples of student goals and related state standards. The student goals for this theme include the following:

- Use appropriate comprehension skills and strategies
- Interpret and respond to text
- Write biographies and autobiographies
- Communicate effectively

These goals support the following state standards:

- Learning to read independently
- Reading, analyzing, and interpreting text
- Types and quality of writing
- Speaking and listening

The assessments listed on the theme planner are examples of diagnostic, formative, and summative measures. Running records are an example of a diagnostic assessment. Formative assessments, which are informal and usually occur on a daily basis, include specific measures such as comprehension strategy applications, and general assessments such as observation and student self-assessment. Summative assessments, which are more formal long-term measures such as projects, are also featured.

Figure 9. Theme-Based Plan for Guided Comprehension: Life Stories: Biography, Autobiography

Goals and Connections to State Standards | Students will

- Use appropriate comprehension skills and strategies. Standard: learning to read independently
- Interpret and respond to text. Standard: reading, analyzing, and interpreting text
- Write biographies and autobiographies. Standard: types and quality of writing
- Communicate effectively. Standard: speaking and listening

Comprehension Strategies

1. Previewing
2. Making Connections
3. Summarizing
4. Summarizing

Teaching Ideas

Bio-Impression
Save the Last Word for Me
Bio-Pyramid
Questions Into Paragraphs (QuIP)

Comprehension Centers

Students will apply the comprehension strategies and related teaching ideas in the following comprehension centers:

Making Books Center
Project Center
Technology Center

Transmediation Center
Theme Center
Writing Center

Comprehension Routines

Students will apply the comprehension strategies and related teaching ideas in the following comprehension routines:

Literature Circles
Reciprocal Teaching
Questioning the Author

Assessment

The following measures can be used for a variety of purposes, including diagnostic, formative, and summative assessment:

Bio-Impression	Running Records
Bio-Pyramid	Save the Last Word for Me
Observation	Self-Assessments
Projects	Student Writing
QuIP	

Text	Theme	Level
1. *A Picture Book of Jackie Robinson*	BIO	K–3
2. *Knots in My Yo-Yo String*	BIO	4–7
3. *Odd Boy Out: Young Albert Einstein*	BIO	K–3
4. *Rosa*	BIO	K–3

Website Resources

Biography
  www.biography.com
Scholastic: Biography Writer's Workshop
  teacher.scholastic.com/writewit/biograph/index.htm
Encyclopedia of World Biography
  www.notablebiographies.com

The Guided Comprehension lessons are based on the following strategies and corresponding teaching ideas:

- Previewing: Bio-Impression
- Making Connections: Save the Last Word for Me
- Summarizing: Bio-Pyramid
- Summarizing: Questions Into Paragraphs (QuIP)

A Picture Book of Jackie Robinson (Adler, 1994), *Knots in My Yo-Yo String* (Spinelli, 1998), *Odd Boy Out: Young Albert Einstein* (Brown, 2004), and *Rosa* (Giovanni, 2005) are the texts used in Stage One for teacher-directed whole-group instruction. Numerous additional theme-related resources, including texts, websites, performances across the curriculum, and a culminating activity, are presented in the Theme Resources at the end of the chapter.

Examples of comprehension centers students use during Stage Two of Guided Comprehension include making books, poetry, technology, theme, and writing. Students also engage in strategy application in comprehension routines such as Literature Circles, Reciprocal Teaching, and Questioning the Author. Sample website resources complete the overview.

In this chapter, all the lessons focus on biography and/or autobiography. The lessons are appropriate for all learners, including English learners, struggling readers, and students with special needs. To accommodate these learners, the lessons include multiple modes of response (such as singing, sketching, and dramatizing) working with partners, books on CD, cross-age experiences, and extra guided instruction. Ideas we used to differentiate instruction in these lessons include the following:

- Content—the information being taught:
  - Using leveled text to accommodate students' abilities in teacher-guided small groups, centers, and routines
  - Providing leveled texts that accommodate student interest and help motivate them to read
- Process—the way in which the information is taught:
  - Preteaching students who may need additional support to use the strategies and skills such as sequencing and generating questions at multiple levels
  - Activating prior knowledge and/or providing background information
  - Scaffolding student learning by using the Guided Comprehension Model
  - Reading the text aloud during Stage One to make it accessible to all students
  - Using visuals to support students' construction of meaning
  - Adapting graphic organizers; providing paragraph frames
  - Encouraging students to work with peers in pairs and small groups to provide additional support
- Product—how the students demonstrate their learning:
  - Integrating alternative modes of representation, such as art, drama, poetry, or music
  - Providing opportunities for students to use computers when creating projects

Guided Comprehension Lessons

Life Stories: Biography, Autobiography
Guided Comprehension Strategy: Previewing
Teaching Idea: Bio-Impression

STAGE ONE: Teacher-Directed Whole-Group Instruction

Text: *A Picture Book of Jackie Robinson* (Adler, 1994)

Explain: I began by explaining the importance of previewing a text before reading, and I thought aloud about what I would read. I said, "Previewing involves activating prior knowledge, predicting, and setting purposes for reading." I reminded students about the Story Impressions we had created previously (see Appendix A, page 244, for a blackline master). I explained that we used sequential clues about published stories to write Story Impressions—what we predicted the story was about. I reminded students that the clues we used in Story Impressions included the narrative elements: characters, setting, problem, attempts to resolve the problem, and resolution. Then I explained that Bio-Impressions were very similar, but this time the sequential clues would be about facts from a person's life instead of story elements. I told the students that thinking about the content of a biography and predicting what we would read about would help get our minds ready to read and understand the text. It would also help us set purposes for reading. I explained that we would be previewing the text by reading a list of clues that would help us predict what we would read about. Then we would write our impression or prediction of what would happen in the biography.

Demonstrate: I shared the title and showed the students the cover of the book. I asked them what they knew about Jackie Robinson. Then I showed students the clues—words and phrases from the biography—that we would use to preview the text and create a Bio-Impression. I reminded students that the clues were connected by arrows and that we would need to use the clues in the order in which they appeared in the list. The clues, which represented events in Jackie Robinson's life, were as follows:

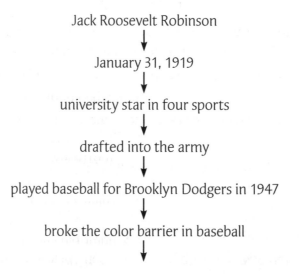

Jack Roosevelt Robinson
↓
January 31, 1919
↓
university star in four sports
↓
drafted into the army
↓
played baseball for Brooklyn Dodgers in 1947
↓
broke the color barrier in baseball
↓

Guided Comprehension: Life Stories: Biography, Autobiography
Previewing: Bio-Impression

Teacher-Directed Whole-Group Instruction

- **Explain** previewing and how to create a Bio-Impression. Focus on using clues to predict information contained in biographies.
- **Demonstrate** a Bio-Impression by introducing the sequential clues for *A Picture Book of Jackie Robinson*. Think aloud about how to use the first two clues to create an opening sentence for the predictive paragraph.
- **Guide** students to contribute to the prediction by looking at the next two clues and creating the next sentence in the impression. Guide students to use the following two words.
- **Practice** using the Bio-Impression to continue predicting the content for the text.
- **Reflect** on how using the Bio-Impression helped to create predictions about text.

Student-Facilitated Comprehension Centers

- **Making Books Center:** Students will create their autobiography page on computers using the Autobiography Organizer and PowerPoint. Students' slides will be combined into a class Autobiography Book.
- **Theme Center:** Create Bio-Impressions for a variety of biographies at different levels. Invite students to use the sequential clues to write the predictive paragraph and then read to learn which predictions are verified.
- **Writing Center:** Encourage students to learn more about the people featured in the biographies they have read and to write about them. Encourage students to write autobiographies using the Autobiography Organizer.

Teacher-Guided Small-Group Instruction

- **Review** the comprehension strategies good readers use. Focus on the importance of predicting before reading and how the Bio-Impression can help us do that. Introduce the sequential clues for the text *The Real McCoy: The Life of an African-American Inventor* and explain that we will use the clues to write a predictive paragraph before reading the text and compare and contrast it to the original biography after reading. Review each clue.
- **Guide** students to start the paragraph by using the first two phrases in a sentence. Record the sentence on a chart and have the student record it on their Bio-Impression blackline. Continue this process with the next two clues.
- **Practice** by having the students work in pairs to finish the Bio-Impression. When they have finished, ask each group to share what they wrote. Students read the biography and then compare and contrast what they wrote with what they read.
- **Reflect** on how previewing using the Bio-Impression helped students create purposes for reading and understand the text.

Student-Facilitated Comprehension Routines

- **Literature Circles:** Provide Bio-Impression sequential clue lists for the texts students read in Literature Circles. Students write Bio-Impressions to preview texts they read for Literature Circles. They share their Bio-Impressions before reading and use them before reading to make predictions and discuss vocabulary. When students finish reading their Literature Circle books, they compare and contrast the original biography with their Bio-Impressions.
- **Reciprocal Teaching:** Provide Bio-Impression sequential clue lists for texts students will read using Reciprocal Teaching. Students can write Bio-Impressions to predict during Reciprocal Teaching. They can also use the word list to guide their summaries of the text.

Teacher-Facilitated Whole-Group Reflection and Goal Setting

- **Share** ideas and insights about previewing using the Bio-Impression; assess students' ability to make meaningful predictions using sequential word lists based on the text.
- **Reflect** on how previewing, and using the Bio-Impression, helped prepare for reading the text
- **Set new goals** or extend existing ones.

National League Rookie of the Year

↓

National League Most Valuable Player

↓

Hall of Fame

↓

October 24, 1972

I read through each of the clues and discussed them with the students. Next, I modeled how to start the predictive paragraph by thinking aloud and saying, "I think that the date listed must be when he was born, so I am going to start my prediction by writing, '*Jack Roosevelt Robinson was born on January 31, 1919.*'" I wrote this on the Bio-Impression chart and invited the students to write it on their copies of the blackline I had provided. Then I said, "The next phrase says *university star in four sports.* So for my next sentence, I will write, '*He attended college and was a star in four different sports. One of them was baseball.*'" I explained that the clue didn't mention baseball, but that I was predicting that was one of the four sports because Jackie Robinson was such an excellent baseball player. I wrote the sentence on the chart, and the students wrote it, too.

Guide: I guided the students to help me write the next sentence. We discussed what *drafted* meant and then we wrote, "*Jackie Robinson didn't volunteer to go into the Army. He was drafted.*" I guided the students to think about the next two phrases, *played baseball for Brooklyn Dodgers in 1947* and *broke the color barrier.* Then they suggested we write, "*He played for the Brooklyn Dodgers in 1947 and broke the color barrier, because black people weren't allowed to play in the major leagues at that time.*"

Practice: The students continued to write the Bio-Impression in pairs, using the rest of the words and phrases. I guided them as needed and when they finished, they shared their impressions. Next, I read aloud *A Picture Book of Jackie Robinson* and we discussed the similarities and differences between our Bio-Impressions and the book David Adler had authored about Jackie Robinson's life. Alyson said, "Our impression was pretty similar, but there were more details about his family in the book." Alejandro said that he liked writing the Bio-Impression because it gave him an idea of what happened in Jackie Robinson's life before he learned everything that was in the book. Steffie said that when we write Story Impressions and Bio-Impressions we get to write our predictions based on the clues we have. They also noted that my predictions about baseball being one of the sports in which Robinson excelled in college was verified in the text. Here is the Bio-Impression that I started and Steve and Aurora completed on their own:

> Jack Roosevelt Robinson was born on January 31, 1919. He attended college and was a star in four different sports. One of them was baseball. Jackie Robinson didn't volunteer to go into the Army. He was drafted. He played for the Brooklyn Dodgers in 1947 and broke the color barrier, because black people weren't allowed to play in the major leagues at that time. While he was playing for the Brooklyn Dodgers, he was named the National League Rookie of the Year and Most Valuable Player. Later he was elected to the Baseball Hall of Fame. Jackie Robinson died on October 24, 1972.

Reflect: We engaged in a discussion about how the clues helped us predict what we knew about Jackie Robinson. Then we talked about how previewing a text this way helped prepare us for reading and made us want to read to find out if our predictions were accurate. We also talked about how previewing vocabulary ahead of time helped make the words easier to know when we encountered them in the text.

STAGE TWO: Teacher-Guided Small-Group Instruction

Text: *The Real McCoy: The Life of an African-American Inventor* (Towle, 1993) (Texts varied according to students' abilities.)

Review: I reviewed with students that as good readers we can preview a text to get our minds ready to read. I also reviewed how we could use sequential clues from a text to create a predictive paragraph called a Bio-Impression. I introduced the book and asked students what they noticed on the cover of the book. I also asked them if they had ever heard the expression "the real McCoy" and what they thought it meant. Several students suggested that it meant "the real thing or the genuine item." Then I shared the list of sequential clues—words and phrases from the biography—that we would use and reviewed them with the students.

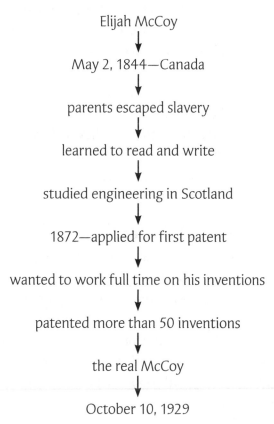

Elijah McCoy

↓

May 2, 1844—Canada

↓

parents escaped slavery

↓

learned to read and write

↓

studied engineering in Scotland

↓

1872—applied for first patent

↓

wanted to work full time on his inventions

↓

patented more than 50 inventions

↓

the real McCoy

↓

October 10, 1929

Guide: I guided the students to look at the first two phrases and think of the first sentence of our predictive paragraph. Because it was similar to the Jackie Robinson example, they had no trouble predicting that the date was probably when he was born. They wrote, "*Elijah McCoy was born on May 2, 1844, in Canada.*" Then we discussed how his parents could have been slaves if they lived in Canada. The students realized that Elijah was born in Canada, but his parents must have escaped slavery in the United States. The students knew that slaves in the United States were not allowed to read and write, but Elijah was. They wrote, "*His parents were slaves from the United States who were able to escape to Canada. In Canada, Elijah was free to learn to read and write.*"

Practice: The students continued to create their predictive paragraphs, with partners. When they were finished, each pair read their Bio-Impression and we used their predictions to set purposes for reading. Students read the biography and then we compared and contrasted the Bio-Impressions with the original text.

Reflect: I asked the students how using the Bio-Impression helped them to preview. They said it helped them learn a little about Elijah McCoy's life even before they read the book. Maria remarked that she and her partner were able to make connections to the clues based on information they had learned about slavery in their social studies class. Robert said that he and his partner enjoyed reading about Elijah, because as they read they learned which of their predictions were verified and which were not.

Student-Facilitated Comprehension Centers

Making Books Center: Each student used a computer to create a page for the class Autobiography Book. Students used the project checklist, the Autobiography Organizer, and PowerPoint. Students' slides were combined into the class book.

Theme Center: I provided sequential clue lists for each biography and autobiography. Students wrote their Bio-Impressions, read the text, and then wrote journal entries about how their impressions and the original biographies were similar and different.

Writing Center: Students used Bio-Impressions they had already written to learn more about the people featured in biographies and autobiographies they had read. For example, Jacquelyn used her Bio-Impression of Jackie Robinson to learn more about his life. She used two bookmarked websites to complete a QuIP (Questions Into Paragraphs) graphic organizer about Jackie Robinson. Then she used the completed organizer to write a paragraph about Jackie Robinson's life.

Student-Facilitated Comprehension Routines

Literature Circles: I provided Bio-Impression clues for the biographies students read in Literature Circles. Students in each group wrote Bio-Impressions and shared their predictions before reading the text. Then they used their impressions to compare and contrast their ideas with the original text.

Reciprocal Teaching: I provided Bio-Impression clues for biographies students read in Reciprocal Teaching. Students used their completed Bio-Impressions to share predictions about the text. They also created questions they had about the books. The list of clues helped them to summarize the important information in the text.

STAGE THREE: Teacher-Facilitated Whole-Group Reflection and Goal Setting

Share: Students shared their work from Stage Two, first in small groups and then with the class. They shared their Bio-Impressions and discussed examples of when their predictions had been confirmed and when they needed to be adjusted.

Reflect: We discussed why previewing is important and how it helps us prepare to read and understand. Cody said that creating Bio-Impressions motivated him to read because he wanted to find out if his predictions were verified. The other students agreed and decided they were comfortable using Bio-Impressions on their own.

Set New Goals: The students enjoyed writing Bio-Impressions. They thought adapting Bio-Impressions for use with other types of informational text would be helpful when reading their social studies and science textbooks. The students thought this would help them think about the content before reading. We decided we would create some Text Impressions for future content area chapters.

Assessment Options

I used observation during whole-group and small-group instruction. I used the checklist I had provided to review students' book pages. I reviewed their completed Bio-Impressions to see if what the students wrote was a reasonable predictive paragraph. This helped me when planning future previewing and writing lessons. I also read and provided feedback on students' self-assessments.

Life Stories: Biography, Autobiography
Guided Comprehension Strategy: Making Connections
Teaching Idea: Save the Last Word for Me

STAGE ONE: Teacher-Directed Whole-Group Instruction

Text: *Knots in My Yo-Yo String* (Spinelli, 1998)

Explain: I began by explaining to my students that making connections is a strategy good readers use while reading. I explained that we can make text–self, text–text, and text–world connections. I explained that Save the Last Word for Me is one way that we can make connections. Then I focused on how these connections help us understand what we are reading.

Demonstrate: I organized students into small groups and introduced Jerry Spinelli's autobiography *Knots in My Yo-Yo String.* I reminded students that autobiographies are life stories people write about themselves. I demonstrated making connections by reading aloud the title and showing the students the cover of the book. I said, "The title and illustration remind me of how much I enjoyed playing with a yo-yo when I was younger. My aunt bought me a Duncan yo-yo for my 10th birthday." Then I asked the students what they knew about yo-yos. I was surprised that so many of them were familiar with the simple toy. We also discussed what students liked to do to have fun. Their responses included playing baseball. They had noticed Jerry Spinelli was wearing a baseball uniform on page 4 of the book. Students also mentioned that they had fun dancing, going to the movies, and playing games on the computer. Next, I looked at the book cover and read the title again. I said, "Knots. I hated when my yo-yo string would get knots. We also used to fly kites down in Ocean City, Maryland, on the beach. That string sometimes got knotted, too." I read the first page aloud to the class and said, "Jerry seems to be really upset because Lucky was hit by a car. When my dog died, I cried and we buried her in our yard." When I read a few more pages, I made another connection. I said, "We also loved to ride our bikes outside every day." Then I demonstrated how to use Save the Last Word for Me. I showed the students an index card and said, "I will write an idea or quote from the book on side 1, and I will write my connection to the idea on side 2." I continued reading aloud. When I stopped I said, "Jerry lived in a row house in the West End of Norristown near a park and a creek. I am going to write that on side 1 of the index card. Now I will turn the card over to side 2. This is where I will write my connection. I am writing that I also lived in a row house but in a smaller town. We had a community park where we spent every day in the summer, either at the pool or the creek, doing arts and crafts, or playing tennis." Then I said that in Save the Last Word for Me, I would be working in a small group. Each member of the group would read side 1 of her card. Next, everyone in the group would comment on what I wrote on side 1. After all have commented, I would read my connection, which I wrote on side 2. I get the last word. That is why this idea is called Save the Last Word for Me.

Guide: As I continued to read aloud the next chapter of the book, I invited students to work with partners to make connections with the story. I guided students to listen for ideas that they could relate to their own experiences and to which they could make connections. I encouraged students to write an idea on side 1 of an index card and to write their connection on the back. Then each group engaged in Save the Last Word for Me. Some of their connections included "*I felt sad and guilty like Jerry Spinelli when I played war with my buddy and I accidentally broke his collarbone*"

Guided Comprehension: Life Stories: Biography, Autobiography
Making Connections: Save the Last Word for Me

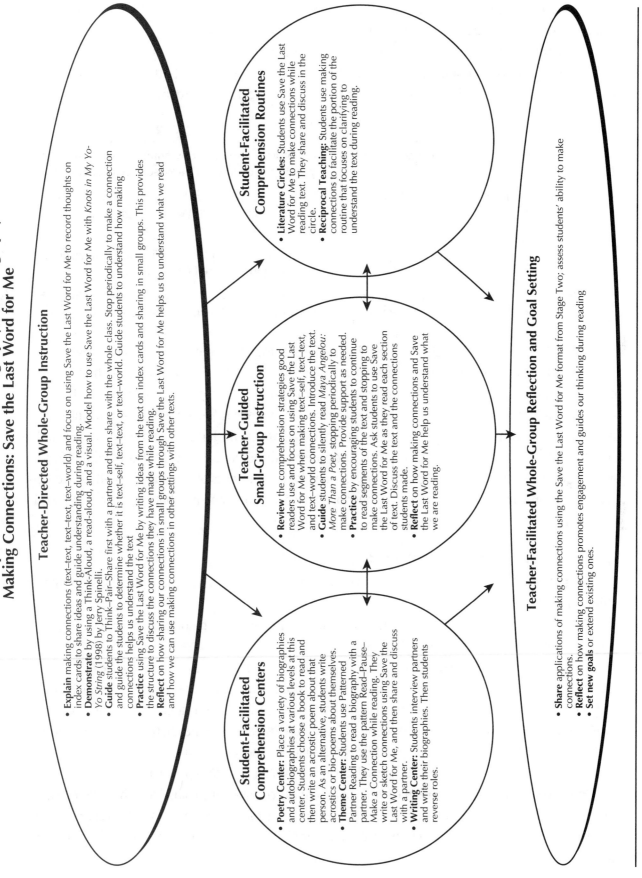

Teacher-Directed Whole-Group Instruction

- **Explain** making connections (text–text, text–text, text–world) and focus on using Save the Last Word for Me to record thoughts on index cards to share ideas and guide understanding during reading.
- **Demonstrate** by using a Think-Aloud, a read-aloud, and a visual. Model how to use Save the Last Word for Me with *Knots in My Yo-Yo String* (1998) by Jerry Spinelli.
- **Guide** students to Think-Pair-Share first with a partner and then share with the whole class. Stop periodically to make a connection and guide the students to determine whether it is text–self, text–text, or text–world. Guide students to understand how making connections helps us understand the text
- **Practice** using Save the Last Word for Me by writing ideas from the text on index cards and sharing in small groups. This provides the structure to discuss the connections they have made while reading.
- **Reflect** on how sharing our connections in small groups through Save the Last Word for Me helps us to understand what we read and how we can use making connections in other settings with other texts.

Student-Facilitated Comprehension Centers

- **Poetry Center:** Place a variety of biographies and autobiographies at various levels at this center. Students choose a book to read and then write an acrostic poem about that person. As an alternative, students write acrostics or bio-poems about themselves.
- **Theme Center:** Students use Patterned Partner Reading to read a biography with a partner. They use the pattern Read–Pause–Make a Connection while reading. They write or sketch connections using Save the Last Word for Me, and then share and discuss with a partner.
- **Writing Center:** Students interview partners and write their biographies. Then students reverse roles.

Teacher-Guided Small-Group Instruction

- **Review** the comprehension strategies good readers use and focus on using Save the Last Word for Me when making text–self, text–text, and text–world connections. Introduce the text.
- **Guide** students to silently read *Maya Angelou: More Than a Poet*, stopping periodically to make connections. Provide support as needed.
- **Practice** by encouraging students to continue to read segments of the text and stopping to make connections. Ask students to use Save the Last Word for Me as they read each section of text. Discuss the text and the connections students made.
- **Reflect** on how making connections and Save the Last Word for Me help us understand what we are reading.

Student-Facilitated Comprehension Routines

- **Literature Circles:** Students use Save the Last Word for Me to make connections while reading text. They share and discuss in the circle.
- **Reciprocal Teaching:** Students use making connections to facilitate the portion of the routine that focuses on clarifying to understand the text during reading.

Teacher-Facilitated Whole-Group Reflection and Goal Setting

- **Share** applications of making connections using the Save the Last Word for Me format from Stage Two; assess students' ability to make connections.
- **Reflect** on how making connections promotes engagement and guides our thinking during reading
- **Set new goals** or extend existing ones.

and *"Jerry talks about being a captive and being tortured during a real war. I can make a connection to Senator John McCain who was a prisoner of war during the Vietnam War."*

Practice: I continued to read the next chapter of the book while students practiced Save the Last Word for Me. The students shared their connections and discussed whether they were text–self, text–text, or text–world. Samples of their connections included the following:

Side 1	Side 2
Jerry enjoyed being a cowboy when he was little. (page 18)	My brother has a cowboy outfit and he wore it last year to the county fair. (text–self connection)
Jerry is a "sports nut" including baseball, football, and basketball. (page 22)	Jerry lived near Philadelphia and the Philadelphia Phillies won the 2008 World Series. (text–world connection)
Jerry won a medal for the 50-yard dash. (page 28)	I won a medal for placing first in our gymnastics competition. (text–self connection)
Jerry felt sorry for himself when he made an error playing shortstop for the "Greensox." (page 30)	In "Casey at the Bat," Casey feels sorry for himself because he struck out. (text–text connection)

Reflect: We began our reflection by discussing how making connections was helping us to relate to Jerry Spinelli's life. The students made many connections to his early life. We had an interesting discussion about how things are different from when Jerry was growing up in the 1950s, and about how many things were still the same. Then we reflected on the importance of using Save the Last Word for Me to make connections. Angela and Jennifer said they liked Save the Last Word for Me because they could choose any idea or quote in the passage. Paul said he liked using it because it was interesting to hear everyone else's comments on the idea he had written on side 1. Everyone decided that making connections keeps us interested in what we are reading and helps us to understand the biographies and autobiographies.

STAGE TWO: Teacher-Guided Small-Group Instruction

Text: *Maya Angelou: More Than a Poet* (Lisandrelli, 1996) (Texts varied according to students' abilities.)

Review: I reminded students about the reading strategies good readers use and reviewed how to make connections using Save the Last Word for Me.

Guide: I introduced the biography *Maya Angelou: More Than a Poet* by showing the cover, reading the title, and asking students to make connections. Samples of their statements included "Maya is at a podium speaking. This reminds me of when we see the President speak." and "I remember seeing Maya doing an interview on television." After everyone shared, students silently read segments of the text, stopping periodically to make connections using Save the Last Word for Me. This time instead of sharing with a small group, they shared with a partner.

Practice: Students silently read Chapter 2 and made connections using Save the Last Word for Me. After each chapter, we discussed their connections. We continued this process until the end of Chapter 5. Examples of the connections students shared in Save the Last Word for Me included the following:

Side 1	Side 2
Maya pretended to be a character from the books. (page 28)	I often do this after I read a story. I enjoyed pretending to be "Julie" in *Julie of the Wolves*. (text–self connection)
After the bombing of Pearl Harbor, West Coast Japanese-Americans, two-thirds of whom were American citizens, were subjected to much hatred. Many were uprooted from their homes and taken to detention camps. (pages 38–39)	I remember reading about the Japanese interment camps last year. Our teacher read Eve Bunting's book *So Far From the Sea* to us. (text–text connection)
Maya went to Big Mary's to pick up her son, but Big Mary and Clyde were not there. (page 59)	In the news, babies are taken all the time. Baby Caylee in Florida has been missing for months. (text–world connection)

Reflect: We engaged in a group retelling of what we had learned about Maya Angelou's life. Next, we discussed her life so far and how we can make connections to it. One student observed how difficult Maya's life has been and compared it with her own. Then we discussed how making connections helped us understand what we read.

Student-Facilitated Comprehension Centers

Poetry Center: Students read a biography or autobiography and wrote an acrostic about that person. Students could also choose to write a bio-poem about themselves or use their first names to write acrostic poems about their lives. This is the acrostic Adriah created:

A student who loves to read

D evoted to my parents and friends

R egrets making some bad decisions

I nterested in going to college

A positive attitude and determination will bring me success

H appy

Theme Center: I placed a variety of biographies and autobiographies at various levels at this center. Students read in pairs, using Patterned Partner Reading with the Read–Pause–Make a Connection pattern. They wrote or sketched their connections using the Save the Last Word for Me format. They shared and discussed their connections with a partner.

Writing Center: Students worked with a partner to write each other's biographies. They began by interviewing each other. When the biographies were complete, each partner made connections to the other's life story.

Student-Facilitated Comprehension Routines

Literature Circles: One group of advanced-level readers chose to read *All God's Children Need Traveling Shoes* (1986) by Maya Angelou. They made connections as they read and shared their thoughts through Save the Last Word for Me. This is an example of Melanie's work:

Side 1: "Hope for the best; be prepared for the worst. You may not get what you pay for, but you will definitely pay for what you get."

Side 2: "When my Mom and me have talks, she says pretty much the same thing." (text–self connection)

Reciprocal Teaching: The students made connections using Save the Last Word for Me and shared them during the portion of the routine that focuses on clarifying.

STAGE THREE: Teacher-Facilitated Whole-Group Reflection and Goal Setting

Share: Students shared their connections from Stage Two in small groups. Then we discussed their applications as a whole class.

Reflect: We reflected on how making connections can promote engagement and guide our reading. We also talked about how we can make all three different types of connections: text–self, text–text, and text–world.

Set New Goals: Students felt confident with their ability to make connections with biographies and autobiographies, so we extended our goal to using Save the Last Word for Me with poetry. We decided to make connections with Maya Angelou's "On the Pulse of Morning" as well as other poems.

Assessment Options

I observed students and listened carefully as they made connections throughout this lesson. I also reviewed their index cards and checked for understanding during their discussions. Students used a graphic organizer and a checklist when writing their autobiographies. I reviewed the organizer and used the checklist to assess what they had written.

Life Stories: Biography, Autobiography
Guided Comprehension Strategy: Summarizing
Teaching Idea: Bio-Pyramid

STAGE ONE: Teacher-Directed Whole-Group Instruction

Text: *Odd Boy Out: Young Albert Einstein* (Brown, 2004)

Explain: I began by explaining summarizing as a reading strategy and focused on the importance of being able to recall the most important information after reading. I explained that the Bio-Pyramid is one way to summarize the lives of people. I told the students that by thinking about the content of a text, and putting it in our own words, we can identify the most important information and share it with others. I explained that we would be summarizing a biography we had already read, using the format of the Bio-Pyramid (see Appendix A, page 265, for a blackline master).

Demonstrate: I briefly recounted the life of Albert Einstein by revisiting the important facts from his life, which I had written on chart paper after we finished reading the book. I demonstrated the Bio-Pyramid and used a Think-Aloud as I reasoned my way through lines 1 and 2. I started with line 1—name—and because there was only one blank, I wrote *Einstein*. I had the students write the name on their blackline after I wrote it on the overhead. Then I thought aloud about line 2. I said, "I need two words to describe Albert Einstein." I explained that I could use two separate words, like *curious* and *thinker*, or I could use a two-word phrase. I told them I wanted to use the phrase, so I wrote "*brilliant scientist*" on line 2. The students wrote the same on line 2 on their Bio-Pyramids. The students were showing that they understood the process so I asked them to help me with line 3—three words describing the person's childhood.

Guide: I guided the students by asking supporting questions such as, "What was something important that happened in his childhood?" Then I said, "Let's look at our list of facts about Einstein's life. Which one of these could we use?" We decided to write "*rebellious in school.*" because Einstein didn't like how he was taught in school. Then I guided the students to think of a problem he had to overcome. We had a discussion about his troubles in school and also how he did not fit in with the other boys, but we kept coming back to the fact that he didn't speak until he was four years old. We decided to write *didn't speak until four.*

Practice: The next three lines summarize accomplishments. We had listed many on our list of facts, so I asked the students to work with a partner to complete lines 5–7. I referred them to the list of facts and I guided pairs as needed. Then they worked with their partner to write eight words to describe a way that the world has benefited from Einstein's accomplishments. Figure 10 shows the Bio-Pyramid I began and Maria and Venetta completed.

Reflect: We engaged in a discussion about what needed to be included in a summary of a biography. Then we reflected on how using the Bio-Pyramid provided a format for summary writing, and how much fun it was to write summaries this way.

STAGE TWO: Teacher-Guided Small-Group Instruction

Text: *Pablo Picasso: Breaking All the Rules* (Kelley, 2002) (Texts varied according to students' abilities.)

Guided Comprehension: Life Stories: Biography, Autobiography Summarizing: Bio-Pyramid

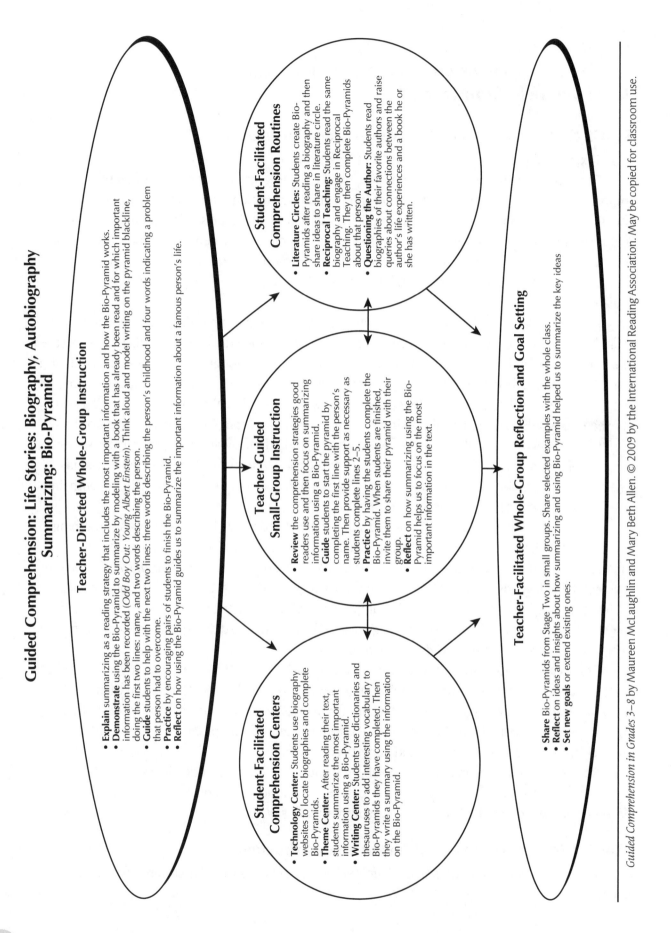

Teacher-Directed Whole-Group Instruction

- **Explain** summarizing as a reading strategy that includes the most important information and how the Bio-Pyramid works.
- **Demonstrate** using the Bio-Pyramid to summarize by modeling with a book that has already been read and for which important information has been recorded (*Odd Boy Out: Young Albert Einstein*). Think aloud and model writing on the pyramid blackline, doing the first two lines: name, and two words describing the person.
- **Guide** students to help with the next two lines: three words describing the person's childhood and four words indicating a problem that person had to overcome.
- **Practice** by encouraging pairs of students to finish the Bio-Pyramid.
- **Reflect** on how using the Bio-Pyramid guides us to summarize the important information about a famous person's life.

Student-Facilitated Comprehension Centers

- **Technology Center:** Students use biography websites to locate biographies and complete Bio-Pyramids.
- **Theme Center:** After reading their text, students summarize the most important information using a Bio-Pyramid.
- **Writing Center:** Students use dictionaries and thesauruses to add interesting vocabulary to Bio-Pyramids they have completed. Then they write a summary using the information on the Bio-Pyramid.

Teacher-Guided Small-Group Instruction

- **Review** the comprehension strategies good readers use and then focus on summarizing information using a Bio-Pyramid.
- **Guide** students to start the pyramid by completing the first line with the person's name. Then provide support as necessary as students complete lines 2–5.
- **Practice** by having the students complete the Bio-Pyramid. When students are finished, invite them to share their pyramid with their group.
- **Reflect** on how summarizing using the Bio-Pyramid helps us to focus on the most important information in the text.

Student-Facilitated Comprehension Routines

- **Literature Circles:** Students create Bio-Pyramids after reading a biography and then share ideas to share in literature circle.
- **Reciprocal Teaching:** Students read the same biography and engage in Reciprocal Teaching. They then complete Bio-Pyramids about that person.
- **Questioning the Author:** Students read biographies of their favorite authors and raise queries about connections between the author's life experiences and a book he or she has written.

Teacher-Facilitated Whole-Group Reflection and Goal Setting

- **Share** Bio-Pyramids from Stage Two in small groups. Share selected examples with the whole class.
- **Reflect** on ideas and insights about how summarizing and using Bio-Pyramid helped us to summarize the key ideas
- **Set new goals** or extend existing ones.

Guided Comprehension in Grades 3–8 by Maureen McLaughlin and Mary Beth Allen. © 2009 by the International Reading Association. May be copied for classroom use.

Figure 10. Bio-Pyramid About Albert Einstein

1. <u>Einstein</u>
Person's name

2. <u>brilliant</u> <u>scientist</u>
Two words describing the person

3. <u>rebellious</u> <u>in</u> <u>school</u>
Three words describing the person's childhood

4. <u>didn't</u> <u>speak</u> <u>until</u> <u>four</u>
Four words indicating a problem the person had to overcome

5. <u>developed</u> <u>the</u> <u>theory</u> <u>of</u> relativity
Five words stating one of his/her accomplishments

6. <u>awarded</u> <u>1921</u> <u>Nobel</u> <u>Prize</u> <u>for</u> <u>Physics</u>
Six words stating a second accomplishment

7. <u>wrote</u> <u>letter</u> <u>to</u> <u>Roosevelt</u> <u>about</u> <u>atom</u> <u>bomb</u>
Seven words stating a third accomplishment

8. <u>Albert</u> <u>Einstein</u> <u>made</u> <u>many</u> <u>great</u> <u>contributions</u> <u>to</u> <u>science</u>
Eight words stating how mankind benefited from his/her accomplishments

Review: I reminded students that as good readers we should be able to summarize the most important information from a text we have read. I reviewed the format of the Bio-Pyramid. Because we had read this book in a previous session, we also reviewed the important things we had learned about Pablo Picasso. We filled in the first line of our Bio-Pyramids by writing *Picasso*.

Guide: I guided the students to think about two words to describe Picasso. We made a list of words—*artist, genius, talented, creative, rule-breaker, painter, sculptor, committed*. We decided to use a phrase from the book: *artistic genius*. Then I prompted students to think of three words to tell something about his childhood. We thought about his father being an artist, that he was talented from a very young age, he was born in Spain, he went to Madrid for art school, and that he was born in 1881. I asked the students to discuss the ideas with a partner and choose three words we could use for line 3 of our Bio-Pyramid. They suggested several choices: *born in 1881, father was artist, talented from birth*. They chose one and recorded it on their line 3. Then I guided them to think about line 4—four words stating a problem the person had to overcome. They shared ideas with a partner and several ideas emerged: *didn't like traditional painting, wanted his own style*, and *broke the art rules*. The students recorded their choice on line 4 and we moved to line 5.

Practice: The students finished line 5 with me and then they worked on their own with a partner to finish lines 6–8. We shared their ideas the next time the group met. Figure 11 shows a completed Bio-Pyramid for Pablo Picasso.

Reflect: I asked students how using the Bio-Pyramid helped them to summarize the key ideas from a biography. They said it helped them to focus on what to include, and they also liked that they had to use a set number of words. They said that made it a little harder to summarize, but also more fun.

Figure 11. Bio-Pyramid About Pablo Picasso

1. <u>Picasso</u>
Person's name

2. <u>artistic</u> <u>genius</u>
Two words describing the person

3. <u>talented</u> <u>from</u> <u>birth</u>
Three words describing the person's childhood

4. <u>didn't</u> <u>like</u> <u>traditional</u> <u>painting</u>
Four words indicating a problem the person had to overcome

5. <u>created</u> <u>new</u> <u>style</u> <u>of</u> <u>art</u>
Five words stating one of his/her accomplishments

6. <u>made</u> <u>about</u> <u>50,000</u> <u>pieces</u> <u>of</u> <u>art</u>
Six words stating a second accomplishment

7. <u>continued</u> <u>painting</u> <u>until</u> <u>the</u> <u>day</u> <u>he</u> <u>died</u>
Seven words stating a third accomplishment

8. <u>people</u> <u>all</u> <u>over</u> <u>the</u> <u>world</u> <u>enjoy</u> <u>his</u> <u>artwork</u>
Eight words stating how mankind benefited from his/her accomplishments

Student-Facilitated Comprehension Centers

Technology Center: Students visited bookmarked websites such as www.biography.com. They read a biography of special interest to them and completed a Bio-Pyramid.

Theme Center: I placed a variety of biographies and autobiographies at different levels at this center. Students chose a book to read and used the Bio-Pyramid format to summarize the key ideas.

Writing Center: I placed several resources for vocabulary at this center. Students used those resources and online dictionaries and thesauruses to add more descriptive language to their Bio-Pyramids. Then they wrote summaries based on the Bio-Pyramids.

Student-Facilitated Comprehension Routines

Literature Circles: Students summarized their biographies using the Bio-Pyramid. They brought completed pyramids to their literature circle and shared ideas. Students had to explain their reasoning for what they chose to include.

Reciprocal Teaching: Students read biographies using Reciprocal Teaching strategies. They then completed Bio-Pyramids about the person featured in the book.

Questioning the Author: Students read biographies of their favorite authors and raised queries about connections between the author's life experiences and a book he or she has written. For example, one student read Gary Paulsen's biography and queried how his life related to the character Brian in *Hatchet*.

STAGE THREE: Teacher-Facilitated Whole-Group Reflection and Goal Setting

Share: Students shared their Bio-Pyramids, first in small groups and then with the class. They shared what they thought was the most important information about the person they had read about.

Reflect: We talked about how summarizing is an important strategy readers can use, and students discussed how they liked the pyramid format. They particularly liked having to rework their ideas to try to stay within the word limit. They also shared ideas about famous people and it motivated other students to want to read those books.

Set New Goals: Students said they could use the Bio-Pyramid for any type of text they read that was about a famous person. They also thought it could be used as a report format when studying famous people in history.

Assessment Options

I used observation during whole-group and small-group instruction. I reviewed and commented on the completed Bio-Pyramids to ensure they featured correct information and accommodated the eight-line structured format.

Life Stories: Biography, Autobiography
Guided Comprehension Strategy: Summarizing
Teaching Idea: Questions Into Paragraphs (QuIP)

STAGE ONE: Teacher-Directed Whole-Group Instruction

Text: *Rosa* (Giovanni, 2005)

Explain: I began by explaining summarizing to the students, noting that when we summarize, we include the important ideas from the text. I pointed out that summarizing informational text is very different from summarizing or retelling stories because retellings include the story elements: characters, setting, problem, attempts to resolve, and resolution. Then I explained Questions Into Paragraphs (QuIP) to students as a way to summarize informational text. I focused on how we use questioning, research, and summarizing to understand new information while we are reading.

Demonstrate: I demonstrated QuIP by using a Think-Aloud, the QuIP graphic organizer (see Appendix A, page 268), and the text. I began by reading aloud the title and showing the students the cover of the book *Rosa*. I showed the cover of the book and thought aloud, "The title tells me this book is about a woman named Rosa. I think it is about Rosa Parks. The illustration made me wonder why the man is looking down at her." Then I asked students what they knew about Rosa Parks. We discussed their responses, which included that she was arrested for not giving up her seat to white people on a bus.

Guide: I guided students to generate ideas by raising a question I had about Rosa Parks. I said, "I have a question about Rosa Parks that I would like to research. My question is, Why is Rosa Parks considered to be the mother of the modern-day civil rights movement in the United States?" I wrote the question in the box labeled 1 on the graphic organizer. Next, I quickly reviewed the levels of questioning we had previously learned (see Chapter 2, page 20) and suggested that students generate questions at higher thinking levels. Then I asked the students to work with partners to generate questions they might have about Rosa Parks. After a few minutes we discussed their ideas. The students generated a variety of questions and we decided to add two of them to our QuIP graphic organizers. I added them to the organizer on the overhead projector, and students added them to their copies. The three questions were as follows:

1. Why is Rosa Parks considered to be the mother of the modern day civil rights movement in the United States?

2. How were Rosa Parks's refusal to give up her seat and the Montgomery Bus Boycott connected?

3. In what ways has the U.S. government acknowledged Rosa Parks's contributions to our world?

I guided students to use two websites about Rosa Parks to gather responses to the questions. I modeled the process by using the first website to respond to question 1. Then I wrote the response in the space provided on the graphic organizer. Students worked with partners to find responses to questions 2 and 3 from the first website. These were the websites I bookmarked for student use:

Rosa and Raymond Parks Institute for Self-Development: www.rosaparks.org/bio.html

Biography.com—Rosa Parks: www.biography.com/search/article.do?id=9433715

Guided Comprehension: Life Stories: Biography, Autobiography

Summarizing: Questions Into Paragraphs (QuIP)

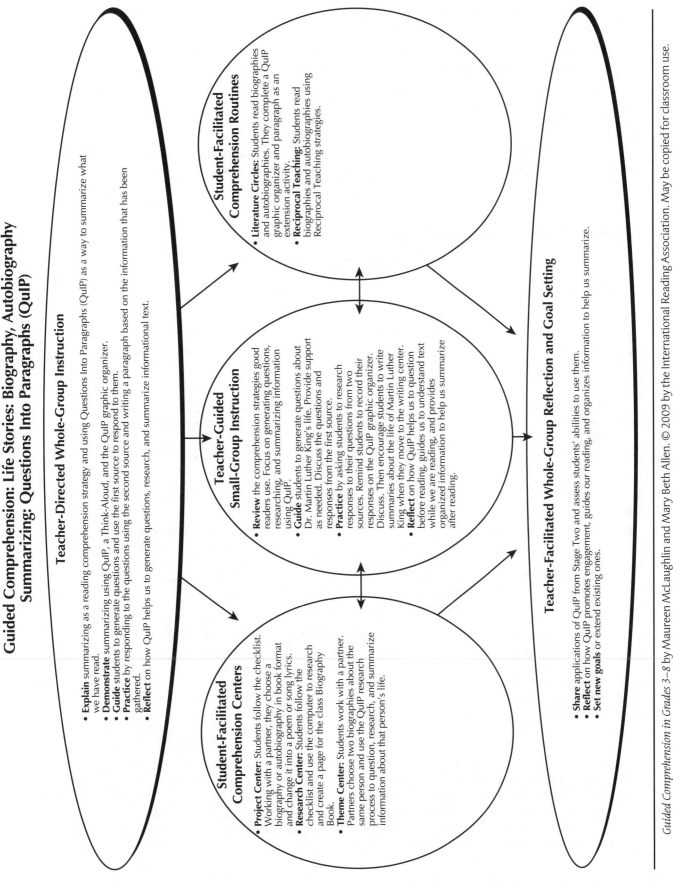

Teacher-Directed Whole-Group Instruction

- **Explain** summarizing as a reading comprehension strategy and using Questions Into Paragraphs (QuIP) as a way to summarize what we have read.
- **Demonstrate** summarizing using QuIP, a Think-Aloud, and the QuIP graphic organizer.
- **Guide** students to generate questions and use the first source to respond to them.
- **Practice** by responding to the questions using the second source and writing a paragraph based on the information that has been gathered.
- **Reflect** on how QuIP helps us to generate questions, research, and summarize informational text.

Student-Facilitated Comprehension Centers

- **Project Center:** Students follow the checklist. Working with a partner, they choose a biography or autobiography in book format and change it into a poem or song lyrics.
- **Research Center:** Students follow the checklist and use the computer to research and create a page for the class Biography Book.
- **Theme Center:** Students work with a partner. Partners choose two biographies about the same person and use the QuIP research process to question, research, and summarize information about that person's life.

Teacher-Guided Small-Group Instruction

- **Review** the comprehension strategies good readers use. Focus on generating questions, researching, and summarizing information using QuIP.
- **Guide** students to generate questions about Dr. Martin Luther King's life. Provide support as needed. Discuss the questions and responses from the first source.
- **Practice** by asking students to research responses to their questions from two sources. Remind students to record their responses on the QuIP graphic organizer. Discuss. Then encourage students to write summaries about the life of Martin Luther King when they move to the writing center.
- **Reflect** on how QuIP helps us to question before reading, guides us to understand text while we are reading, and provides organized information to help us summarize after reading.

Student-Facilitated Comprehension Routines

- **Literature Circles:** Students read biographies and autobiographies. They complete a QuIP graphic organizer and paragraph as an extension activity.
- **Reciprocal Teaching:** Students read biographies and autobiographies using Reciprocal Teaching strategies.

Teacher-Facilitated Whole-Group Reflection and Goal Setting

- **Share** applications of QuIP from Stage Two and assess students' abilities to use them.
- **Reflect** on how QuIP promotes engagement, guides our reading, and organizes information to help us summarize.
- **Set new goals** or extend existing ones.

Figure 12 shows the QuIP organizer and paragraph Sadie and Max completed in response to the three questions.

Practice: Students practiced by responding to the three questions using information from the second website. We discussed the responses and then the students worked on their own to write QuIP summaries. When they finished and we shared a few examples, I invited students to relax as I read aloud *Rosa*. Then we discussed the book and compared and contrasted it to the information we found on the websites.

Reflect: We began our reflection by discussing how important good questions are when we need to find information. Then we discussed using more than one research source and how easy

Figure 12. QuIP Organizer and Paragraph

Topic: Rosa Parks

Questions	Answers	
	Source A: Rosa and Raymond Parks Institute for Self-Development www.rosaparks.org/bio.html	Source B: Biography.com www.biography.com/search/article.do?id=9433715
1. Why is Rosa Parks considered to be the mother of the modern day civil rights movement in America?	She stood up for herself and her people by not giving up her seat on a bus for a white person.	Rosa Parks and 3 other black people were asked to give up their seats on a bus so a white man could sit down. The others moved. Rosa Parks refused to give up her seat and the bus driver had her arrested.
2. How were Rosa Parks' refusal to give up her seat and the Montgomery Bus Boycott connected?	After Rosa Parks was arrested the black people who lived in Montgomery organized a bus boycott that lasted 381 days. Martin Luther King Jr. was the spokesperson for the boycott.	The Montgomery Bus Boycott began after Rosa Parks was convicted of violating a local law. 40,000 people boycotted the buses.
3. In what ways has the United States government acknowledged Rosa Parks' contributions to our world?	President Clinton awarded Rosa Parks the Medal of Freedom.	Rosa Parks was awarded the Congressional Gold Medal of Honor.

Rosa Parks is considered to be the mother of the civil rights movement because she refused to give up her seat to a white person when the bus driver asked her to. The bus driver told the police and Rosa Parks was arrested for disorderly conduct. Black people in Montgomery organized a bus boycott after Rosa Parks was convicted. The boycott lasted for 381 days and the spokesperson was Martin Luther King, Jr. When President Clinton was in office, Rosa Parks was awarded the Medal of Freedom and the Congressional Gold Medal of Honor for her courage.

it was to write summaries based on our completed QuIPs. Michael said that the QuIP made it very easy to write a paragraph because all the information was important enough to include. Louis remarked that he will remember the information about Rosa Parks for a long time because he found it in response to our own questions. Students agreed that the QuIP provide a good way for us to organize the information we wanted to learn.

STAGE TWO: Teacher-Guided Small-Group Instruction

Texts: *M.L.K.: Journey of a King* (Bolden, 2007) and *Who Was Martin Luther King Jr.?* (Bader & Harrison, 2007) (Texts varied according to students' abilities.)

Review: I reminded students about the strategies good readers use and focused on questioning and summarizing using QuIP.

Guide: I introduced the texts about Martin Luther King Jr. and guided the students to work with partners to generate questions they would like to include on our QuIP graphic organizer. We discussed their suggestions and added three questions to our QuIP:

1. What is known about Martin Luther King's education?

2. Why is Dr. King's "I Have a Dream" speech so famous?

3. How would you describe Martin Luther King Jr.'s contributions to our world?

Practice: Students read the texts silently and used them to respond to the QuIP questions. After our small-group time ended, students went to the writing center and wrote paragraphs based on their completed QuIPs. This is Jenny's QuIP paragraph:

> Martin Luther King, Jr. became a minister after he went to a theological seminary and earned his doctorate at Boston University. Many people think that his "I Have a Dream" speech contained a very powerful message of hope for America. He led a peaceful march on Washington, DC and gave the speech to 250,000 people. Martin Luther King, Jr. contributed to our world by leading a nonviolent civil rights movement. He received the Nobel Peace Prize in 1964 and was assassinated in 1968.

Reflect: We discussed what we had learned about Martin Luther King Jr. Jesse pointed out that there was a timeline in the back of one of the texts that helped us to understand the events of King's life in chronological order. We reflected on the role good questions play when we are completing QuIPs. We discussed how questioning and recording the information we researched helped us learn new information and organize it so we remember what we have read. Then students moved on to the writing center to write paragraphs based on their completed QuIPs.

Student-Facilitated Comprehension Centers

Project Center: I provided a checklist at this center for students to follow as they created their transmediations. Students worked with partners to select a biography or autobiography in book format and change it into a poem or song lyrics. If time permitted, students illustrated their transmediations.

Research Center: I provided checklists for students to follow as they completed their biography pages. Students used completed QuIPs as starting points for learning more about the people they were investigating. The resources students used included biographies and autobiographies I had placed at the center as well as websites I had bookmarked. The students presented their research as a page in our class biography book.

Theme Center: Students worked in pairs to read two biographies of the same person. Students generated their questions together on the QuIP graphic organizer and then read the books together to find the information. They recorded their answers on the QuIP and wrote summary paragraphs.

Student-Facilitated Comprehension Routines

Literature Circles: Students read their biographies and completed QuIPs as an extension activity. They discussed their completed QuIPs and wrote their paragraphs in their Guided Comprehension Journals.

Reciprocal Teaching: The students used their questions and summaries during the portion of the routine that focuses on these strategies.

STAGE THREE: Teacher-Facilitated Whole-Group Reflection and Goal Setting

Share: Students shared their QuIPs, transmediations, and research projects from Stage Two in small groups. Then we discussed examples as a whole class.

Reflect: We reflected on how QuIP questions guide our research and reading and how the organizer makes it easier to write a summary.

Set New Goals: Students felt confident with their ability to use QuIPs to question and summarize research, so we extended our goal to using this technique with other forms of expository text. We decided to use QuIPs to learn about endangered species for our upcoming science unit on animals.

Assessment Options

I used observation throughout the lesson. I listened carefully to students' questions and reviewed their responses and paragraphs. I used checklists, which I provided at the centers, when assessing students' transmediations and research projects. I also read and provided feedback on students' center self-assessments.

Theme Resources

Books

Adams, M.M. (2005). *The life and times of Cleopatra*. Hockessin, DE: Mitchell Lane.

Atalay, B., & Wamsley, K. (2009). *Leonardo's universe: The Renaissance world of Leonardo da Vinci*. Washington, DC: National Geographic.

Bankston, J. (2003). *Venus Williams*. Bear, DE: Mitchell Lane.

Brophy, D.B. (2009). *Michelle Obama: Meet the First Lady*. New York: Collins.

Carpenter, A.S. (2003). *Lewis Carroll: Through the looking glass*. Minneapolis, MN: Lerner Publications.

Christopher, M. (1998). *On the field with...Mia Hamm*. New York: Little, Brown.

Christopher, M. (2004). *On the court with...Yao Ming*. New York: Little, Brown.

Cobb, V. (2005). *Harry Houdini*. New York: DK Children.

Collins, K. (2004). *Sojourner Truth: Equal rights advocate*. New York: Rosen.

DeMauro, L. (2006). *Presidents of the United States*. New York: HarperCollins.

Denenberg, D., & Roscoe, L. (2006). *50 American heroes every kid should meet*. Minneapolis, MN: Millbrook Press.

Foster, F.S. (2007). *T: An auto-biography*. Farmington, NH: River Road Press.

Fradin, D.B. (2002). *Who was Ben Franklin?* New York: Grosset & Dunlap.

Gibson, K.B. (2006). *The life and times of Catherine the Great*. Hockessin, DE: Mitchell Lane.

Glass, M. (2004). *Benjamin Franklin: Early American genius*. New York: Rosen.

Gunderson, J. (2007). *Sacagawea: Journey into the west*. Mankato, MN: Capstone Press.

Humphrey, S.M. (2005). *Dare to dream! 25 extraordinary lives*. Amherst, NY: Prometheus.

Kaplan, H.S. (2004). *John F. Kennedy*. New York: DK Children.

King, D.C. (2006). *Charles Darwin*. New York: DK Children.

McPherson, S.S. (1995). *Ordinary genius: The story of Albert Einstein*. Minneapolis, MN: Carolrhoda.

Márquez, H. (2005). *Roberto Clemente: Baseball's humanitarian hero*. Minneapolis, MN: Carolrhoda.

Mattern, J. (2006). *Princess Diana*. New York: DK Children.

Mattern, J. (2007). *Peyton Manning*. Hockessin, DE: Mitchell Lane.

O'Connor, B. (2003). *Leonardo da Vinci: Renaissance genius*. Minneapolis, MN: Carolrhoda.

Olmstead, K. (2008). *Jacques Cousteau: A life under the sea*. New York: Sterling.

Pastan, A. (2004). *Martin Luther King, Jr.* New York: DK Children.

Thomas, G. (2008). *Yes we can: A biography of Barack Obama*. New York: Feiwel & Friends.

Time for Kids biography series. New York: HarperCollins.

Wilkinson, P. (2005). *Gandhi: The young protester who founded a nation*. Washington, DC: National Geographic.

Whiting, J. (2006). *Aristotle*. Hockessin, DE: Mitchell Lane.

Who was...? book series. New York: Grosset & Dunlap.

Woog, A. (2003). *Bill Gates*. San Diego, CA: KidHaven Press.

Websites

Biography
   www.biography.com

BiographyBase
> www.biographybase.com

BiographyBiography.com: How to Write a Biography
> www.biographybiography.com/howtowriteabiography.html

Biography Shelf
> www.biographyshelf.com

Encyclopedia of World Biography
> www.notablebiographies.com

Leonardo Da Vinci: Artist, Inventor, and Universal Genius of the Renaissance
> www.leonardo-history.com

Nobelprize.org
> nobelprize.org/nobel_prizes/peace/laureates/1964/king-bio.html

The Official Website of The British Monarchy
> www.royal.gov.uk/output/page151.asp

Scholastic: Biography Writer's Workshop
> teacher.scholastic.com/writewit/biograph/index.htm

Scholastic: Writing an Autobiography
> www2.scholastic.com/browse/lessonplan.jsp?id=24

Smithsonian.com: Who Was Cleopatra?
> www.smithsonianmag.com/history-archaeology/biography/cleopatra.html

The White House
> www.whitehouse.gov/history/presidents/jk35.html

Performance Extensions Across the Curriculum

Social Studies

- Choose a person who has played a prominent role in U.S. history and research that person's biography. Share what you learn through a presentation mode such as a picture book, poem, or PowerPoint slideshow.

- Working with a partner, read two biographies about a great military leader of your choice. Create interview questions and responses based on what you learned from your reading. Digitally record and share the interview in a *Meet the Press* or press conference format.

Science

- Visit a website that focuses on biographies of great scientists, such as World of Biography (www. worldofbiography.com/Scientists-inventors-biography.asp). Choose one scientist from the 18th, 19th, and 20th centuries and read their biographies. Add information about each to our Scientists of the Past descriptive timeline/mural.

- Select a scientist, and using a total of three library and online sources, create a page for him or her in our class *Scientists of the Ages* PowerPoint book.

Math

- Use at least two bookmarked website sources, such as Biographies of Women Mathematicians (www.agnesscott.edu/lriddle/women/women.htm) to create a biography for a woman mathematician of your choice. Select a presentation mode for the information you gather.
- Work in a small group to create a tri-fold presentation about a mathematician associated with our current topic of study. Use a minimum of three sources.

Art

- Research using a minimum of three sources, and then create a picture book biography of your favorite author.
- Using the Autobiography Organizer, create and illustrate your autobiography.

Music

- Choose a familiar tune and write lyrics based on your autobiography.
- Create a PowerPoint slide presentation for a biography you have read or written and integrate music to enhance the information.
- Work with a partner to create a transmediation by changing a biography picture book into song lyrics.

Culminating Activity

Every Life Has a Story: Invite parents and community members to participate in a theme celebration titled *Every Life Has a Story*. Display students' projects from the biography/ autobiography theme. Invite students to dramatize scenes from selected biographies. Encourage parents, community members, and students to share their favorite life memories. Create a variety of stations where students can explain their biography projects from across the curriculum to the visitors. Provide refreshments, and offer visitors interactive opportunities to give feedback on the celebration, such as writing comments on a class mural or e-mailing comments to students on class computers. Students will autograph copies of the class book *Our Awesome Autobiographies* and give them as gifts to their families.

CHAPTER 8

Identity: Who Are You?

We are all familiar with the song "Who Are You." It was originally a hit for The Who and is now the theme song of the popular television series *CSI: Crime Scene Investigation*. The lyrics of the chorus, which repeatedly question, "Who are you?" might remind us of our lifelong quests to discover our identities. Because we and our students seek to learn about ourselves, we can readily identify with the themes within this chapter: appreciating individual uniqueness, accepting ourselves and others, and balancing life responsibilities.

The sample Theme-Based Plan for Guided Comprehension: Identity: Who Are You? (see Figure 13) offers an overview of the thinking and resources that support this theme. It presents a sampling of goals, state standards, assessments, texts, website resources, comprehension strategies, teaching ideas, comprehension centers, and comprehension routines. The plan begins by delineating examples of student goals and related state standards. The student goals for this theme include the following:

- Use appropriate comprehension skills and strategies

- Interpret and respond to text

- Communicate effectively

These goals support the following state standards:

- Learning to read independently

- Reading, analyzing, and interpreting text

- Types and quality of writing

- Speaking and listening

The assessments listed on the theme planner are examples of diagnostic, formative, and summative measures. Running records are an example of a diagnostic assessment. Formative assessments, which are informal and usually occur on a daily basis, include specific measures such as comprehension strategy applications, and general assessments such as observation and student self-assessment. Summative assessments, which are more formal long-term measures such as projects, are also featured.

The Guided Comprehension lessons are based on the following strategies and corresponding teaching ideas:

Figure 13. Theme-Based Plan for Guided Comprehension: Identity: Who Are You?

Goals and Connections to State Standards

Students will

- Use appropriate comprehension skills and strategies. Standard: learning to read independently
- Interpret and respond to text. Standard: reading, analyzing, and interpreting text
- Communicate effectively. Standard: types and quality of writing; speaking and listening

Assessment

The following measures can be used for a variety of purposes, including diagnostic, formative, and summative assessment:

Draw and Label Visualizations   Projects
Evaluative Questioning   Running Records
Narrative Pyramids   Self-Assessments
Observation   Student Writing
Paired Questioning

Text	Title	Theme	Level
1.	*Papa's Mark*	Identity	K–3
2.	*My Name Is Not Isabella*	Identity	K–3
3.	*The Miraculous Journey of Edward Tulane*	Identity	4–7
4.	*Sleeping Freshmen Never Lie*	Identity	YA

Website Resources

Annenberg Media
www.learner.org/workshops/tml/workshop1/teaching3.html
Great Peacemakers
    www.greatpeacemakers.com
Scholastic
    teacher.scholastic.com/activities/immigration/index.htm

Comprehension Strategies

1. Self-Questioning
2. Visualizing
3. Summarizing
4. Evaluating

Teaching Ideas

Paired Questioning
Draw and Label Visualizations
Narrative Pyramids
Evaluative Questioning

Comprehension Centers

Students will apply the comprehension strategies and related teaching ideas in the following comprehension centers:

Art Center   Research Center
Drama Center   Technology Center
Making Books Center   Theme Center
Poetry Center   Writing Center

Comprehension Routines

Students will apply the comprehension strategies and related teaching ideas in the following comprehension routines:

Literature Circles
Reciprocal Teaching
Questioning the Author

- Self-Questioning: Paired Questioning
- Visualizing: Draw and Label Visualizations
- Summarizing: Narrative Pyramids
- Evaluating: Evaluative Questioning

Papa's Mark (Battle-Lavert, 2003), *My Name Is Not Isabella* (Fosberry, 2008), *The Miraculous Journey of Edward Tulane* (DiCamillo, 2006), and *Sleeping Freshmen Never Lie* (Lubar, 2005) are the texts used in Stage One for teacher-directed whole-group instruction. Numerous additional theme-related resources, including texts, websites, performances across the curriculum, and a culminating activity, are presented in the Theme Resources at the end of the chapter.

Comprehension centers students use during Stage Two of Guided Comprehension include art, drama, making books, poetry, research, technology, theme, and writing. Students also engage in strategy application in comprehension routines such as Literature Circles, Reciprocal Teaching, and Questioning the Author. Sample website resources complete the overview.

All the lessons in this chapter focus on identity. The lessons are appropriate for all learners, including English learners, struggling readers, and students with special needs. To accommodate these learners, the lessons include multiple modes of response (such as singing, sketching, and dramatizing) working with partners, books on CD, cross-age experiences, and extra guided instruction. Ideas we used to differentiate instruction in these lessons include the following:

- Content—the information being taught:
  - Using theme-related leveled books in teacher-guided small groups
  - Providing multiple levels of text for students' use in Guided Comprehension centers and routines

- Process—the way in which the information is taught:
  - Preteaching students who may need additional support to use the strategies and skills such as generating questions at multiple levels
  - Using visuals and adapted graphic organizers to support student thinking
  - Encouraging students to work with peers to provide additional support

- Product—how the students demonstrate their learning:
  - Integrating alternative modes of representation, such as sketching and dramatizing
  - Providing opportunities for students to create projects
  - Providing opportunities for students to use computers when creating projects or contributing to class projects

Guided Comprehension Lessons

Identity: Who Are You?
Guided Comprehension Strategy: Self-Questioning
Teaching Idea: Paired Questioning

STAGE ONE: Teacher-Directed Whole-Group Instruction

Text: *Papa's Mark* (Battle-Lavert, 2003)

Explain: I began by explaining self-questioning as a comprehension strategy that involves generating questions to guide our reading. Next, I explained Paired Questioning. I said, "When we use Paired Questioning, we work with partners to generate and respond to questions after we have read a segment of text silently. When we finish reading the text, we take turns explaining what we believe to be the important information in the story. We agree or disagree about what we think is important. After that, we have a class discussion about the text and talk about how we used Paired Questioning."

Demonstrate: I began demonstrating Paired Questioning by introducing *Papa's Mark*, a picture book about Simms, a young black boy, who teaches his father how to write his full name so he can write it instead of signing "X" when he votes for the first time. I reminded students that we were continuing to read books related to our identity theme. I said, "In this lesson, we will focus on the identity of young people who take on adult jobs. For example, in *Papa's Mark*, Simms, a young student, takes on the role of the teacher." Then I read aloud the title and showed the students the cover of the book. I said, "The title and illustration remind me of how my mother and I used to study together. My mother helped me learn to read and write. We studied almost every night." I asked the students if they studied with their parents. We discussed the students' responses, which included that they studied with grandparents and siblings as well as parents. Then I looked at the book cover and read the title again. I said, "As I look more closely at the cover, I see that the boy's hand seems to be guiding his father's hand. I wonder if the boy is helping his father to study? Let's read the book to find out." Then I reminded the students that we would be engaging in Paired Questioning as we read. Next, Chrissie, a student I had previously asked to help me demonstrate, joined me at the front of the room. Chrissie and I each had our own copies of the book—as did the students—and we read the first segment silently. Then I read aloud a segment that included pages 5 and 6 and said, "This illustration shows us the town that Simms lives in. It looks like a small town surrounded by farms. The text tells us that it is time to vote. So, my question for Chrissie is, 'Why do you think Simms is so excited about the election?'" Chrissie responded, "I think that this election is important." Chrissie turned the page and looked at the illustration. She said, "We see Simms and Papa riding to the General Store. I wonder what they are going to buy. So, my question for Ms. Gibb is, 'What do you think they will buy?'" I said, "I think they will buy food because it says in the story that they can smell oranges and onions."

Then I looked at the next illustration and said, "Simms has what seems to be a shopping list. They are going shopping." I read the text aloud and said, "Now I know why Simms is so excited about the election. Papa is going to vote for the first time. Why do you think Papa hasn't voted before? I

Guided Comprehension: Identity: Who Are You?
Self-Questioning: Paired Questioning

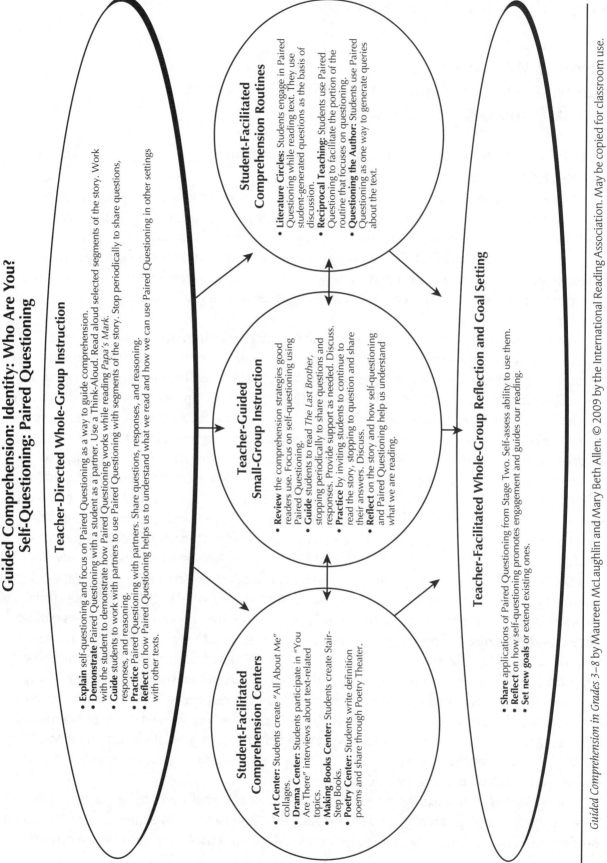

Teacher-Directed Whole-Group Instruction

- **Explain** self-questioning and focus on Paired Questioning as a way to guide comprehension.
- **Demonstrate** Paired Questioning with a student as a partner. Use a Think-Aloud. Read aloud selected segments of the story. Work with the student to demonstrate how Paired Questioning works while reading *Papa's Mark*.
- **Guide** students to work with partners to use Paired Questioning with segments of the story. Stop periodically to share questions, responses, and reasoning.
- **Practice** Paired Questioning with partners. Share questions, responses, and reasoning.
- **Reflect** on how Paired Questioning helps us to understand what we read and how we can use Paired Questioning in other settings with other texts.

Student-Facilitated Comprehension Centers

- **Art Center:** Students create "All About Me" collages.
- **Drama Center:** Students participate in "You Are There" interviews about text-related topics.
- **Making Books Center:** Students create Stair-Step Books.
- **Poetry Center:** Students write definition poems and share through Poetry Theater.

Teacher-Guided Small-Group Instruction

- **Review** the comprehension strategies good readers use. Focus on self-questioning using Paired Questioning.
- **Guide** students to read *The Last Brother*, stopping periodically to share questions and responses. Provide support as needed. Discuss.
- **Practice** by inviting students to continue to read the story, stopping to question and share their answers. Discuss.
- **Reflect** on the story and how self-questioning and Paired Questioning help us understand what we are reading.

Student-Facilitated Comprehension Routines

- **Literature Circles:** Students engage in Paired Questioning while reading text. They use student-generated questions as the basis of discussion.
- **Reciprocal Teaching:** Students use Paired Questioning to facilitate the portion of the routine that focuses on questioning.
- **Questioning the Author:** Students use Paired Questioning as one way to generate queries about the text.

Teacher-Facilitated Whole-Group Reflection and Goal Setting

- **Share** applications of Paired Questioning from Stage Two. Self-assess ability to use them.
- **Reflect** on how self-questioning promotes engagement and guides our reading.
- **Set new goals** or extend existing ones.

Guided Comprehension in Grades 3–8 by Maureen McLaughlin and Mary Beth Allen. © 2009 by the International Reading Association. May be copied for classroom use.

think maybe it was because he was an African American. African Americans did not always have the right to vote."

Guide: I invited the students to work with partners to generate and respond to paired questions as they read the text the silently while I read aloud the next segment of the story. We repeated the process with another segment of text. Then we briefly discussed the text and Paired Questioning.

Practice: Students continued reading segments silently as I read aloud. Students practiced creating paired questions independently. Students asked questions and responded to their partners' questions. Examples of their paired questions included "Why is Papa writing an "X" for his name?" and "Why does Simms know how to write, but Papa does not?"

We discussed that in the time period in which the story occurs, people signed an "X" when they were not able to write their names. The students inferred that the story may have taken place soon after slavery ended. When we read the next segment of the story, we verified that slavery may have ended recently because Papa says, "Freedom don't come easy." The students and I continued reading and the students continued using Paired Questioning until we came to the end of the story. Then I revisited my initial question about the boy helping his father to study and confirmed that the Simms did indeed help Papa learn to write his name.

Reflect: We began our reflection by thinking about the outcome of the story. The students were happy that Papa learned how to write his name and didn't have to make an "X" anymore. The students questioned why Papa had not learned to write his name in school. That prompted discussions about slavery and the importance of education. Next, we reflected on how using Paired Questioning helped us understand what we are reading. Then we reflected on how we could use Paired Questioning with other texts in other settings.

STAGE TWO: Teacher-Guided Small-Group Instruction

Text: *The Last Brother: A Civil War Tale* (Noble, 2006) (Texts varied according to students' abilities.)

Review: I reminded students about the strategies good readers use and then focused on self-questioning. I briefly recalled an example of Paired Questioning from Stage One.

Guide: I introduced the story *The Last Brother*, which is about a young boy serving as a bugler in the Union Army during the U.S. Civil War. Gabe, the main character, joins the army with one of his brothers after his two older brothers die in the war. I asked the students why they thought we were reading this book in our identity theme. Several responded that the book is about the identity of a young person who takes on an adult job by joining the army. Others noted that the book was also about Gabe's identity as a family member. Then I showed the cover of the book, read the title, and invited students to engage in Paired Questioning. Examples of their questions included "Why is such a young boy in an army uniform?" and "Is he the last brother left in his family?"

After everyone in the small group had shared, students read *The Last Brother* silently, pausing at designated stopping points to engage in Paired Questioning with partners. Examples of their paired questions included the following:

- Why do you think Gabe wanted to be in the war?
- Why do you think the recruiting officer believed Gabe when he said he was 18?
- Why do you think the army branded Lancer?

After the students had read two segments, we discussed the text and a few of their questions.

Practice: Students continued to read segments, stopping periodically to engage in Paired Questioning, until they reached the end of the book. Examples of students' Paired Questionings included the following:

- Why do you think the armies used bugles for battle commands?
- Why do you think Gabe and Orlee were able to be friends even though they were on different sides of the war?
- Do you think the campfires along Cemetery Ridge fooled the Confederate soldiers?

Reflect: After the students finished reading and questioning, we discussed the story. We reflected on how the author, Trinka Hakes Noble, represented Gabe and Orlee as children whose identity involved having jobs that only adults in this country do today. In the story, Gabe went from being the youngest child in his family to being treated just like any other adult soldier by commanding officers. He joined the army because after his brothers died, he thought he was responsible for his family. When he meets Orlee, we realize that both boys wanted to be soldiers, like adults, but they also wanted to play, like children. One student, Brandon, observed, "Even though the boys were in the army like adults, they were still able to fish and swim together just like normal kids." Next, we reflected that just like Simms in *Papa's Mark*, Gabe and Orlee went from being the children in their families to taking on adult roles. Simms became a teacher while Gabe and Orlee became soldiers. Several of the students wondered if Simms and Gabe went back to being treated like kids after their "adult" jobs were over or if they were still treated like adults. Then we discussed how Paired Questioning helped us understand what we read.

Student-Facilitated Comprehension Centers

Art Center: Students had a choice of how to create their projects at this center. They could create "All About Me" poster collages using magazines and newspapers I provided at the center and photos they had brought from home. As an alternative choice, they could create an "All About Me" PowerPoint slideshow in which they imported clip art and photos.

Drama Center: Students worked in pairs to create a "You Are There" interview focused on a theme-related topic. For example, Joseph and Abby focused on a topic in which they became interested while reading *Papa's Mark*. They gathered information about the history of African Americans voting in the United States and generated interview questions. Then they dramatized what they learned through a "You Are There" interview format.

Making Books Center: Students worked on their own to create stair-step books. In stair-step books, students use a timeline to show step by step how times have changed from the time in which the books they chose to read took place to a particular point in history. The books are designed to flip from step to step. Students included a minimum of four events and used photos or clipart to complement their text. For example, Freddy, a student who had read *Papa's Mark*, began with Frederick Douglass in 1872 and then added steps such as the passing of the Civil Rights Act of 1964 and the National Voting Rights Act of 1965. The final step in his book was the election of the first African American U.S. president. A page from Freddy's stair-step book appears in Figure 14.

Figure 14. Page From Freddy's Stair-Step Book

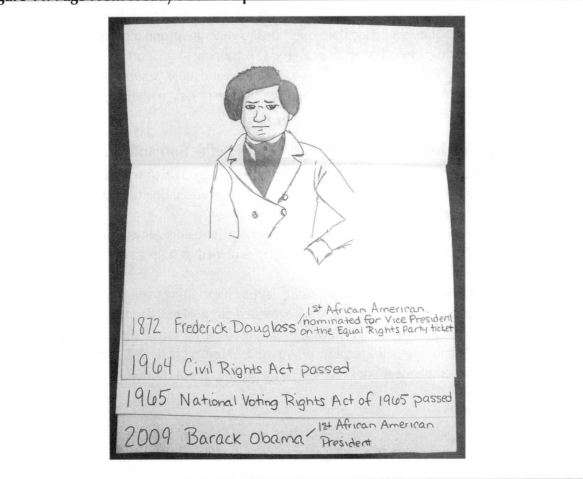

Poetry Center: Students created definition poems (see Appendix B, page 295) using identity or a topic from their reading as a focus. Students shared their poems with the class during a Poetry Theater Presentation we held during Stage Three. The following example of a definition poem was written by Karen Bell.

Who am I?

A fifth grader

A reader

A writer

A sports fan

A dancer

A puzzle solver

A daughter

A sister

An American

That is who I am!

Student-Facilitated Comprehension Routines

Literature Circles: The students read their books and used sticky notes to record questions as they read on their own. Then they used their questions to generate group discussion.

Reciprocal Teaching: The students used Paired Questioning in the portion of the routine that focuses on questioning. Then they discussed their responses and ideas to support their thinking.

Questioning the Author: The students used Paired Questioning to generate queries about the text. They also shared their responses and reasoning.

STAGE THREE: Teacher-Facilitated Whole-Group Reflection and Goal Setting

Share: Students shared their Paired Questionings from Stage Two in small groups, and then we discussed their applications as a whole class. Next, we enjoyed sharing the definition poems created at the poetry center in our Poetry Theater Presentation.

Reflect: We reflected on how self-questioning can promote engagement and guide our reading. We also reflected on how working with partners helped to support our thinking and how well we could use Paired Questioning.

Set New Goals: Everyone felt confident using Paired Questioning to engage in self-questioning while reading a narrative text, so we extended our goal to using this technique with informational text. We decided to use Paired Questioning to learn more about other topics in our theme, including tolerance and self-acceptance. We used websites I had bookmarked to access informational text to complement books we would be reading about these topics.

Assessment Options

I used observation and listened carefully to students' Paired Questions and responses throughout this lesson. I reviewed and commented on students' poems, stair-step books, and self-assessments from Stage Two. During Teacher-Guided Small-Group Instruction, I also periodically administered running records and fluency checks.

Identity: Who Are You?
Guided Comprehension Strategies: Making Connections and Visualizing
Teaching Idea: Drawing Connections

STAGE ONE: Teacher-Directed Whole-Group Instruction

Text: *My Name Is Not Isabella* (Fosberry, 2008)

Explain: I began by explaining that making connections is thinking about the text in relation to ourselves, other texts, and the world. When we make connections, we link what we are reading to what we already know. Then I explained that visualizing is a reading comprehension strategy that we use to create mental pictures while we are reading. Next, I explained Drawing Connections, noting that it supports both strategies and is a way to use visual representations to demonstrate links between the text and the reader. Then I focused on how Drawing Connections helps us understand what we are reading.

Demonstrate: I began by introducing *My Name Is Not Isabella*, a book in which Isabella decides that she wants to be someone else. She tries on the identities of various famous women, but in the end, she decides that she—Isabella—is the best fit. The students and I discussed that this book worked well in our identity theme because many of us did not like our names when we were younger. Then I demonstrated Drawing Connections by reading aloud the title and showing the students the cover of the book. I said, "I can make a connection to the book. The title and illustration remind me of all the different kinds of jobs I wanted to have when I grew up. When I was a young girl I wanted to be a fireman. Later, I decided that I wanted to be an archaeologist." Then I asked the students what they want to be when they grow up. We discussed the students' responses, which included being a doctor, teacher, police officer, and President of the United States. Then I looked at the book cover and read the title again. I said, "There is a girl on the cover, but the title is *My Name Is Not Isabella*. I wonder what her name is. Let's read the book to find out."

I read the first pages aloud to the class and said, "The girl's mother wakes up a girl named Isabella, but the girl in the picture says she is not Isabella. I think she might be pretending to be someone else. Have you ever pretended to be someone else? I can make a connection to that. When I was very young, I pretended to be a garbage person. I dressed up in overalls, put on my rain boots, and got a pair of rubber gloves because I did not want to have dirty hands. I went around to quite a few of the neighbors' houses and dragged their garbage cans to my house before my mother saw what I was doing and made me stop. When I close my eyes I can still picture myself as that garbage person." Next, using the Drawing Connections graphic organizer (see Appendix A, page 252), I drew a quick sketch of myself in overalls picking up a garbage can. Then I wrote, "I pretended to be a garbage person and took out the neighbors' garbage and ours." When I turned the page, I responded to my question by looking at the picture and reading the text. I said, "The girl is pretending to be an astronaut named Sally. That reminds me of an astronaut named Neil Armstrong. He was the first man to walk on the moon." Then I made a quick sketch of an astronaut walking on the moon on the Drawing Connections blackline and wrote, "Neil Armstrong was the first astronaut to walk on the moon." Figure 15 shows my completed Drawing Connections blackline.

Guided Comprehension Instruction: Identity: Who Are You?
Making Connections and Visualizing: Drawing Connections

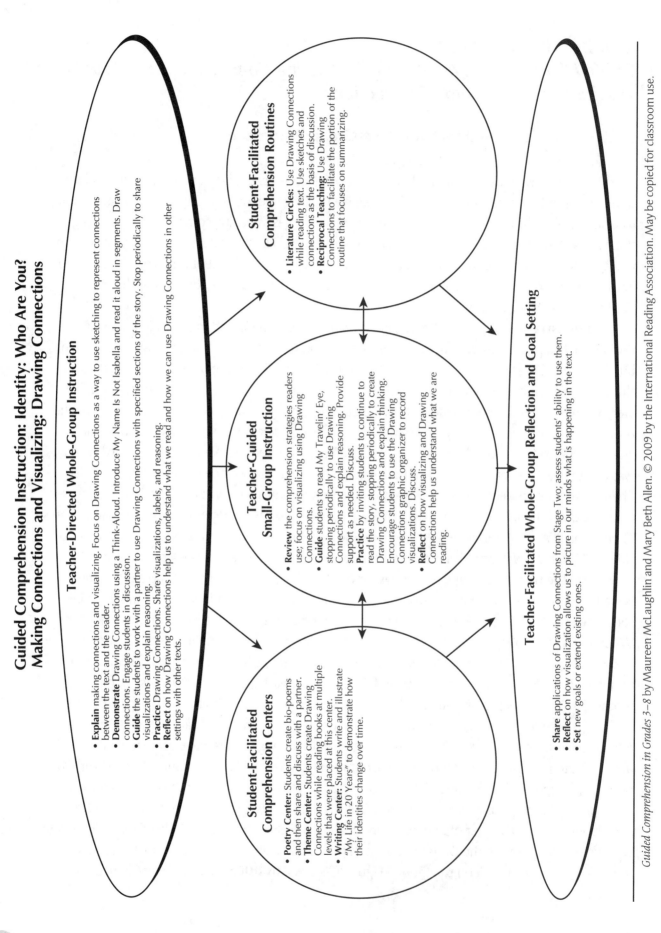

Teacher-Directed Whole-Group Instruction

- **Explain** making connections and visualizing. Focus on Drawing Connections as a way to use sketching to represent connections between the text and the reader.
- **Demonstrate** Drawing Connections using a Think-Aloud. Introduce My Name Is Not Isabella and read it aloud in segments. Draw connections. Engage students in discussion.
- **Guide** the students to work with a partner to use Drawing Connections with specified sections of the story. Stop periodically to share visualizations and explain reasoning.
- **Practice** Drawing Connections. Share visualizations, labels, and reasoning.
- **Reflect** on how Drawing Connections help us to understand what we read and how we can use Drawing Connections in other settings with other texts.

Student-Facilitated Comprehension Centers

- **Poetry Center:** Students create bio-poems and then share and discuss with a partner.
- **Theme Center:** Students create Drawing Connections while reading books at multiple levels that were placed at this center.
- **Writing Center:** Students write and illustrate "My Life in 20 Years" to demonstrate how their identities change over time.

Teacher-Guided Small-Group Instruction

- **Review** the comprehension strategies readers use; focus on visualizing using Drawing Connections.
- **Guide** students to read My Travelin' Eye, stopping periodically to use Drawing Connections and explain reasoning. Provide support as needed. Discuss.
- **Practice** by inviting students to continue to read the story, stopping periodically to create Drawing Connections and explain thinking. Encourage students to use the Drawing Connections graphic organizer to record visualizations. Discuss.
- **Reflect** on how visualizing and Drawing Connections help us understand what we are reading.

Student-Facilitated Comprehension Routines

- **Literature Circles:** Use Drawing Connections while reading text. Use sketches and connections as the basis of discussion.
- **Reciprocal Teaching:** Use Drawing Connections to facilitate the portion of the routine that focuses on summarizing.

Teacher-Facilitated Whole-Group Reflection and Goal Setting

- **Share** applications of Drawing Connections from Stage Two; assess students' ability to use them.
- **Reflect** on how visualization allows us to picture in our minds what is happening in the text.
- **Set** new goals or extend existing ones.

Guided Comprehension in Grades 3–8 by Maureen McLaughlin and Mary Beth Allen. © 2009 by the International Reading Association. May be copied for classroom use.

Figure 15. Completed Drawing Connections Blackline

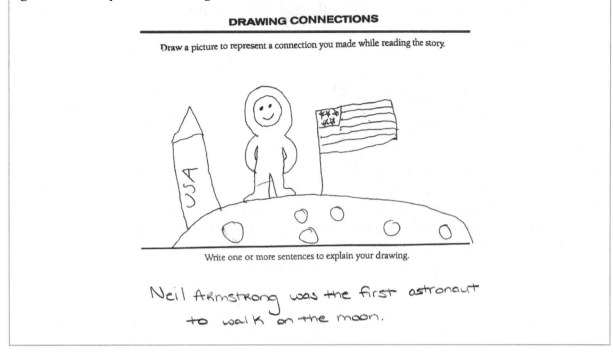

I read the next page to the class. The girl told her mother that she was not Sally. I said, "I wonder who she will pretend to be next." I continued through the next few pages, Drawing Connections between the famous figures based on who Isabella pretended to be and me.

Guide: As I continued to read aloud the next few segments, I guided the students to work with partners to engage in Drawing Connections. I guided the students to visualize as they read and to make connections with the characters. Students shared their connections with partners and then we discussed the students' reasoning as a whole class.

Practice: I continued to share the book while students practiced Drawing Connections on their own. Students shared their sketches and discussed their reasoning. Samples of their Drawing Connections included a sketch of Martin Luther King Jr. with the statement "Martin Luther King, Jr. was friends with Rosa Parks" and a sketch of a doctor with the statement "I had to go to the doctor yesterday. My doctor's name is Dr. Y." We continued this process of Drawing Connections for segments of text until we came to the last section of the book. At that point, I revisited my initial question about what the girl's name really was—Isabella.

Reflect: We began our reflection by discussing the outcome of the story. The students stated that they thought the girl's name might really be Isabella. They wondered why Isabella pretended to be other people. That led to a discussion about how we look up to people we want to be like, but need to be ourselves at the same time. Then we reflected on using Drawing Connections and how making connections helped us to understand the story and stay involved in it.

STAGE TWO: Teacher-Guided Small-Group Instruction

Text: *My Travelin' Eye* (Kostecki-Shaw, 2008) (Texts varied according to students' abilities.)

Review: I reminded students about the strategies good readers use and our focus on visualizing and making connections. Then I briefly recalled an example of Drawing Connections from Stage One.

Guide: I began by introducing *My Travelin' Eye*, a book in which Jenny Sue, who has a "lazy eye," gets new glasses and an eye patch. Jenny Sue has trouble adjusting to her new look, but makes the best of it when she decorates her eye patches to make them as special as she is. The students and I discussed how *My Travelin' Eye* might relate to our identity theme. The students suggested that many of us had experienced times when we had to wear a cast or an eye patch. They also said that other things like getting new glasses or a different haircut can take time to get used to. Next, I guided students to make connections to the cover. Examples of their responses included "I wear glasses" and "My mom wears glasses like the girl on the cover." After everyone had shared, they read a segment of *My Travelin' Eye*, stopping at two points to engage in Drawing Connections.

Practice: After each section of the book, students used the Drawing Connections graphic organizer to communicate about the connections and mental pictures they were creating while reading. After each section, they shared their sketches with a partner. We continued this process until the end of the story. A Drawing Connections example from *My Travelin' Eye* is shown in Figure 16.

Reflect: We reflected on how the author showed us that it was difficult for Jenny Sue to deal with the glasses and patch she needed to help her lazy eye and that she felt more comfortable when she created her "fashion-patches." One student observed, "Jenny Sue found a cool way to wear her glasses. When I had to wear a cast last year it was itchy and I didn't like it. It wasn't so bad when my friends started drawing and writing their names on it." Then we discussed how visualizing and Drawing Connections helped us understand what we read.

Figure 16. Drawing Connections Example From *My Travelin' Eye*

Student-Facilitated Comprehension Centers

Poetry Center: Students created bio-poems about friends, family, or themselves using the bio-poem blackline (see Appendix B, page 295). Then they shared and discussed their poems with a partner. In this example, Judy wrote about her uncle:

Thomas
Veteran
Loyal, hard-working, dedicated, brave
Lover of family, friends, and dogs
Who enjoyed the news, work, and being an uncle
Who believed in our country
Who wanted to help others, improve life, and reach his goals
Who used his mind, his heart, and hard work
Who gave us freedom
Who said, "If you can dream it, you can make it happen."
Burke

Theme Center: I placed theme-related books at a variety of levels at this center. I also provided blacklines to use. Students self-selected books and completed Drawing Connections as they read.

Writing Center: Students wrote and illustrated "My Life in 20 Years," in which they described their identities at that time. They wrote about the people they became, the educations they earned, the jobs they held, and the families they had.

Student-Facilitated Comprehension Routines

Literature Circles: The students used Drawing Connections as they read, and then shared them during discussion.

Reciprocal Teaching: The students integrated Drawing Connections in the portions of the routine that focused on questioning and summarizing.

STAGE THREE: Teacher-Facilitated Whole-Group Reflection and Goal Setting

Share: Students shared their Drawing Connections from Stage Two in small groups. Then we discussed their applications as a whole class.

Reflect: We reflected on how making connections and visualizing can help us understand what we read. We also discussed how sketching helped us to express our ideas.

Set New Goals: Students felt confident with their ability to use Drawing Connections while reading narrative text, so we decided to extended our goal to using this technique with informational text. We decided to use Drawing Connections to learn about people who had to overcome difficulties in their lives.

Assessment Options

I reviewed the students' Drawing Connections throughout this lesson. I observed the students during discussion, during whole-group and small-group instruction, and as they presented their work from Stage Two. I reviewed their work from the centers and routines, as well as their self-assessments. In addition, I periodically used running records and fluency checks.

Identity: Who Are You?
Guided Comprehension Strategy: Summarizing
Teaching Idea: Narrative Pyramid

STAGE ONE: Teacher-Directed Whole-Group Instruction

Text: *The Miraculous Journey of Edward Tulane* (DiCamillo, 2006)

Explain: I began by explaining summarizing as extracting the important ideas from what we are reading. Next, I described how we can use the Narrative Pyramid to summarize stories. I explained that we would need to focus on story elements—characters, setting, problem, attempts to resolve the problem, and solution—and be careful to use only the number of words indicated in each line.

Demonstrate: Before I began demonstrating, I explained that although I usually read texts in segments when we are learning strategies, today we would be using Chapters 1 through 4 of the book I had been reading as the class read-aloud. Then I re-introduced *The Miraculous Journey of Edward Tulane,* the story of a ceramic rabbit that travels and along the way learns how to love himself and others. Next, the students and I discussed how this book related to our identity theme. We agreed that the book was about self-acceptance and love of others, two aspects of identity that we all hoped to be able to achieve. Then I encouraged the students to help me retell Chapters 1 through 4 to refresh our memories of the story.

After a brief discussion, I distributed the Narrative Pyramid blacklines (see Appendix A, page 267). Then I asked the students to focus on the format, as I began completing my copy on the board. I said, "To complete the first line, I will need to choose a character. In the second line, I will need to describe that character using only two words." Then I thought aloud about which character I would choose. I thought about Edward, Abeline, and Pellegrina as possibilities. Then I said, "Abeline is a very important character in this section of the story because she is Edward's owner. I think I will choose her." After writing *Abeline* on the first line of the Narrative Pyramid on the board, I thought aloud about two words to describe her. I said, "Abeline is a *rich girl*, so I could write that, but she is also Edward's devoted owner." I decided to write *devoted owner* on line 2. For the next line of the Narrative Pyramid, I said, "Now I need to write three words describing the setting. Let's remember that because I am writing about the setting, I can write about the time period in which the story takes place or the location or both." Then I said, "We know that Abeline is moving to a new place, so I think we should use the time period. I remember a part of the story when Edward had his watch vacuumed up by the maid, so I think the story could take place today." Then Anthony, a student, said, "But in the story it also says they are taking a ship to England instead of flying there. I think it might be in the past." After more discussion, I wrote "*around mid-20th century*" for the time period in which the story takes place on line 3. Next, we discussed line 4 of the Narrative Pyramid. I said, "For line 4, we will need to determine the problem in this section. I think that how Edward feels is a problem because he feels that he is not treated well by Abeline's family. He feels as if he should be treated as a person." Student suggestions for how Edward was being treated included "disrespected" and "demeaned." So, on line 4 I wrote, "*The family disrespected Edward.*"

Guide: For line 5 I guided students to work with partners to create a five-word phrase that describes one event that happens during this section of the story. Responses included "The dog almost ate him" and "His suit stained with drool." We discussed the phrases and the students'

Guided Comprehension Instruction: Identity: Who Are You?
Summarizing: Narrative Pyramid

Teacher-Directed Whole-Group Instruction

- **Explain** summarizing and focus on the Narrative Pyramid as a way to summarize when reading.
- **Demonstrate** the first four lines of the Narrative Pyramid on chart paper, returning to *The Miraculous Journey of Edward Tulane* for information.
- **Guide** students to work with a partner to complete lines 5 and 6 of the Narrative Pyramid with specified sections of the story. Share lines 5 and 6 and explain reasoning.
- **Practice** by completing lines 7 and 8 of the Narrative Pyramid. Share and explain reasoning.
- **Reflect** on what has happened so far in the story and how using the Narrative Pyramid helps us to summarize story elements. Reflect on how we can use the Narrative Pyramid in other settings with other texts.

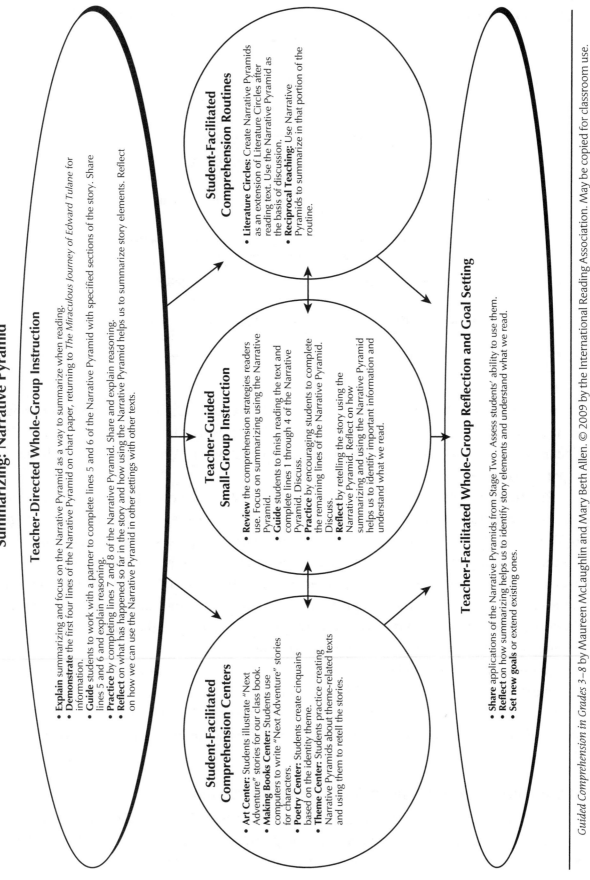

Student-Facilitated Comprehension Routines

- **Literature Circles:** Create Narrative Pyramids as an extension of Literature Circles after reading text. Use the Narrative Pyramid as the basis of discussion.
- **Reciprocal Teaching:** Use Narrative Pyramids to summarize in that portion of the routine.

Teacher-Guided Small-Group Instruction

- **Review** the comprehension strategies readers use. Focus on summarizing using the Narrative Pyramid.
- **Guide** students to finish reading the text and complete lines 1 through 4 of the Narrative Pyramid. Discuss.
- **Practice** by encouraging students to complete the remaining lines of the Narrative Pyramid. Discuss.
- **Reflect** by retelling the story using the Narrative Pyramid. Reflect on how summarizing and using the Narrative Pyramid helps us to identify important information and understand what we read.

Student-Facilitated Comprehension Centers

- **Art Center:** Students illustrate "Next Adventure" stories for our class book.
- **Making Books Center:** Students use computers to write "Next Adventure" stories for characters.
- **Poetry Center:** Students create cinquains based on the identity theme.
- **Theme Center:** Students practice creating Narrative Pyramids about theme-related texts and using them to retell the stories.

Teacher-Facilitated Whole-Group Reflection and Goal Setting

- **Share** applications of the Narrative Pyramids from Stage Two. Assess students' ability to use them.
- **Reflect** on how summarizing helps us to identify story elements and understand what we read.
- **Set new goals** or extend existing ones.

Figure 17. Narrative Pyramid for *The Miraculous Journey of Edward Tulane* (Chapters 1–4)

1. <u>Abeline</u>
Character's name

2. <u>Devoted</u>   <u>owner</u>
Two words describing the character

3. <u>Around</u> <u>mid-20th</u> <u>century</u>
Three words describing the setting

4. <u>The</u>   <u>family</u>   <u>disrespected</u>   <u>Edward</u>.
Four words stating the problem

5. <u>The</u>   <u>dog</u>   <u>almost</u>   <u>ate</u>   <u>him</u>.
Five words describing one event

6. <u>Edward</u>   <u>lost</u>   <u>his</u>   <u>gold</u>   <u>pocket</u>   <u>watch</u>.
Six words describing another event

7. <u>Pellegrina</u>   <u>told</u>   <u>Edward</u>   <u>that</u>   <u>he</u>   <u>disappointed</u>   <u>her</u>.
Seven words describing a third event

8. <u>Abeline</u>   <u>told</u>   <u>Edward</u>   <u>she</u>   <u>will</u>   <u>love</u>   <u>him</u>   <u>always</u>.
Eight words describing a solution to the problem

reasoning as a whole class. We chose *The dog almost ate him*, and the students continued working with partners as they completed line 6. Examples of their responses for line 6 included "The maid vacuumed and dusted Edward" and "He lost his gold pocket watch." We chose to add the latter response to our Narrative Pyramid.

Practice: Students practiced writing phrases for line 7 on their own. Then they shared their statements and discussed their reasoning. Examples of their responses for line 7 included "Pellegrina told Edward that he disappointed her" and "Edward thought Pellegrina's story was very gruesome." We chose to include the line about Pellegrina in our Narrative Pyramid. For line 8, students wrote an eight-line phrase to explain how the problem of Edward's treatment was solved in this section of the book. Students made several suggestions, including "Abeline told Edward she will love him always" and "Edward is traveling on *Queen Mary* to England." We wrote the statement about Abeline to complete our Narrative Pyramid, which appears in Figure 17.

Reflect: We began by reflecting on this portion of the story. The students were able to offer multiple examples that Abeline loved Edward, but they were not sure how Edward felt about Abeline. The students wondered why Pellegrina was disappointed with Edward. Then we reflected on how using the Narrative Pyramid helped us to organize and summarize important aspects of the story.

STAGE TWO: Teacher-Guided Small-Group Instruction

Text: *The Lemonade Club* (Polacco, 2007) (Texts varied according to students' abilities.)

Review: I reminded students about the strategies that good readers use. Then I focused on summarizing and briefly recalled our Narrative Pyramid from Stage One.

Figure 18. Narrative Pyramid About *The Lemonade Club*

1. <u>Marilyn</u>
Character's name

2. <u>friend</u>   <u>student</u>
Two words describing the character

3. <u>fifth</u>   <u>grade</u>   <u>class</u>
Three words describing the setting

4. <u>Two</u>   <u>friends</u>   <u>have</u>   <u>cancer</u>
Four words stating the problem

5. <u>Marilyn</u>   <u>learns</u>   <u>about</u>   <u>her</u>   <u>cancer</u>
Five words describing one event

6. <u>Class</u>   <u>shaves</u>   <u>heads</u>   <u>to</u>   <u>support</u>   <u>Marilyn</u>
Six words describing another event

7. <u>The</u>   <u>girls</u>   <u>learn</u>   <u>about</u>   <u>Miss</u>   <u>Wichelman's</u>   <u>cancer</u>
Seven words describing a third event

8. <u>Marilyn</u>   <u>and</u>   <u>Miss</u>   <u>Wichelman</u>   <u>both</u>   <u>live</u>   <u>without</u>   <u>cancer</u>
Eight words describing a solution to the problem

Guide: I re-introduced *The Lemonade Club*, a story about remaining positive when a friend and a teacher both get cancer, and students joined me in retelling the part of the story they had already read. Next, we discussed how *The Lemonade Club* related to our identity theme. The students suggested that the book was about accepting ourselves and others—no matter what happens. Several of the students provided examples of friends and family who had become very ill with cancer and other diseases. They noted how important it was to remain positive in such situations. Then I guided the students to read the last eight pages. We discussed the positive outcome of the story and students worked with partners to complete lines 1–4 of the Narrative Pyramid.

Practice: Students practiced by completing lines 5–8 of their Narrative Pyramids. Figure 18 shows Hailey and Juan's completed Narrative Pyramid about *The Lemonade Club*.

Reflect: Students shared their Narrative Pyramids and used them to retell the story. Next, we discussed the story and how the author was able to show how Miss Wichelman, Marilyn, and Traci stayed true to the Lemonade Club's belief that if life gives us lemons—challenges, difficulties—we should make lemonade—stay positive, make the best of it. Then we discussed how summarizing and using the Narrative Pyramid helped us understand what we read.

Student-Facilitated Comprehension Centers

Art Center: Students created illustrations for their "Next Adventure" stories, which were then included in the story that became part of our class book.

Making Books Center: Students worked with partners on class computers to write "_____'s Next Adventure" for the character of their choice. The students included their stories in our class book.

Poetry Center: Students created cinquains about peoples' identities. In the following cinquain, Carl wrote about President Barack Obama.

Obama
One Word: Noun

powerful intelligent
Two Adjectives Describing Line 1

deciding appointing signing
"ing" Words Telling Actions of Line 1

bringing change to America
Four-Word Phrase Describing a Feeling Related to Line 1

President
One Word: Synonym or Reference to Line 1

Theme Center: I placed a variety of titles at different levels at this center. I also provided Narrative Pyramid blacklines for the students to use. Students practiced creating Narrative Pyramids about theme-related texts they selected and using them to retell the stories.

Student-Facilitated Comprehension Routines

Literature Circles: When they finished reading their books, the students completed Narrative Pyramids as an extension activity. They shared them and used them to retell the story.

Reciprocal Teaching: The students completed Narrative Pyramids to emphasize summarizing after they had finished reading the text.

STAGE THREE: Teacher-Facilitated Whole-Group Reflection and Goal Setting

Share: Partners shared their Narrative Pyramids and the stories for our class book they completed during Stage Two. Then we discussed their applications as a whole class.

Reflect: We reflected on how summarizing can help us extract the important information from what we have read and how we can use Narrative Pyramids to summarize stories.

Set New Goals: Students felt confident with their ability to use the Narrative Pyramid and to engage in summarizing while reading a narrative text, so we extended our goal to using the Bio-Pyramid, a similar technique. We decided to begin by summarizing informational text in biographies of historical figures who learned about themselves as they overcame adversity.

Assessment Options

I used observation, listening carefully to students' responses and reasoning, throughout this lesson. I reviewed their strategy applications, creative writing, and self-assessments, providing feedback as necessary. I also completed periodic fluency checks and running records.

Identity: Who Are You?
Guided Comprehension Strategy: Evaluating
Teaching Idea: Evaluative Questioning

STAGE ONE: Teacher-Directed Whole-Group Instruction

Text: *Sleeping Freshmen Never Lie* (Lubar, 2005)

Explain: I began by explaining that evaluating is a reading comprehension strategy that helps us to make judgments about text. I reminded students that when we evaluate, we make judgments and support our thinking with sound reasoning. Then I explained how to structure evaluative questions using signal words or phrases such as *what do you think* and *defend*, *judge*, or *justify* your response.

Demonstrate: I used a read-aloud and a Think-Aloud to demonstrate how to create and use evaluative questions. I began by introducing the book *Sleeping Freshmen Never Lie* in which Scott, the main character, attempts to balance a new school, new friends, girls, extracurricular activities, and the fact that his mother is having another baby. The students and I discussed how this book related to our identity theme. They suggested that Scott was searching for his identity through everything that was going on in his life. The students noted that they could relate to a lot of what Scott was experiencing.

The students immediately made connections to going to high school as soon as they finish middle school. After a brief discussion, I began reading the first three chapters aloud. As I read, I stopped periodically to think aloud about evaluative questions I had as I was reading. I wrote the questions on the overhead. For example, I thought aloud, "What do you think about Scott's first day of high school? Justify your response." I wrote the question on the overhead and underlined the signal words *what do you think* and *justify.* Next, I demonstrated that responding to evaluative questions involved what I had read in the book, but it also involved what I had known about the high school experience before I read. I responded to the evaluative question. I said, "Scott's first day seemed to be overwhelming and confusing. He was overwhelmed by the amount of reading he was going to have to do. He said, 'I was beginning to calculate my reading load by the pound instead of by the page' (p. 18). He also seemed confused for much of the day. He was put in different classes than his friends were. He didn't understand Spanish at all, and he almost missed his bus. I think that Scott had a very rough day!" Then I continued to read aloud, stopping periodically to respond to evaluative questions I had generated while reading. I stopped again after Chapter 4, when Scott's parents informed him that they were going to have another baby. Scott started a journal to his future sibling: "Right now, I can sort of cope, because you're not real. After you're born, I'll probably hate you. So it's good that I'm doing this now. Maybe it'll make up for all the rotten things I'll do to you later." My evaluative question this time was, "How would you defend Scott's attitude toward his new sibling?" The students and I discussed possible responses and decided that Scott was taken aback by the situation and was not prepared for what his parents had told him, especially after his first day of high school.

Guide: As I continued to read aloud, I guided students to work in pairs to use the signal words to create evaluative questions. Many of their questions focused on the beginning of Chapter 6 when Scott is writing in the journal for his unborn brother. One entry read, "So, you formless clump

Guided Comprehension Instruction: Identity: Who Are You? Evaluating: Evaluative Questioning

Teacher-Directed Whole-Group Instruction

- **Explain** evaluating and focus on Evaluative Questioning as a way to make judgments about text.
- **Demonstrate** using a Think-Aloud and a read-aloud. Write evaluative questions on the overhead. Discuss possible answers.
- **Guide** students to work with a partner to generate evaluative questions with a specified section of the story. Continue to read aloud. Share questions and explain responses.
- **Practice** by continuing to read aloud. Encourage students to generate additional evaluative questions and share possible answers.
- **Reflect** on how using Evaluative Questioning helps us to think critically about the story and how we can use Evaluative Questioning in other settings with other texts.

Student-Facilitated Comprehension Centers

- **Research Center:** Students select a person from the biographies at the center and generate a list of evaluative questions they would use to interview that individual.
- **Technology Center:** Students work with partners to create PowerPoint slides for the class Identity Theme slideshow.
- **Theme Center:** Students select titles from a variety of theme-related books at multiple levels and create evaluative questions as they read.

Teacher-Guided Small-Group Instruction

- **Review** the comprehension strategies readers use. Focus on evaluating using Evaluative Questioning and the text *Zen and the Art of Faking It.*
- **Guide** students in pairs to generate evaluative questions using sections of the text. Discuss.
- **Practice** by encouraging students to finish reading the book and generate evaluative questions. Discuss.
- **Reflect** on how Evaluative Questioning helped us to think critically about the text.

Student-Facilitated Comprehension Routines

- **Literature Circles:** Use Evaluative Questioning while reading text. Use the evaluative questions as the basis of critical discussion.
- **Reciprocal Teaching:** Use Evaluative Questioning to facilitate the portion of the routine that focuses on questioning.
- **Questioning the Author:** Use Evaluative Questioning to query the author. Discuss responses.

Teacher-Facilitated Whole-Group Reflection and Goal Setting

- **Share** applications of evaluative questioning from Stage Two. Assess students' ability to use them.
- **Reflect** on how evaluating helps us to think critically.
- **Set new goals** or extend existing ones.

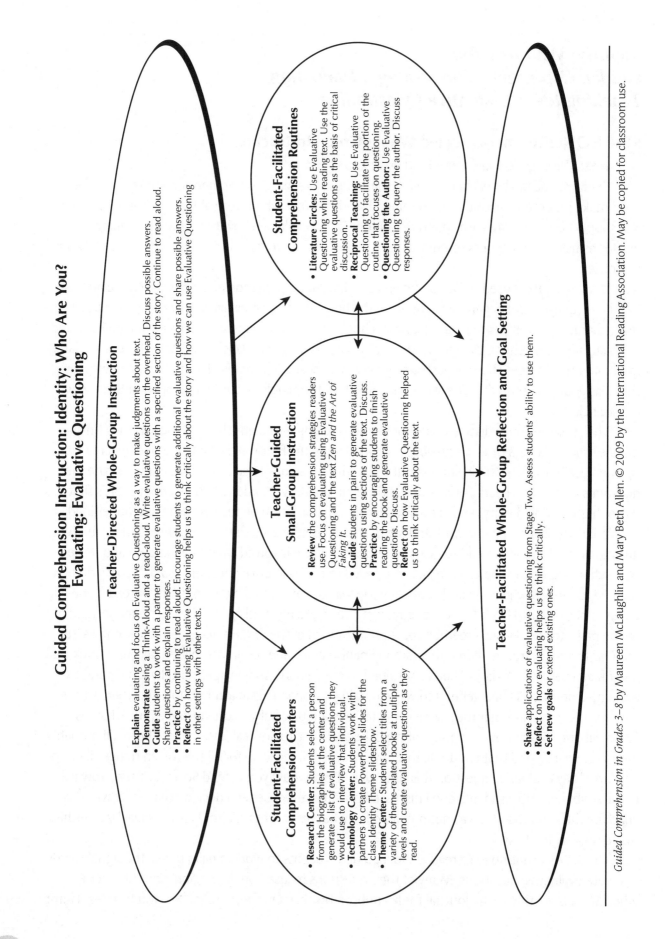

Guided Comprehension in Grades 3–8 by Maureen McLaughlin and Mary Beth Allen. © 2009 by the International Reading Association. May be copied for classroom use.

of cells, you're probably wondering whether I learned anything today. You bet. Listen carefully. This is important. Never try to impress anyone. Especially not a girl. It won't work. You'll just end up feeling stupid." Students generated questions asking Scott to justify why he is giving his future sibling such advice. We shared and discussed questions and possible responses. This resulted in a discussion about how relationships with one person (Scott's experience with a girl) can impact our relationships with others (his unborn brother). We thought this indicated that Scott was getting closer with his unborn brother because of his life experiences.

Practice: As I continued to read sections of *Sleeping Freshmen Never Lie* aloud, students worked on their own to create evaluative questions and formulate possible responses. The students liked creating their own questions instead of answering questions created by others. I observed that even students with limited abilities were able to create and respond to evaluative questions.

Reflect: I encouraged the students to reflect on how creating evaluative questions helped them to make judgments about text. Naomi said, "I seem to create the questions really easily, but I have to think about how I will answer them. I can't just find them in the book. I like when I can use what I already know and what I have read to answer a question."

STAGE TWO: Teacher-Guided Small-Group Instruction

Text: *Zen and the Art of Faking It* (Sonnenblick, 2007) (Texts varied according to students' abilities.)

Review: I reminded students about our focus on evaluating and briefly recalled examples of evaluative questions students had generated during Stage One.

Guide: I introduced *Zen and the Art of Faking It*, a book in which San Lee adopts a new identity every time he moves. As he enters a new school and contemplates who he wants to be at this school, he is mistaken for a Zen Master and follows that path where it leads him. I explained that this book was about a boy who moved from school to school, and as he moved, he changed his identity to fit in with certain crowds. In this story, he is trying to figure out who he wants to be in his newest school. We briefly discussed how this book supported our theme and what it is like to be a new student in school. Then I guided students' reading of the first few chapters. I asked them to create evaluative questions as they read and to think about possible responses. Several of the students focused on a passage from Chapter 2 when San Lee thinks, "On my second day of school, I was still trying out who to be in Pennsylvania: a skater, like I'd been in Cali? A Bible-thumper, like I'd been in Alabama? A rich preppy kid, like I'd been in Houston? A macho pretend-jock, like I'd been in Germany? People were always telling kids to be themselves, but either they didn't mean it or they didn't tell you how to go about doing it when everyone else was trying to push and pull you into line." Students' questions focused on justifying San's decision to alter his personality. Other students commented on San's initial evaluation of Woody and tried to justify his judgments of her. They also made personal connections to San's thinking. Many students commented that a number of factors, including our clothing, can determine who wants to be friends with us.

Practice: The students practiced by continuing to read the next three chapters of *Zen and the Art of Faking It*, creating evaluative questions as they read. We discussed their evaluative questions and possible answers. Questions included, "Justify San's challenging Jones during his social studies class." "Defend San's decision to learn about Zen to create a new identity." "Do you think that San's learning Woody Guthrie songs is a good way to impress Woody? Defend your response." "Justify how Woody can tell that San is 'so—I don't know—real'." The students' queries resulted in a lively discussion about how we view ourselves and how others view us.

Reflect: We discussed the story and talked about how people reinvent themselves just like San did. One student, Ray, stated, "Emily justified giving herself a new identity so that she could stay connected to her mom." Next we discussed how Evaluative Questioning helped us to think critically about what we read.

Student-Facilitated Comprehension Centers

Research Center: I provided a stack of short biographies at this center. The biographies focused on people in whom students had expressed interest. (I knew this from reading their Interest Inventories—see Appendix D, page 314.) Students self-selected a person, read the biography, and generated a list of evaluative questions they would ask if they had the opportunity to interview that individual.

Technology Center: Students worked with partners or on their own to create six PowerPoint slides about their identities—three about each of them. They used clip art, sound, and animation. When they finished their slides, they added them to the class Identity Slideshow. We saved the file and shared it during Stage Three. Inez's slide about her family is featured in Figure 19.

Theme Center: I left a wide variety of theme-related books at various levels at this center. Students worked with partners to self-select identity books of interest and create and respond to evaluative questions as they read.

Student-Facilitated Comprehension Routines

Literature Circles: Students created and responded to evaluative questions while reading text. They used the questions as the basis of critical discussion.

Figure 19. Inez's PowerPoint Slide

Reciprocal Teaching: Students used Evaluative Questioning to facilitate the portion of the routine that focuses on questioning.

Questioning the Author: Students used Evaluative Questioning to question the author. This was particularly meaningful because QtA requires students to read from a critical perspective.

STAGE THREE: Teacher-Facilitated Whole-Group Reflection and Goal Setting

Share: Students shared their evaluative questions from Stage Two in small groups. Then we discussed their applications as a whole class.

Reflect: We reflected on how evaluating can help us think critically about what we have read and how well Evaluative Questioning helped us to have a deeper understanding of what we read.

Set New Goals: Students felt confident with their ability to use Evaluative Questioning while reading a narrative text, so we extended our goal to using this technique with informational text. We decided to begin by using Evaluative Questioning when we research using informational literacy.

Assessment Options

I used observation, listening carefully to students' evaluative questions and reasoning, throughout this lesson. I reviewed students' PowerPoint slides and theme folders, which included their interview questions and self-assessments. I also completed running records and fluency checks as needed.

Theme Resources

Books

Anderson, L.H. (2009). *Fear of falling.* New York: Puffin.

Anderson, M.T. (2006). *The astonishing life of Octavian Nothing, traitor to the nation: Volume I: The pox party.* Cambridge, MA: Candlewick.

Barker, M.P. (2008). *A difficult boy.* New York: Holiday House.

Bartoletti, S.C. (1999). *Kids on strike!* Boston: Houghton Mifflin.

Bartoletti, S.C. (2008). *The boy who dared.* New York: Scholastic.

Choldenko, G. (2004). *Al Capone does my shirts.* New York: Putnam.

Clements, A. (2007). *No talking.* New York: Simon & Schuster.

Curtis, C.P. (2005). *Bud, not Buddy.* New York: Yearling.

Frank, A. (1993). *Anne Frank: The diary of a young girl.* New York: Bantam.

Gold, A.L. (2000). *A special fate: Chiune Sugihara, hero of the Holocaust.* New York: Scholastic.

Hidier, T.D. (2002). *Born confused.* New York: Scholastic.

Hobbs, V. (2005). *Defiance.* New York: Farrar, Straus and Giroux.

Hoose, P. (2009). *Claudette Colvin: Twice toward justice.* New York: Melanie Kroupa Books.

Hoose, P. (2001). *We were there, too! Young people in U.S. history.* New York: Farrar, Straus and Giroux.

Hughes, P. (2004). *The Breaker Boys.* New York: Farrar, Straus and Giroux.

Kinney, J. (2007). *Diary of a wimpy kid.* New York: Abrams.

Korman, G. (2007). *Schooled.* New York: Hyperion.

Lansdowne, Y., & Horton, A. (2008). *Pitch black.* El Paso, TX: Cinco Puntos Press.

Lord, C. (2008). *Rules.* New York: Scholastic.

Lowry, L. (1998). *Number the stars.* New York: Laurel Leaf.

Park, F., & Park, G. (1998). *My freedom trip: A child's escape from North Korea.* Honesdale, PA: Boyds Mills Press.

Paulsen, G. (2006). *Hatchet.* New York: Aladdin.

Pearsall, S. (2007). *Crooked river.* New York: Yearling.

Pfitzenmaier, A. (2008). *Cheating fate.* Saskatoon, SK: Thistledown Press.

Rodman, M.A. (2004). *Yankee girl.* New York: Farrar, Straus and Giroux.

Salisbury, G. (2005). *Under the blood-red sun.* New York: Laurel Leaf.

Schmidt, G.D. (2007). *The Wednesday wars.* New York: Clarion.

Spinnelli, J. (2007). *Eggs.* New York: Little, Brown.

Tan, S. (2007). *The arrival.* New York: Arthur A. Levine.

van der Rol, R., & Verhoeven, R. (1995). *Anne Frank, beyond the diary: A photographic remembrance.* New York: Puffin.

Venkatraman, P. (2008). *Climbing the stairs.* New York: Putnam.

Warren, A. (2008). *Escape from Saigon: How a Vietnam War orphan became an American boy.* New York: Farrar, Straus and Giroux.

Wyeth, S.D. (2002). *Something beautiful.* New York: Dragonfly.

Yep, L., & Yep, K.S. (2008). *The dragon's child: A story of Angel Island.* New York: HarperCollins.

Woodson, J. (2007). *Feathers.* New York: Putnam.

Websites

Annenberg Media: Workshop 1: Engagement and Dialogue
   www.learner.org/workshops/tml/workshop1/teaching3.html

Children's Books That Break Gender Role Stereotypes
   journal.naeyc.org/btj/200303/Books4Children.pdf

Great Peacemakers
   www.greatpeacemakers.com

Scholastic Student Activities: Immigration: Stories of Yesterday and Today
   teacher.scholastic.com/activities/immigration/index.htm

Scholastic: Teaching "Diversity": A Place to Begin
   content.scholastic.com/browse/article.jsp?id=3499

Student Performances Across the Curriculum

Social Studies

- Create a Webquest that classmates can work through to help understand their identities. Webquests can deal with cultural identity, community identity, self-acceptance, or family customs.

- Read a variety of resources about a culture and then write a series of first-person diary entries that describe the routines and experiences within that culture.

Science

- Explore the scientific contributions of people of different cultures.

Mathematics

- Use geometric shapes, patterns, and colors to create personal crests. Each shape, pattern, or color represents something that is unique to the identity of the creator.

- Collaborate in small groups to create and present PowerPoint slideshows about the identities of famous mathematicians.

Art

- Create electronic collages that depict various aspects of friends' lives—interests, family, hobbies, pets, aspirations, and so on. As an alternative, create collages for characters/people in a theme-based book.

- Explore art from different cultures. Use it to discuss "art as identity" and explain how it is culturally relevant.

Music

- Select and record background music for self-created poems, books, and PowerPoint slideshows. Play the music when the work is shared.

- Investigate the music of different cultures and time periods. Share songs and artists as examples of cultural identity.

- Using an identity theme, create a Lyric Summary (see Appendix A) about a novel or famous person.

Culminating Activity

Who Are We? Invite parents and community members to participate in a theme celebration titled *Who Are We?* Exhibit student projects, such as class poetry books, stair-step books, and All About Me collages from the identity theme. Encourage parents, community members, and students to share their identities. Create a variety of stations where students can explain the identity theme and what they learned. Provide refreshments, and offer interactive opportunities for parents to give feedback on the celebration, such as e-mailing comments to students on class computers. At the end of the celebration, students will present their parents with copies of the class poetry book, *Who Are We?*

CHAPTER 9

Poetry: Extraordinary Wonder

Poetry is wonder, beauty, and laughter. It is the genre responsible for the incessant giggling that occurs whenever we read Shel Silverstein, Judith Viorst, and Jack Prelutsky poems. It is the genre that helps us to see wonder in ordinary things when we read Robert Frost's "Stopping by Woods on a Snowy Evening" and to see ourselves when we read Maya Angelou's "Still I Rise." It is the genre that moves us to tears when we read the haunting poems written by children of the Holocaust in *I Never Saw Another Butterfly* (Volavkova, 1993). In our teaching, poetry is a wonderful resource. It cultivates creativity, nurtures thinking, and motivates students to find the poets within.

The sample Theme-Based Plan for Guided Comprehension: Poetry: Extraordinary Wonder (see Figure 20) offers an overview of the thinking and resources that support this theme. It presents a sampling of goals, state standards, assessments, texts, website resources, comprehension strategies, teaching ideas, comprehension centers, and comprehension routines. The plan begins by delineating examples of student goals and related state standards. The student goals for this theme include the following:

- Use appropriate comprehension skills and strategies
- Interpret and respond to text
- Write poetry
- Communicate effectively

These goals support the following state standards:

- Learning to read independently
- Reading, analyzing, and interpreting text
- Types and quality of writing
- Speaking and listening

The assessments listed on the theme planner are examples of diagnostic, formative, and summative measures. Running records are an example of a diagnostic assessment. Formative assessments, which are informal and usually occur on a daily basis, include specific measures such as comprehension strategy applications, and general assessments such as observation and student self-assessment. Summative assessments, which are more formal long-term measures such as projects, are also featured.

Figure 20. Theme-Based Plan for Guided Comprehension: Poetry: Extraordinary Wonder

Goals and Connections to State Standards | Students will

- Use appropriate comprehension skills and strategies. Standard: learning to read independently
- Interpret and respond to text. Standard: reading, analyzing, and interpreting text
- Write poetry. Standard: types and quality of writing
- Communicate effectively. Standard: speaking and listening

Assessment

The following measures can be used for a variety of purposes, including diagnostic, formative, and summative assessment:

Anticipation/Reaction Guide	Projects
Concept of Definition Map	Running Records
Lyric Retelling	Self-Assessments
Observation	Student Writing
Photographs of the Mind	

Text	Title	Theme	Level
1.	*I Never Saw Another Butterfly*	Poetry	YA
2.	*The Poet Slave of Cuba*	Poetry	4–7
3.	*Joyful Noise: Poems for Two Voices*	Poetry	4–7
4.	*Where the Sidewalk Ends*	Poetry	4–7

Website Resources

Giggle Poetry
    www.gigglepoetry.com
Jack Prelutsky: How to Write a Funny Poem
    www.jackprelutsky.com/flash/pdf_docs
How to Write a Funny Poem
    www.poetry.org

Comprehension Strategies

1. Previewing
2. Knowing How Words Work
3. Monitoring
4. Summarizing

Teaching Ideas

Anticipation/Reaction Guide
Concept of Definition Map
Photographs of the Mind
Lyric Retelling

Comprehension Centers

Students will apply the comprehension strategies and related teaching ideas in the following comprehension centers:

Listening Center	Theme Center
Making Books Center	Writing Center
Poetry Center	
Project Center	

Comprehension Routines

Students will apply the comprehension strategies and related teaching ideas in the following comprehension routines:

Literature Circles
Reciprocal Teaching
Questioning the Author

The Guided Comprehension lessons are based on the following strategies and corresponding teaching ideas:

- Previewing: Anticipation/Reaction Guide
- Knowing How Words Work: Concept of Definition Map
- Monitoring: Photographs of the Mind
- Summarizing: Lyric Retelling

I Never Saw Another Butterfly: Children's Drawings and Poems From Terezin Concentration Camp 1942–1944 (Volavkova, 1993), *The Poet Slave of Cuba: A Biography of Juan Francisco Manzano* (Engle, 2006), *Joyful Noise: Poems for Two Voices* (Fleischman, 1988), and *Where the Sidewalk Ends* (Silverstein, 1974) are the texts used in Stage One for teacher-directed whole-group instruction. Numerous additional theme-related resources, including texts, websites, performances across the curriculum, and a culminating activity, are presented in the Theme Resources at the end of the chapter.

Examples of comprehension centers students use during Stage Two of Guided Comprehension include listening, making books, poetry, project, theme, and writing. Students also engage in strategy application in comprehension routines such as Literature Circles, Reciprocal Teaching, and Questioning the Author. Sample website resources complete the overview.

In this chapter, all the lessons focus on poetry. The lessons are appropriate for all learners, including English learners, struggling readers, and students with special needs. To accommodate these learners, the lessons include multiple modes of response (such as singing, sketching, and dramatizing) working with partners, books on CD, cross-age experiences, and extra guided instruction. Ideas we used to differentiate instruction in these lessons include the following:

- Content—the information being taught:
  - Providing leveled texts that accommodate student interest
  - Making leveled text available to students working in Guided Comprehension centers and routines

- Process—the way in which the information is taught:
  - Preteaching skills and strategies to students who may need additional support
  - Reading the poems aloud during Stage One and Stage Two to make them accessible to students and provide good fluent reading models
  - Using visuals to support students' construction of meaning
  - Encouraging students to work with peers to provide additional support
  - Scaffolding learning in Stages One and Two

- Product—how the students demonstrate their learning:
  - Integrating alternative modes of representation, such as art, poetry, or music
  - Providing opportunities for students to create projects
  - Providing opportunities for students to use computers when creating projects or contributing to class projects

Guided Comprehension Lessons

Poetry: Extraordinary Wonder
Guided Comprehension Strategy: Previewing
Teaching Idea: Anticipation/Reaction Guide

STAGE ONE: Teacher-Directed Whole-Group Instruction

Text: *I Never Saw Another Butterfly: Children's Drawings and Poems From Terezin Concentration Camp 1942–1944* (Volavkova, 1993)

Explain: I began by explaining previewing, and by focusing on the Anticipation/Reaction Guide. I said, "Previewing is a reading comprehension strategy that involves activating background knowledge, predicting, and setting purposes for reading." Then I said, "One way we can preview text is to use an Anticipation/Reaction Guide. Anticipation/Reaction Guides help us to activate prior knowledge, make connections to text, set purposes for reading, and develop more accurate understandings of informational text." Next, I showed students the Anticipation/Reaction Guide we would be using during Stage One. I pointed out that the guide consisted of three statements that related to a short informational text. I explained that the statements may or may not be true. I said, "Before reading the text, we read the statements and indicate whether we agree or disagree with each. Then we share our responses. Next, we read the text. After reading, we revisit the statements, decide whether our thinking has changed, and mark the statements accordingly. After that, we discuss again, explaining any changes that may have occurred in our thinking. We use Anticipation/ Reaction Guides before and after reading informational texts."

Demonstrate: I demonstrated by using a Think-Aloud, a read-aloud, the Anticipation/Reaction Guide, and an overhead projector. I began by reading the statements that appeared on the guide and showing where we place a checkmark to indicate whether we agreed or disagreed with each statement. I read the first statement, "*Holocaust* is a word of Greek origin meaning 'sacrifice by fire,'" and thought aloud. I said, "I am not sure about the origin of the word, but I know from what we learned in social studies that many people were sacrificed or put to death during the Holocaust, so I am going to agree with this statement." Then I placed a check in the *agree* column.

Guide: I distributed copies of the Anticipation/Reaction Guide and guided students to work with partners to respond to the next statement. It said, "Millions of Jewish people died during the Holocaust." The partners discussed the statement. They all agreed with it, based on information they had learned in social studies. Next, I read the third statement: "The Jewish people were the only ones persecuted during the Holocaust." The students discussed this statement with their partners and most indicated they agreed that it was true.

Practice: Students practiced by reading the four-paragraph "Introduction to the Holocaust" from the student link on the United States Holocaust Memorial Museum website (www.ushmm .org/education/forstudents/).

Next, we revisited the Anticipation/Reaction Guide and discussed whether our thinking about the three statements had changed. The students were quick to point out that the definition of the word *Holocaust* was correct. They had also confirmed that millions of Jewish people died during

Guided Comprehension: Poetry: Extraordinary Wonder
Previewing: Anticipation/Reaction Guide

Teacher-Directed Whole-Group Instruction

- **Explain** previewing as a reading comprehension strategy and focus on the Anticipation/Reaction Guide.
- **Demonstrate** by using a Think-Aloud, a read-aloud, an Anticipation/Reaction Guide, and an overhead projector. Complete a response to the first statement.
- **Guide** students to work with partners to respond to statements 2 and 3 on the Anticipation/Reaction Guides. Discuss.
- **Practice** by reading information provided on website. Encourage students to revisit the Anticipation/Reaction Guide and indicate if reading changed their thinking. Discuss.
- **Reflect** on the Holocaust and Holocaust poems written by children. Reflect on how previewing and the Anticipation/Reaction Guides help us understand what we read and how we can use them in other settings.

Student-Facilitated Comprehension Centers

- **Poetry Center:** Students write a poem in a self-selected format to be published in our class poetry book.
- **Project Center:** Students create PowerPoint slides for the class poetry anthology: *Favorite Poets, Favorite Poems.*
- **Theme Center:** Students complete Anticipation/Reaction Guides with poems and related informational articles.

Teacher-Guided Small-Group Instruction

- **Review** comprehension strategies and focus on previewing, using Anticipation/Reaction Guides.
- **Guide** students to complete the Anticipation/Reaction Guide. Discuss their responses and guide them to listen to the "I Have a Dream" speech and read two Langston Hughes poems.
- **Practice** by inviting students to revisit the Anticipation/Reaction Guide, changing and adding information as necessary. Discuss.
- **Reflect** on how previewing and the Anticipation/Reaction Guides help us understand what we read.

Student-Facilitated Comprehension Routines

- **Literature Circles:** Complete a topic-related Anticipation/Reaction Guide before reading. Read and discuss the book. Revisit the guide and revise responses as necessary.
- **Reciprocal Teaching:** Students completed Anticipation/Reaction Guides for the texts they were reading.
- **Questioning the Author:** Students completed Anticipation Guides before raising questions about the author's message.

Teacher-Facilitated Whole-Group Reflection and Goal Setting

- **Share** completed Anticipation/Reaction Guides, poems, and projects from Stage Two.
- **Reflect** on how previewing and Anticipation/Reaction Guides help us comprehend and how we can use them in other settings.
- **Set new goals** or extend existing ones.

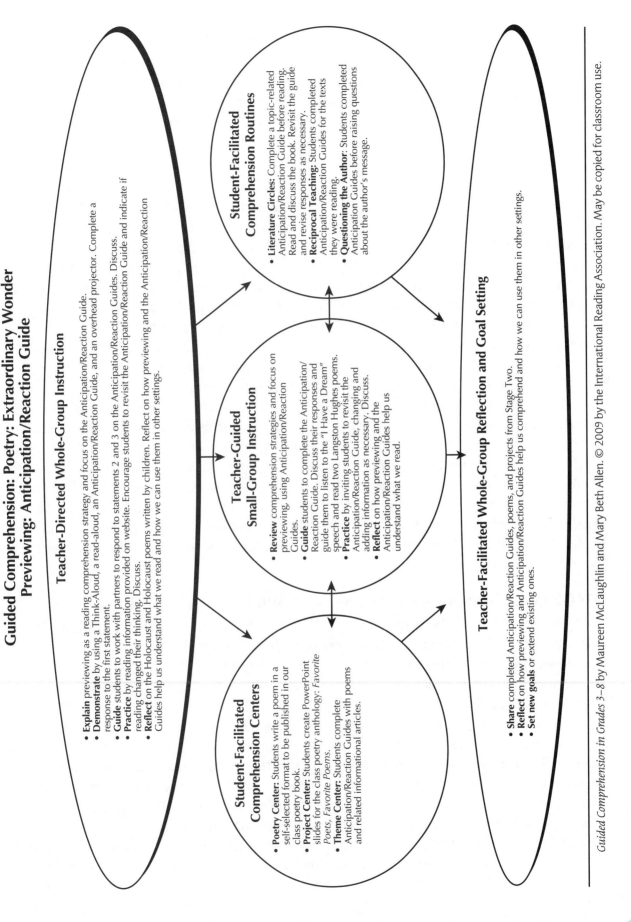

Figure 21. Joseph's Anticipation/Reaction Guide About the Holocaust

Agree	Disagree	
✓	_____	1. *Holocaust* is a word of Greek origin meaning "sacrifice by fire."
✓	_____	2. Millions of Jewish people died during the Holocaust.
✓	X	3. The Jews were the only people persecuted during the Holocaust.

the Holocaust, but their thinking had changed about the third statement. They learned through their reading that in addition to Jewish people, the Nazis also persecuted a variety of other groups including Roma (Gypsies), mentally and physically disabled people, and Soviet prisoners of war. They indicated the change in their thinking about the third statement by placing an "X" in the *disagree* column. Then I introduced *I Never Saw Another Butterfly* and shared two poems written by Jewish children in the Terezin Concentration Camp. The students and I discussed that their social studies textbook doesn't really provide information about children during the Holocaust. Students were very interested in the poems. I read "Homesick," in which the poet writes about the homes the children were forced to leave, and "The Butterfly," in which the poet sadly notes that butterflies don't live in the concentration camps. Then we discussed the poems.

Reflect: We reflected on how we used the Anticipation/Reaction Guide to help us to preview text and how important it is to have background knowledge and be able to make connections to the poems and other texts we read. Angela, one of the students, said, "Learning about the Holocaust can be sad. I remember when I read Anne Frank's diary. That made me sad, too. Today it was sad to think about the children who wrote the poems, but it is good that we are able to read them. Their words are still here, even though they are gone." At the conclusion of this part of the lesson, I left multiple copies of *I Never Saw Another Butterfly* at the theme center. Many students chose this book during independent reading. Figure 21 shows the Anticipation/Reaction Guide Joseph completed during Stage One.

STAGE TWO: Teacher-Guided Small-Group Instruction

Text: *The Collected Poems of Langston Hughes* (Hughes, 1995) and Martin Luther King Jr.'s "I Have a Dream" speech (1963) (Texts varied according to students' abilities.)

Review: I reminded students about comprehension strategies active readers use and focused on previewing and using Anticipation/Reaction Guides. I also referenced the guide we had completed in Stage One.

Guide: I explained to students that we would be completing an Anticipation/Reaction Guide, listening to Martin Luther King's "I Have a Dream" speech, and reading two Langston Hughes poems—"Dreams" and "Dream Deferred." I guided the students to complete the Anticipation/ Reaction Guide. I suggested that we read the statements silently and indicate whether we agree or disagree. When we completed the guides, we discussed each statement. The first said, "Abraham Lincoln gave The Emancipation Proclamation." All the students agreed that he had. The second statement said, "Americans have always been free to pursue their dreams." Some students thought this was true, because they believed they were free to pursue their dreams. Others disagreed with this statement because they thought that even now there are people who are too poor to pursue

Figure 22. Beth's Anticipation/Reaction Guide About Freedom and Dreams

Agree	Disagree	
✓	_____	1. Abraham Lincoln gave "The Emancipation Proclamation."
✓	X	2. Americans have always been free to pursue their dreams.
✓	_____	3. The United States government believes that all people are created equal.

their dreams. The third statement said, "The United States government believes that all people are created equal." The students thought this was true and that it might be in the U.S. Declaration of Independence. After we discussed our responses, we listened to a recording of Martin Luther King Jr. giving his "I Have a Dream" speech. We discussed the speech and then I read aloud the poems "Dreams" and "Dream Deferred" to provide a fluent reading and so students could listen for pleasure. We discussed the Langston Hughes poems. The students thought that both poems were powerful. They were particularly moved by Hughes's idea that a dream deferred could fester and explode. Then students practiced the poems and read them to a partner.

Practice: Students practiced by revisiting the Anticipation/Reaction Guides. They decided that the first statement was correct, based on their prior knowledge and King's reference to Lincoln in his speech. Many students changed their thinking about the second statement based on King's speech and the Hughes poem "Dream Deferred." King's speech also confirmed their thinking that statement three was true. If their thinking had changed, students placed an "X" in that column. Figure 22 shows the Anticipation/Reaction Guide that Beth completed.

Reflect: We reflected on how previewing and Anticipation/Reaction Guides help us to understand text and make connections between what we know and what we read. Then we discussed how we could use Anticipation/Reaction Guides in our content area classes.

Student-Facilitated Comprehension Centers

Poetry Center: Students chose from a wide range of possibilities, including form poems, list poems, and shape poems, and wrote about an informational topic of their choice. Completed poems were displayed in our classroom and later published in our class poetry book.

Project Center: I placed a wide variety of poetry resources at multiple levels at this center. Students chose their favorite poet and poem. Then they used computers to create two PowerPoint slides for our class poetry anthology *Favorite Poets, Favorite Poems*. The first slide contained a three-paragraph biography of their favorite poet; the second slide featured the favorite poem. Students began the projects at the center and completed them as a class project.

Theme Center: I placed a variety of poems paired with short informational articles and related Anticipation/Reaction Guides at this center. Students worked with partners to complete the guides, read the text, and discuss.

Student-Facilitated Comprehension Routines

Literature Circles: I prepared Anticipation/Reaction Guides for the biographies each of the Literature Circle groups had selected to read. Students individually completed the guides before they began reading biographies. When they met in Literature Circles, the students used the guides to enhance discussion.

Reciprocal Teaching: I prepared Anticipation/Reaction Guides for the informational texts students were reading. Students completed the guides, discussed them, read the text, and revisited the guides to discuss whether their thinking had changed.

Questioning the Author: Prior to engaging in QtA, the students completed Anticipation/Reaction Guides based on the informational text they would be reading. They discussed the guides, read the text, and revisited the guides to indicate changes in their thinking. Then the students raised queries such as "What is the author trying to tell us?" and "Why is the author telling us that?"

STAGE THREE: Teacher-Facilitated Whole-Group Reflection and Goal Setting

Share: Students shared their Anticipation/Reaction Guides and poems in small groups. Then we discussed selected examples as a whole class. We also discussed our favorite poets and poems. When the class poetry anthology was completed, we projected it on a screen and applauded after students discussed the poets and poems they chose to include. When the class poetry book was completed, we provided copies for parents.

Reflect: We reflected on how previewing and using Anticipation/Reaction Guides helped us to understand what we read. We also talked about how well we could use the guides in other subject areas.

Set New Goals: Students felt good about using Anticipation/Reaction Guides, so we decided to extend our use of them to informational text in science and math.

Assessment Options

I used observation throughout the lessons, carefully watching how students worked with others and how well they worked on their own. I reviewed and commented on the students' Anticipation/Reaction Guides. I also read and commented on their poems and projects. I reviewed their self-assessments and conferenced with them as necessary. In addition, I completed periodic fluency checks and running records.

Poetry: Extraordinary Wonder
Guided Comprehension Strategy: Knowing How Words Work
Teaching Idea: Concept of Definition Map

STAGE ONE: Teacher-Directed Whole-Group Instruction

Texts: *The Poet Slave of Cuba: A Biography of Juan Francisco Manzano* (Engle, 2006) and *Narrative of the Life of Frederick Douglass* (Douglass, 2004)

Explain: I began by explaining knowing how words work and focusing on the Concept of Definition Map. I said, "Knowing how words work is a reading comprehension strategy that involves understanding words through strategic vocabulary development. The Concept of Definition Map is one way to strategically determine word meanings. When we use this map, we complete this graphic organizer" (see Appendix A, page 259). Then I showed the students the organizer on the overhead projector and distributed copies. I continued to explain. I said, "As we can see on the organizer, the focus word appears in the center. The other parts of the map provide information about the focus word—a definition, a description, examples, and a comparison." I also noted that we can add what we already know about the topic to the Concept of Definition Map before reading, and we can verify the information and add other facts after reading. Next, I explained that when the map is complete, we can use it to write a definition or summary of the focus word.

Demonstrate: I demonstrated by using a Think-Aloud, a read-aloud, the graphic organizer, and an overhead projector. I began by introducing the Concept of Definition Map graphic organizer. I read aloud the various categories of information we would need to complete it. I wrote *slave*, the topic for our Concept of Definition Map, in the center oval and explained that we would need to provide information for each category on the map. I read aloud the next category of information: "What is it?" I thought aloud, saying, "When I think about the slaves we had in our country, I remember learning that they were owned by other people. For example, prior to the Civil War, plantation owners in the South would buy slaves to work their land. The plantation owners controlled the slaves and made them live according to the owners' rules." Then, in the section labeled "What is it?" I wrote "a person owned and controlled by another." Next, I went back to the center oval and said, "A slave is a person who is owned and controlled by another."

Guide: I guided students to work with partners as we completed the next section of the Concept of Definition Map: "How would you describe it?" I said, "Let's think about how we would describe a slave." The partners discussed and then they suggested several words to describe a slave, including *imprisoned servant, hard worker, bad conditions*, and *no freedom*. We decided we would use *imprisoned servant, bad conditions*, and *no freedom*. Next, I prompted students to complete the next part of the Concept of Definition Map. I said, "This section of the map asks us to provide examples of slavery. I think we can change that question to make it more meaningful. I suggest we replace it with 'What are three countries that have had slaves?'" The students quickly started discussing that the United States had slaves in the past, but it was not the only country that did. So we listed two countries we knew had slaves at some point in their history. We wrote *United States* and *Egypt*. We left the third choice blank because students weren't sure which other country to add. I said, "This is fine for now. We can revisit this section after we read." Then we discussed what we would add in the space labeled Comparison. I reminded the students that when we look for comparisons, we

Guided Comprehension: Poetry: Extraordinary Wonder
Knowing How Words Work: Concept of Definition Map

Teacher-Directed Whole-Group Instruction

- **Explain** knowing how words work and focus on the Concept of Definition Map.
- **Demonstrate** by using a Think-Aloud, a read-aloud, a graphic organizer, and an overhead projector.
- **Guide** students to work with partners to contribute to Concept of Definition Maps.
- **Practice** by encouraging students to contribute ideas on their own to the remaining segments of maps. Read aloud the poem about Juan Francisco Marzano and excerpts from Frederick Douglass's autobiography. Discuss and revisit the map. Create a Concept of Definition Map Summary.
- **Reflect** on how this strategy and Concept of Definition Maps help us understand what we read and how we can use them in other settings.

Student-Facilitated Comprehension Centers

- **Poetry Center:** Students write definition poems about informational topics, and display their poems in a class poetry gallery.
- **Project Center:** Students create PowerPoint transmediations, changing poems into picture books.
- **Theme Center:** Students complete Concept of Definition Maps and read theme-related texts.
- **Writing Center:** Students use completed Concept of Definition Maps to generate research questions and write paragraphs using Questions Into Paragraphs (QuIP).

Teacher-Guided Small-Group Instruction

- **Review** comprehension strategies and focus on knowing how words work, using Concept of Definition Maps.
- **Guide** students to begin completing the Concept of Definition Map. Discuss responses.
- **Practice** by inviting students to complete the map. Read Alice Walker's poem in picture book format. Discuss excerpts from books about World War II and the Vietnam War. Discuss the text and revisit the Concept of Definition Map, revising as necessary. Create an oral Concept of Definition Map Summary. Discuss.
- **Reflect** on how knowing how words work and the Concept of Definition Maps help us understand what we read.

Student-Facilitated Comprehension Routines

- **Literature Circles:** Students complete a topic-related Concept of Definition Map before reading. They read and discuss the book, and then revisit the map and create an oral Concept of Definition Map Summary.

Teacher-Facilitated Whole-Group Reflection and Goal Setting

- **Share** completed Concept of Definition Maps and Summaries, poems, QuIPs, and projects from Stage Two.
- **Reflect** on how knowing how words work and Concept of Definition Maps help us comprehend and how we can use the maps in other settings.
- **Set new goals** or extend existing ones.

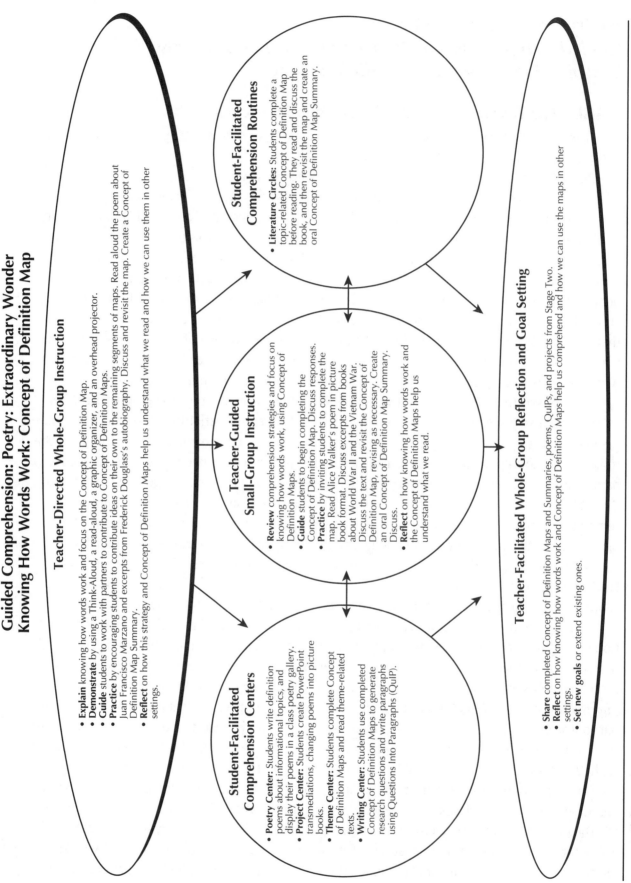

Guided Comprehension in Grades 3–8 by Maureen McLaughlin and Mary Beth Allen. © 2009 by the International Reading Association. May be copied for classroom use.

are looking for topics that are similar. The students suggested that we should write *prisoner* in that section because slaves could not escape. I went back to the center oval and read the information we had on our map at that point.

Practice: I introduced the poem "Juan," which was written about Juan Francisco Manzano, a Cuban slave who was also a poet. This resulted in quite a discussion because students had learned in history class that slaves in our country were not allowed to read or write. The students wondered when Manzano found time to write. We took a few minutes to access his biography and learned that he was born into slavery in Havana, Cuba, in 1797. He remained enslaved for 40 years and somehow managed to publish two small books of poems during that time. I explained to the students that the poem we would be reading would not be one of Manzano's poems, but rather a poem written by Margarita Engle, an author who had written Manzano's biography in poetry. Next, I introduced the poem titled "Juan," in which Engle tells readers about Manzano's life through a simply phrased description of where he lived, what fruits and flowers he smelled, and how he sketched funny shapes because he did not know how to write. I read the poem aloud for the students. Then we read the poem chorally and discussed what we were visualizing as we read. Students noted they could see the rustic courtyard and the square patch of blue sky. They could imagine smelling the scents of the fruits and blossoms. After we discussed the poem, students noted that it was great that the author wrote Manzano's biography in poetry. Next, I read aloud a few excerpts from *Narrative of the Life of Frederick Douglass*. We discussed what we had learned from Douglass's autobiography. Then we revisited our Concept of Definition Map. Students immediately suggested that we add *Cuba* as our third country that had slaves. I added it to the map with a different color marker to remind us that we added it after reading. Then we used what we had learned about Frederick Douglass to verify the information we had written on our Concept of Definition Map. We used our completed map to write a Concept of Definition Map Summary. Figure 23 shows our completed Concept of Definition Map and Concept of Definition Map Summary about slaves.

Reflect: We reflected on how we used the Concept of Definition Map to help us understand how words work and comprehend what we read. The students were genuinely engaged in learning about Juan Francisco Manzano's life, and in reading Engle's poems about him. They also were motivated to learn more about Frederick Douglass's life. I put several books about him at the theme center and many students read them during independent reading. Finally, we talked about how we could use the Concept of Definition Maps with other texts in other settings.

STAGE TWO: Teacher-Guided Small-Group Instruction

Text: *Why War Is Never a Good Idea* (Walker, 2007) (Texts varied according to students' abilities.)

Review: I reminded students about comprehension strategies active readers use, and focused on knowing how words work and using Concept of Definition Maps. I also referenced the map we had completed in Stage One.

Guide: I gave the small group of students Concept of Definition Map graphic organizers (see Appendix A, page 259) and explained that our focus word would be *war*. We briefly discussed some things we knew about war, and then I guided the students to work with a partner to provide information about war for the first two categories. We discussed the partners' responses to "What

Figure 23. Concept of Definition Map and Summary About Slaves

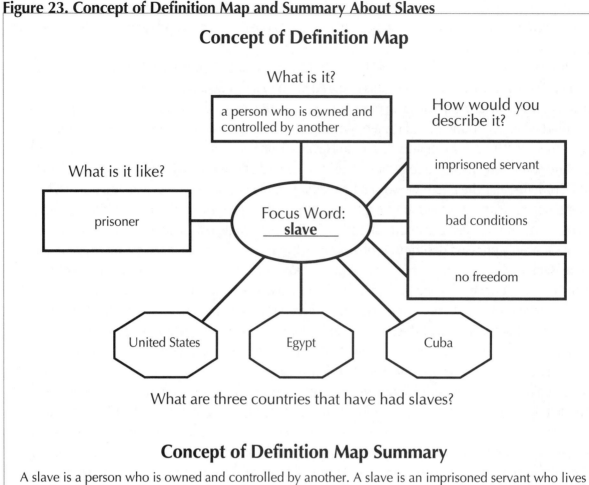

Concept of Definition Map

What is it?

a person who is owned and controlled by another

How would you describe it?

imprisoned servant

bad conditions

no freedom

What is it like?

prisoner

Focus Word: **slave**

United States

Egypt

Cuba

What are three countries that have had slaves?

Concept of Definition Map Summary

A slave is a person who is owned and controlled by another. A slave is an imprisoned servant who lives in bad conditions and has no freedom. The United States, Egypt, and Cuba are examples of countries that have had slaves. A slave is similar to a prisoner.

is it?" Possibilities included *combat* and *battle*. They were their responses on their maps. Then we discussed, "How would you describe it?" *Fighting, killing,* and *bombing* were among the partners' responses.

Practice: Students practiced by completing the Concept of Definition Maps they had begun with partners. They thought about the next question: "What are some examples?" They discussed possibilities such as *Iraq, Vietnam,* and *World War II.* Then they focused on the comparison. The students suggested that we use *conflict* as the comparison. When the maps were complete, we created an oral Concept of Definition Map Summary. Next, I introduced Alice Walker's picture book *Why War Is Never a Good Idea.* The book is a transmediation—one medium that has been changed into another. In this case, Alice Walker's poem has been changed into a picture book illustrated by Stefano Vitale. I read the book to provide a fluent reading of the poem, and then the students read it. We discussed the poem and made connections to our Concept of Definition Map. Next, I read excerpts from the books about World War II and the Vietnam War, and we discussed how the information in the books supported what we had included in our map. I placed these books and others at the theme center, where students could choose them for independent reading.

Reflect: We reflected on how Concept of Definition Maps help us understand how words work and how to make connections between what we know and what we have read. Jerry, one of the students, said, "I liked the way we were able to use the map to connect what we knew about war to the poem." Suze said, "When you read the poem, I was picturing it in my head. Then when we read the poem in the book, we got to see the illustrations. It was cool to see what the illustrator pictured when he read the poem." Finally, we discussed how we could use Concept of Definition Maps and Concept of Definition Map Summaries to help us understand texts in other settings.

Student-Facilitated Comprehension Centers

Poetry Center: Students wrote definition poems (see Appendix B, page 295, for reproducible blackline) about informational topics such as slavery, war, inventions, explorations, and historic events. Students had access to a number of books I had placed at the center and to a number of websites I had bookmarked for them. Completed poems were displayed in a class poetry gallery.

Project Center: I placed project rubrics and a wide variety of poems at this center. Students used them to create PowerPoint transmediations by turning one of their favorite poems into an electronic picture book. Students began the projects at the center and completed them as a class project.

Theme Center: I placed a variety of poetry books and books about topics we had studied during our theme at this center. The books represented a wide variety of reading levels. Within each poetry book, I selected a few poems and provided related Concept of Definition Maps. I provided the focus word for each blackline. I also provided these for the other books. Students completed the maps, and then they read the poems and books. After reading, students revisited the maps and revised them as necessary. Next, they wrote summaries based on their completed maps.

Writing Center: Students used their completed Concept of Definition Map Summaries to generate three research questions and write paragraphs. They used the Questions Into Paragraphs (QuIP) graphic organizer (see Appendix A, page 268) to record their questions and information from two sources.

Student-Facilitated Comprehension Routines

Literature Circles: Students individually completed Concept of Definition Maps and Summaries before they began reading a variety of books. They shared their map information and summaries during group discussion.

STAGE THREE: Teacher-Facilitated Whole-Group Reflection and Goal Setting

Share: Students shared their Concept of Definition Maps and Summaries from Stage Two in small groups. Then we discussed selected examples as a whole class. Then the small groups walked through our poetry gallery, stopping to hear each group member read his or her definition poem. We viewed the PowerPoint projects toward the end of the theme.

Reflect: We reflected on how knowing how words work and using Concept of Definition Maps helped us to understand what we read. We also talked about how well we could use the maps and that they seemed to work best with informational topics.

Set New Goals: We decided to continue working on knowing how words work by learning about semantic maps, which were more flexible in structure.

Assessment Options

I used observation throughout the lesson. I reviewed and commented on students' Concept of Definition Maps and Summaries, as well as their self-assessments, during the lesson. I also read and commented on their poems and completed running records and fluency checks as needed.

Poetry: Extraordinary Wonder
Guided Comprehension Strategies: Monitoring and Visualizing
Teaching Idea: Photographs of the Mind

STAGE ONE: Teacher-Directed Whole-Group Instruction

Text: *Joyful Noise: Poems for Two Voices* (Fleischman, 1988)

Explain: I began by explaining that monitoring involves asking, "Does this make sense?" and clarifying by adapting strategic processes. Then I explained that visualizing is creating pictures in our minds based on what we are reading. Next, I explained how Photographs of the Mind works. I said, "While we are reading, we stop at predetermined points to sketch what we are visualizing at that point. The sketching provides a way for us to share our visualizations." Then I shared the blackline (see Appendix A, page 258) and said, "We usually stop and sketch at four different points."

Demonstrate: I demonstrated using a Think-Aloud, a read-aloud, and an overhead projector. I introduced *Joyful Noise: Poems for Two Voices* and explained that we would be reading "Honeybees." I noted that this poem was written to be read by two voices, so Chris, a student I had previously invited to help me, and I read the poem aloud to provide a fluent reading model. We briefly discussed the poem with the class and then Chris and I reread to the first stopping point and sketched and shared our visualizations. The first section of the poem is about the differences between when the queen bee and the worker bee awake and how soon they begin to work. In our first sketches, which we placed in the first square on the blackline, Chris sketched a simple little bee guarding the hive and an elaborate queen bee being fed by other bees. My sketch was strikingly similar. I reminded students that we didn't need to be artists to sketch our ideas. I also noted that using simple lines and shapes worked very well.

Guide: Chris and I read the poem aloud to the second stopping point and invited students to work with partners to engage in Photographs of the Mind. We encouraged them to place their sketches in the second boxes on their blacklines. This section talks about different tasks that the worker bee did while the queen bee was pampered. The students sketched their visualizations and shared them with a partner. We repeated this process with the third section of the poem, which talks about all the worker bee does while the queen lays eggs and is adored.

Practice: Chris and I read the final section of the poem, and the students practiced by completing the final section of Photographs of the Mind. Then they shared and discussed their sketches. We discussed the poem and students remarked about how much they enjoyed poems with two voices. The students took a few minutes to practice reading "Honeybees" and then they read it aloud with a partner. Students enjoyed monitoring their understanding through Photographs of the Mind.

Reflect: We reflected on how monitoring and visualizing help us understand what we read. Then we discussed how we could use Photographs of the Mind with other kinds of texts in other settings. Students indicated that they enjoyed this technique because it gave them a fun way to share their thinking. Figure 24 shows Chris's completed Photographs of the Mind for "Honeybees."

Guided Comprehension: Poetry: Extraordinary Wonder
Monitoring and Visualizing; Photographs of the Mind

Teacher-Directed Whole-Group Instruction

- **Explain** monitoring and focus on Photographs of the Mind.
- **Demonstrate** Photographs of the Mind using a Think-Aloud, a read-aloud, a graphic organizer, and a copy of "Honeybees."
- **Guide** students to work with partners to use Photographs of the Mind while listening to or reading poetry. Share and discuss.
- **Practice** engaging in Photographs of the Mind. Share and discuss.
- **Reflect** on how monitoring and Photographs of the Mind help us understand what we read and how we can use Photographs of the Mind with other text.

Student-Facilitated Comprehension Centers

- **Listening Center:** Students listen or read along as partners read selected poems. Partners stop at designated points to share and discuss.
- **Poetry Center:** Students work with partners to write a brief story poem for two voices.
- **Theme Center:** Students select poems with partners. They read the poems and complete Photographs of the Mind.

Teacher-Guided Small-Group Instruction

- **Review** the comprehension strategies good readers use, and focus on monitoring and using Photographs of the Mind.
- **Guide** students to begin reading "Seventh-Grade Soap Opera" and in completing Photographs of the Mind.
- **Practice** by encouraging students to continue to read the poem, stopping at designated points to complete Photographs of the Mind and share and discuss their sketches.
- **Reflect** on how monitoring and Photographs of the Mind help us understand what we are reading.

Student-Facilitated Comprehension Routines

- **Literature Circles:** Students use Photographs of the Mind while reading selected chapters of the Literature Circle book. Students share and discuss with the group.
- **Reciprocal Teaching:** Students use Photographs of the Mind in the portion of the routine that focuses on summarizing.
- **Questioning the Author:** While reading, students sketch ideas to question the author.

Teacher-Facilitated Whole-Group Reflection and Goal Setting

- **Share** applications of Photographs of the Mind and poems. Invite students to self-assess their ability to use them.
- **Reflect** on how monitoring and Photographs of the Mind guide our understanding during reading.
- **Set new goals** or extend existing ones.

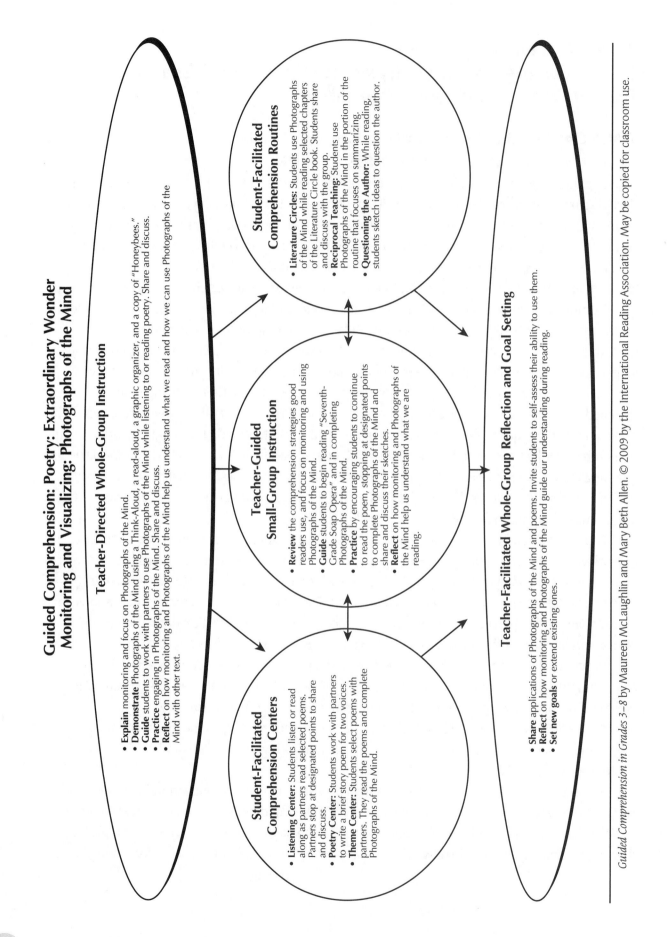

Figure 24. Chris's Completed Photographs of the Mind for "Honeybees"

STAGE TWO: Teacher-Guided Small-Group Instruction

Text: *Big Talk: Poems for Four Voices* (Fleischman, 2000) (Texts varied according to students' abilities.)

Review: I reviewed the comprehension strategies good readers use and then focused on using Photographs of the Mind as a way to use visualizing and sketching to monitor our thinking.

Guide: Then I introduced "Seventh-Grade Soap Opera" from *Big Talk: Poems for Four Voices* by Paul Fleischman. This poem is a four voice "he said–she said" accounting of middle school life. I played a recording I had previously made with other teachers to provide a fluent reading for students. We discussed the poem and students commented that it sounded just like every day at the middle school. Then I guided each of the students to practice reading the lines for just one of

Figure 25. Brandon's Photographs of the Mind for "Seventh-Grade Soap Opera"

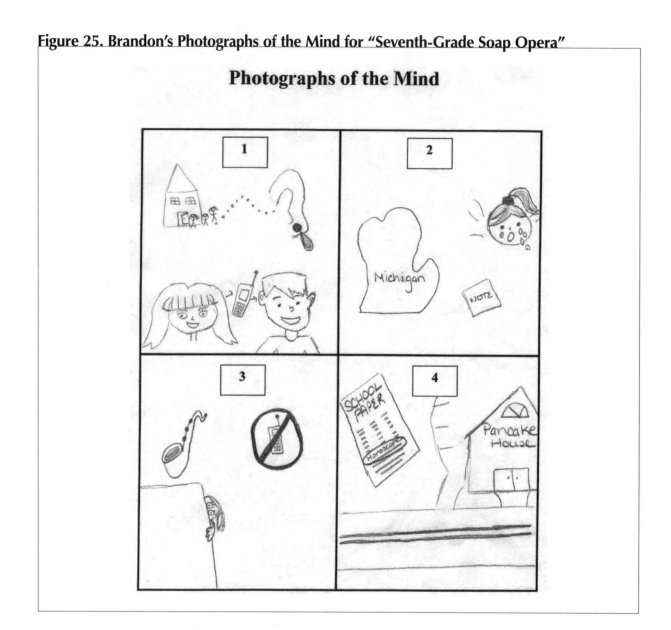

the voices in the poem. After practicing a few times, they read the poem. Then I played the reading again, stopping at two predetermined points so they could sketch and share their Photographs of the Mind. Students shared their sketches and ideas with partners.

Practice: I continued playing the recording of the poem, stopping at two additional points for students to complete their Photographs of the Mind. Then they shared and discussed with all the group members. Figure 25 shows Brandon's Photographs of the Mind based on "Seventh-Grade Soap Opera."

Reflect: We reflected on how using Photographs of the Mind to share our visualizations helped us understand text. The students agreed that the sketching provided a way for us to share the pictures inside our minds. They noted that sketching and sharing ideas made it easy to monitor their understanding.

Student-Facilitated Comprehension Centers

Listening Center: Students listened to poems for multiple voices. They worked with partners, stopping at designated points to engage in Photographs of the Mind, share, and discuss.

Poetry Center: Students worked with partners to create brief story poems for two voices. When the students finished writing, they displayed their poems in the poetry gallery. They also recorded their poems for the class.

Theme Center: I placed a variety of types and levels of poems (lyric, narrative, free verse, form, humorous, etc.—both published and student-authored) at this center. Students self-selected a poem and read it for pleasure. Then they read it a second time, stopping at designated points to create Photographs of the Mind.

Student-Facilitated Comprehension Routines

Literature Circles: Students worked with partners to read selected chapters and complete Photographs of the Mind. They used their sketches as the basis of discussion of those sections.

Reciprocal Teaching: Students used Photographs of the Mind to summarize text they read.

Questioning the Author: While reading, students sketched ideas to query the author about purpose and intent.

STAGE THREE: Teacher-Facilitated Whole-Group Reflection and Goal Setting

Share: Students shared and discussed their Photographs of the Mind applications and their writing from Stage Two in small groups. Then they either played the recording of their poem for two voices or read it aloud for the whole class. The students especially enjoyed sharing these poems.

Reflect: We reflected on how monitoring and visualizing help us understand what we read. Students noted that sketching really helps them to understand what they are reading. Then they self-assessed their ability to use this and similar techniques.

Set New Goals: Students felt comfortable using Photographs of the Mind with poetry, so we decided to extend our goal of monitoring and visualizing to narrative and informational text.

Assessment Options

I observed students in all stages of Guided Comprehension, focusing on their ability to work with others and understand what they read. I reviewed and commented on their Photographs of the Mind, and I read and commented on their poems. I also completed fluency checks and running records as necessary.

Poetry: Extraordinary Wonder
Guided Comprehension Strategy: Summarizing
Teaching Idea: Lyric Retelling

STAGE ONE: Teacher-Directed Whole-Group Instruction

Text: *Where the Sidewalk Ends* (Silverstein, 1974)

Explain: I began by reminding students that we had already learned that when we summarize, we should include the important information from the text. Next, I focused on retelling and reviewed the narrative elements. I shared the Lyric Retelling blackline master (see Appendix A, page 266) and noted that when we wrote our Lyric Retellings, we would need to include the important points from the story—the characters, setting, problem, attempts to resolve the problem, and resolution. I also reminded students that we would need to retell what happened in the story in the correct sequence. Next, I explained that our Lyric Retellings would be different from other retellings in two ways: (1) We would be choosing a song that everyone knew and writing our retellings as new lyrics—or words—for that song, and (2) Instead of reading stories, we would be reading story poems.

Demonstrate: I demonstrated by using a Think-Aloud, an overhead projector, and a read-aloud of "The Crocodile's Toothache" by Shel Silverstein. In that poem, a crocodile that has a toothache goes to a dentist who pulls out random teeth, not caring which one is causing the pain. In response, the crocodile snaps his mouth closed while the dentist is working inside. I introduced the poem by reading its title, and discussing dentists and toothaches with the students. Because the students were very familiar with Shel Silverstein poems, they knew there would be something humorous about the poem. Next, I read the poem aloud and shared Silverstein's illustration of the crocodile in the dentist's chair. I thought aloud as I wrote. I began by saying, "To begin my Lyric Retelling, I need to think about who the characters are and where the story takes place. I think the characters are the crocodile and the dentist and it looks as if the story takes place in the dentist's office." Next, I said, "Now I need to figure out the problem in this story." I restated the title and said, "I think the problem is that the crocodile has a toothache." The students agreed. Then I asked them what attempts were made to try to resolve the problem. The students all suggested that the dentist pulled out a lot of teeth. Next, I asked how the story was resolved. The students agreed that the problem was resolved when the crocodile snapped closed its mouth while the dentist was still inside. They believed that because the dentist was pulling the wrong teeth, the crocodile decided to get rid of the dentist by snapping closed his mouth.

Guide: When we had completed our list of narrative elements, I guided the students to choose a song we could use to create our Lyric Retelling. I explained that although we usually write Lyric Retellings in small groups, we would write this one as a whole class because we were just learning how to do it. I reminded the students that everyone needed to know the song the class chose. Then they decided on the theme song from *The Brady Bunch* television series. I suggested that we all sing that song with its original lyrics and the students were happy to do so. We decided to begin our Lyric Retelling with these lyrics: "It's a story about a crocodile and a dentist who had an office of his own." We sang that line and decided that it worked well. Then we wrote the rest of our song. This is our Lyric Retelling for "The Crocodile's Toothache" to the tune of "The Brady Bunch."

Guided Comprehension: Poetry: Extraordinary Wonder Summarizing; Lyric Retelling

Teacher-Directed Whole-Group Instruction

- **Explain** summarizing and focus on Lyric Retelling.
- **Demonstrate** Lyric Retelling using a story poem the class has read, a Think-Aloud, and a read-aloud.
- **Guide** students to work with partners to contribute ideas to the Lyric Retelling. Discuss.
- **Practice** by working with students to complete the Lyric Retelling. Discuss. Sing the Lyric Retelling.
- **Reflect** on how summarizing using Lyric Retelling helps us understand what we read and how we can use it with narrative and informational text.

Student-Facilitated Comprehension Centers

- **Making Books Center:** Students work with partners to create poems for the class book of story poems.
- **Poetry Center:** Students write cinquains based on self-selected topics.
- **Theme Center:** Students select story poems with partners. They read poems and complete Lyric Retellings.

Teacher-Guided Small-Group Instruction

- **Review** the comprehension strategies good readers use and focus on summarizing and using Lyric Retelling.
- **Guide** students to read a story poem and begin writing a Lyric Retelling.
- **Practice** by encouraging students to complete and sing their Lyric Retelling.
- **Reflect** on how summarizing and Lyric Retelling help us understand what we are reading.

Student-Facilitated Comprehension Routines

- **Literature Circles:** Students use Lyric Retelling as an extension activity for Literature Circles. They share their work with the class.
- **Reciprocal Teaching:** Students write Lyric Retellings about books they read.

Teacher-Facilitated Whole-Group Reflection and Goal Setting

- **Share** Lyric Retellings and poems created in Stage Two. Encourage students to assess their ability to use them.
- **Reflect** on how summarizing and Lyric Retelling help us to understand what we are reading.
- **Set new goals** or extend existing ones.

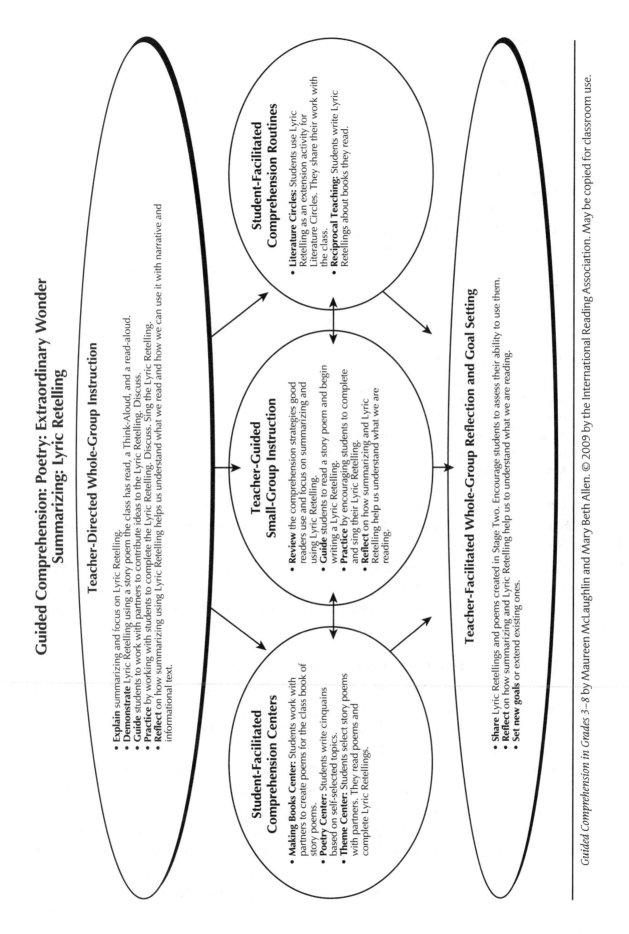

Guided Comprehension in Grades 3–8 by Maureen McLaughlin and Mary Beth Allen. © 2009 by the International Reading Association. May be copied for classroom use.

Lyric Retelling for "The Crocodile's Toothache"

It's a story about a crocodile
And a dentist who had an office of his own.
The crocodile had a toothache like we've all had,
And he could not stand the pain.

It's a story about a crocodile
That went to the dentist's office.
He hoped the dentist could stop the pain
And help him feel better.

So the crocodile and the dentist made an appointment
And the crocodile showed up right on time.
The dentist knew the crocodile was in pain
And his job was to take the pain away...to take the pain away...to take the pain away.
His job was to take the pain away.

It's a story about a dentist
Who started pulling out a lot of crocodile teeth.
He didn't seem to care if they were healthy,
He just kept pulling them out.

It's a story about a crocodile
Who did not like losing so many teeth.
He was still a big strong animal,
So he snapped his mouth and the dentist was gone.
He snapped his mouth...he snapped his mouth...he snapped his mouth
And now the dentist is not around.

Practice: We practiced by singing the Lyric Retelling as I had recorded it on the overhead transparency. The students learned how to use lyrics to summarize stories or story poems and looked forward to writing more.

Reflect: We reflected on how using Lyric Retellings to summarize helped us understand what we were reading. We learned and had a great deal of fun writing and singing. As Ramone, one of the students, observed, "Shel Silverstein writes really funny poems, but writing Lyric Retellings about his poems is even more fun."

STAGE TWO: Teacher-Guided Small-Group Instruction

Text: *A Pizza the Size of the Sun* (Prelutsky, 1996) (Texts varied according to students' abilities.)

Review: I began by reviewing the strategies good readers use and focusing on summarizing. Then I reviewed the process for creating Lyric Retellings, referenced our Lyric Retelling from Stage One, and distributed the organizer to the students.

Guide: I introduced Jack Prelutsky's poem "I Think My Computer Is Crazy" by sharing the title and discussing it with the students. We decided that we had all experienced times when our computers did not do what we needed them to do. Then I read the poem aloud for the students' listening pleasure and to provide a fluent reading. We discussed it. The students especially enjoyed the last stanza, in which the author wrote that the computer was "buzzing like bees" and "begging for cheese." Of course, their favorite part was when the author decided the computer wouldn't work because his brother "inserted bologna into the floppy disk drive." Next, I guided the students to practice reading the poem for a few minutes and then read it aloud with a partner. Then I guided the students to list information about the narrative elements. They worked as a small group and we all wrote the list. The students decided the character was the writer of the poem and the setting was the writer's house. They suggested that the problem was that the computer wasn't working and attempts to resolve it resulted in its "churning out drivel," "making disheartening noises," "buzzing like billions of bees" and "begging for cheese." We agreed that the brother putting bologna in the disk drive was the resolution. Next, we chose our song. The students in the group decided to write their Lyric Retelling to the tune of "Old McDonald Had a Farm." They referred to their list of story elements as they wrote their Lyric Retelling and I guided them through the process.

Lyric Retelling of "I Think My Computer Is Crazy"

My computer has gone crazy
And I don't know what to do.
It used to help me do my homework right,
And I don't know what to do.

My computer makes noises day and night
And I don't know what to do
It makes weird noises and buzzes like bees
And I don't know what to do.

With a buzz-buzz here and a buzz-buzz there,
Here a buzz, there a buzz, everywhere a buzz-buzz,
My computer has gone crazy
And I don't know what to do.

My computer has gone crazy
And now it is begging for cheese
I think my computer will never work again
Because of my brother's bologna.

With a buzz-buzz here and a cheese-cheese there
Bologna here and bologna there.
I think my computer has gone crazy
And will never work again.

Practice: The students practiced by singing their Lyric Retelling. There was a lot of giggling, as there often is when reading a Jack Prelutsky poem. Then we reflected on how to create Lyric Retellings and how they helped us understand what we read. Everyone agreed that writing Lyric Retellings was fun and that they helped us to remember what we had read.

Student-Facilitated Comprehension Centers

Making Books Center: Students worked with partners to create four-stanza poems for our class book of story poems. I provided Story Map blacklines (see Appendix A, page 255) to help the students organize the narrative elements they would use in their story poems.

Poetry Center: Students used the cinquain blackline (see Appendix B, page 294) to write cinquains about topics of their choice. They began their writing by brainstorming a word and its synonym because that is how cinquains begin and end. This is Mandy's cinquain:

Summer
One word—Noun

<u>hot</u> <u>sunny</u>
Two Adjectives Describing Line 1

<u>tanning</u> <u>swimming</u> <u>relaxing</u>
"ing" Words Telling Actions of Line 1

<u>Happy</u> <u>there's</u> <u>no</u> <u>school</u>
Four-Word Phrase Describing a Feeling Related to Line 1

<u>Season</u>
One Word—Synonym or Reference to Line 1

Theme Center: Students worked in groups of four to create Lyric Retellings either for story poems or for books. They selected music, wrote lyrics, and practiced performing their Lyric Retelling. They sang their Lyric Retelling for the class during Stage Three.

Student-Facilitated Comprehension Routines

Literature Circles: Students used their Lyric Retellings as extension activities for the books they had just finished reading. They revisited the narrative elements of the story by completing a Story Map. They wrote their Lyric Retelling, practiced it, and sang it for the class during Stage Three.

Reciprocal Teaching: Students engaged in Reciprocal Teaching and then recorded the narrative elements on the Story Map blackline. They wrote their Lyric Retellings and shared them with the class in Stage Three.

STAGE THREE: Teacher-Facilitated Whole-Group Reflection and Goal Setting

Share: Students shared their poems and sang their Lyric Retellings from Stage Two to the class. It was a fun sharing session because the students enjoyed singing as well as being audience members.

Reflect: We reflected on our understanding of summarizing and our ability to create Lyric Retellings. The students enjoyed writing and singing the Lyric Retellings.

Set New Goals: We decided that we all felt very comfortable creating Lyric Retellings for poems and stories. So, we extended our goal to learn how to summarize using Lyric Summaries with informational text.

Assessment Options

I observed students throughout the Guided Comprehension process and reviewed and commented on their Lyric Retellings, cinquains, and story poems. I also reviewed the students' self-assessments and completed running records as needed.

Theme Resources

Books

Bagert, B. (Ed.). (1995). *Poetry for young people: Edgar Allen Poe*. New York: Sterling.

Bolin, F.S. (Ed.). (2008). *Poetry for young people: Emily Dickinson*. New York: Sterling.

Clinton, C. (1998). *I, too, sing America: Three centuries of African American poetry*. Boston: Houghton Mifflin.

Dakos, K. (1995). *If you're not here, please raise your hand: Poems about school*. New York: Aladdin.

Donegan, P. (2003). *Haiku*. Boston: Tuttle.

Fletcher, R. (2002). *Poetry matters: Writing a poem from the inside out*. New York: HarperTrophy.

Franco, B. (2006). *Math poetry: Linking language and math in a fresh way*. Tucson, AZ: Good Year Books.

Janeczko, P.B. (1994). *Poetry from A to Z: A guide for young writers*. New York: Simon & Schuster.

Kastan, D.S., & Kastan, M. (Eds.). (2008). *Poetry for young people: William Shakespeare*. New York: Sterling.

Paschen, E., & Mosby, R.P. (Eds.). (2001). *Poetry speaks: Hear great poets read their own works from Tennyson to Plath*. Naperville, IL: Sourcebooks. (CDs included)

Paschen, E., & Raccah, D. (Eds.). (2005). *Poetry speaks to children*. Naperville, IL: Sourcebooks. (CD included)

Prelutsky, J. (1984). *The new kid on the block*. New York: Greenwillow.

Prelutsky, J. (1990). *Something big has been here*. New York: Greenwillow.

Prelutsky, J. (2008). *My dog may be a genius*. New York: Greenwillow.

Prelutsky, J. (2008). *Pizza, pigs, and poetry: How to write a poem*. New York: Greenwillow.

Roessel, D., & Rampersad, A. (Eds.). (2006). *Poetry for young people: Langston Hughes*. New York: Sterling.

Schmidt, G.D. (Ed.). (2008). *Poetry for young people: Robert Frost*. New York: Sterling.

Silverstein, S. (2004). *Where the sidewalk ends: The poems and drawings of Shel Silverstein* (30th anniversary ed.). New York: HarperCollins.

Wilson, E.G. (Ed.). (2007). *Poetry for young people: Maya Angelou*. New York: Sterling.

Websites

Giggle Poetry: Hundred of Poems to Read & Rate
www.gigglepoetry.com

How to Write a Funny Poem by Jack Prelutsky
www.jackprelutsky.com/flash/pdf_docs/HowToWriteAFunnyPoem.pdf

Modern American Poetry: The Poets
www.english.uiuc.edu/maps/poets.htm

PoemHunter.com
www.poemhunter.com

Poetry.com
rhyme.poetry.com

Poetry.org
   www.poetry.org

PoetryTeachers.com
   www.poetryteachers.com

Poets.org From the Academy of American Poets
   www.poets.org/index.php

Shel Silverstein.com
   www.shelsilverstein.com/indexSite.html

Performance Extensions Across the Curriculum

Social Studies

- Read poetry about historical events or famous people. Write a definition poem about historical events or adapt the poem format to write about people who have contributed to history.

- Use PowerPoint to create and illustrate an acrostic poem about a famous American leader. Contribute your poem to a class book of acrostic poems.

Science

- Use Douglas Florian's books of poems (*Mammalabilia*; *Comets, Stars, the Moon, and Mars*) as models to create a science poem and illustration. Include the poem and illustration in a class book.

- Use the list poems from Georgia Heard's *Falling Down the Page: A Book of List Poems* (2008) or Paul Janeczko's *A Kick in the Head: An Everyday Guide to Poetic Forms* (2009) as models to write a list poem or form poem about science topics.

Mathematics

- Create math poems or Lyric Retellings to help remember math facts.

- Create shape poems to explain geometric concepts or geometry in everyday life.

Art

- View paintings and sculptures. Then create poems to express your interpretations of the art

- Create a work of art to complement a poem you have written.

Music

- Rewrite the lyrics to existing songs, incorporating information from your life.

- Create or choose music to complement a poem you have written.

Culminating Activity

We Are Poets! Encourage students to design and deliver invitations to their parents and families for the culminating activity *We Are Poets!* Then plan an engaging and informative celebration of poetry. Display poems and projects created during the poetry theme. Display hard copies of student-authored poems in the class poetry gallery. Students can serve as guides and explain the different types of poems they created. Present students' electronic projects by using an LCD projector. Students can narrate the slideshows. Create different stations where students can serve as guides. For example, students at one station could explain how they learned to write form poems and invite visitors to write acrostic poems using their first names. Invite the parents, community members, and students to share their favorite poets and poems. Provide refreshments, and offer interactive ways for parents to comment on the celebration. Murals on which parents can write messages to the class or computers through which they can send e-mail messages to the class generally work well. At the conclusion of the celebration, students will present their parents with copies of a class book, *We Are Poets!* The volume should include an original poem written by each class member.

CHAPTER 10

Fantasy: Unbridled Imagination

Fantasy nurtures our sense of wonder and dares us to seek new experiences. Whether we are reading C.S. Lewis's *Prince Caspian* (1951) or Stephenie Myer's *Twilight* (2005)—books that were written more than half a century apart—we are moved to think beyond the usual and explore the boundaries of our imaginations. This genre, which features themes of internal and external quests and struggles between good and evil, truly is fantastic.

The sample Theme-Based Plan for Guided Comprehension: Fantasy: Unbridled Imagination (see Figure 26) offers an overview of the thinking and resources that support this theme. It presents a sampling of goals, state standards, assessments, texts, website resources, comprehension strategies, teaching ideas, comprehension centers, and comprehension routines. The plan begins by delineating examples of student goals and related state standards. The student goals for this theme include the following:

- Use appropriate comprehension skills and strategies
- Interpret and respond to text
- Write fantasy stories
- Communicate effectively

These goals support the following state standards:

- Learning to read independently
- Reading, analyzing, and interpreting text
- Types and quality of writing
- Speaking and listening

The assessments listed on the theme planner are examples of diagnostic, formative, and summative measures. Running records are an example of a diagnostic assessment. Formative assessments, which are informal and usually occur on a daily basis, include specific measures such as comprehension strategy applications, and general assessments such as observation and student self-assessment. Summative assessments, which are more formal long-term measures such as projects, are also featured.

The Guided Comprehension lessons are based on the following strategies and corresponding teaching ideas:

- Self-Questioning: "I Wonder" Statements
- Visualizing: Open-Mind Portraits

Figure 26. Theme-Based Plan for Guided Comprehension: Fantasy: Unbridled Imagination

Goals and Connections to State Standards   Students will

- Use appropriate comprehension strategies. Standard: learning to read independently
- Interpret and respond to text. Standard: reading, analyzing, and interpreting text
- Write fantasy stories. Standard: types and quality of writing
- Communicate effectively. Standard: speaking and listening

Assessment

The following measures can be used for a variety of purposes, including diagnostic, formative, and summative assessment:

Double-Entry Journals   Running Records
"I Wonder" Statements   Say Something
Observation   Self-Assessments
Open-Mind Portraits   Student Writing
Projects

Text	Title	Theme	Level
1.	*The Seventh Crystal*	Fantasy	4–7
2.	*Twilight*	Fantasy	YA
3.	*Prince Caspian*	Fantasy	4–7
4.	*Polar Bears Past Bedtime*	Fantasy	K–3

Website Resources

Scholastic
    www.scholastic.com/harrypotter
Scholastic Internet Field Trip: Worlds of Fantasy Online
    teacher.scholastic.com/fieldtrp/childlit/fantasy.htm
How to Teach Fantasy Writing
    www.ehow.com/how_2194806_teach-writing.html

Comprehension Strategies

Teaching Ideas
"I Wonder" Statements
Open-Mind Portraits
Double-Entry Journals
Say Something

1. Self-Questioning
2. Visualizing
3. Monitoring
4. Monitoring

Comprehension Centers

Students will apply the comprehension strategies and related teaching ideas in the following comprehension centers:

Listening Center   Technology Center
Making Books Center   Theme Center
Project Center   Writing Center
Science Center

Comprehension Routines

Students will apply the comprehension strategies and related teaching ideas in the following comprehension routines:

Literature Circles
Reciprocal Teaching
Questioning the Author

- Monitoring: Double-Entry Journals

- Monitoring: Say Something

The Seventh Crystal (Paulsen, 1996), *Twilight* (Meyer, 2005), *Prince Caspian* (Lewis, 1951), and *Polar Bears Past Bedtime* (Osborne, 1998) are the texts used in Stage One for teacher-directed whole-group instruction. Numerous additional theme-related resources, including texts, websites, performances across the curriculum, and a culminating activity, are presented in the Theme Resources at the end of the chapter.

Comprehension centers students use during Stage Two of Guided Comprehension include listening, making books, project, science, technology, theme, and writing. Students also engage in strategy application in comprehension routines such as Literature Circles, Reciprocal Teaching, and Questioning the Author. Website resources complete the overview.

In this chapter, all the lessons focus on fantasy. The lessons are appropriate for all learners, including English learners, struggling readers, and students with special needs. To accommodate these learners, the lessons include multiple modes of response (such as singing, sketching, and dramatizing) working with partners, books on CD, cross-age experiences, and extra guided instruction. Ideas we used to differentiate instruction in these lessons include the following:

- Content—the information being taught:

  - Using leveled text to accommodate students' abilities in teacher-guided small groups

  - Making leveled text available to students working in Guide Comprehension centers and routines

  - Providing leveled texts that accommodate student interest (for example, some students related to the medieval times and dragon slayers created by Gary Paulsen, some preferred the imaginary worlds created by Chris Van Allsburg, and others enjoyed David Weisner's wordless picture books and Magic Tree House titles)

- Process—the way in which the information is taught:

  - Preteaching students who may need additional support to use the strategies and skills such as sequencing and generating questions at multiple levels

  - Reading the text aloud during Stage One to make it accessible to all students

  - Using visuals to support students' construction of meaning to direct students' attention

  - Using graphic organizers and color highlighting or numbering the sections

  - Encouraging students to work with peers to provide additional support

  - Scaffolding learning in Stages One and Two

- Product—how the students demonstrate their learning:

  - Integrating alternative modes of representation, such as art, drama, poetry, or music

  - Providing opportunities for students to create projects

  - Providing opportunities for students to use computers when creating projects or contributing to class projects

Guided Comprehension Lessons

Fantasy: Unbridled Imagination
Guided Comprehension Strategy: Self-Questioning
Teaching Idea: "I Wonder" Statements

STAGE ONE: Teacher-Directed Whole-Group Instruction

Text: *The Seventh Crystal* (Paulsen, 1996)

Explain: I began by explaining self-questioning as a comprehension strategy in which we generate questions to guide our thinking while reading. Then I explained that using "I Wonder" Statements is one way to self-question. I said, "When we wonder, we question what may happen or what a character may do. Then we think about why we are questioning that may happen. For example, if a character does something, we may wonder what will happen because he took that action. When we wonder, we predict whether something will occur, provide reasons for our thinking, and then read to find out if our wondering is verified."

Demonstrate: I used a read-aloud and a Think-Aloud to demonstrate "I Wonder" Statements as I read aloud Gary Paulsen's *The Seventh Crystal*, a book in which teenage boys find themselves in a video game that was delivered mysteriously with no return address. I read aloud the title and showed students the cover of the book. I said, "The title and illustration remind me of medieval times because this character is wearing a tunic and has a sword in his hand. I think this book involves time travel, so it must be a fantasy. I wonder who the two-headed creature with the fangs and wings is because his eyes look scary." Then I asked the students if they play video games. We discussed the games they played, which included *Star Wars*, *Batman*, *Spiderman*, and *Iron Man*. Then I looked at the book cover and read the title a second time. I said, "I wonder what the seventh crystal is. I wonder if it will lead the boys back to medieval times because of what is pictured on the cover. Let's read the book to find out." I read aloud the first chapter (four pages) to the class. I said, "Chris seems to be worried that two bullies who are classmates are out to get him. I wonder if they will be waiting for him after school." When I continued reading the second chapter, I confirmed my wondering. The bullies were still waiting for Chris, but he didn't get hurt because the teacher came by when the bullies were about to jump him. Next, I read the first page of the third chapter, which was about where Chris lives and what he does when he is home. I said, "Chris lives with his grandmother. I wonder if he tells her about the boys." Then I read the next page and responded to my wondering. I said, "Chris goes right upstairs and begins to play a video game, so he doesn't tell his grandmother about the bullies." I continued through the next few pages of Chapter 3 creating "I Wonder" Statements about Chris, his neighborhood friend Jimmy, and the video games he was playing.

Guide: Through Chapters 4 and 5 of the book, I continued to read aloud, and guided students to create "I Wonder" Statements with partners and share them. We discussed the "wonders" and the students' reasoning as a whole class.

Practice: I continued to read aloud Chapters 6 and 7 of the book while students practiced creating "I Wonder" Statements on their own. By this point, the teenage friends were inside the

Guided Comprehension: Fantasy: Unbridled Imagination
Self-Questioning: "I Wonder" Statements

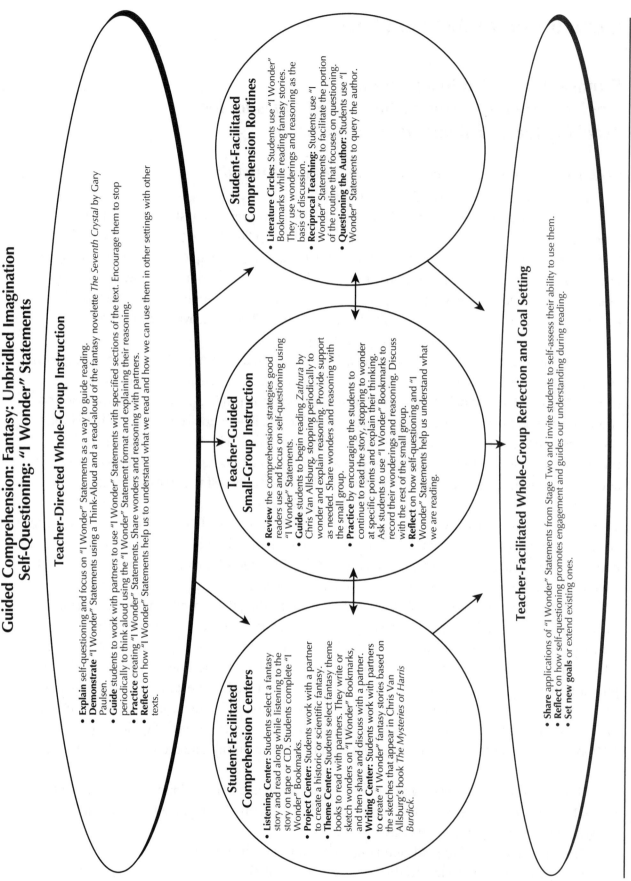

Teacher-Directed Whole-Group Instruction

- **Explain** self-questioning and focus on "I Wonder" Statements as a way to guide reading.
- **Demonstrate** "I Wonder" Statements using a Think-Aloud and a read-aloud of the fantasy novelette *The Seventh Crystal* by Gary Paulsen.
- **Guide** students to work with partners to use "I Wonder" Statements with specified sections of the text. Encourage them to stop periodically to think aloud using the "I Wonder" Statement format and explaining their reasoning.
- **Practice** creating "I Wonder" Statements. Share wonders and reasoning with partners.
- **Reflect** on how "I Wonder" Statements help us to understand what we read and how we can use them in other settings with other texts.

Student-Facilitated Comprehension Centers

- **Listening Center:** Students select a fantasy story and read along while listening to the story on tape or CD. Students complete "I Wonder" Bookmarks.
- **Project Center:** Students work with a partner to create a historic or scientific fantasy.
- **Theme Center:** Students select fantasy theme books to read with partners. They write or sketch wonders on "I Wonder" Bookmarks, and then share and discuss with a partner.
- **Writing Center:** Students work with partners to create "I Wonder" fantasy stories based on the sketches that appear in Chris Van Allsburg's book *The Mysteries of Harris Burdick*.

Teacher-Guided Small-Group Instruction

- **Review** the comprehension strategies good readers use and focus on self-questioning using "I Wonder" Statements.
- **Guide** students to begin reading *Zathura* by Chris Van Allsburg, stopping periodically to wonder and explain reasoning. Provide support as needed. Share wonders and reasoning with the small group.
- **Practice** by encouraging the students to continue to read the story, stopping to wonder at specific points and explain their thinking. Ask students to use "I Wonder" Bookmarks to record their wonderings and reasoning. Discuss with the rest of the small group.
- **Reflect** on how self-questioning and "I Wonder" Statements help us understand what we are reading.

Student-Facilitated Comprehension Routines

- **Literature Circles:** Students use "I Wonder" Bookmarks while reading fantasy stories. They use wonderings and reasoning as the basis of discussion.
- **Reciprocal Teaching:** Students use "I Wonder" Statements to facilitate the portion of the routine that focuses on questioning.
- **Questioning the Author:** Students use "I Wonder" Statements to query the author.

Teacher-Facilitated Whole-Group Reflection and Goal Setting

- **Share** applications of "I Wonder" Statements from Stage Two and invite students to self-assess their ability to use them.
- **Reflect** on how self-questioning promotes engagement and guides our understanding during reading.
- **Set new goals** or extend existing ones.

video game and had been transported back in time. I stopped periodically and students shared their wonderings and discussed their reasoning. Examples of their "I Wonder" Statements included "I wonder if the compass will help them find their way because they have been transported back in time" and "I wonder why the giant knight beheaded the fruit seller because there doesn't seem to be a reason." As we read on to verify the first statement, the students noted that the compass was indeed leading the boys up a steep hill and across the path. Then flamethrowers appeared. When I finished reading Chapter 7, we verified that the knight killed the fruit seller because Mogg, the evil leader of the place where the boys had been transported, demanded loyalty.

Reflect: We began our reflection by discussing the story to this point. The students were surprised that Chris and Jimmy were really back in medieval times just like Chris's video game. The students wondered when Chris and Jimmy would find the seventh crystal and if it would help them to get back home. We had an interesting discussion about who Mogg is and if Chris and Jimmy would also be hurt by Mogg's knights. Next, we reflected on using "I Wonder" Statements and how they keep us interested in what we are reading and how creating "I Wonder" Statements help us to understand the story. Then I explained to students that they could find out how the story ended by either reading copies of *The Seventh Crystal* that I placed at the theme center or listening to the story on tape at the listening center. By the end of the day, all the students had read or listened to the ending.

STAGE TWO: Teacher-Guided Small-Group Instruction

Text: *Zathura* (Van Allsburg, 2002) (Texts varied according to students' abilities.)

Review: I reminded students about our focus on self-questioning and briefly recalled an example of our wonderings from Stage One.

Guide: I introduced *Zathura*, a book in which two brothers, Walter and Danny, learn to appreciate each other as they find themselves playing a game that takes them on adventures through space, time, and dimension. I showed the cover and title of the book and asked the students to create oral "I Wonder" Statements. Examples of their statements included "I wonder who the boys are because I cannot tell from the cover" and "I wonder if they will have an adventure together, because it looks like maybe they will." After everyone had shared, the students began reading the first section of *Zathura*. This time they recorded their wonderings and reasoning on "I Wonder" Bookmarks. When the students had read the first section, we stopped and discussed their wonderings.

Practice: Students practiced by continuing to read and record their "I Wonder" Statements on their "I Wonder" Bookmarks (see Appendix A, page 245, for a blackline). After each segment, we discussed their wonderings and reasoning. We continued this process until the end of the story. One of Blake's "I Wonder" Bookmarks appears in Figure 27.

Reflect: We discussed the story and reflected on how fantasy took the boys into an exciting adventure. One student observed that the boys were playing together in the end and that was what the young brother really had wanted. Then we discussed how self-questioning and "I Wonder" Statements helped us understand what we read.

Student-Facilitated Comprehension Centers

Listening Center: I placed a number of fantasy books at different levels at this center. Students selected a fantasy story and read along while listening to the story on tape or CD. They stopped periodically to record their wonderings and reasoning on "I Wonder" Bookmarks.

Figure 27. Blake's "I Wonder" Bookmark

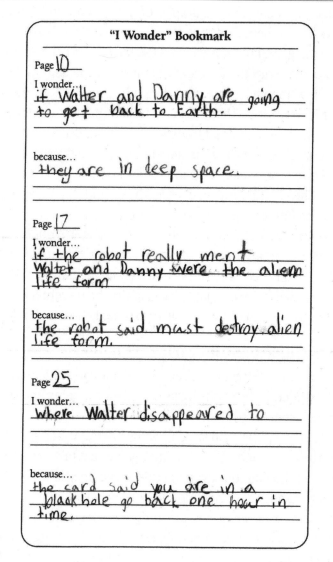

"I Wonder" Bookmark

Page 10

I wonder...
if Walter and Danny are going to get back to Earth.

because...
they are in deep space.

Page 17

I wonder...
if the robot really ment Walter and Danny were the alien life form

because...
the robot said must destroy alien life form.

Page 25

I wonder...
where Walter disappeared to

because...
the card said you are in a black hole go back one hour in time.

Project Center: Students worked with partners to create historic or scientific fantasies featuring characters they had read about in the fantasy theme. I placed a number of fantasy books at the center to engage students' thinking. First, they created an illustration that represented the history- or science-related fantasy they were creating. Then they outlined their fantasy story. Students began this project in the center and continued developing it outside of class. The students shared their illustrations and outlines in Stage Three and their projects at the conclusion of our fantasy theme.

Theme Center: I placed a number of fantasy books at a variety of levels, including wordless picture books such as David Weisner's *Tuesday* (1997), *Sector 7* (1999), and *Flotsam* (2006), at this center. Students worked in pairs to read another fantasy book. They used Patterned Partner Reading and wrote or sketched their wonders on the "I Wonder" Bookmarks. They shared and discussed their wonderings and reasoning with their partners.

Writing Center: Students worked with partners to write "I Wonder" fantasy stories based on the pictures in Chris Van Allsburg's *The Mysteries of Harris Burdick*. When they completed their stories, the students shared them with another set of partners.

Student-Facilitated Comprehension Routines

Literature Circles: The students read fantasy books on their independent levels and recorded their wonderings and reasoning on "I Wonder" Bookmarks. They used their wonders as the basis for discussion. One group read *Harry Potter and the Deathly Hallows* (Rowling, 2007). Some of their responses for Chapter 1 were as follows:

- I wonder who these two men are...because they had not been mentioned before.
- I wonder what these two men are plotting...because I think they are against Harry.
- I wonder why Snape is speaking with Voldemort...because I thought he was on Harry's side.
- I wonder why Snape is speaking with Voldemort, I hope he didn't go back to Voldemort's side...because he was once part of Voldemort's army.
- I wonder how Voldemort is going to attempt to kill Harry...because I know he won't be successful.
- I wonder why the Malfoys didn't speak up...because it seemed as if they didn't agree with Voldemort's idea to kill Harry and he didn't want them to use his wand to do it.

Reciprocal Teaching: The students used oral "I Wonder" Statements and discussed their reasoning in the portion of the routine that focuses on questioning.

Questioning the Author: Students used oral "I Wonder" Statements to query the author about the intended message. Sample queries included, "I wonder what the author is trying to tell us" and "I wonder how the author could have made that clearer."

STAGE THREE: Teacher-Facilitated Whole-Group Reflection and Goal Setting

Share: Students shared their "I Wonder" Statements and writings from Stage Two in small groups. Then we discussed their applications as a whole class.

Reflect: We reflected on how self-questioning can promote engagement and guide our reading. We also reflected on how we can use "I Wonder" Statements during reading to help us to understand text.

Set New Goals: Students felt confident with their ability to use "I Wonder" Statements to engage in self-questioning while reading fantasies, so we extended our goal to using this technique with other texts. We decided to use "I Wonder" Statements to learn about the Revolutionary War in social studies class. We also decided to learn other techniques for self-questioning, such as Question–Answer Relationships (QAR).

Assessment Options

I used observation throughout this lesson. I listened carefully to students' wonders and reasoning. I also reviewed and commented on their "I Wonder" Bookmarks, fantasy stories, project illustrations and outlines, and self-assessments.

Fantasy: Unbridled Imagination
Guided Comprehension Strategy: Visualizing
Teaching Idea: Open-Mind Portrait

STAGE ONE: Teacher-Directed Whole-Group Instruction

Text: *Twilight* (Meyer, 2005)

Explain: I began by explaining that visualizing is a reading comprehension strategy in which we create text-related pictures in our minds while we read. Then I explained that creating Open-Mind Portraits provides us with a way to use sketching to express our visualizations. Then I focused on how we could use visualizing and Open-Mind Portraits to help us understand what we are reading.

Demonstrate: I began by introducing *Twilight* by Stephenie Myer. I showed the cover and asked students to make some predictions and inferences, based on the illustration and the title. They said, "The story might be scary because it probably happens at twilight" and "Maybe it happens at school because there is an apple on the cover." We used these predictions to set a purpose for reading. Next, I read aloud the first chapter, stopping periodically to discuss the main character, Bella, and the thoughts and feelings she had when she moved to a new town and had to go to a new school. At the end of the chapter, we discussed her intrigue with the strange family at school, and in particular, the one named Edward. Then I began demonstrating how to create an Open-Mind Portrait. First, I sketched a portrait of Bella. Next, I cut it out and traced the portrait on blank sheets of paper. I thought aloud about some of the thoughts and feelings that Bella showed in the opening chapter. First, she was apprehensive about moving in with her dad and about her first day at the new school. I thought aloud about ways I could represent that feeling in the Open-Mind Portrait using simple lines and shapes. I decided I would draw some zigzag lines inside the Open-Mind Portrait to represent shaking and being afraid. Next, I thought aloud about Bella's perception of Edward's treatment of her in biology class. She was perplexed and quite hurt by his abruptness and avoidance of her. I thought aloud about how I could represent this and decided to use question marks because she didn't understand why he treated her that way and tears because she was hurt by the way he treated her. Then I sketched the question marks and tears in the Open-Mind Portrait.

Guide: As I began reading Chapter 2, I guided the students to think about Bella. Then I read the chapter aloud, stopping periodically to discuss Bella's feelings and thoughts with the students. When I finished reading, I guided the students to work with partners to add a portrait to the Open-Mind Portrait I had begun about Bella. I used questions such as, "How do you think Bella felt when...?" and "When she said..., what do you think she was thinking?" I helped students verbalize Bella's thoughts and feelings, and then guided them to decide what kind of sketch or symbol they could use to represent her feelings. I read another chapter and again guided the students to add to their Open-Mind Portraits.

Practice: Students practiced on their own as I read another chapter aloud. Then students recorded their ideas about Bella's thoughts and feelings. Students shared their sketches and discussed the reasoning for their thinking.

Reflect: We began our reflection by discussing Bella as she was represented in the sketches we had put in our Open-Mind Portraits. We discussed how this process helped us to think about the

Guided Comprehension: Fantasy: Unbridled Enthusiasm
Visualizing: Open-Mind Portraits

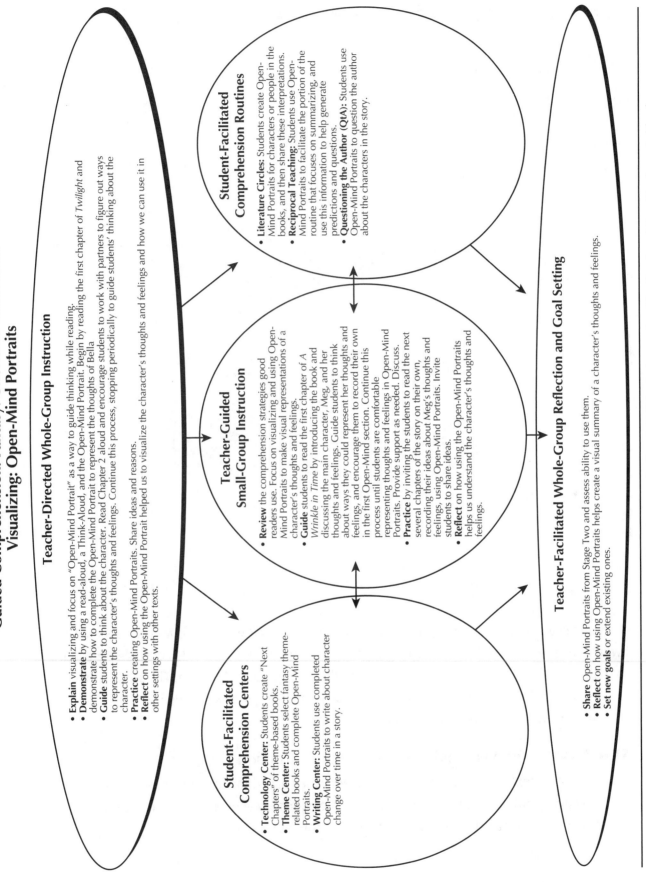

Teacher-Directed Whole-Group Instruction

- **Explain** visualizing and focus on "Open-Mind Portrait" as a way to guide thinking while reading.
- **Demonstrate** by using a read-aloud, a Think-Aloud, and the Open-Mind Portrait. Begin by reading the first chapter of *Twilight* and demonstrate how to complete the Open-Mind Portrait to represent the thoughts of Bella.
- **Guide** students to think about the character. Read Chapter 2 aloud and encourage students to work with partners to figure out ways to represent the character's thoughts and feelings. Continue this process, stopping periodically to guide students' thinking about the character.
- **Practice** creating Open-Mind Portraits. Share ideas and reasons.
- **Reflect** on how using the Open-Mind Portrait helped us to visualize the character's thoughts and feelings and how we can use it in other settings with other texts.

Student-Facilitated Comprehension Routines

- **Literature Circles:** Students create Open-Mind Portraits for characters or people in the books, and then share these interpretations.
- **Reciprocal Teaching:** Students use Open-Mind Portraits to facilitate the portion of the routine that focuses on summarizing, and use this information to help generate predictions and questions.
- **Questioning the Author (QtA):** Students use Open-Mind Portraits to question the author about the characters in the story.

Teacher-Guided Small-Group Instruction

- **Review** the comprehension strategies good readers use. Focus on visualizing and using Open-Mind Portraits to make visual representations of a character's thoughts and feelings.
- **Guide** students to read the first chapter of *A Wrinkle in Time* by introducing the book and discussing the main character, Meg, and her thoughts and feelings. Guide students to think about ways they could represent her thoughts and feelings, and encourage them to record their own in the first Open-Mind section. Continue this process until students are comfortable representing thoughts and feelings in Open-Mind Portraits. Provide support as needed. Discuss.
- **Practice** by inviting the students to read the next several chapters of the story on their own, recording their ideas about Meg's thoughts and feelings, using Open-Mind Portraits. Invite students to share ideas.
- **Reflect** on how using the Open-Mind Portraits helps us understand the character's thoughts and feelings.

Student-Facilitated Comprehension Centers

- **Technology Center:** Students create "Next Chapters" of theme-based books.
- **Theme Center:** Students select fantasy theme-related books and complete Open-Mind Portraits.
- **Writing Center:** Students use completed Open-Mind Portraits to write about character change over time in a story.

Teacher-Facilitated Whole-Group Reflection and Goal Setting

- **Share** Open-Mind Portraits from Stage Two and assess ability to use them.
- **Reflect** on how using Open-Mind Portraits helps create a visual summary of a character's thoughts and feelings.
- **Set new goals** or extend existing ones.

Figure 28. Students' Open-Mind Portraits for *Twilight*

story and characters more deeply. Then I explained that *Twilight* would be our new class read-aloud. I would read aloud a section a day until we finished the book, and we would continue contributing to the Open-Mind Portrait and discussing how Bella emerged as a character. The students were delighted. They liked *Twilight* and were highly motivated to learn how it ended. Excerpts from students' Open-Mind Portraits appear in Figure 28.

STAGE TWO: Teacher-Guided Small-Group Instruction

Text: *A Wrinkle in Time* (L'Engle, 1962) (Texts varied according to students' abilities.)

Review: I reminded students about the strategies good readers use and our focus on visualizing. Then I recalled the Open-Mind Portrait from Stage One.

Guide: I introduced *A Wrinkle in Time* by showing the cover and title of the book and asking students to make predictions or inferences. I also asked them to look at the Table of Contents and generate more predictions and inferences. I reminded students that we would be thinking about the main character, Meg, and in particular what she was thinking or feeling. Then I guided the students to read the first six pages of Chapter 1 silently. After they finished reading, we discussed how Meg felt about herself, her brothers, and her parents. I guided the students to think about ways they could represent her feelings with symbols and sketches. The students finished the chapter and we used sketches within the Open-Mind Portrait to summarize Meg's thoughts and feelings. Then I guided students to make predictions about what might happen in Chapter 2.

Practice: The students read the next chapter on their own and recorded some symbols and sketches to represent Meg's thoughts and feelings. Then we discussed their ideas. I guided the students to elaborate on their interpretations of Meg's thoughts and feelings and how they documented them in the Open-Mind Portrait. We used the portrait to summarize the chapter and make new predictions. The students and I continued reading *A Wrinkle in Time* in subsequent sessions.

Reflect: We reflected on how the Open-Mind Portrait helped us to understand what we read. The students said it helped them to understand the characters better and to remember what was happening in the story. Excerpts from students' Open-Mind Portraits appear in Figure 29.

Student-Facilitated Comprehension Centers

Technology Center: Students worked with partners to develop "Next Chapters," PowerPoint slideshows of what happened after a fantasy book they had read ended. They shared their projects with the class in Stage Three.

Theme Center: I placed a variety of fantasy books at different reading levels at this center. Students selected books and used Open-Mind Portraits to capture ideas about characters during independent reading. They shared their completed portraits in Stage Three.

Writing Center: Students used the Open-Mind Portraits to provide ideas for writing about how characters changed through the books. The sketches and symbols provided the students with specific thoughts and feelings, which they were able to use as the basis of their writing.

Student-Facilitated Comprehension Routines

Literature Circles: The students read their books and used their Guided Comprehension Journals to record the main character's thoughts and feelings using Open-Mind Portraits. They used the completed portraits as the basis for discussion.

Reciprocal Teaching: The students used the Open-Mind Portraits for the summarizing section. They were able to generate questions and predictions after sharing their portraits with others in their group.

Questioning the Author: Students read to a specific section of the text, recorded their interpretations about the character on the Open-Mind Portrait, and then used it to discuss key ideas, points for clarification, and author language.

Figure 29. Students' Open-Mind Portraits for *A Wrinkle in Time*

STAGE THREE: Teacher-Facilitated Whole-Group Reflection and Goal Setting

Share: Students shared their Open-Mind Portraits from Stage Two in small groups. Then we discussed their applications as a whole class.

Reflect: We reflected on how visualizing and inferring a character's thoughts and feelings can help us think more deeply about a character and provide good information for predictions and inferences.

Set New Goals: Students really liked Open-Mind Portraits because they liked being able to sketch the information. We decided to list page numbers and specific text information the next time, so students could revisit the text more quickly.

Assessment Options

I used observation during whole-group and small-group instruction. I was also able to review and comment on students' Open-Mind Portraits. This enabled me to informally assess students' ability to use Open-Mind Portraits and determine what I would need to do to help them understand this process better.

Fantasy: Unbridled Imagination
Guided Comprehension Strategy: Monitoring
Teaching Idea: Double-Entry Journals

STAGE ONE: Teacher-Directed Whole-Group Instruction

Text: *Prince Caspian* (Lewis, 1951)

Explain: I began by explaining that monitoring is a reading comprehension strategy that involves asking, "Does this make sense?" and clarifying by adapting strategic processes to accommodate the response. Next, I explained that Double-Entry Journals may be used in different ways, but today we would use them to help us monitor our thinking through our reactions and responses. Then I said, "When using Double-Entry Journals, we can write an idea from the text and then give our reflection or reaction or we can write a quotation—the exact words of the author— and then give our reflection or reaction."

Demonstrate: I demonstrated by using a Think-Aloud and a read-aloud of chapters from *Prince Caspian* by C.S. Lewis. In the book, the four children, Peter, Susan, Edmund, and Lucy, return to Narnia to help Caspian battle Miraz so he can be the rightful heir to the throne. We had been using this book during the times I read aloud to the class each day. We engaged in informal retelling to review the events of Chapters 8 and 9 in which the children left the island and Lucy saw Aslan. Next, we previewed Chapter 10 by discussing the title and illustrations in the chapter. Then I read the first section of Chapter 10 and thought aloud as I demonstrated how we monitor our thoughts during reading. I said, "In this section we learned about how they took a route that was not as demanding as the one through the fir woods and they were able to walk along the river. Of course, then the way became more demanding. When I read the phrase *those cliffs remained cruel*, I found myself visualizing how steep and sheer they must have been. *Cruel* is an unusual word to use to describe cliffs, but in this case it helped me to understand that they could not possibly find a way to climb them." I used the overhead and a transparency of the Double-Entry Journal blackline (see Appendix A, pages 250–251) to record my quote/idea from the text and reflection/reaction. I wrote, "those cliffs remained cruel," and on the right-hand side I reflected on how C.S. Lewis's use of language helped me to understand the it was impossible to use the cliffs.

Guide: Next, I read another section of text as the students followed along. I invited them to work with partners to choose an idea or quotation and then provide their reflection/reaction. We discussed their responses and I recorded a few examples on the Double-Entry Journal blackline overhead transparency. For example, Maria and Alex wrote something Aslan had said to Lucy when they met up while the others were sleeping. Lucy thought that Aslan, a lion, was much bigger than when she had last seen him. Aslan said, "But every year you grow, you will find me bigger." In their reaction to this quotation, the students said that they could tell that Aslan cared about Lucy because of the way he spoke to her. Both students had heard similar statements from family members and were able to make connections—Maria to her grandfather, who she only saw once a year, and Alex to a brother who had been away in military service. Other students readily related to Maria and Alex's choices and their reasoning. I continued reading aloud and the students continued to complete their Double-Entry Journals. We repeated this process with a few sections.

Practice: I continued to read aloud as students followed along. I encouraged them to practice completing entries for their Double-Entry Journals on their own. I provided support as requested.

Guided Comprehension: Fantasy: Unbridled Imagination
Monitoring: Double-Entry Journals

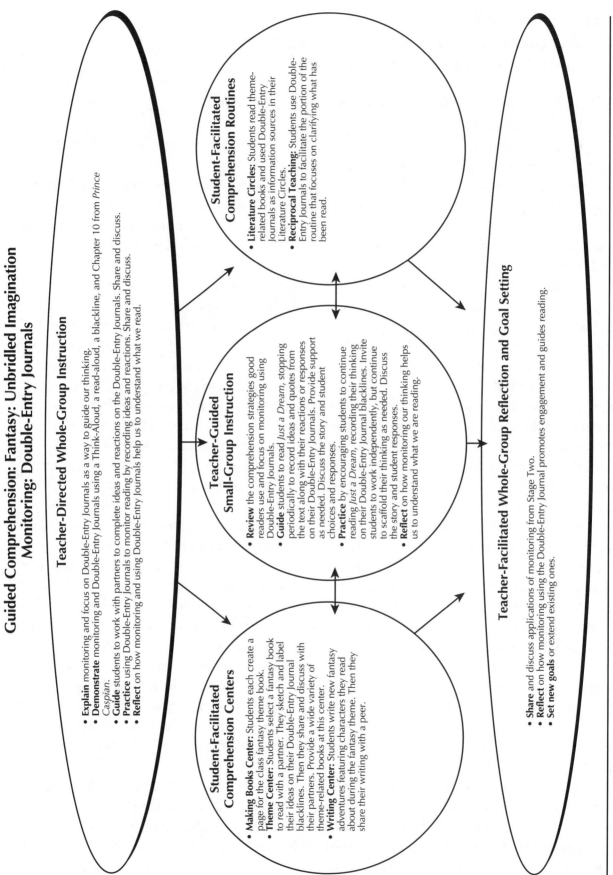

Teacher-Directed Whole-Group Instruction

- **Explain** monitoring and focus on Double-Entry Journals as a way to guide our thinking.
- **Demonstrate** monitoring and Double-Entry Journals using a Think-Aloud, a read-aloud, a blackline, and Chapter 10 from *Prince Caspian*.
- **Guide** students to work with partners to complete ideas and reactions on the Double-Entry Journals. Share and discuss.
- **Practice** using Double-Entry Journals to monitor reading by recording ideas and reactions. Share and discuss.
- **Reflect** on how monitoring and using Double-Entry Journals help us to understand what we read.

Student-Facilitated Comprehension Centers

- **Making Books Center:** Students each create a page for the class fantasy theme book.
- **Theme Center:** Students select a fantasy book to read with a partner. They sketch and label their ideas on their Double-Entry Journal blacklines. Then they share and discuss with their partners. Provide a wide variety of theme-related books at this center.
- **Writing Center:** Students write new fantasy adventures featuring characters they read about during the fantasy theme. Then they share their writing with a peer.

Teacher-Guided Small-Group Instruction

- **Review** the comprehension strategies good readers use and focus on monitoring using Double-Entry Journals.
- **Guide** students to read *Just a Dream*, stopping periodically to record ideas and quotes from the text along with their reactions or responses on their Double-Entry Journals. Provide support as needed. Discuss the story and student choices and responses.
- **Practice** by encouraging students to continue reading *Just a Dream*, recording their thinking on their Double-Entry Journal blacklines. Invite students to work independently, but continue to scaffold their thinking as needed. Discuss the story and student responses.
- **Reflect** on how monitoring our thinking helps us to understand what we are reading.

Student-Facilitated Comprehension Routines

- **Literature Circles:** Students read theme-related books and used Double-Entry Journals as information sources in their Literature Circles.
- **Reciprocal Teaching:** Students use Double-Entry Journals to facilitate the portion of the routine that focuses on clarifying what has been read.

Teacher-Facilitated Whole-Group Reflection and Goal Setting

- **Share** and discuss applications of monitoring from Stage Two.
- **Reflect** on how monitoring using the Double-Entry Journal promotes engagement and guides reading.
- **Set new goals** or extend existing ones.

Then we discussed their choices and responses. We continued this until we reached the end of the chapter.

Reflect: Following discussion, we reflected on what we knew about monitoring and how using Double-Entry Journals helped us to monitor our thoughts and make responses to the text during reading. Then the students asked that I continue to read *Prince Caspian* so they could learn how the story ends. I continued to read aloud a chapter each day.

The following are excerpts from the Double-Entry Journal we created during Stage One:

Quote/Idea From Text	Reflection/Reaction
"It was maddening, because everyone knew that once they were out of the gorge on that side, they would have only a smooth slope and a fairly short walk to Caspian's headquarters." (p. 131)	They should have listened to Lucy. I wonder why they didn't. Maybe because she's the youngest. I hope they can get there. It's taking a long time.
"…won a glorious victory…." (p. 133)	I think the boys remembering their "glorious victory" from hundreds of years ago foreshadows that they will go to battle and be victorious again.

STAGE TWO: Teacher-Guided Small-Group Instruction

Text: *Just a Dream* (Van Allsburg, 1990)

Review: I reviewed the strategies good readers use and then focused on monitoring and Double-Entry Journals. I reminded students about a few examples we had created during Stage One.

Guide: I began by doing a quick picture walk through the opening sections of *Just a Dream*, because Chris Van Allsburg's illustrations contribute greatly to the story. This is a book in which Walter and his bed are transported through time to the future, where he sees what happens because he did not take good care of the Earth. Students made predictions that included, "Walter is having a dream that will take him into the future" and "Walter is being moved to a world that is not as nice as ours, because he did not help to take care of it." Next, I guided students as they read the first section of text (pages 1–10). Then they created entries for their Double-Entry Journals. After they completed their entries, they shared their ideas. For example, Monica had written this quotation on the left side of her journal blackline: "Walter went to bed wishing he lived in the future." Then on the right side she wrote, "I think Walter is going to enter a world of the future. He hasn't been taking good care of his world." On the left side of his Double-Entry Journal, Thomas wrote, "When Walter woke up, his bed was in the middle of a garbage dump and he was about to be plowed by a bulldozer." On the right side, he wrote, "Walter wouldn't take time to sort the garbage and now he is living in the garbage dump. He should have taken the time to recycle." We repeated this process with the next section (pages 11–26).

Practice: Students practiced by continuing to read subsequent sections and creating entries for their Double-Entry Journals. We stopped periodically to discuss their ideas. For example, in the section that included pages 27–34, Ananya wrote on the left side of her Double-Entry Journal, "Walter woke up and his bed was near the Grand Canyon and a woman on a horse was telling him that no one had seen the canyon for a long time because the air pollution was too bad." On the right side she wrote, "Air pollution that is that bad is exactly what is going to happen if we don't all take care of our world. I remember that there was a lot of air pollution in China just before the Olympics. It was because they have so many cars."

Reflect: We began by reflecting on the story. Students felt the book made a powerful argument in support of caring for the environment. We talked about what we do to help the environment—from recycling to volunteering on litter pick-up crews. Students also reflected on how writing entries on their Double-Entry Journal blacklines helped them to monitor their reading and comprehend the text. Finally, we discussed how we could use Double-Entry Journals when reading other types of books.

Student-Facilitated Comprehension Centers

Making Books Center: At this center, students used computers to create pages for our class fantasy theme book. They used PowerPoint and were able to import graphics from websites I had bookmarked. Students created their pages about books they had read during the fantasy theme. We shared the book electronically during Stage Three.

Theme Center: I placed a wide variety of fantasy titles at various levels at this center. These titles included books such as *Frindle* (Clements, 1996), *Maximum Ride: The Angel Experiment* (Patterson, 2005), *The Magnificent Mummy Maker* (Woodruff, 1994), *The Summer I Shrank My Grandmother* (Woodruff, 1992), and *The Lion, the Witch and the Wardrobe* (Lewis, 2005). Students worked with partners to select and read a book. As they read, they stopped periodically to create entries on their Double-Entry Journal blacklines and discuss them. At this center, they sketched their ideas instead of writing them and then wrote their reactions. They shared and discussed their ideas with their partners.

Writing Center: Students worked with partners either to create new characters and write mini-fantasy stories or to create new fantasy stories for characters they had read about during our fantasy theme. Titles of students' stories included *Ironspiderbatman Saves the Middle School*, *Students Stuck in Narnia*, and *Midnight—The Newest Story in the Twilight Series*.

Student-Facilitated Comprehension Routines

Literature Circles: Students read their books and used Double-Entry Journal blacklines to record ideas and quotations from the text along with their reflections/reactions They used their entries as the basis of discussion.

Reciprocal Teaching: Students used their monitoring of the text through their reflections/reactions on their Double-Entry Journals to facilitate the portion of the routine that focuses on clarifying what has been read.

STAGE THREE: Teacher-Facilitated Whole-Group Reflection and Goal Setting

Share: We discussed how monitoring helps to us to clarify the information in the text. A number of students commented that using Double-Entry Journals helped them to think about and understand the story better. When asked if we had achieved our comprehension goal, they responded positively. When I asked how we knew this, they suggested we share our Double-Entry Journals. We did this in small groups and then each small group shared a few ideas with the whole class. Finally, we viewed and discussed our student-authored electronic fantasy theme book.

Everyone applauded after each author explained his or her page. We were all very proud of our book.

Reflect: Students reflected on how monitoring using the Double-Entry Journal promotes clarifying what we read and guides our understanding of the text.

Set New Goals: Students felt confident with their ability to use monitoring through the Double-Entry Journal format with narrative text, so we thought we would try it with informational text. We decided to use Double-Entry Journals to monitor our comprehension in our science unit on rocks and minerals.

Assessment Options

I used observation throughout this lesson and listened carefully to students' discussions about monitoring. I also reviewed and commented on their work from Stage Two, which included the pages they had created for our class book, as well as other work they had done in the centers and routines.

Fantasy: Unbridled Imagination
Guided Comprehension Strategy: Monitoring
Teaching Idea: Say Something

STAGE ONE: Teacher-Directed Whole-Group Instruction

Text: *Polar Bears Past Bedtime* (Osborne, 1998)

Explain: I began by explaining the importance of monitoring comprehension while reading and making sure that we can understand what we are reading. I told the students that good readers know that reading needs to make sense and that we use different strategies to ensure that we are making meaning. I explained how we would be reading the text in sections and using Say Something, in which we would choose something important in what we are reading and say it to a partner, who would also Say Something to us. I explained that our goal was to make sure we were thinking while we read.

Demonstrate: I introduced *Polar Bears Past Bedtime* by showing the cover and asking students to notice what was on it. We discussed that there were two children dressed warmly and there was also a large polar bear. The students also noticed the surprised expression on the children's faces. I encouraged them to use their knowledge of the adventures of Jack and Annie and the Magic Tree House, in addition to the clues on the cover, to make a prediction about what might happen in this story. They said "Jack and Annie are going to go to the North Pole. It looks like something is frightening them. Maybe something is trying to hurt the bear or the kids. Maybe Jack and Annie will do something to help save the polar bears." Then we looked at the Table of Contents and used the chapter titles to add to our knowledge. I asked the students to share more predictions. We used these predictions to set purposes for reading and then I read the first chapter aloud. At the end of the chapter, I explained to the students that I was going to "Say Something" to them to help me monitor my thinking and stay engaged with the story. I told them that I learned that Jack and Annie saw an owl and it led them to the tree house. When they got there, Morgan le Fay, the enchantress librarian, pulled out a scroll with a riddle for them to solve. She also handed them a book about the Arctic. From this information, and from what I know about the adventures that Jack and Annie have had in other stories, I think that the tree house is going to take them to the Arctic and they will have to solve a riddle about polar bears.

Guide: I asked the students if they had any other ideas they wanted to add. Next, I asked them to think about the next chapter with me, and get ready to Say Something after I read it to them. I read the short chapter aloud and when I was finished reading, I guided the students to Say Something to summarize the information we just heard. I used questions such as, "What have we learned about Jack and Annie? What is the riddle they need to solve? What have they noticed so far?" I asked them to Say Something to their partners. Then some of the students shared their ideas with the class. I continued this process with the next chapter.

Practice: I continued to read the next chapter. Then I asked students to stop to Say Something. I reduced the amount of guiding I did as the students became more comfortable using Say Something.

Reflect: We began our reflection by discussing how this story was similar to and different from other Magic Tree House stories. We discussed how monitoring by stopping and thinking throughout the book was helpful to us as readers and thinkers. All the students wanted to know

Guided Comprehension: Fantasy: Unbridled Imagination
Monitoring: Say Something

Teacher-Directed Whole-Group Instruction

- **Explain** monitoring and focus on Say Something as a way to guide thinking during reading.
- **Demonstrate** using Say Something by reading the first chapter of the Magic Tree House book *Polar Bears Past Bedtime* using a Think-Aloud and modeling how to monitor thinking by engaging in sharing ideas about the text, particularly new information.
- **Guide** students to monitor while reading Chapter 2 aloud. Encourage students to Say Something to a partner. Continue this process, stopping within and at the end of each chapter to guide students' thinking about the story line.
- **Practice** using Say Something as a way to monitor thinking during reading. Share ideas, specifically important points and information that is new.
- **Reflect** on how using Say Something helped to monitor thinking while reading and how students can use it with other texts.

Student-Facilitated Comprehension Routines

- **Literature Circles:** Students use Say Something as a framework for discussion. Encourage students to focus on words, connections, and summary statements.
- **Reciprocal Teaching:** Students use Say Something and focus on the four strategies: predicting, questioning, clarifying, and summarizing.
- **Questioning the Author:** Students use Say Something to question the author's intent and message.

Teacher-Guided Small-Group Instruction

- **Review** the comprehension strategies good readers use and focus on monitoring by engaging in Say Something.
- **Guide** students to read the first chapter of the Magic Tree House book *Good Morning, Gorillas* silently, use text clues, think about what happened that was important, and then Say Something to their partners. Share ideas with the group. Continue this process until students understand how to continually monitor their understanding while reading the text.
- **Practice** by asking students to read the next chapter silently. At the end of the chapter, ask students to Say Something to a partner about the important information from the chapter.
- **Reflect** on how using Say Something helps our thinking while reading.

Student-Facilitated Comprehension Centers

- **Project Theme:** Students research polar bears using QuIP and multiple sources, including books and websites.
- **Science Center:** Students choose an informational book such as *Polar Bears and the Arctic* and periodically "Say Something" to a peer who is reading the same book.
- **Theme Center:** Invite students to do Patterned Partner Reading using the Read–Pause–Say Something pattern.

Teacher-Facilitated Whole-Group Reflection and Goal Setting

- **Share** ideas and insights gained from using Say Something to monitor understanding. Assess students' ability to monitor their reading.
- **Reflect** on how monitoring and using Say Something helped students make meaning from the text
- **Set new goals** or extend existing ones.

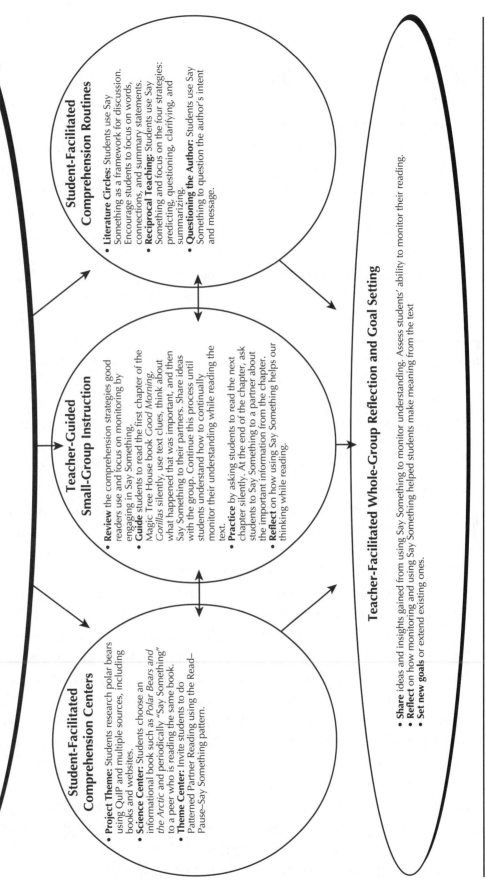

how the story ended, so I explained that I would continue to share *Polar Bears Past Bedtime* as our class read-aloud.

STAGE TWO: Teacher-Guided Small-Group Instruction

Text: *Good Morning, Gorillas* (Osborne, 2002) (Texts varied according to students' abilities.)

Review: I reviewed the strategies good readers use. Next, I reminded students about the importance of monitoring our thinking while we read, and how we used Say Something to help us monitor.

Guide: I introduced the text by showing the cover and title of the book and asking students to discuss things they saw on the cover. I also had them look at the Table of Contents and we discussed what we found there. Then I asked them to use that information to make predictions about what might happen in the story. I asked students to Say Something to a partner, and then share those ideas with the rest of the group. Next, I asked students to read the first chapter silently. After they finished reading, I asked students to think about what we learned so far. Then they engaged in Say Something with their partners. We discussed how the stories in the Magic Tree House series start in a similar way and how we could use our experiences with these texts to guide our thinking. The students then read Chapter 2 silently and repeated the process of thinking and then using Say Something to verbalize their thoughts.

Practice: Students read Chapter 3 on their own and used Say Something to share their ideas with a partner. They also shared with the group. We continued this process as we finished reading the story.

Reflect: We reflected by discussing how using Say Something helped us to understand the text. Then students suggested they could use Say Something when they were doing Patterned Partner Reading (see Appendix A, page 220) because it helped them clarify their thinking and provided a way for them to talk about the book. The pattern would be Read–Pause–Say Something.

Student-Facilitated Comprehension Centers

Project Center: Students researched the effects of global warming on polar bears using the Questions Into Paragraphs (QuIP) graphic organizer (see Appendix A, page 268). They generated three research questions and researched using books I had placed at the center and websites I had bookmarked. Books included *The Last Polar Bear: Facing the Truth of a Warming World* (Kazlowski, 2008) and *Polar Bear, Why Is Your World Melting?* (Wells, 2008). Examples of websites included World View of Global Warming (www.worldviewofglobalwarming.org), National Wildlife Federation: Polar Bears and Global Warming (www.nwf.org/polarbearsandglobalwarming/), and Polar Bears Global Warming: Effects of Global Warming (www.bearplanet.org/global-warming-polar-bears.shtml).

Science Center: Students read *Polar Bears and the Arctic* (Osborne & Boyce, 2007), the companion book to *Polar Bears Past Bedtime*, and other informational titles such as *The World of the Polar Bear* (Rosing, 2006), *Polar Bears* (Gibbons, 2002), and *Do Penguins Get Frostbite? Questions and Answers About Polar Animals* (Berger & Berger, 2000a). The students used sticky notes to record their "Say Somethings" and shared them with a partner periodically.

Theme Center: I placed a variety of fantasy books at different levels at this center. Students used Say Something as they engaged in Patterned Partner Reading of self-selected books, using the pattern Read–Pause–Say Something. They stopped periodically to Say Something.

Student-Facilitated Comprehension Routines

Literature Circles: As students read their books, they used sticky notes to record "Say Somethings" they wanted to share. They contributed their ideas to group discussion in their Literature Circle.

Reciprocal Teaching: Students used Say Something as a way to guide their discussions on the four Reciprocal Teaching strategies. They used different colored sticky notes and wrote summaries, things they wanted to clarify, questions, and predictions. They used the information they wrote to guide their discussion of each section of text.

Questioning the Author: Students read a specific section of the text, recording first what they thought was the big idea of that part of the book. They then recorded questions that would help them delve into the author's purpose and message. They used this information to Say Something to one another and guide their discussion.

STAGE THREE: Teacher-Facilitated Whole-Group Reflection and Goal Setting

Share: Students shared ideas from their reading and their work from Stage Two, first in small groups and then with the class.

Reflect: We reflected on how monitoring helps us understand what we are reading. We also discussed how Say Something helped us to monitor our understanding of the books we read.

Set New Goals: Students really liked Say Something because it got them talking. They decided it would be a good thing to use when reading science and social studies textbooks, because they could read those chapters in sections and discuss what they read. They thought Say Something might make those texts more interesting to read.

Assessment Options

I used observation during whole-group and small-group instruction. I was also able to review and comment on students' writing. This helped me to know what the students were thinking and how I could guide them in future lessons.

Theme Resources

Books

Alexander, L. (2003). *Time cat: The remarkable journeys of Jason and Gareth*. New York: Henry Holt.

Batson, W.T. (2005). *The door within* (The Door Within Trilogy, no. 1). Nashville, TN: Thomas Nelson.

Benchimol, B. (2008). *Jadyn and the magic bubble: I met Ghandi!* Manhattan Beach, CA: East West Discovery Press.

Carroll, L. (2008). *Alice's adventures in Wonderland*. New York: Puffin.

Colfer, E. (2002). *Artemis Fowl* (Artemis Fowl, book 1). New York: Hyperion.

Colfer, E. (2003). *The Arctic incident* (Artemis Fowl, book 2). New York: Hyperion.

Colfer, E. (2008). *The time paradox* (Artemis Fowl, book 6). New York: Hyperion.

Curry, J.L. (2005). *The black canary*. New York: Margaret K. McElderry.

DeMeulemeester, L. (2007). *The secret of Grim Hill*. Montreal, QC: Lobster Press.

Dubrovin, B. (2007). *Fantasy fair: Bright stories of imagination*. Masonville, CO: Storycraft.

Kane, D., & Wood, C. (2008). *Aríel's journey* (The Ice Horse Adventures series, book 1). Amherst, OH: Blue Ink Press.

Knotoff, K.E. (2007). *The Island of Rouge*. Baltimore: PublishAmerica.

L'Engle, M. (1962). *A Wrinkle in Time*. New York: Farrar, Straus and Giroux.

Lewis, C.S. (1994). The Chronicles of Narnia boxed set. New York: HarperTrophy.

Lister, R., & Baker, A. (2005). *The story of King Arthur*. Boston: Kingfisher.

Paolini, C. (2007). *Eldest* (Inheritance, book 2). New York: Knopf.

Paolini, C. (2007). *Eragon* (Inheritance, book 1). New York: Laurel Leaf.

Paolini, C. (2008). *Brisingr* (Inheritance, book 3). New York: Knopf.

Tolkien, J.R.R. (2002). The Lord of the Rings boxed set. Boston: Houghton Mifflin.

Vanderwood, J.A. (2006). *Through the rug*. Bloomington, IN: AuthorHouse.

Websites

English Online: Science Fiction and Fantasy Unit Plan
www.english.unitecnology.ac.nz/resources/units/sci_fi/home.html

Fantasy Books—Grade 3
www.edina.k12.mn.us/concord/classrooms/media/readinglists/Fantasygr3.pdf

Fantasy Books for Grades 5–8
www.oaklandlibrary.org/links/kids/Booklists/fantasy.html

Harry Potter: The Official Site
www.harrypotter.warnerbros.com

How to Teach Fantasy Writing
www.ehow.com/how_2194806_teach-fantasy-writing.html

J.K. Rowling Official Website
www.jkrowling.com

Kim's Korner for Teacher Talk: Fantasy
www.kimskorner4teachertalk.com/readingliterature/genres/fantasy/fantasy.htm

Life After Harry Potter
>www.life-after-harry-potter.com

Scholastic: Harry Potter Book Series
>www.scholastic.com/harrypotter/

Scholastic Internet Field Trip: Worlds of Fantasy Online
>teacher.scholastic.com/fieldtrp/childlit/fantasy.htm

Student Performances Across the Curriculum

Social Studies

- Research information about the setting of one of the fantasy stories and present it in travel brochure format (electronic or hard copy).

- Create an illustrated timeline for a time travel book. Include date/time and descriptions of events in chronological order.

Science

- Investigate one the concepts from a fantasy story you have read, such as time travel, aliens, or vampires. Write a critique of the science that supports or refutes the possibility that the concept you chose actually exists.

- Work with a partner to create a planet that could serve as the setting for a galactic fantasy. Describe the planet and create a physical representation. Then write a fantasy story that takes place there.

Mathematics

- Work with a partner to create a mathematical fantasy in which the characters and setting are mathematical terms and the fantasy involves geometric shapes.

Art

- Make a 3-D model or a painting of an important scene or character from a fantasy you have read. Title it and write a description of it.

- Create a transmediation of a fantasy book as a picture book. Include the story elements and complementary illustrations.

Music

- Work with a partner to write a fantasy rap based on two or more fantasies you have read by the same author.

- Work with a small group to create a Lyric Retelling based on a fantasy you have read.

Culminating Activity

Flights of Fantasy: Invite parents and community members to participate in a theme celebration titled *Flights of Fantasy.* Display students' projects, including class fantasy books, students' "Next Chapter" fantasy stories, and their stories about the characters they created during the fantasy theme. Encourage parents, community members, and students to share their favorite fantasy books and authors. Create a series of "flights of fantasy" by inviting small groups of students to share brief presentations about their favorite fantasy authors, books, and themes. Provide refreshments, and offer interactive opportunities, such as murals on which parents can write their comments about the celebration or computers through which they can send e-mail messages to the class. At the conclusion of the celebration, students will present their parents with copies of the class book *Our Favorite Fantasy Stories*, which includes an original fantasy story written by each class member.

Resources That Support Guided Comprehension

Focus: Resources that underpin the Guided Comprehension Model and facilitate its use in grades 3–8.

Comprehension Strategies, Teaching Ideas, and Blacklines: A wide variety of ideas for teaching comprehension strategies that can be used before, during, and after reading are featured in this section. Organized by comprehension strategy, the teaching ideas are presented in a step-by-step instructional format. Teaching examples and reproducible blackline masters are also included in this section. (Appendix A)

Resources for Organizing and Managing Comprehension Centers and Routines: Various reproducible blackline masters to facilitate classroom organization and management, as well as graphic organizers that support a number of center activities, are presented in this section. Student self-assessments for Guided Comprehension centers and routines are also included. (Appendix B)

101 Literature Response Prompts: An array of ideas to motivate students to respond to literature is presented. The prompts provide myriad ideas to engage students' thinking and stimulate their creativity. (Appendix C)

Informal Assessments: Informal assessments, ranging from attitude and motivation surveys to observation guides, are featured. (Appendix D)

Leveled Book Resources: Sources of leveled texts, including websites and publishers' materials, are presented in this section. (Appendix E)

Guided Comprehension Lesson Planning Forms: Guided Comprehension planning forms for themes and lessons are presented. (Appendix F)

Teaching Ideas
and Blackline Masters

TEACHING IDEAS AT A GLANCE

Teaching Idea	When to Use	Comprehension Strategy	Text
Previewing			
Anticipation/Reaction Guide	Before After	Previewing Monitoring	Narrative Informational
Predict-o-Gram	Before After	Previewing Summarizing	Narrative
Prereading Plan (PreP)	Before After	Previewing Making Connections	Informational
Probable Passages	Before	Previewing Making Connections	Narrative
Questioning the Text	Before During	Previewing Making Connections Summarizing	Narrative Informational
Semantic Map	Before After	Previewing Knowing How Words Work Summarizing	Narrative Informational
Story Impressions	Before	Previewing Making Connections	Narrative
Text Introductions	Before	Previewing Knowing How Words Work Making Connections	Narrative Informational
Self-Questioning			
"I Wonder" Statements	Before During After	Self-Questioning Previewing Making Connections	Narrative Informational
K–W–L and K–W–L–S	Before During After	Self-Questioning Previewing Making Connections	Informational
Paired Questioning	During After	Self-Questioning Making Connections Monitoring	Narrative Informational
Question–Answer Relationships (QAR)	During After	Self-Questioning Making Connections Monitoring	Narrative Informational
Thick and Thin Questions	Before During After	Self-Questioning Making Connections	Narrative Informational
Making Connections			
Coding the Text	During	Making Connections	Narrative Informational
Connection Stems	After	Making Connections	Narrative Informational
Double-Entry Journal	Before During After	Making Connections Monitoring Summarizing	Narrative Informational
Drawing Connections	During After	Making Connections Visualizing	Narrative Informational
Save the Last Word for Me	After	Making Connections Evaluating	Narrative Informational

(continued)

TEACHING IDEAS AT A GLANCE (continued)

Teaching Idea	When to Use	Comprehension Strategy	Text
Visualizing			
Gallery Images	After	Visualizing Making Connections	Informational
Graphic Organizers/ Visual Organizers	Before During After	Visualizing Making Connections Summarizing	Narrative Informational
Guided Imagery	Before After	Visualizing Making Connections	Narrative Informational
Open-Mind Portrait	After	Visualizing Making Connections	Narrative Informational
Photographs of the Mind	During	Visualizing Monitoring	Narrative Informational
Sketch to Stretch	After	Visualizing Making Connections	Narrative Informational
Knowing How Words Work			
Concept of Definition Map	Before After	Knowing How Words Work	Narrative Informational
Context Clues	During	Knowing How Words Work	Narrative Informational
Decoding by Analogy	During	Knowing How Words Work	Narrative Informational
List–Group–Label	Before After	Knowing How Words Work Previewing Making Connections	Informational
Possible Sentences	Before After	Knowing How Words Work Previewing Monitoring Summarizing	Informational
RIVET	Before	Knowing How Words Work Previewing	Informational
Semantic Feature Analysis	Before After	Knowing How Words Work Making Connections	Narrative Informational
Vocabulary by Analogy	During	Knowing How Words Work	Narrative Informational
Vocabulary Self-Collection Strategy	After	Knowing How Words Work Making Connections	Narrative Informational
Monitoring			
Bookmark Technique	During After	Monitoring Knowing How Words Work Making Connections Evaluating	Narrative Informational
INSERT	During	Monitoring Making Connections	Informational
Patterned Partner Reading	During	Monitoring Making Connections Evaluating	Narrative Informational
Say Something	During	Monitoring Making Connections	Narrative Informational
Think-Alouds	Before During After	All	Narrative Informational

(continued)

TEACHING IDEAS AT A GLANCE (continued)

Teaching Idea	When to Use	Comprehension Strategy	Text
Summarizing			
Bio-Pyramid	After	Summarizing Making Connections Monitoring	Informational
Lyric Retelling	After	Summarizing	Narrative Informational
Narrative Pyramid	After	Summarizing Making Connections Monitoring	Narrative
Paired Summarizing	After	Summarizing Making Connections Monitoring	Narrative Informational
QuIP (Questions Into Paragraphs)	Before During After	Summarizing Self-Questioning	Informational
Retelling	After	Summarizing	Narrative
Summary Cubes	Before During After	Summarizing	Narrative Informational
Evaluating			
Contrast Chart	After	Evaluating	Narrative Informational
Discussion Web	After	Evaluating Making Connections	Narrative Informational
Evaluative Questioning	During After	Evaluating Self-Questioning	Narrative Informational
Journal Responses	During After	Evaluating Making Connections Summarizing	Narrative Informational
Meeting of the Minds	After	Evaluating	Narrative Informational
Mind and Alternative Mind Portrats	During After	Evaluating	Narrative Informational
Persuasive Writing	Before During After	Evaluating	Narrative Informational
Comprehension Routines			
Directed Reading–Thinking Activity/Directed Reading–Listening Activity	Before During After	Previewing Making Connections Monitoring	Narrative Informational
Literature Circles	After	Making Connections Knowing How Words Work Monitoring Summarizing Evaluating	Narrative Informational
Questioning the Author (QtA)	During	Making Connections Self-Questioning Monitoring	Narrative Informational
Reciprocal Teaching	Before During After	Previewing Self-Questioning Monitoring Summarizing	Narrative Informational

TEACHING IDEAS

Anticipation/Reaction Guide

Purposes: To set purposes for reading texts; to activate prior knowledge and help make connections with the text.

Comprehension Strategies: Previewing, Monitoring

Text: Narrative, Informational   **Use:** Before and After Reading

Procedure: (Begin by explaining and demonstrating Anticipation/Reaction Guides.)

1. Select a text for the students to read.

2. Create three to five general statements for the students to respond to with "agree" or "disagree." Create statements that are intuitively sound but may be disconfirmed by reading the text, or that appear intuitively incorrect but may be proven true by reading the text.

3. Ask students to read the statements and indicate agreement or disagreement by placing a check in the appropriate column.

4. Introduce the text to the students.

5. Ask students to read the text to confirm or disconfirm their original responses.

6. After reading, encourage students to revisit their predictions and modify, if necessary.

Example: (*Martin's Big Words: The Life of Dr. Martin Luther King, Jr.* [2001] by Doreen Rappaport)

Agree   Disagree

_____   _____   1. Martin Luther King, Jr. became a minister.

_____   _____   2. Martin Luther King, Jr. was inspired by the teachings of Mahatma Gandhi.

_____   _____   3. Martin Luther King, Jr. participated in the Montgomery bus boycott.

_____   _____   4. Martin Luther King, Jr. believed in peaceful protest not violence.

Source: Readence, J.E., Bean, T.W., & Baldwin, R. (2000). *Content area reading: An integrated approach* (7th ed.). Dubuque, IA: Kendall/Hunt.

Predict-o-Gram

(See blackline, page 241.)

Purposes: To make predictions about a story using narrative elements; to introduce vocabulary.

Comprehension Strategies: Previewing, Summarizing

Text: Narrative   **Use:** Before and After Reading (revisit)

Procedure: (Begin by explaining and demonstrating Predict-o-Grams.)

1. Select vocabulary from the story to stimulate predictions. Vocabulary should represent the story elements: characters, setting, problem, action, solution.

2. Ask students to work with partners to decide which story element the word tells about and write each word on the Predict-o-Gram in the appropriate place.

3. Introduce the story and invite students to read it.

4. Revisit the original predictions with students and make changes as necessary. Use the resulting information to summarize or retell the story.

Example: (*Safe at Home* [2006] by Sharon Robinson)

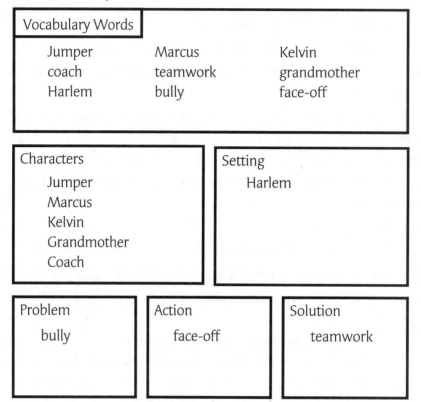

Vocabulary Words

Jumper	Marcus	Kelvin
coach	teamwork	grandmother
Harlem	bully	face-off

Characters
- Jumper
- Marcus
- Kelvin
- Grandmother
- Coach

Setting
- Harlem

Problem
- bully

Action
- face-off

Solution
- teamwork

Source: Blachowicz, C.L. (1986). Making connections: Alternatives to the vocabulary notebook. *Journal of Reading, 29*, 643–649.

Prereading Plan (PreP)

Purposes: To activate prior knowledge about a topic; to introduce new vocabulary and make connections.

Comprehension Strategies: Previewing, Making Connections

Text: Informational   **Use:** Before and After Reading

Procedure: (Begin by explaining and demonstrating PreP.)

1. Provide students with a cue word or idea to stimulate thinking about the topic.

2. Ask students to brainstorm words or concepts related to the topic. Write all ideas.

3. After all the words and ideas are listed, go back to each word and ask the contributor why she suggested that word. Clarify ideas or elaborate on concepts.

4. Read the text.

5. After reading, revisit the original list of words and revise as necessary.

TEACHING IDEAS

Example: (*Volcanoes* [1988] by Seymour Simon)

Cue Word: *Volcanoes*

- *Lava* (Lava flows out of a volcano when it erupts.)
- *Tectonic plates* (Tectonic plates collide into each other and pull apart.)
- *Volcanologists* (Volcanologists can tell the types of eruptions that have occurred.)

Source: Langer, J. (1981). From theory to practice: A prereading plan. *Journal of Reading, 25*, 152–156.

Probable Passages

(See blackline, page 242.)

Purposes: To make predictions using story elements; to introduce vocabulary; to use story vocabulary to make connections with story structure.

Comprehension Strategies: Previewing, Making Connections

Text: Narrative   **Use:** Before Reading

Procedure: (Begin by explaining and demonstrating Probable Passages.)

1. Introduce key vocabulary from the story to students. (Choose vocabulary that represents the elements of the story: characters, setting, problem, attempts to resolve, and resolution.)

2. Invite students to use the key vocabulary to create probable sentences to predict each element in the story. (Providing a story frame/story map facilitates this process.)

3. Encourage students to use their probable sentences to create a story and share it with the class.

4. Introduce the story and read it.

5. Compare and contrast Probable Passages with the story. Confirm or modify original predictions.

Example: (*Cinderella Penguin: Or, the Little Glass Flipper* [1992] by Janet Perlman)

Key Vocabulary: *penguins, invitation, palace, glass flipper, fit*

Story Map: Use the words to create a probable sentence to predict each story element.

Setting:	The story will take place in a palace.
Characters:	The penguins will be the characters in this story.
Problem:	The penguins will receive an invitation to a ball, but Cinderella Penguin will not be able to go.
Attempts to resolve the problem:	The penguin fairy godmother will provide clothes and transportation for Cinderella Penguin.
Solution:	Cinderella Penguin will marry the penguin prince and live happily ever after.

TEACHING IDEAS

Probable Passage:

> This is a story about a penguin named Cinderella who wants to go the ball at the palace. The penguin Fairy Godmother comes to Cinderella's rescue and she is able to go to the ball. She loses her glass flipper at the ball when she leaves at midnight, but the Prince finds it and learns that it fits Cinderella. They live happily ever after.

Source: Adapted from Wood, K. (1984). Probable passages: A writing strategy. *The Reading Teacher, 37,* 496–499.

Questioning the Text

(See blackline, page 243.)

Purposes: To use knowledge of text structures and text supports to facilitate comprehension; to make connections and summarize information.

Comprehension Strategies: Previewing, Making Connections, Summarizing

Text: Narrative, Informational   **Use:** Before and During Reading

Procedure: (Begin by explaining and demonstrating Questioning the Text.)

1. Think aloud by asking some or all the following questions before reading the text:

   - What is the text structure? Narrative? Informational? What clues help me know this?
   - What questions will this text answer?
   - What questions do I have for this text?
   - What clues does the front cover (title, cover art, author) offer? The contents page?
   - What do the physical aspects (size, length, print size) of the book tell me?
   - Is the author familiar? What do I know about the author? What connections can I make?
   - Is the topic familiar? What do I know about the topic? What connections can I make?
   - What clues do the genre and writing style provide for me?
   - Is there a summary? What does it help me know?
   - What does the information on the back cover tell me?

2. Provide small groups of students with a text and the questions. Guide students to question the text.

3. Discuss the information students compile.

4. Summarize the information. Have students add to this information during reading.

Note: Encourage students to question the text before and during reading to enhance their comprehension.

Example: (*Fields of Fury: The American Civil War* [2002] by James M. McPherson)

Think aloud:

- <u>What is the text structure?</u> Informational

- <u>What clues help me know this?</u> The title says it is about the American Civil War. On the inside cover there is a timeline of actual events from the Civil War.

TEACHING IDEAS

- <u>What questions will this text answer?</u>

  When did the Civil War begin?
  How did the Civil War begin, and what were the causes of it?
  Who fought in the Civil War?
  What were the most historically influential battles?
  Who lead the troops for the Confederates? Union?
  How did the Civil War end?

- <u>What questions do I have for this text?</u>

  Were women allowed to fight in the Civil War?
  If not, what roles did women play?

- <u>What clues does the front cover offer?</u>

  The book is about the Civil War.
  The book has a color picture of people in uniform fighting with swords and on horses.
  The time is not recent because the soldiers are wearing old uniforms and people do not fight on horses anymore.

- <u>What clues does the content page offer?</u> The content page has a list of the topics that are covered in the book. There are no chapters but there are separate sections for different topics.

- <u>What do the physical aspects of the book tell me?</u> This is not a chapter book because it is only 86 pages long and the book's shape is large. There are pictures on all the pages, and the text is written in a larger font.

- <u>Is the author familiar?</u> No. What do I know about the author? The author has also written another book about a war and is a Pulitzer Prize–winning author. He is a Civil War expert according to the back panel. What connections can I make? This book will probably be well written if he won an award for his other book that is similar to this one. He also seems to be well-informed about the topic.

- <u>Is the topic familiar?</u> Yes. What do I know about the topic? I learned about the Civil War in my History class. What connections can I make? The book will probably repeat some information that I have already learned about the Civil War, but I am hoping there will also be new information.

- <u>What clues do the genre and writing style provide for me?</u> This is an informational text. It is a picture book, so illustrations support what the author has to say.

- <u>Is there a summary?</u> What does it help me to know? There is a timeline that provides a good overview of important events in the Civil War.

- <u>What does the information on the back cover tell me?</u> There are quotes about other books about the Civil War that the author has written.

Source: McLaughlin, M., & Allen, M.B. (2002). *Guided Comprehension: A teaching model for grades 3–8*. Newark, DE: International Reading Association.

TEACHING IDEAS

Semantic Map

Purposes: To activate and organize knowledge about a specific topic.

Comprehension Strategies: Previewing, Knowing How Words Work, Summarizing

Text: Narrative, Informational   **Use:** Before and After Reading

Procedure: (Begin by explaining and demonstrating Semantic Maps.)

1. Select a focus word that relates to the main idea or topic of a text; write it on a chart, overhead, or chalkboard; and draw an oval around it.

2. Ask students what comes to mind when they think of the focus word. Write students' responses.

3. Invite students to review the list of responses and suggest subtopics that emerge.

4. Add the subtopics to the Semantic Map, draw ovals around them, and use lines to connect them to the focus word.

5. Visit each subtopic and ask students which of their original responses support each subtopic. Record these ideas beneath each subtopic.

6. Read the text and revise the Semantic Map to reflect new knowledge.

Example: (*Fight for Freedom: The American Revolutionary War* [2004] by Benson Bobrick)

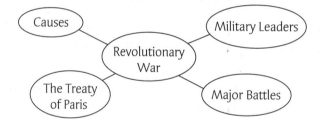

Source: Johnson, D.D., & Pearson, P.D. (1984). *Teaching reading vocabulary* (2nd ed.). New York: Holt, Rinehart and Winston.

Story Impressions

(See blackline, page 244.)

Purposes: To provide a framework for narrative writing; to encourage predictions about the story; to make connections between story vocabulary and story structure.

Comprehension Strategies: Previewing, Making Connections

Text: Narrative   **Use:** Before Reading

Procedure: (Begin by explaining and demonstrating Story Impressions.)

1. Provide students with a list of words that provide clues about the story. Choose words that relate to the narrative elements—characters, setting, problem, attempts to resolve, and resolution. Clues may be up to 5 words long. The maximum number of clues is 10.

2. List the clues in the order in which they appear in the story. Connect them with downward arrows. Share the list of sequential clues with the students.

TEACHING IDEAS

3. Ask students to work in small groups to use the sequential clues to write Story Impressions.

4. Invite small groups to share their Story Impressions with the class and discuss them.

5. Read the original story to the class and ask students to compare and contrast their Story Impressions with the original story.

Example: (*Meteor!* [1987] by Patricia Polacco)

Clues:

falling star

↓

grandparents

↓

grandchildren

↓

house shaking

↓

crash

↓

telephone calls

↓

relatives and townspeople spread news

↓

celebration

↓

magical

Story Impression: My brother and I were staying at our grandparents' farmhouse when the house started shaking. We heard a crash and we all ran outside to see what had happened. Our grandparents said a star had fallen from the sky. When it landed on the farm, it created a big crater. Our grandparents started calling relative and friends to tell them what had happened. The people they called told other people and soon there were a lot of visitors at the farm. We had a big celebration and everyone said it was a magical night.

Adaptations: Create Bio-Impressions or Text Impressions using informational text. Create Poem Impressions using story poems.

Source: McGinley, W., & Denner, P. (1987). Story impressions: A prereading/prewriting activity. *Journal of Reading, 31*, 248–253.

Text Introductions

Purposes: To introduce story, characters, vocabulary, and style of a book prior to reading; to promote prediction and anticipation of a story; to make new texts accessible to readers.

Comprehension Strategies: Previewing, Knowing How Words Work, Making Connections

TEACHING IDEAS

Text: Narrative, Informational   **Use:** Before Reading

Procedure: (Begin by explaining and demonstrating Text Introductions.)

1. Preview the text and prepare the introduction. Focus on points that will help make the text accessible to students. These may include text structure, specific vocabulary, language patterns, etc.

2. Introduce the topic, title, and characters.

3. Ask students what connections they can make to the cover and text illustrations.

4. Do a Picture Walk and invite students to make connections and predictions. Introduce the plot up to a point, but do not give away the ending.

5. Introduce a few vocabulary words students will not be able to determine from context. Also introduce sentence structures or repetitive sentence patterns that will be helpful to the readers.

6. Invite students to read the text. Then engage in discussion and other activities.

Example: (*Superdog: The Heart of a Hero* [2004] by Caralyn Buehner)

- <u>Introduce the text:</u> This story is about a dog named Dexter who is so small that other animals don't want to play with him. Dexter the dog has big dreams though. He has always dreamed of becoming a superhero.

- <u>Ask students to make connections:</u> Have you ever wanted to be a superhero? Have you ever had a special dream about accomplishing your goals?

- <u>Do a Picture Walk and invite students to make connections and predictions:</u> At the beginning of the story we learn that Dexter is a dog who is small in stature and, as the book says, looks "like a plump sausage sitting on four little meatballs." Dexter was so small that other dogs forgot to invite him to play. Cleevis the tomcat liked to stand over Dexter just to show how small Dexter really was. Dexter knew he was small but he had big dreams. Every night Dexter would dream about becoming a hero. (*Making connections with your students: What kind of dreams do you have?*) Dexter decided that he wanted to stop dreaming to be a hero. Dexter started training and exercising every day because he knew that a hero needed to have big, strong muscles. (*Making connections with your students: Dexter knew how he could accomplish his dreams. How do you think you could start achieving yours?*) Training to become a superhero was exhausting, but Dexter never gave up. He was determined to become a hero. Then the day came that Dexter got his superhero costume in the mail and he was ready to be a superhero. (*Making connections with your students: How does it feel when you set a goal for yourself and then you accomplish that goal?*)

- <u>Introduce a few vocabulary words to students:</u> While we are reading, we want to make sure that we understand the important words, so we're going to focus on just two words: *fatigue* and *desperate.*

    When the author tells us that Dex is in serious training to become a superhero, we learn that he continues to train even though it is very difficult. Then we read a sentence that states, "The mighty Dex pressed on, through wind and rain and storm and fatigue" (p. 6). We know that Dex was outside and the weather was not good, but he continued on through the wind, rain, storm, and fatigue. We know that *wind*, *rain*, and *storm* are weather words. We know that it is harder to continue training when the weather is bad, so what do you think *fatigue* means? If you were outside during bad weather, and you continued to train, how do you think you would feel? Yes, *fatigue* means "tiredness" or "exhaustion." Dex was tired from all the training and especially from doing it in bad weather. So Dex continued on even though the weather was bad and he was very tired.

Another sentence states, "It was clearly a desperate situation" (p. 18). We know from the illustrations that Cleevis was stuck in a tree. The author describes that as "a desperate situation." What do you think that means? Yes, the situation seemed hopeless. They knew the situation was not good and that Cleevis could be injured or killed.

- Now it is time for each of us to read the story. Let's remember to make connections as we read. We'll discuss *Superdog* when we finish.

Source: Adapted from Clay, M.M. (1991). Introducing a new storybook to young readers. *The Reading Teacher*, 45, 264–273.

"I Wonder" Statements

Purposes: To encourage self-questioning; to provide a model for active thinking during the reading process.

Comprehension Strategies: Self-Questioning, Previewing, Making Connections

Text: Narrative, Informational   **Use:** Before, During, and After Reading

Procedure: (Begin by explaining and demonstrating "I Wonder" Statements.)

1. Model for students how to wonder. Do this orally and in writing, beginning your thoughts with "I wonder…." Wonder about life experiences or the world, as well as events in stories or facts presented in texts.

2. Guide students to wonder about the world, their lives, story events, and ideas presented in texts.

3. Provide students with a format for sharing their wonderings orally or in writing, including "I Wonder" Bookmarks.

4. Share wonders and discuss them with text support, if possible.

5. Encourage students to wonder throughout the reading of a story or content area text. Use students' "I Wonder" Statements to provide structure for further reading or research.

Example: (*Papa's Mark* [2003] by Gwendolyn Battle-Lavert)

Before Reading:
- I wonder who Papa is.
- I wonder what mark he needs to make.
- I wonder what the mark is for.

During Reading:
- I wonder why Papa signed the paper with an X.
- I wonder why Papa won't let his son teach him to write his name at first.
- I wonder why the men of color were afraid to vote.

TEACHING IDEAS

After Reading:
- I wonder why women of color were not allowed to vote when the men were.
- I wonder what kinds of problems they faced when they first attempted to vote.
- I wonder who Papa voted for and why.

Alternative Format: "I Wonder" Bookmarks (See blackline, page 245.)

Source: Harvey, S., & Goudvis, A. (2000). *Strategies that work: Teaching comprehension to enhance understanding.* York, ME: Stenhouse.

Know–Want to Know–Learn (K–W–L)

(See blacklines, pages 246–247.)

Purposes: To activate students' prior knowledge about a topic; to set purposes for reading; to confirm, revise, or expand original understandings related to a topic.

Comprehension Strategies: Self-Questioning, Previewing, Making Connections

Text: Informational   **Use:** Before, During, and After Reading

Procedure: (Begin by explaining and demonstrating K–W–L.)

1. Ask students to brainstorm everything they know, or think they know, about a specific topic. Write, or ask students to write, these ideas in the *K* column.

2. Next, invite students to write or tell some things they want to know about the topic. List these in the *W* column.

3. Encourage students to read the text. (As they read, they can jot down new ideas, facts, or concepts they learn in the *L* column.)

4. List or have students list what they learned in the *L* column.

5. Revisit the *K* column to modify or confirm original understandings.

6. Revisit the *W* column to check if all questions have been answered.

7. Discuss the completed K–W–L. Use it to summarize the topic.

Example: (*A Dinosaur Named Sue: The Story of the Colossal Fossil* [2000] by Pat Relf)

Topic: Tyrannosaurus Rex Dinosaurs

K (What I know or think I know)	W (What I want to know)	L (What I learned)
carnivores extinct	How big were they?	They were 40 feet long or the size of a school bus.
	What kind of teeth did they have? How did they use their teeth?	They had huge, jagged teeth that showed they were meat-eaters
	How long did dinosaurs live on Earth?	They lived on Earth about 65 million years.

Source: Ogle, D. (1986). K-W-L: A teaching model that develops active reading of expository text. *The Reading Teacher, 39,* 564–570.

TEACHING IDEAS

Adaptation: Know–Want to Know–Learned–Still Want to Know (K–W–L–S)

Extend K–W–L by inviting students to list what they <u>still</u> want to know in a fourth column. Develop a plan to help them find answers to these questions.

Source: Sippola, A.E. (1995). K-W-L-S. *The Reading Teacher, 48,* 542–543.

Paired Questioning

Purpose: To engage in questioning and active decision making during the reading of a narrative or informational text.

Comprehension Strategies: Self-Questioning, Making Connections, Monitoring

Text: Narrative, Informational   **Use:** During and After Reading

Procedure: (Begin by explaining and demonstrating Paired Questioning.)

1. Introduce a text and encourage students to read the title or subtitle of a manageable section, put the reading material aside, and ask a question related to the title or subtitle. Each partner provides a reasonable answer to the question.

2. Encourage students to silently read a predetermined (by teacher or students) section of text and take turns asking a question about the reading. If needed, they can use the text when asking or responding to the question. Students reverse roles and continue reading and asking questions until the text is finished.

3. After the text is read, invite each partner to explain what he or she believes to be the important and unimportant ideas in the text. Encourage the students to share their reasoning. Then the partner agrees or disagrees with the choices and offers support for his or her thinking.

Example: (*Growing Up in Coal Country* [1996] by Susan Campbell Bartoletti)

pp. 10–13

After Reading the Chapter Title "The Breaker Boys":

    Student 1: Who were the breaker boys?
    Student 2: The book title talked about coal, so maybe the breaker boys broke up coal in the mines.
    Student 1: Why were there kids working in the mines?
    Student 2: They could fit into small places.

After Reading a Section:

    Student 1: What was a coal breaker?
    Student 2: It was a tall structure where coal was broken and sorted.
    Student 1: How old did kids have to be to work in coal mines?
    Student 2: Kids were supposed to be 12, but people got around the laws and kids as young as 5 worked.

Source: Vaughn, J., & Estes, T. (1986). *Reading and reasoning beyond the primary grades.* Boston: Allyn & Bacon.

TEACHING IDEAS

Question–Answer Relationships (QAR)

(See blackline, page 248.)

Purposes: To promote self-questioning; to answer comprehension questions by focusing on the information source needed to answer the question.

Comprehension Strategies: Self-Questioning, Making Connections, Monitoring

Text: Narrative, Informational   **Use:** During and After Reading

Procedure: (Begin by explaining and demonstrating QAR.)

1. Introduce the QAR concept and terminology. Explain that there are two kinds of information:

   In the Book—The answer is found in the text.

   In My Head—The answer requires input from the student's understandings and background knowledge.

   Explain that there are two kinds of QARs for each kind of information:

   In the Book:

   Right There—The answer is stated in the passage.

   Think and Search—The answer is derived from more than one sentence or paragraph but is stated in the text.

   In My Head:

   On My Own—The answer is contingent on information the reader already possesses in his or her background knowledge.

   Author and Me—The answer is inferred in the text, but the reader must make the connections with his or her own prior knowledge.

2. Use a Think-Aloud to practice using QAR with a text. Model choosing the appropriate QAR, giving the answer from the source, and writing or telling the answer.

3. Introduce a short passage and related questions. Have groups or individuals work through the passages and the questions. Students answer the questions and tell the QAR strategy they used. Any justifiable answer should be accepted.

4. Practice QAR with additional texts.

Principles of Teaching QAR: Give immediate feedback; progress from shorter to longer texts; guide students from group to independent activities; provide transitions from easier to more difficult tasks.

Example: (*Americans Who Tell the Truth* [2005] by Robert Shetterly)

In the Book:

Right there—In which speech did Lincoln say America is a country "of the people, by the people, for the people"? The Gettysburg Address

Think and Search—What does it mean to stand up for the promise of America? It means we shape history and we must have the hope and courage to get involved.

TEACHING IDEAS

In My Head:

On My Own—Martin Luther King Jr. said, "Non-violence is a powerful and just weapon which cuts without wounding and ennobles the man who wields it." Can you think of an example where this is true? During the Montgomery Bus Boycott black people peacefully made a statement without resorting to violence.

Author and Me—What does Eleanor Roosevelt mean when she says, "No one can make you feel inferior without your consent"? She means that you should not let others dictate who you are. People can be cruel and someone may tell you that you are not good enough, but it is ultimately your decision to decide whether you are.

Source: Raphael, T. (1986). Teaching children Question–Answer Relationships, revisited. *The Reading Teacher, 39*, 516–522.

Thick and Thin Questions

(See blackline, page 249.)

Purposes: To create questions pertaining to a text; to help students discern the depth of the questions they ask and are asked; to use questions to facilitate understanding a text.

Comprehension Strategies: Self-Questioning, Making Connections

Text: Narrative, Informational   **Use:** Before, During, and After Reading

Procedure: (Begin by explaining and demonstrating Thick and Thin Questions.)

1. Teach the students the difference between thick questions and thin questions. Thick questions deal with the big picture and large concepts. Answers to thick questions are involved, complex, and open-ended. Thin questions deal with specific content or words. Answers to thin questions are short (often 1, 2, or 3 words) and close-ended. Thick questions usually require higher order thinking; thin questions require literal responses.

2. Guide students to work with partners to create Thick and Thin Questions. Read a portion of text and prompt students with stems such as "Why..." or "What if..." for thick questions and "How far..." and "When..." for thin questions.

3. Encourage students to create Thick and Thin Questions for the texts they are reading. They can use the blackline master, write the questions in their Guided Comprehension Journals, or write their thick questions on larger sticky notes and their thin questions on smaller sticky notes.

4. Share questions and answers in small and large groups.

Example: (*Elephants* [2002] by M. Cole)

Thick: Why do elephants coat their skin with mud? It protects them from sunburn, cuts, and insect bites.

Thin: When do male calves leave their family group? They leave their families at about age 13.

Source: Lewin, L. (1998). *Great performances: Creating classroom-based assessment tasks.* Alexandria, VA: Association for Supervision and Curriculum Development.

TEACHING IDEAS

Coding the Text

Purposes: To make connections while reading; to actively engage in reading.

Comprehension Strategy: Making Connections

Text: Narrative, Informational   **Use:** During Reading

Procedure: (Begin by explaining and demonstrating Coding the Text.)

1. Explain that we can make three different kinds of connections: text–self, text–text, and text–world.

2. Think aloud as you model examples of each type of connection.

3. Read aloud while demonstrating how to code a section of text that elicits a connection. Use a sticky note, a code (T–S = text–self, T–T = text–text, T–W = text–world), and a few words to describe the connection.

4. Invite students to work with partners, read additional sections, and code the text. Ask them to share their connections with the class.

5. Encourage students to code the text using sticky notes to record their ideas.

Example: (*The City of Ember* [2003] by Jeanne DuPrau)

<u>Text–Self:</u> This text reminds me not to take things for granted.
<u>Text–Text:</u> This story reminds me of *The Giver* by Lois Lowry. In both stories, the new generations do not know about the world outside their communities.
<u>Text–World:</u> My connection to the world is that if we become too cautious in trying to preserve our society, we can lose track of the things that make life worth living.

Source: Harvey, S., & Goudvis, A. (2000). *Strategies that work: Teaching comprehension to enhance understanding.* York, ME: Stenhouse.

Connection Stems

Purposes: To provide a structure to make connections while reading; to encourage reflection during reading.

Comprehension Strategy: Making Connections

Text: Narrative, Informational   **Use:** After Reading

Procedure: (Begin by explaining and demonstrating Connection Stems.)

1. After reading a section of text aloud, show students a sentence stem, and think aloud about the process you use for completing it. Use text support and personal experiences to explain the text–self, text–text, or text–world connection.

2. Read another section of text aloud and guide the students to complete the stem orally with a partner.

3. Invite students to read a short text in pairs and work together to complete Connection Stems.

4. Discuss the completed stems.

TEACHING IDEAS

Connection Stems:

- That reminds me of...
- I remember when...
- I have a connection to...
- An experience I have had like that...
- I felt like that character when...
- If I were that character, I would...

Example: (*Leonardo's Shadow: Or, My Astonishing Life as Leonardo da Vinci's Servant* [2006] by Christopher Grey)

- If I were Giacomo, I would have demanded that da Vinci help me find my parents from the beginning.
- I have felt like Giacomo when he was annoyed that da Vinci hadn't been working on the Last Supper like he was supposed to. I felt like this when I was working on a group project. Everyone in the group did their work and then we had to wait for one person to finish because she hadn't even begun to work on her section of the project.

Source: Adapted from Harvey, S., & Goudvis, A. (2000). *Strategies that work: Teaching comprehension to enhance understanding.* York, ME: Stenhouse.

Double-Entry Journal

(See blacklines, pages 250–251.)

Purposes: To provide a structure for reading response; to make decisions about significant aspects of text and reflect on personal connections to the text.

Comprehension Strategies: Making Connections, Monitoring, Summarizing

Text: Narrative, Informational   **Use:** Before, During, and After Reading

Procedure: (Begin by explaining and demonstrating Double-Entry Journals.)

1. Provide students with a Double-Entry Journal blackline.

2. Model the procedure by writing a quote, phrase, or idea in the left column and providing corresponding examples of reflective comments in the right column. (Encourage text–self, text–text, or text–world connections.)

3. Invite students to read (or listen to) a text or part of a text.

4. Ask students to select a key event, idea, word, quote, or concept from the text and write it in the left column.

5. In the right column, ask students write their response or connection to the item in the left column.

6. Use Double-Entry Journals as a springboard for discussion of text.

Adaptation: Use a different Double-Entry Journal format and ask students to create a summary and reflection.

TEACHING IDEAS

Example: (*Al Capone Does My Shirts* [2004] by Gennifer Choldenko)

Idea/Text From Story	My Connection
pp. 3–6 Moving to Alcatraz	This section of text reminds me of how it feels to be in a new place and how uncomfortable it can feel, whether it is a new home or Alcatraz.

Source: Tompkins, G.E. (2006). *Literacy for the 21st century: A balanced approach* (4th ed.). Upper Saddle River, NJ: Prentice Hall.

Drawing Connections

(See blackline, page 252.)

Purposes: To provide a structure to make connections while reading; to use visual representations to express connections.

Comprehension Strategies: Making Connections, Visualizing

Text: Narrative, Informational **Use:** During and After Reading

Procedure: (Begin by explaining and demonstrating Drawing Connections.)

1. Demonstrate how to draw visual representations (pictures, shapes, lines) to communicate connections with text.

2. Read a section of text and think aloud about a connection you can make. Model creating a visual representation of your thoughts. Think aloud as you write a sentence or paragraph explaining the connection you made.

3. Read another section of text to students and ask them to create visual representations of their connections to the text. Next, ask them to write a sentence or paragraph explaining their connection. Finally, invite them to share their drawings with and explain their connections to a partner.

4. Encourage students to engage in Drawing Connections when they are reading on their own.

Adaptation: Instead of connections, have students sketch their visualizations.

Example: (*The Silver Cup* [2007] by Constance Leeds)

Chapter 1: "The Silver Smith" pp. 1–7

 I drew a picture of a young girl looking unsure about herself. Anna is very excited to go to town until she visits the Silversmith. She sees a young girl that is pretty and well-dressed. Anna can't understand the young girl's language and wonders if the girl is talking about her. I think that everyone feels self-conscious at some point, and Anna is no different.

Source: McLaughlin, M., & Allen, M.B. (2002). *Guided Comprehension: A teaching model for grades 3–8.* Newark, DE: International Reading Association.

TEACHING IDEAS

Save the Last Word for Me

Purposes: To provide a structure to discuss the information and ideas in the text; to make connections to and evaluations of the information presented in the text.

Comprehension Strategies: Making Connections, Evaluating

Text: Narrative, Informational   **Use:** After Reading

Procedure: (Begin by explaining and demonstrating Save the Last Word for Me.)

1. Introduce a text and invite students to read it.

2. After reading, ask them to complete an index card with the following information:

   Side 1—Students select an idea, phrase, quote, concept, fact, etc. from the text that evokes a response. It can be something new, something that confirms previous ideas, or something they disagree with. Students write their selection on side 1 and indicate the page number where it can be found in the text.
   Side 2—Students write their reaction to what they wrote on side 1.

3. Have students gather in small groups to discuss the ideas they have written for Save the Last Word for Me.

4. Students should discuss using the following procedure: A student reads side 1 of his card and each student in the group responds to the information shared. The student who authored the card gets the last word by sharing side 2 of his card, which contains his explanation of what was written on side 1.

5. Repeat the process until everyone in the group has shared.

Example: (*One Thousand Tracings: Healing the Wounds of World War II* [2007] by Lita Judge)

Side 1—Quote from *One Thousand Tracings* p. 4: "With tears in her eyes, Mama gathered wool socks, sweaters, and her own winter coat. She placed all these things and cans of meat, sugar, and tea in a box."

Side 2—Reaction: I chose this quote because it reminded me of how kind and giving people can be. This family did not have very much food or clothing but they made sacrifices in order to help their German friends who were in need. They were caring people and they organized others to help.

Source: Short, K.G., Harste, J.C., & Burke, C. (1996). *Creating classrooms for authors and inquirers.* Portsmouth, NH: Heinemann.

Gallery Images

Purposes: To create mental images while reading; to provide a format for sharing visualizations.

Comprehension Strategies: Visualizing, Making Connections

Text: Informational   **Use:** After Reading

TEACHING IDEAS

Procedure: (Begin by explaining and demonstrating Gallery Images.)

1. Explain the concept of using images to represent information. Show two to four examples of different images representing content area concepts.

2. In small groups, ask students to read a section of informational text and visualize—create mental images as they read. Then ask students to create two to four images on poster-size paper to represent the content. Ask them to label their sketches.

3. Share the images and their labels with the class. Use a classroom wall to display Gallery Images.

4. Encourage students to create images in content areas they study.

Example: (*Earthquakes* [1991] by Seymour Simon)

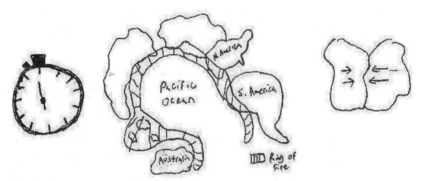

Every 30 seconds there is an earthquake somewhere in the world.

Four-fifths of earthquakes occur along the rim of the Pacific Ocean. This area is called the Ring of Fire.

Earthquakes are caused by colliding plates or stresses in underlying rocks.

Source: Ogle, D.M. (2000). Make it visual: A picture is worth a thousand words. In M. McLaughlin & M.E. Vogt (Eds.), *Creativity and innovation in content area teaching* (pp. 55–71). Norwood, MA: Christopher-Gordon.

Graphic Organizers/Visual Organizers

(See blacklines, pages 253–257.)

Purposes: To provide a visual model of the structure of text; to provide a format for organizing information and concepts.

Comprehension Strategies: Visualizing, Making Connections, Summarizing

Text: Narrative, Informational   **Use:** Before, During, and After Reading

Procedure: (Begin by explaining and demonstrating Graphic Organizers/Visual Organizers.)

1. Introduce the Graphic Organizer to students. Demonstrate how it works by reading a piece of text and noting key concepts and ideas on the organizer.

2. Ask students to work with partners to practice using the Graphic Organizer with ideas from an independently read text. Share ideas with the class.

TEACHING IDEAS

3. Choose organizers that match text structures and thinking processes.

4. Encourage students to use graphic organizers to help them think through text.

Example: (*Wolves* [2009] by Seymour Simon)

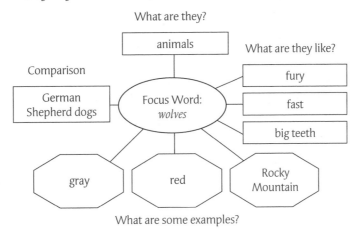

Guided Imagery

Purposes: To create mental images; to provide occasions to discuss visualizations.

Comprehension Strategies: Visualizing, Making Connections

Text: Narrative, Informational   **Use:** Before and After Reading

Procedure: (Begin by explaining and demonstrating Guided Imagery.)

1. Ask students to turn to partners and describe to each other the mental images they create when you provide a verbal stimulus of things with which the students are familiar—a birthday party, a favorite pet, or a fireworks display. Provide time for students to elaborate on their mental pictures.

2. Introduce the text students will be reading next. Invite them to preview the text by focusing on illustrations, charts, or any other graphics.

3. Explain to students that they should close their eyes, breathe deeply, and relax. Guide the students to think more deeply about the topic they will read about. Provide a detailed description of the setting, the action, sensory images, emotions, etc.

4. Ask students to open their eyes and work with partners to share the pictures they made in their minds. Monitor and respond to any questions.

5. Invite students to write or draw information gleaned from Guided Imagery.

6. Finally, ask students to read the text and modify or enhance their writing or sketching as necessary.

Example: (*Louis Sockalexis: Native American Baseball Pioneer* [2007] by Bill Wise)

<u>Before Reading:</u> I think the text will tell the story of Louis Sockalexis. From the title, I know he is Native American and plays baseball. I think the story will take place in the country on a reservation.

TEACHING IDEAS

The reservation will be deep within a forest far from white civilization. I think that one day he will see men playing baseball and want to play, too. The game will fascinate him and he will practice to get good at the sport. He will face difficulties in his dream of becoming a pro-baseball player. The white men on his team will not accept him at first and he'll have to prove himself to be an asset to the team. I think in the end he will become a really great player and inspire other minorities to play ball. <u>After Reading:</u> The story takes place in the country. Louis Sockalexis is from Maine. When Sockalexis is twelve he sees some boys playing baseball and is asked to join them. He falls in love with the game and faces a lot of objections to his dreams of becoming a baseball player. His father disapproves and many people don't want a Native American to play in a "white man's sport." Sockalexis ignores the jeers and becomes even more determined to prove them all wrong. In June of 1897, at New York's Polo Grounds, Sockalexis faced off against Rusie and hit a home run, proving his worth to all those that opposed his dream. Louis Sockalexis was the first Native American baseball player.

Source: Lasear, D. (1991). *Seven ways of teaching: The artistry of teaching with multiple intelligences.* Palatine, IL: Skylight.

Open-Mind Portrait

Purposes: To create and represent personal meanings for a story; to understand a character's perspective or point of view.

Comprehension Strategies: Visualizing, Making Connections

Text: Narrative, Informational   **Use:** After Reading

Procedure: (Begin by explaining and demonstrating Open-Mind Portraits.)

1. Invite students to draw and color a portrait of a character from a story or a famous person from a biography.

2. Ask students to cut out the portrait and use it to trace on one or several sheets of paper to create one or more blank head shapes.

3. Staple the color portrait and the blank sheets together.

4. On the blank pages, students should draw or write about the person's thoughts and feelings throughout the text.

5. Share Open-Mind Portraits in book clubs, Literature Circles, or class meeting time.

Adaptation: Students fold a large sheet of paper (11" × 17") in half. On one half, they draw a portrait of a character from the book. On the other half, they draw the same shape of the portrait but do not fill in facial features. Instead, they fill the head with words and pictures to represent the thoughts and feelings of the character.

Example: (*Hillary Rodham Clinton: Dreams Taking Flight* [2008] by Kathleen Krull)

<u>Open-Mind Portrait of Hillary Clinton:</u>

TEACHING IDEAS

Messages Written on Subsequent Pages:

- As a child Hillary dreamed of becoming an astronaut, but in 1961 women weren't permitted in that field.
- Hillary loved learning and was inspired by meeting Martin Luther King, Jr.
- Hillary was proud to become the wife of President Bill Clinton and proud to mother their daughter.
- Hillary was proud to serve the people. She became a senator.
- Hillary is still following her dream of becoming president.

Source: Tompkins, G.E. (2006). *Literacy for the 21st century: A balanced approach* (4th ed.). Upper Saddle River, NJ: Prentice Hall.

Photographs of the Mind

(See blackline, page 258.)

Purposes: To visualize while reading text; to monitor understanding.

Comprehension Strategies: Visualizing, Monitoring

Text: Narrative, Informational   **Use:** During Reading

Procedure: (Begin by explaining and modeling Photographs of the Mind.)

1. Introduce the text to be read.

2. Read the text or invite students to read the text.

3. At four designated or self-selected points in the text, have students stop and sketch a visualization related to the reading.

4. Ask students to share the sketch with a partner during each stop.

Example: (*Aunt Flossie's Hats (and Crab Cakes Later)* [2001] by Elizabeth Fitzgerald Howard)

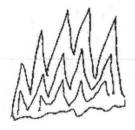 Aunt Flossie remembers the night she wore that hat. She witnessed the great fire of Baltimore. Every time she sees the hat, she can still smell the smoke in her memory.

Source: Keene, E.O., & Zimmermann, S. (2007). *Mosaic of thought: Teaching comprehension in a reader's workshop* (2nd ed.). Portsmouth, NH: Heinemann.

Sketch to Stretch

Purposes: To create, represent, and share personal meanings for a narrative or informational text; to summarize understandings through sketches.

TEACHING IDEAS

Comprehension Strategies: Visualizing, Making Connections

Text: Narrative, Informational   **Use:** After Reading

Procedure: (Begin by explaining and demonstrating Sketch to Stretch.)

1. After reading or listening to text, ask students to sketch what the text means to them.

2. Encourage students to experiment and assure them there are many ways to represent personal meanings.

3. Organize students in groups of three to five.

4. Each person in the group shares his or her sketch. As the sketch is shared, all other group members give their interpretation of the sketch. Once everyone has shared, the artist tells his or her interpretation.

5. Repeat Step 4 until everyone in the group has had a chance to share.

Example: (*Looking at Liberty* [2003] by Harvey Stevenson)

 A personal meaning I got from the text is that the Statue of Liberty is a sign of peace for the United States of America.

 A personal meaning I got from the text is that the Statue of Liberty is a representation of friendship. She represents the promise that in America you shouldn't be judged on race, ethnicity, disability, or age and that all of the people of America should get along.

Source: Short, K.G., Harste, J.C., & Burke, C. (1996). *Creating classrooms for authors and inquirers.* Portsmouth, NH: Heinemann.

Concept of Definition Map

(See blackline, page 259.)

Purposes: To make connections with new words and topics and build personal meanings by connecting the new information with prior knowledge.

Comprehension Strategy: Knowing How Words Work

Text: Informational   **Use:** Before and After Reading

Procedure: (Begin by explaining and demonstrating a Concept of Definition Map.)

1. Select or have student(s) select a word to be explored and place the word in the center of the map. (Example: *flotsam*)

2. Ask students to determine a broad category that best describes the word and write it in the *What is it?* section. (Example: *debris*)

TEACHING IDEAS

3. Encourage student(s) to provide some words that describe the focus word in the *What is it like?* section. (Examples: *garbage, wreckage, pollution*)

4. Have students provide some specific examples of the word in the *What are some examples?* section. (Examples: *plastic bags, Styrofoam food containers, soda pack rings*)

5. Ask students to determine a comparison. (Example: *jetsam*)

6. Discuss the Concept of Definition Map.

7. Read the text. Revisit the map. Make modifications or additions.

8. Encourage students to write a Concept of Definition Map Summary after completing the map.

Example: (*Tracking Trash: Flotsam, Jetsam, and the Science of Ocean Motion* [2007] by Loree Griffin Burns)

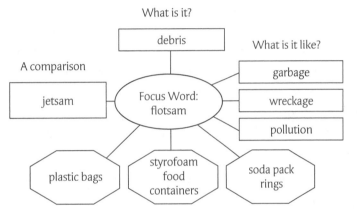

Source: Schwartz, R., & Raphael, T. (1985). Concept of definition: A key to improving students' vocabulary. *The Reading Teacher, 39*, 198–205.

Context Clues

Purposes: To use semantics and syntax to figure out unknown words; to use a variety of cueing systems to make sense of text.

Comprehension Strategy: Knowing How Words Work

Text: Narrative, Informational   **Use:** During Reading

Procedure: (Begin by demonstrating how to use Context Clues to figure out word meanings.)

1. Explain to students the eight types of Context Clues and give examples of each:

    Definition—provides a definition that often connects the unknown word to a known word
    Example/Illustration—provides an example or illustration to describe the word
    Compare/Contrast—provides a comparison or contrast to the word
    Logic—provides a connection (such as a simile) to the word
    Root Words and Affixes—provides meaningful roots and affixes that the reader uses to determine meaning

TEACHING IDEAS

Grammar—provides syntactical cues that allow for reader interpretation
Cause and Effect—cause and effect example allows the reader to hypothesize meaning
Mood and Tone—description of mood related to the word allows readers to hypothesize meaning

2. Read aloud and think aloud to demonstrate using one or more of the clues to determine the meaning of a difficult or unfamiliar word in the text. (Use a Think-Aloud to demonstrate the most effective type of clue based on the context of the sentence.) Readers use several of the clues to figure out unknown words.

3. If the context does not provide enough information, demonstrate other strategies for figuring out the meaning of the word.

Example: (*Diary of a Spider* [2005] by Doreen Cronin)

From page 12: "Mom said I was getting too big for my own skin. So I molted."
The word we are trying to define is *molted*. We can begin by looking at the Grammar clue and trying to figure out what part of speech *molted* is. The mother said he was getting too big for his own skin. So he *molted*. So, we know that molted is a *verb*, but we still do not know what *molted* means. The most effective Context Clue may be Example/Illustration because there is an illustration in the book that shows the spider holding what appears to be another spider, but it is just spider skin. From this illustration, we can determine the definition of *molted*. The spider is holding up his old skin, so *molted* means "to shed or lose skin."

Source: Vacca, R.T., & Vacca, J.L. (2008). *Content area reading: Literacy and learning across the curriculum* (9th ed.). Boston: Allyn & Bacon.

Decoding by Analogy

Purpose: To use graphic cues in rime to decode unfamiliar words.

Comprehension Strategy: Knowing How Words Work

Text: Narrative, Informational   **Use:** During Reading

Procedure: (Begin by explaining and demonstrating Decoding by Analogy.)

1. Teach students high-frequency words that have common spelling patterns.

2. Keep a word wall of these example words.

3. Model for students, using a Think-Aloud, how to use these patterns to decode unfamiliar words.

4. Provide opportunities for students to practice decoding new words by analogy in context. Prompt students with verbal cues if necessary.

5. Encourage students to use this strategy as a way to decode new words and spell conventionally.

TEACHING IDEAS

Example: (*The Wright Brothers: Inventors of the Airplane* [2000] by Wendie C. Old)

new word = *extraordinary*

I don't recognize this word, but I do recognize parts of it. I recognize *extra*, *or*, and *in*. I can use these patterns to decode this word; I read *extra-or-in...extraordin...extraordinary*. Now I will read the sentence and make sure *extraordinary* makes sense.

Source: Gaskins, I.W., Ehri, L.C., Cress, C., O'Hara, C., & Donnelly, K. (1996). Procedures for word learning: Making discoveries about words. *The Reading Teacher, 50*, 2–18.

List–Group–Label

Purposes: To activate prior knowledge about a topic; to develop clearer understandings about concepts.

Comprehension Strategies: Knowing How Words Work, Previewing, Making Connections

Text: Informational   **Use:** Before and After Reading

Procedure: (Begin by explaining and demonstrating List–Group–Label.)

1. Write a cue word or phrase on the board or overhead.

2. Ask students to brainstorm words or concepts related to the topic. Write down all ideas.

3. Lead a discussion about whether any words should be eliminated, and if so, why?

4. Divide the class into groups of three or four. Invite groups to cluster the words and give each cluster a descriptive term.

5. Encourage groups to share their clusters and give reasons for their choices. (There are no wrong answers if clusters and labels can be justified.)

6. Introduce the text and ask students to read it. Afterward, invite students to revisit their clusters and modify, if necessary.

Example: (*Children of the Gold Rush* [1999] by Claire Murphy & Jane G. Haigh)

Cue Phrase: Yukon Gold Rush

Location	Challenges	Purposes
Alaska	Harsh climate	Mining
	Dangerous trails	Wealth
	Supplies	Change
	Hard work	
	Separation of family members	
	Competition	
	Death	

Source: Maring, G., Furman, G., & Blum-Anderson, J. (1985). Five cooperative learning strategies for mainstreamed youngsters in content area classrooms. *The Reading Teacher, 39*, 310–313.

TEACHING IDEAS

Possible Sentences

Purposes: To improve understanding of text and key concepts presented in the text; to use vocabulary to make predictions about the content.

Comprehension Strategies: Knowing How Words Work, Previewing, Monitoring, Summarizing

Text: Informational   **Use:** Before and After Reading

Procedure: (Begin by explaining and demonstrating Possible Sentences.)

1. Choose six to eight words from the text that may be difficult and list them on the board or overhead.

2. Choose another four to six words from the text that may be more familiar to the students and list them on the board or overhead.

3. Define the words. If possible, invite the students do this by using their background knowledge.

4. Ask the students (individuals or groups) to develop sentences using at least two of the words in each sentence. Write all contributed sentences on the board.

5. Ask students to read the text to confirm, modify, or extend the information contained in the sentences on the board.

6. After reading, revisit the original sentences and revise as needed. Add any new information to the list.

7. Use the revised list as the basis for creating summaries.

Example: (*Remember Pearl Harbor: American and Japanese Survivors Tell Their Stories* [2001] by Thomas B. Allen)

Vocabulary Words:

anti-submarine nets—steel nets intended to entangle enemy submarines
casualties—death/injuries caused during war or accidents
monument—a statue dedicated to some event or person of importance
veterans—people retired from military service
air craft carriers—warships that carry planes

Sentences:

- There is a *monument* dedicated to World War II *veterans* and those that lost their lives at Pearl Harbor.

- The United States used many *air craft carriers* and *anti-submarine nets* to help protect soldiers during World War II.

- Although *anti-submarine nets* were used to protect bases from enemy attacks, there were still *casualties*.

Source: Stahl, S., & Kapinus, B. (1991). Possible sentences: Predicting word meaning to teach content area vocabulary. *The Reading Teacher, 45*, 36–43.

TEACHING IDEAS

RIVET

Purposes: To activate prior knowledge of a topic; to make predictions; to introduce vocabulary; to model spelling of specific vocabulary words.

Comprehension Strategies: Knowing How Words Work, Previewing

Text: Informational   **Use:** Before Reading

Procedure: (Begin by explaining and demonstrating RIVET.)

1. Choose six to eight interesting and important words from the selection to be read.

2. Create a visual representation of the words in a numbered list, leaving lines for each letter in the words. (You may want to provide students with a copy of this.)

3. Fill in the letters of the first word, one by one. Ask students to fill in their sheets or copy the words along with you. Ask students to predict what the word might be.

4. Continue this process for each word on the list.

5. Make sure students understand word meanings. Encourage them to share.

6. Invite students to make predictions about the text, using the lists of words. Record the predictions.

7. Encourage students to ask questions prompted by the list of words. Record the questions.

8. Read the text. Revisit predictions to confirm or modify. Answer questions on the list.

Example: (*Do Tornadoes Really Twist? Questions and Answers About Tornadoes and Hurricanes* [2000] by Melvin Berger & Gilda Berger)

1. __ __ __ __ __ __ __ __ __ (tornadoes)
   T O

2. __ __ __ __ __ __ __ __ __ __ (hurricanes)
   H U R

3. __ __ __ __ __ __ (funnel)
   F U

4. __ __ __ __ (wind)
   W

5. __ __ __ __ __ __ (swells)
   S W

6. __ __ __ (eye)
   E

Source: Cunningham, P.M. (1995). *Phonics they use: Words for reading and writing.* New York: HarperCollins.

TEACHING IDEAS

Semantic Feature Analysis

(See blackline, page 260.)

Purposes: To make predictions about attributes related to specific vocabulary words or concepts; to set a purpose for reading or researching; to confirm predictions.

Comprehension Strategies: Knowing How Words Work, Making Connections

Text: Narrative, Informational   **Use:** Before and After Reading

Procedure: (Begin by explaining and demonstrating Semantic Feature Analysis.)

1. Select a topic and some words or categories that relate to that topic. List the words in the left-hand column of the Semantic Feature Analysis chart.

2. Choose characteristics that relate to one or more of the related words. List those across the top row of the chart.

3. Ask students make predictions about which characteristics relate to each word by placing a + if it is a characteristic, a − if it is not, and a ? if they are not sure.

4. Discuss students' predictions. Have them explain why they chose the characteristics.

5. Introduce the text and ask students to read about the topic and modify their charts as necessary.

6. Encourage students to share completed charts in small groups and then discuss as a class.

Example: (*Rain Forest* [1992] by Barbara Taylor)

+ = yes

− = no

? = don't know

Characteristics / Categories	Lives in trees	Needs to live in a moist place	Lays eggs	Has sticky suckers fingers and toes	Can see in the dark	Can fly	Is poisonous
Gliding Gecko	+	−	+	−	+	−	−
Tiger Centipede	−	+	+	−	+	−	+
Dart Frog	−	+	+	+	?	−	+
Postman Caterpillar	?	−	+	−	−	−	+
Fruit Bat	+	−	+	−	−	+	−
Tarantula	−	−	+	−	?	−	+
Rainbow Bird	+	−	+	−	−	+	−

Source: Johnson, D.D., & Pearson, P.D. (1984). *Teaching reading vocabulary* (2nd ed.). New York: Holt, Rinehart and Winston.

TEACHING IDEAS

Vocabulary by Analogy

Purposes: To help students make connections between words they know and new words; to help students use roots, prefixes, and suffixes to figure out the meaning of unknown words.

Comprehension Strategy: Knowing How Words Work

Text: Narrative, Informational   **Use:** During Reading

Procedure: (Begin by explaining and demonstrating Vocabulary by Analogy.)

1. Teach students the meanings of common roots, prefixes, and suffixes, and provide examples of each, for example:

   Roots—*graph, psych, scope, script*
   Prefixes—*tele, pre, trans, un*
   Suffixes—*ology, ship, ment, hood*

2. Keep a word wall or individual word charts of these examples.

3. Model for students, using a Think-Aloud, how to use these parts of words to figure out the meaning of unfamiliar words.

4. Provide opportunities for students to practice figuring out new vocabulary by analogy in context. Prompt students with verbal cues if necessary. Refer them to use the class word wall as a resource.

5. Encourage students to use this strategy to figure out the meaning of new words they meet while reading.

Example: (*Tracking Trash: Flotsam, Jetsam, and the Science of Ocean Motion* [2007] by Loree Griffin Burns)

new word = *oceanographers*

I don't know this word, but I recognize *ocean* and I know some other parts of it from our word wall. I see the root *graph* and I know that means "write." I also know that *er* means "one who." So, I can figure out that *oceanographers* are people who write about—or perhaps study—the ocean.

Source: McLaughlin, M., & Allen, M.B. (2002). *Guided Comprehension: A teaching model for grades 3–8.* Newark, DE: International Reading Association.

Vocabulary Self-Collection Strategy (VSS)

Purposes: To motivate students to engage in vocabulary study; to expand vocabulary.

Comprehension Strategies: Knowing How Words Work, Making Connections

Text: Narrative, Informational   **Use:** After Reading

Procedure: (Begin by explaining and demonstrating VSS.)

1. Invite student groups or individual students to select words from a previously read text that they would like to study or learn more about. The teacher also chooses a word.

2. Ask students to share the word, the context, where it was found, what they think it means, and why the class should study it.

TEACHING IDEAS

3. Accept all nominated words and record them. Encourage more discussion about the words.

4. Narrow the list to a predetermined number for study and refine definitions.

5. Ask students to record final wordlists and definitions in their vocabulary journals.

6. Plan lessons to reinforce the words' meanings and uses.

7. Use the words in follow-up assignments and other learning experiences.

Example: (*Savvy* [2008] by Ingrid Law)

1. Invite students to select words from Chapter 1 of *Savvy* after they read the first chapter.

Examples of words students might choose:

Momentum   p. 2
Unkempt   p. 5
Broody   p. 7
Hibernating   p. 8

2. Invite students to share the word, the context, where it was found, what they think it means, and why the class should study it.

Examples of possible student responses:

Unkempt, page 5; used in the context "...running one hand through his dark shock of *unkempt* hair with a crackle of static." I think *unkempt* means *sloppy* or *messy*. The class should study *unkempt* because it is a word we encounter in our reading and could use when talking or writing.

3. Encourage discussions about this other student-suggested words.

4. Narrow the list and refine definitions:

Word	Definition
Momentum	the power to increase or develop at an ever-growing pace
Unkempt	messy or disorderly, unpolished, tangled or matted in need of combing
Broody	thoughtful or gloomy
Hibernating	to be in a dormant state resembling sleep

(Students removed the word *console* from the list.)

Source: Haggard, M.R. (1986). The vocabulary self-collection strategy: Using student interest and world knowledge to enhance vocabulary growth. *Journal of Reading, 29*, 634–642.

Bookmark Technique

(See blacklines, pages 261–262.)

Purposes: To monitor comprehension while reading; to make evaluative judgments about aspects of text.

Comprehension Strategies: Monitoring, Knowing How Words Work, Making Connections, Evaluating

Text: Narrative, Informational   **Use:** During and After Reading

TEACHING IDEAS

Procedure: (Begin by explaining and demonstrating the Bookmark Technique.)

1. As students read, ask them to make decisions and record specific information on each Bookmark, including the page and paragraph where the information is located.

   Bookmark 1—Write and/or sketch about the part of the text that you found most interesting.
   Bookmark 2—Write and/or sketch something you found confusing.
   Bookmark 3—Write a word you think the whole class needs to discuss.
   Bookmark 4—Indicate a chart, map, graph, or illustration that helped you to understand what you were reading.

2. Use the completed bookmarks to promote discussion about the text.

Example: (*Giraffes Can't Dance* [2001] by Giles Andreae & Guy Parker-Rees)

Bookmark 1	Bookmark 2	Bookmark 3	Bookmark 4
The part of the text that I found most interesting was when Gerald talked with the cricket and the cricket gave him the good advice that sometimes he just needs a different song to dance to. (p. 16)	I found the part of the book confusing when all of the animals made fun of Gerald. I did not understand why they made fun of him just because he could not dance. (p. 12)	*Waltzing*—I think waltzing is a type of dance where you move about in a circular motion. I think that we should discuss this word as a class so we will understand what kind of dance the giraffes are doing. (p. 7)	The illustration that helped me understand what I was reading showed Gerald dancing in front of everyone toward the end of the book. All the animals thought he was a good dancer then and they wanted Gerald to teach them how to dance the way he did. (p. 26)

Source: McLaughlin, M., & Allen, M.B. (2002). *Guided Comprehension: A teaching model for grades 3–8.* Newark, DE: International Reading Association.

INSERT (Interactive Notation System to Effective Reading and Thinking)

(See blacklines, pages 263–264.)

Purposes: To provide opportunities for reflection; to make connections between prior knowledge and text content.

Comprehension Strategies: Monitoring, Making Connections

Text: Informational   **Use:** During Reading

Procedure: (Begin by explaining and demonstrating INSERT.)

1. Introduce a topic and ask students to brainstorm lists of what they already know about it.

TEACHING IDEAS

2. Teach students the following modified notation system:

If an idea:	Put this notation in the margin:
• confirms what you thought (makes you say "I knew that.")	✓ Insert a checkmark
• contradicts what you thought (makes you say "I thought differently.")	– Insert a minus sign
• is new to you (makes you say "I didn't know that!")	+ Insert a plus sign
• confuses you (makes you question "What does this mean?")	? Insert a question mark

3. Encourage students to use the notation system in the margins of an informational article or on the INSERT Bookmarks as they read various parts of the text.

4. After the students finish reading and inserting the symbols, use that information as the basis of discussion, to seek more information, to answer questions, or to raise new questions.

Example: (*The Best Book of Mummies* [1998] by Philip Steele)

p. 10

The Next World

The ancient Egyptians believed that when they died they would travel to the Next World, the Kingdom of Osiris. They believed this kingdom was a wonderful place, and that whoever managed to reach it would live forever. However, the journey to the Next World was long and hard. **?** On the journey, the dead needed food and drink. Their bodies had to be whole and strong. **+** And the priests had to chant spells to protect them.

Source: Vaughn, J., & Estes, T. (1986). *Reading and reasoning beyond the primary grades*. Boston: Allyn & Bacon.

Patterned Partner Reading

Purposes: To provide a structure for reading interactively with another; to promote strategic reading.

Comprehension Strategies: Monitoring, Making Connections, Evaluating

Text: Narrative, Informational   **Use:** During Reading

Procedure: (Begin by explaining and demonstrating Patterned Partner Reading.)

1. Instruct students to select a text and a partner with whom they will read or assign partners.

2. Partners should determine the amount of text to be read and choose a pattern such as the following to use as they engage in the reading:

Read–Pause–Ask Questions—partners read a page silently and then ask each other a question about that page before moving on

Predict–Read–Discuss—partners make predictions about material, read to confirm or disconfirm their predictions, discuss the outcome, and renew the cycle

Read–Pause–Retell—partners read, stop to think, and take turns retelling what they have read to a given point

TEACHING IDEAS

Read–Pause–Make Connections—partners read a predetermined amount and then tell the text–self, text–text, or text–world connections they have made

Read–Pause–Visualize—partners read a portion of the text and describe the pictures they have created in their minds

You Choose days—partners select which pattern to use

Example: (*The Encyclopedia of Awesome Oceans* [2002] by Michael Bright)

Read–Pause–Ask Questions:

p. 14: Penguins
Student One: What is a krill?
Student Two: Why can't penguins fly?

Source: Adapted from Cunningham, P., & Allington, R. (1999). *Classrooms that work: They can all read and write* (2nd ed.). New York: Addison-Wesley.

Say Something

Purposes: To make connections with texts during reading; to enhance comprehension of written material through short readings and oral discussion.

Comprehension Strategies: Monitoring, Making Connections

Text: Narrative, Informational   **Use:** During Reading

Procedure: (Begin by explaining and demonstrating Say Something.)

1. Instruct pairs of students to select text to read.

2. Designate a stopping point for reading.

3. Ask students to read to the stopping point and then "Say Something" about the text to their partner.

4. Allow pairs to choose the next stopping point. (If the text has subheadings, these make good stopping points.) Students repeat Steps 3 and 4 until they have finished reading the text.

Example: (*Do Penguins Get Frostbite? Questions and Answers About Polar Animals* [2000] by Melvin Berger & Gilda Berger)

Stopping Point: p. 8

Student 1: It says that the male cares for the young. That is unusual.
Student 2: The male group works together to keep themselves and the eggs warm. They form a giant incubator and take turns being in the center.

Source: Adapted from Short, K.G., Harste, J.C., & Burke, C. (1996). *Creating classrooms for authors and inquirers*. Portsmouth, NH: Heinemann.

TEACHING IDEAS

Think-Alouds

Purpose: To provide a model for active thinking during the reading process.

Comprehension Strategies: Previewing, Visualizing, Monitoring, Self-Questioning, Making Connections, Knowing How Words Work, Summarizing, Evaluating

Text: Narrative, Informational   **Use:** Before, During, and After Reading

Procedure: (Begin by explaining and demonstrating Think-Alouds.)

1. Introduce the text. Select a passage to read aloud to the students. The passage should require some strategic thinking in order to clarify understandings.

2. Before reading, encourage students to work with partners to make predictions for the story or chapter and explain their reasoning. (For example, "From the title [or cover], we can predict... because....")

3. During reading, encourage students to think aloud to demonstrate strategies such as

   - Making/confirming/modifying predictions ("We were thinking _____, but now we predict _____."; "We thought that was what was going to happen because _____.")

   - Visualizing—making pictures in our minds ("What we are seeing in our minds right now is _____.")

   - Making connections ("This reminds us of _____"; This is like a _____.")

   - Monitoring ("This is confusing. We need to reread or read on or ask someone for help."; "This is not what we expected.")

   - Figuring out unknown words ("We don't know that word, but it looks like _____."; "That word must mean _____ because _____.")

4. After guiding them to practice with partners several times, encourage students to use this technique on their own.

Example: (*Whale Journey* [1998] by Vivian French)

<u>Before reading, share your predictions and explain your reasoning:</u> From the title, *Whale Journey*, we can predict that the story is going to be about one or more whales taking a trip somewhere. We can predict that it will be about a journey through the ocean during a day or a year. We do not know how many whales because neither the title nor the illustration tell us. By looking on the back cover we see there are three whales, two larger whales and one smaller whale. The journey will probably include these three whales. One may be the baby with its mother and father whale. We do not know but hopefully will find out as we read.

<u>Model some of these strategies:</u>

- Making predictions—It seems like this whale is having a baby.

- Confirming predictions—"a tail emerging, and then, with a slither, he is born." You can use the description given to you in this sentence to confirm that yes the whale did have a baby.

TEACHING IDEAS

- Visualizing—After reading this passage, what are you seeing in your mind right now? I see a mother whale and her new baby whale.
- Making Connections—This reminds me of when my mom had my younger brother/sister.

Source: Davey, B. (1983). Think-aloud—demonstrating the cognitive processes of reading comprehension. *Journal of Reading, 27*, 44–47.

Bio-Pyramid

(See blackline, page 265.)

Purposes: To summarize a person's life; to provide a format for summary writing.

Comprehension Strategies: Summarizing, Making Connections, Monitoring

Text: Informational   **Use:** After Reading

Procedure: (Begin by explaining and demonstrating the Bio-Pyramid.)

1. After reading about a person's life, show students the format for writing Bio-Pyramids.

    Line 1—person's name
    Line 2—two words describing the person
    Line 3—three words describing the person's childhood
    Line 4—four words indicating a problem the person had to overcome
    Line 5—five words stating one of his or her accomplishments
    Line 6—six words stating a second accomplishment
    Line 7—seven words stating a third accomplishment
    Line 8—eight words stating how mankind benefited from the accomplishments

2. Create a Bio-Pyramid as a class.

3. In small groups or pairs invite students to create Bio-Pyramids.

4. Use the completed Bio-Pyramids to promote discussion and summarize the person's life.

Example: (*Talkin' About Bessie: The Story of Aviator Elizabeth Coleman* [2002] by Nikki Grimes)

Bessie
Determined woman
Poverty-stricken Texas community
Racism and gender discrimination
Attended Caudron School of Aviation
Became the world's first African-American aviatrix
Lost her life in an aviation accident
Challenged us to dream and reach our goals.

Source: Macon, J.M. (1991). *Literature response.* Paper presented at the Annual Literacy Workshop, Anaheim, CA.

TEACHING IDEAS

Lyric Retelling/Lyric Summary

(See blackline, page 266.)

Purposes: To provide an alternative format for narrative text retellings or informational text summaries; to provide opportunities to use multiple modalities when creating summaries; to link content learning and the arts.

Comprehension Strategy: Summarizing

Text: Narrative and Informational   **Use:** After Reading

Procedure: (Begin by explaining and demonstrating Lyric Retellings/Lyric Summaries.)

1. Review summarizing with the students. Ask them to note the types of information that comprise narrative or informational summaries. Choose a topic and brainstorm a list of related information.

2. Introduce the musical aspect of Lyric Retellings/Lyric Summaries by explaining to students that summaries can also be written as song lyrics to familiar tunes (popular, rock, jazz, children's songs).

3. Choose a melody with which students are familiar and use the brainstormed list to write lyrics. Write the first line and then encourage pairs of students to suggest subsequent lines. When the Lyric Retelling/Lyric Summary is completed, sing it with the class.

4. Ask small groups of students to brainstorm a list of facts they know about a story they have read or a content area topic they have studied. Invite them to choose a melody everyone in the group knows and create their own Lyric Retellings/Lyric Summaries.

5. Invite the students to sing their completed summaries for the class.

Example: (*Volcanoes* [1988] by Seymour Simon)

Sung to "London Bridge Is Falling Down"

> The magma is piling up, piling up, piling up.
> The magma is piling up deep within the earth's crust.
>
> Steam and gas are building up, building up, building up.
> Steam and gas are building up. There is going to be a explosion.
>
> The volcano is going to erupt, going to erupt, going to erupt.
> The volcano is going to erupt along the Pacific Ocean.
>
> Lava and ash are raining down, raining down, raining down.
> Lava and ash are raining down. Evacuate the town.
>
> The lava is turning to rock, turning to rock, turning to rock.
> The lava is turning to rock and new land is formed.

Source: McLaughlin, M., & Allen, M.B. (2002). *Guided Comprehension: A teaching model for grades 3–8.* Newark, DE: International Reading Association.

TEACHING IDEAS

Narrative Pyramid

(See blackline, page 267.)

Purposes: To summarize a narrative text; to provide a format for summary writing.

Comprehension Strategies: Making Connections, Monitoring, Summarizing

Text: Narrative   **Use:** After Reading

Procedure:

1. After reading a story, show students the format for writing narrative pyramids.

> Line 1—character's name
> Line 2—two words describing the character
> Line 3—three words describing the setting
> Line 4—four words stating the problem
> Line 5—five words describing one event
> Line 6—six words describing another event
> Line 7—seven words describing a third event
> Line 8—eight words describing the solution to the problem

2. Create a Narrative Pyramid as a class.

3. Have students create Narrative Pyramids in small groups or pairs for a story they have read.

4. Use the completed pyramids as the basis for discussion.

Example: (*The City of Ember* [2003] by Jeanne DuPrau)

Lina

Curious kind

Underground city Ember

Ember   City   is   dying

Lina   gets   a   messenger   job

Finds   document   leading   out   of   Ember

Lina   and   Doon   escape   city   of   Ember

Kids   drop   the   escape   instructions   down   to   Ember

Source: Waldo, B. (1991). Story pyramid. In J.M. Macon, D. Bewell, & M.E. Vogt (Eds.), *Responses to literature: Grades K–8* (pp. 23–24). Newark, DE: International Reading Association.

Paired Summarizing

Purposes: To provide a format for pairs to summarize narrative or informational text and to articulate understandings and confusions.

Comprehension Strategies: Making Connections, Monitoring, Summarizing

Text: Narrative, Informational   **Use:** After Reading

TEACHING IDEAS

Procedure: (Begin by explaining and demonstrating Paired Summarizing.)

1. Ask pairs of students to read a selection, and invite each student to write a summary or retelling. They may refer to the text to help cue their memory, but they should not write while they are looking at the text.

2. Ask partners to trade the retellings or summaries that they wrote and read each other's work. Encourage each student to write a summary of the other partner's paper.

3. Encourage students to compare and contrast their summaries. The discussion should focus on
   • Articulating what each reader understands
   • Identifying what they collectively cannot come to understand
   • Formulating clarification questions for classmates and the teacher

4. Invite students to share understandings and questions in a small-group or whole-class discussion.

Example: (*Fields of Fury: The American Civil War* [2002] by James M. McPherson)

pp. 86–87: Reconstruction

<u>Student 1 Summary:</u> March 4, 1865, began the Reconstruction period. After the Civil War the South lay in ruins. President Lincoln asked that the high ranking officials be pardoned because he wanted to create peace with the South. However; Lincoln never got to establish his Reconstruction ideas, because he was assassinated by John Wilkes Booth. His Vice-President, Andrew Johnson, took over. President Johnson was too lenient with the South and they reelected the same political parties into office and created black codes so they could almost use African Americans as slaves again. Congress got angry and took control over the Reconstruction. Southerners still resented African Americans and found new ways to keep them as second class citizens. They enforced Jim Crow laws and Segregation. Reconstruction ended in 1877.

<u>Student 2 Summary of First Summary:</u> Reconstruction of the South began after the Civil War. The South was destroyed and President Lincoln was in charge of rebuilding it. Lincoln, however; was assassinated and so the job fell to his Vice-President, Andrew Johnson. Johnson attempted to bring order to the South, but he ran into problems. The South kept creating laws to keep African Americans in their control.

Source: Vaughn, J., & Estes, T. (1986). *Reading and reasoning beyond the primary grades.* Boston: Allyn & Bacon.

QuIP (Questions Into Paragraphs)

(See blackline, page 268.)

Purpose: To provide a framework for initiating research and structuring writing.

Comprehension Strategies: Summarizing, Self-Questioning

Text: Informational   **Use:** Before, During, and After Reading

TEACHING IDEAS

Procedure: (Begin by explaining and demonstrating QuIP.)

1. Invite students to choose a topic to explore and write the topic at the top of the QuIP grid.

2. Ask students to generate three broad questions related to the topic.

3. Students should locate and read two sources to find the answers to their questions. They write the titles of the sources in spaces provided on the grid.

4. Students record answers to the questions in the spaces provided on the grid.

5. Students synthesize information into a paragraph. (Demonstrating synthesizing and paragraph writing facilitates this process.)

6. Students share their paragraphs in pairs or small groups.

Examples: (*The Encyclopedia of Awesome Oceans* [2002] by Michael Bright and *Ocean Watch: Protecting Our Planet* [2001] by Martyn Bramwell)

QuIP Research Grid

Topic: Oceans

Questions	Answers	
	Source A: Bright, M. (2002). *The encyclopedia of awesome oceans.*	**Source B:** Bramwell, M. (2001). *Ocean watch: Protecting our planet.*
Question A How many different oceans are there in the world?	There are 5 oceans on the planet, divided into the Pacific, Atlantic, Indian, Antarctic and Arctic Oceans. (pp. 92–93)	The Pacific, Atlantic, Indian, Arctic, and Antarctic are all linked in one vast mass of water. (p. 10)
Question B What are some ways in which humans have caused harm to the oceans?	Fishing fleets overfish not only fish but also krill. Krill is an essential part of most food chains in the Antarctic. (p. 12)	Chemicals from agriculture and industry are now spread far and wide through the oceans. Some whales and fish have been hunted almost to extinction. (p. 8)
Question C What is the most fearsome animal in the ocean?	The great white shark is a monster man-eater and the largest predatory fish in the sea. It is the number one people killer. (p. 74)	The great white shark is at the top of the food chain. It can only be killed by humans, old age, or disease. (p. 17)

<u>Paragraph based on the QuIP organizer:</u> The Earth contains five oceans; the Atlantic, Pacific, Indian and Arctic. Humans harm oceans by over-fishing and polluting. The most fearsome creature found in the ocean is the great white shark. The great white shark is the largest predatory fish in the sea and at the top of the food chain. Sharks can only be killed by old age, disease or humans.

Source: McLaughlin, E.M. (1987). QuIP: A writing strategy to improve comprehension of informational structure. *The Reading Teacher, 40,* 650–654.

TEACHING IDEAS

Retelling

(See blackline, page 269.)

Purposes: To promote reflection about narrative text; to provide a format for summarizing narrative text structure.

Comprehension Strategy: Summarizing

Text: Narrative   **Use:** After Reading

Procedure: (Begin by explaining and demonstrating Retelling.)

1. Explain to the students the purpose of retelling a story and the major elements that are included (characters, setting, problem, attempts to resolve, resolution).

2. Demonstrate a Retelling after reading a story aloud. Discuss the components you included. (A story map or other Graphic Organizer may help.)

3. Read another story to the students, and then ask them to form groups and retell the story. (You may want to give each student in the group a card listing a specific story element, such as characters, setting, problem, attempts to resolve, resolution.)

4. Share information with the class and record it on a chart or overhead. Review the Retellings to ensure all elements are addressed.

5. Encourage students to do Retellings orally, in writing, or through sketching or dramatization to demonstrate understanding of a narrative text.

Example: (*Murphy Meets the Treadmill* [2001] by Harriet Ziefert)

Murphy, a yellow lab dog, and his owner, Cheryl, are the main characters. The story takes place at their house and on their front porch. Murphy has eaten too much and that made him gain weight. Cheryl decides Murphy should exercise and get healthy.

Cheryl wants Murphy to get on the scale, but he refuses. She decides to start feeding him healthy food and exercising with him. Then she buys a treadmill. Murphy starts to enjoy using the treadmill and is proud to be getting in shape. All of his friends admire his dedication to his new healthy lifestyle. Murphy meets a new friend and travels around the world as a famous treadmilling dog.

Source: Morrow, L.M. (1985). Retelling stories: A strategy for improving children's comprehension, concept of story, and oral language complexity. *The Elementary School Journal, 85*(5), 647–661.

Summary Cubes

(See blackline, page 270.)

Purpose: To provide a structure for summarizing factual information or retelling key points of a story.

Comprehension Strategy: Summarizing

Text: Narrative, Informational   **Use:** Before, During, and After Reading

TEACHING IDEAS

Procedure: (Begin by explaining and demonstrating Summary Cubes.)

1. Explain the idea of cubing to the students. Describe the information that goes on each side of the cube.

2. Demonstrate through read-aloud and Think-Aloud the process of determining key ideas about either narrative or informational text to write on the cube. Show the students how to assemble the cube.

3. Guide the students to work with partners to read text and create Summary Cubes.

4. Share ideas with the class. Display Summary Cubes.

5. Encourage students to create their own cubes as follow-ups to reading narrative and informational texts.

   Information for cubes:

	Option 1	Option 2	Option 3	Option 4
Side 1	Who?	Title	Animal	Topic
Side 2	What?	Characters	Habitat	Subtopic 1 and details
Side 3	Where?	Setting	Food	Subtopic 2 and details
Side 4	When?	Problem	Physical description	Subtopic 3 and details
Side 5	Why?	Solution	Classification	Summary
Side 6	How?	Theme	Illustration	Illustration

Adaptation: Complete the Bio-Cube detailed at the Read Write Think website: www.readwritethink.org/lessons/lesson_view.asp?id=1028.

Example: (*Mama Played Baseball* [2003] by David A. Adler)

Side 1—Title: *Mama Played Baseball*
Side 2—Characters: Mama, Amy, Grandpa, Grandma, Father
Side 3—Setting: During World War II
Side 4—Problem: Mama needs a job while her husband fights in the war.
Side 5—Solution: She gets a job playing baseball.
Side 6—Theme: Reaching for your dreams

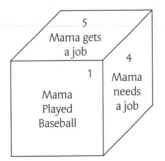

Source: McLaughlin, M., & Allen, M.B. (2002). *Guided Comprehension: A teaching model for grades 3–8.* Newark, DE: International Reading Association.

TEACHING IDEAS

Contrast Chart

(See blackline, page 271.)

Purposes: To contrast two views of an issue; to analyze authors' and illustrators' choices and how they impact perspective

Comprehension Strategy: Evaluating

Text: Narrative, Informational   **Use:** After Reading

Procedure: (Begin by explaining and demonstrating Contrast Charts.)

1. After reading, ask students to determine a perspective of the story or issue expressed in the text. Ask them to write ideas that characterize that perspective in the left-hand column of the chart. They should use specific words, phrases, or events from the text to support ideas.

2. Students should determine another view of the story or issue that contrasts the first perspective and write contrasts in the right-hand column of the chart. Recommend that they be sure to record the contrasts directly opposite original perspective.

3. Have students share and discuss contrasts with a partner, small group, or whole class.

Example: (*Fight for Freedom: The American Revolutionary War* [2004] by Benson Bobrick)

The Americans	The British
The Colonists were outraged by the taxes. "No taxation without representation is tyranny."	The British backed the Colonists during the French and Indian War. The British Parliament had colonists pay taxes and house and shelter soldiers.
Many people left Britain to find freedom and the colonies wanted to create a government of their own.	The colonies were still a part of Britain, so they had to obey British rules.
Taxes on tea caused the colonists to revolt and throw tea into the harbor. This is known as the Boston Tea Party.	After the Boston Tea Party, King George the III felt he could no longer trust the people in Massachusetts and passed laws such as the Restraining Acts. British troops were also placed in Boston.
To gain their independence the Colonists began the revolution.	

Source: Adapted from Tompkins, G. E. (2006). *Literacy for the 21st century: A balanced approach* (4th ed.). Upper Saddle River, NJ: Prentice Hall.

TEACHING IDEAS

Discussion Web

(See blackline, page 272.)

Purposes: To provide a structure for conversing about a topic; to provide opportunities for critical thinking.

Comprehension Strategies: Evaluating, Making Connections

Text: Narrative, Informational   **Use:** After Reading

Procedure: (Begin by explaining and demonstrating Discussion Webs.)

1. Select a topic that can be discussed from two different perspectives. Create a statement or question about it and write the question in the space indicated on the Discussion Web.

2. Encourage students to work in pairs and read text supporting each side of the argument. Ask them to record their yes (pro) and no (con) reasons in the spaces provided on the Discussion Web.

3. Encourage the students to discuss the question and the arguments for and against. Then ask the students to come to a conclusion, as a pair, and justify their thinking.

4. Remind students to write their conclusion and rationale at the bottom of the web.

5. Encourage pairs to share their conclusions and rationales with the class. Then the class comes to a conclusion and offers a rationale.

Example: (*Rosa* [2005] by Nikki Giovanni)

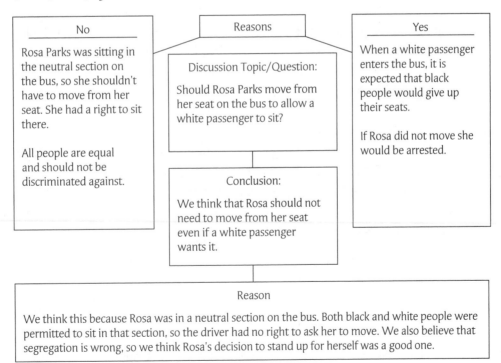

Source: Alvermann, D. (1991). The discussion web: A graphic aid for learning across the curriculum. *The Reading Teacher, 45*, 92–99.

TEACHING IDEAS

Evaluative Questioning

Purpose: To promote self-questioning and evaluative thinking.

Comprehension Strategy: Evaluating, Self-Questioning

Text: Narrative, Informational   **Use:** During and After Reading

Procedure: (Begin by explaining and demonstrating Evaluative Questioning.)

1. Explain the importance of multiple levels of questioning, focusing on evaluative questions. (See Chapter 2.)

2. Model creating and responding to evaluative questions using a read-aloud and Think-Aloud. Explain the signal words and cognitive operations used to form and respond to evaluative questions.

   Signal words: *defend, judge, justify*
   Cognitive operations: valuing, judging, defending, justifying

3. Using a common text, guide small groups of students to read the text and create an evaluative question. One at a time, ask groups to share their question and encourage other students to respond. Discuss the cognitive processes students used to answer each question.

4. Provide opportunities for students to use evaluative questions to engage in reflection and conversations about the texts they read.

Example: (*Growing Up in Coal Country* [1996] by Susan Campbell Bartoletti)

<u>Do you think the coal miner's decision to strike against the coal companies was justifiable? (Defend your response.)</u> Coal mining was a dangerous job. Men could be trapped under debris or be killed in an explosion. They worked long hours and received very little pay. The workers wanted shorter days and more pay for their work and better living conditions. These demands are reasonable and should be granted. In today's times conditions such as these would not go unnoticed. The coal companies were taking advantage of their workers.

<u>Do you support the sheriff and deputies' decision to end the protest of 1897 with violence? (Justify your response.)</u> A group of 400 angry workers marched to Lattimer Patch that day. I think the sheriff and deputies did what they did because they feared the workers would riot. Groups such as the Molly Maguires would burn company bridges or derail coal cars. I think the sheriff and deputies didn't know how the protesters would react and feared the worst.

Source: Ciardiello, A.V. (1998). Did you ask a good question today? Alternative cognitive and metacognitive strategies. *Journal of Adolescent & Adult Literacy, 42*, 210–219.

Journal Responses

Purposes: To respond in writing to the texts they are reading; to provide opportunities for reflection and critical thinking.

Comprehension Strategies: Evaluating, Making Connections, Summarizing

Text: Narrative, Informational   **Use:** During and After Reading

TEACHING IDEAS

Procedure: (Begin by explaining and demonstrating Journal Responses.)

1. Provide students with a journal or a system for keeping their responses.

2. Show students examples of good responses to texts. Help students identify aspects of thoughtful reading responses.

3. Read aloud a portion of text and think aloud through a thoughtful response. Discuss with students why it was thoughtful.

4. Read aloud another portion of text and encourage students to write a thoughtful response. Share with partners.

5. For independent reading, ask students to write the date and the title of the text or chapter at the top of the page or in the left margin.

6. After reading a text, or listening to one, use Journal Responses as one of many methods students use to respond to what they read. Journal Responses can include reactions, questions, wonderings, predictions, connections, or feelings.

   Possible Journal Response prompts:

   - What was the most interesting part of what you read? Explain.
   - How did this make you feel? Explain.
   - What was important in the chapter? How do you know?
   - What is something new you learned? Explain.
   - What connection(s) did you make? Explain.

7. Encourage students to share responses in groups or with the whole class.

Example: (*Whale Journey* [1998] by Vivian French)

Journal Response Prompt: What was your favorite part? (Explain.) I like the part where the whales encountered the whale watching boat. I thought this was an interesting section because I got to read about the experience from the whale's perspective. The whales were afraid of the boat and tasted the oil from the boat in the water. I have been whale watching before and it is kind of interesting to think about the experience through a whale's eyes.

Meeting of the Minds

Purposes: To support a point of view with facts from reading; to promote debate and evaluative thinking.

Comprehension Strategy: Evaluating

Text: Narrative, Informational   **Use:** After Reading

Procedure: (Begin by explaining and demonstrating Meeting of the Minds.)

1. Teach students how to participate in Meeting of the Minds, a debate format between two characters or people that have differing viewpoints on a topic.

2. Choose a few students to help model the procedure. Give each one a role—moderator, characters (at least two), and summarizer. The moderator poses questions to which the characters respond. The

Guided Comprehension in Grades 3–8 by Maureen McLaughlin and Mary Beth Allen.
© 2009 by the International Reading Association. May be copied for classroom use.

TEACHING IDEAS

characters must support their points of view with references from the text. The summarizer recaps the information presented. Prepare the students to use a debate format to respond to predetermined questions. Model Meeting of the Minds for the whole class with these students. Discuss the process with the students, seeking questions, generating reflections, and summarizing benefits.

3. Divide the class into groups of 8 to 10. Invite 4 or 5 students to participate in Meeting of the Minds while the other students act as audience members. Then ask the students to reverse the roles. Invite students to participate in Meeting of the Minds with various narrative and informational topics occasionally throughout the year.

Example: (*Remember Pearl Harbor: American and Japanese Survivors Tell Their Stories* [2001] by Thomas B. Allen)

Meeting of the Minds
Topic: Pearl Harbor

Moderator:	Why are your two countries so hostile toward one another?
Japanese Representative:	Japan wishes to expand its territories. We wish to become a country of power. We were invading China and gaining more power when America began its threats. They stopped buying our products and cut off oil exports to our country.
American Representative:	We were on good terms with China. President Roosevelt decided we would back China and advised Japan to stop its takeover of China. America had been sending missionaries to China for some time to bring Christianity to China's people. The American people were sympathetic to China's plight.
Moderator:	Who began the first attack?
Japanese Representative:	We thought if we destroyed America's naval ships at Pearl Harbor that the U.S. would be unable to fight back and would be forced to let us continue expanding our empire. Japan sent its bombers to Pearl Harbor, with its pilots using the radio station's signal as a guide. We also sent submarines to keep us informed.
American Representative:	The Japanese began dropping torpedoes. Shrapnel flew everywhere. Some of our planes at the base made it into the air to fight against our attackers. More than 2,400 Americans were killed and 1,100 were wounded. We rebuilt our ship and will never forget the brave people that died that day. Japan signed the papers of surrender in 1945.
Summarizer:	Japan sought to destroy United States planes and ships so that it would be unopposed in its conquest of China. The Japanese were successful in surprising the United States and blew up many ships. America lost many lives at the Pearl Harbor base. America retaliated by sending aircraft carriers to attack Japan. Japan surrendered in 1945.

Source: Adapted from Richard-Amato, P.A. (1988). *Making it happen: Interaction in the second language classroom.* New York: Longman.

TEACHING IDEAS

Mind and Alternative Mind Portraits

(See blackline, page 273.)

Purpose: To examine a topic or issue from two perspectives; to examine a story through two characters.

Comprehension Strategy: Evaluating

Text: Narrative, Informational   **Use:** During and After Reading

Procedure: (Begin by explaining and modeling Mind and Alternative Mind Portraits.)

1. Introduce, read, and discuss the text.

2. Work with the students to determine a perspective that is prevalent. Then contemplate a perspective that is not presented equally or is silenced or missing from the text.

    Mind Portrait—Encourage students to label the portrait to represent the perspective of one person or character. Inside the portrait, encourage students to write, draw, or collage ideas and experiences that delineate that person's perspective.

    Alternative Mind Portrait—Encourage students to label the portrait to represent the alternative perspective of a person or character. Inside the portrait, encourage students to write, draw, or collage ideas and experiences that delineate that person's perspective.

3. Invite students to share and discuss portraits to compare and contrast perspectives.

Adaptations: Narratives and Alternative Narratives; Photographs and Alternative Photographs; Videos and Alternative Video

Example: (*Prince Caspian* [1951] by C.S. Lewis)

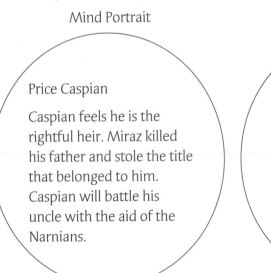

Mind Portrait

Price Caspian

Caspian feels he is the rightful heir. Miraz killed his father and stole the title that belonged to him. Caspian will battle his uncle with the aid of the Narnians.

Alternative Mind Portrait

Miraz

Miraz is Caspian's uncle. He killed Caspian's father and took his place as ruler. Miraz feels he is the best ruler for their land and now that he has a son as an heir, Caspian must die.

Source: McLaughlin, M. (2002). *Guided Comprehension in action: Lessons for grades 3–8*. Newark, DE: International Reading Association.

TEACHING IDEAS

Persuasive Writing

Purposes: To express points of view with supporting ideas; to foster understanding of multiple perspectives on a topic.

Comprehension Strategy: Evaluating

Text: Narrative, Informational   **Use:** Before, During, and After Reading

Procedure: (Begin by explaining and demonstrating Persuasive Writing.)

1. Introduce a topic by reading an article that contains two points of view about the same issue.

2. Use a Think-Aloud to share the different perspectives about the topic.

3. Then choose a side and write persuasively to defend your choice. Think aloud throughout this process. Be certain to support your argument with facts.

4. Discuss your writing with the students and encourage them to express their ideas about the topic.

5. Then guide the students to engage in Persuasive Writing by sharing a different article and scaffolding their ability to write persuasively.

6. Provide additional opportunities for students to engage in practice by using current events, character choices, and historical events in other instructional settings.

Example: (*Tracking Trash: Flotsam, Jetsam, and the Science of Ocean Motion* [2007] by Loree Griffin Burns)

I think the third section of *Tracking Trash* is the most important because it explains how harmful all of the trash that travels through the ocean is. I was surprised to learn about the abandoned fishing nets that Loree Burns described as tangled plastic as long as a school bus and how ocean animals can become tangled in them and die. The nets can also attract predators that can become tangled. These masses of plastic can also damage coral reefs. Everyone from people who go to the beach to those who use oceans for business should be required not to litter. We need our oceans to live and they are becoming more and more polluted.

Source: McLaughlin, M., & Allen, M.B. (2002). *Guided Comprehension: A teaching model for grades 3–8.* Newark, DE: International Reading Association.

COMPREHENSION ROUTINES

Directed Reading–Thinking Activity (DR–TA)/ Directed Listening–Thinking Activity (DR–LA)

Purposes: To encourage students to make predictions about a story or text; to use the author's clues to make meaningful connections and predictions; to foster active reading or listening of a text.

Comprehension Strategies: Previewing, Making Connections, Monitoring

Text: Narrative, Informational   **Use:** Before, During, and After Reading

Procedure: (Begin by explaining and demonstrating DR–TA or DL–TA.)

1. Invite students to look at the title and/or cover of a book and ask, "What do you think this story (or book) is about? Explain your thinking." Students respond with predictions and reasons for their thinking. This helps activate prior knowledge.

2. Ask students to read to a designated stopping point in the text, review their predictions, make new predictions, and explain the reasons for the new predictions.

3. Repeat Step 3 until the text is finished.

4. Encourage students to reflect on their predictions, stating what was helpful, what was surprising, and what was confusing.

   Other ideas for using DR–TA:

   • Students can predict orally, in writing, or by illustrating.

   • For DL–TA, students listen to the story. The reader stops at various preselected places and asks students to review predictions, make new ones, and explain their reasoning.

Source: Stauffer, R. (1975). *Directing the reading–thinking process*. New York: Harper & Row.

Literature Circles

(See Chapter 2 and blacklines, pages 284–286.)

Purposes: To provide a structure for student talk about texts from a variety of perspectives; to provide opportunities for social learning.

Comprehension Strategies: Making Connections, Knowing How Words Work, Monitoring, Summarizing, Evaluating

Text: Narrative, Informational   **Use:** After Reading

Procedure: (Begin by explaining and demonstrating Literature Circles.)

1. Invite students to select books to read and to join groups based on their text selections.

2. Ask groups to meet to develop a schedule—how much they will read, when they will meet, etc.

3. Encourage students to read the predetermined amount of text independently, taking notes as they read. Students can keep their notes in their Guided Comprehension Journals. The notes can reflect the students' role in the Literature Circle or their personal connections to the text. Roles within the Literature Circles should vary from meeting to meeting.

4. Encourage students to continue to meet according to the group schedule to discuss ideas about the text until the book is completed.

5. Provide opportunities for students to participate in Literature Circles in Stage Two of Guided Comprehension.

Source: Daniels, H. (1994). *Literature circles: Voice and choice in the student-centered classroom*. York, ME: Stenhouse.

Questioning the Author (QtA)

(See Chapter 2 and blackline, page 296.)

Purposes: To facilitate understanding of text; to use questions to promote discussion for the purpose of collaboratively constructing meaning from text.

Comprehension Strategies: Making Connections, Self-Questioning, Monitoring

Text: Narrative, Informational   **Use:** During Reading

Procedure: (Begin by explaining and demonstrating QtA.)

1. Read the text to determine major understandings and potential problems.

2. Determine segments within the text to use for discussion. These segments should be chosen because of their importance in helping students to construct meaning related to the major understandings that have been determined in Step 1.

3. Create queries that will lead the students to the major understandings. Develop initiating queries to start the discussion. Anticipate student responses to these queries to determine follow-up queries. Use these to focus and move the discussion.

4. Guide the students to read the text, using the queries to facilitate discussion during reading.

5. When students become proficient at QtA, have them use it in Stage Two of Guided Comprehension as an independent comprehension routine.

   Sample Queries:

   Initiating
   - What is the author trying to say here?
   - What is the author's message?
   - What is the author talking about?

   Follow-up
   - What does the author mean here?
   - Did the author explain this clearly?
   - Does this make sense with what the author told us before?
   - How does this connect with what the author had told us here?
   - Does the author tell us why?
   - Why do you think the author tells us this now?

Narrative

- How do things look for this character now?
- How has the author let you know that something has changed?
- How has the author settled this for us?
- Given what the author has already told us about the character, what do you think he's up to?

Source: Beck, I.L., McKeown, M.G., Hamilton, R.L., & Kucan, L. (1997). *Questioning the Author: An approach to enhancing student engagement with text*. Newark, DE: International Reading Association.

Reciprocal Teaching

(See Chapter 2 and blacklines, pages 297–299.)

Purposes: To provide a format for using comprehension strategies—predicting, self-questioning, monitoring, and summarizing—in a small-group setting; to facilitate a group effort to bring meaning to a text; to monitor thinking and learning.

Comprehension Strategies: Previewing, Self-Questioning, Monitoring, Summarizing

Text: Narrative, Informational   **Use:** Before, During, and After Reading

Procedure: (Begin by explaining and demonstrating Reciprocal Teaching.)

1. Explain the procedure and each of the four reading comprehension strategies: predicting, self-questioning, monitoring, summarizing.

2. Model thinking related to each of the four strategies by using an authentic text and thinking aloud.

3. With the whole class, guide students to engage in similar types of thinking by providing responses for each of the strategies. Sentence stems, such as the following, facilitate this:

   Predicting
   - I think...
   - I bet...
   - I wonder...
   - I imagine...
   - I suppose...

   Questioning
   - What connections can I make?
   - How does this support my thinking?

   Clarifying
   - I did not understand the part where...
   - I need to know more about...

   Summarizing
   - The important ideas in what I read are...

4. Place students in groups of four and provide each group with copies of the same text to use as the basis for Reciprocal Teaching.

5. Assign each student one of the four strategies and the suggested prompts.

6. Invite students to engage in Reciprocal Teaching using the process that was modeled.

7. Ask students to reflect on the process and their comprehension of the text.

8. Provide opportunities for the students to engage in Reciprocal Teaching in Stage Two of Guided Comprehension as an independent comprehension routine.

Source: Palincsar, A.S., & Brown, A.L. (1986). Interactive teaching to promote independent learning from text. *The Reading Teacher, 39,* 771–777.

PREDICT-O-GRAM

Vocabulary Words

Characters	Setting

Problem	Action	Solution

PROBABLE PASSAGES

Setting:

Characters:

Problem:

Events:

Solution:

QUESTIONING THE TEXT

1. What is the text structure (e.g., narrative, informational)? What clues help me know this?

   _____

2. What questions will this text answer?

   _____

3. What questions do I have for this text?

   _____

4. What clues does the cover (title, cover art, author) offer? What does the contents page tell me?

   _____

5. What do the physical aspects (size, length, print size) of the book tell me?

   _____

6. Is the author familiar? What do I know about the author? What connections can I make?

   _____

7. Is the topic familiar? What do I know about the topic? What connections can I make?

   _____

8. What clues do the genre and writing style provide for me?

   _____

9. Is there a summary? What does it help me know?

   _____

10. What does the information on the book jacket tell me?

    _____

    Summary of what I now know about the text:

    _____

    _____

    _____

STORY IMPRESSIONS

Title: _____

Words

Prediction

Guided Comprehension in Grades 3–8 by Maureen McLaughlin and Mary Beth Allen. © 2009 by the International Reading Association. May be copied for classroom use.

"I WONDER" BOOKMARK

"I Wonder" Bookmark

Page _____

I wonder...

_____

_____

_____

because...

_____

_____

_____

Page _____

I wonder...

_____

_____

_____

because...

_____

_____

_____

Page _____

I wonder...

_____

_____

_____

because...

_____

_____

_____

K–W–L

Topic: _____

K (What I know or think I know)	W (What I want to know)	L (What I learned)

K–W–L–S

Topic: _____

K (What I know or think I know)	W (What I want to know)	L (What I learned)	S (What I still want to know)

Guided Comprehension in Grades 3–8 by Maureen McLaughlin and Mary Beth Allen. © 2009 by the International Reading Association. May be copied for classroom use.

QUESTION–ANSWER RELATIONSHIPS (QAR)

<u>In the Text</u>

- Right There—the answer is within one sentence in the text.

- Think and Search—the answer is contained in more than one sentence from the text.

<u>In My Head</u>

- Author and You—the answer needs information from the reader's background knowledge and the text.

- On Your Own—the answer needs information from only the reader's background knowledge.

THICK AND THIN QUESTIONS

Text: _____

Page	Thin Questions	Thick Questions

DOUBLE-ENTRY JOURNAL

Idea	Reflection/Reaction

DOUBLE-ENTRY JOURNAL

Idea/Text From Story	My Connection

DRAWING CONNECTIONS

Draw a picture to represent a connection you made while reading the story.

Write one or more sentences to explain your drawing.

SEQUENCE CHAIN

Title

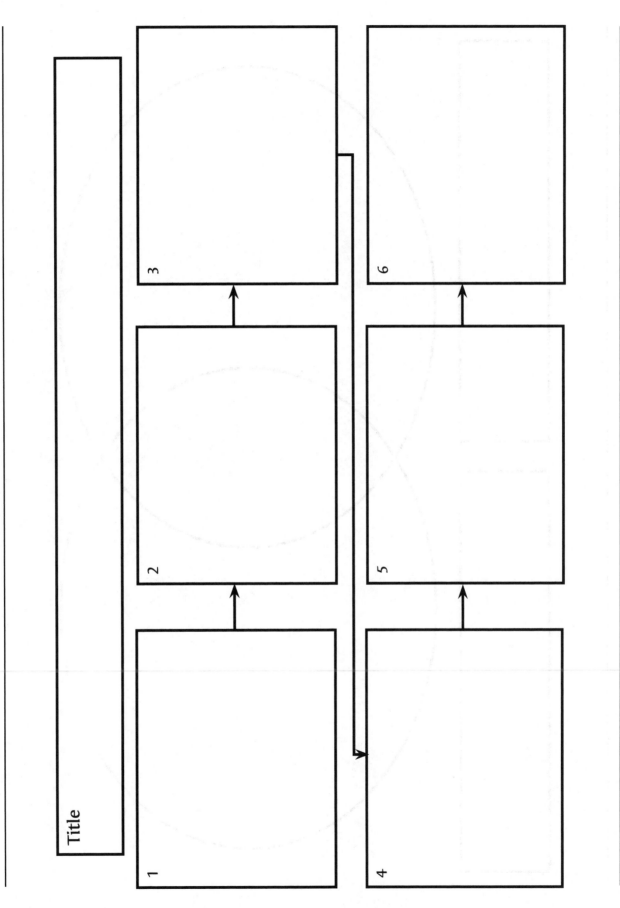

1

2

3

4

5

6

VENN DIAGRAM

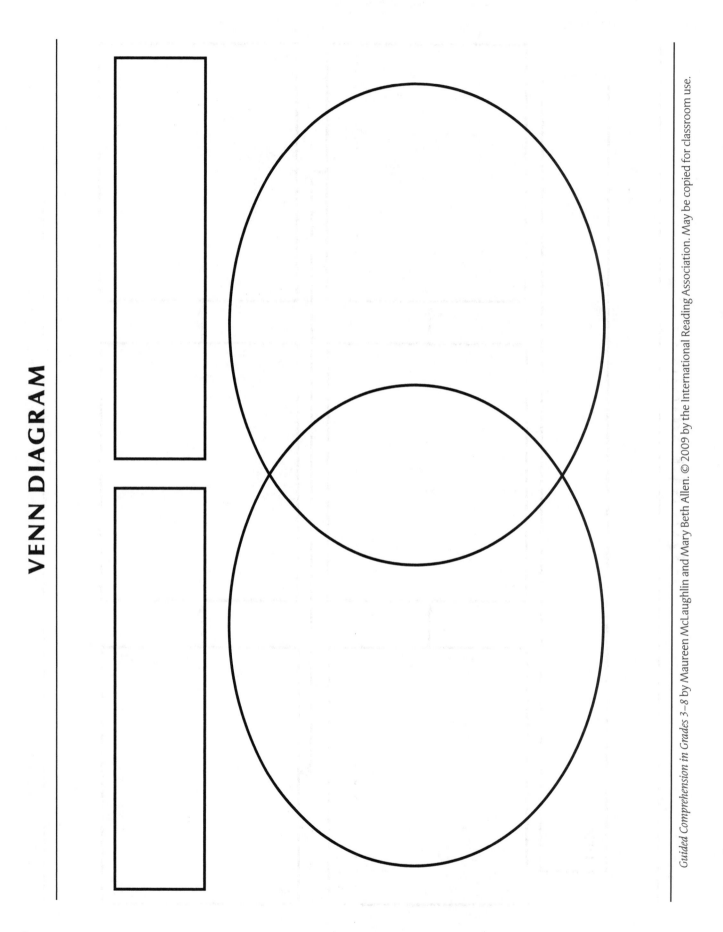

STORY MAP

Title/Chapter: _____

Setting	Characters

Problem

Event 1

Event 2

Event 3

Event 4

Event 5

Solution

Theme

MAIN IDEA TABLE

Main Idea

COMPARE/CONTRAST MATRIX

Story Elements

Title	Characters	Setting	Problem	Solution

PHOTOGRAPHS OF THE MIND

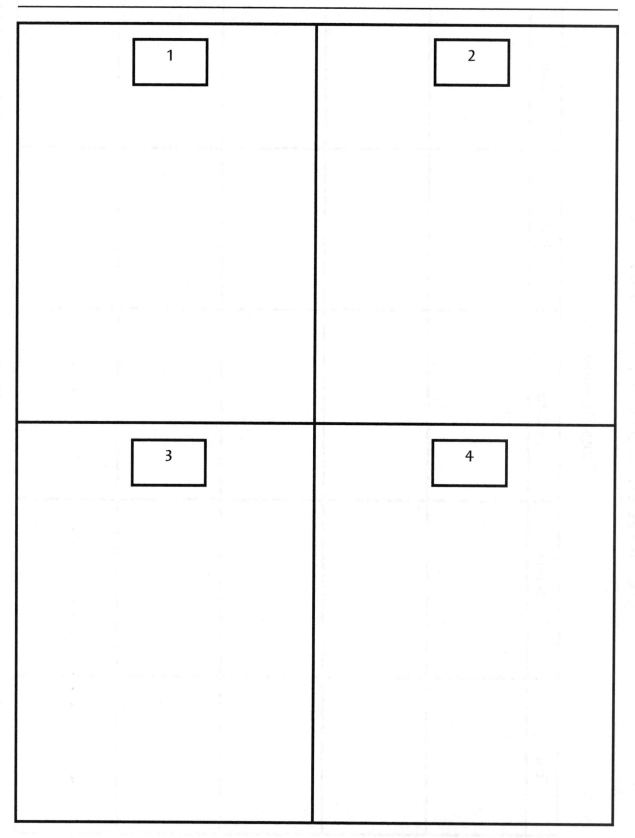

CONCEPT OF DEFINITION MAP

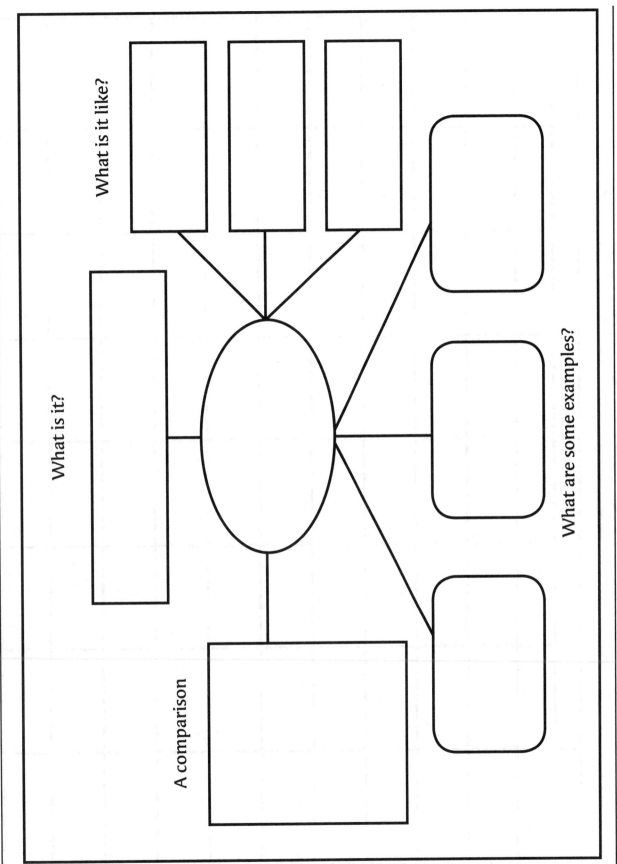

What is it?

What is it like?

A comparison

What are some examples?

SEMANTIC FEATURE ANALYSIS

Categories	Characteristics									

BOOKMARK TECHNIQUE

Bookmark 1

Name: _____

Date: _____

The part I found most interesting was...

Page: _____

Paragraph: _____

Bookmark 2

Name: _____

Date: _____

Something that confused me was...

Page: _____

Paragraph: _____

BOOKMARK TECHNIQUE

Bookmark 3

Name: _____

Date: _____

A word I think the whole class needs to talk about is...

I think it means...

Page: _____

Paragraph: _____

Bookmark 4

Name: _____

Date: _____

The illustration, chart, map, or graph that helped me understand what I was reading was...

It helped me to understand because...

Page: _____

Paragraph: _____

INSERT BOOKMARKS

INSERT Bookmark 1

✓ = I knew that!

+ = I didn't know that!

− = I thought differently.

? = What does this mean?

Page: _____

I knew that!

Page: _____

I knew that!

INSERT Bookmark 2

✓ = I knew that!

+ = I didn't know that!

− = I thought differently.

? = What does this mean?

Page: _____

I didn't know that!

Page: _____

I didn't know that!

INSERT BOOKMARKS

INSERT Bookmark 3

✓ = I knew that!

+ = I didn't know that!

− = I thought differently.

? = What does this mean?

Page: _____

I thought differently.

Page: _____

I thought differently.

INSERT Bookmark 4

✓ = I knew that!

+ = I didn't know that!

− = I thought differently.

? = What does this mean?

Page: _____

What does this mean?

Page: _____

What does this mean?

BIO-PYRAMID

1. _____
   Person's name

2. _____
   Two words describing the person

3. _____
   Three words describing the person's childhood

4. _____
   Four words indicating a problem the person had to overcome

5. _____
   Five words stating one of his or her accomplishments

6. _____
   Six words stating a second accomplishment

7. _____
   Seven words stating a third accomplishment

8. _____
   Eight words stating how mankind benefited from his or her accomplishments

Guided Comprehension in Grades 3–8 by Maureen McLaughlin and Mary Beth Allen. © 2009 by the International Reading Association. May be copied for classroom use.

LYRIC RETELLING/LYRIC SUMMARY

Text: _____

Tune: _____

Verse 1:

_____

_____

_____

_____

_____

Verse 2:

_____

_____

_____

_____

_____

Refrain (or Verse 3):

_____

_____

_____

_____

_____

_____

_____

NARRATIVE PYRAMID

1. _____
   Character's name

2. _____
   Two words describing the character

3. _____
   Three words describing the setting

4. _____
   Four words stating the problem

5. _____
   Five words describing one event

6. _____
   Six words describing another event

7. _____
   Seven words describing a third event

8. _____
   Eight words describing a solution to the problem

QuIP RESEARCH GRID

Topic: _____

Questions	Answers	
	Source A:	Source B:
1.		
2.		
3.		

RETELLING

Retelling for _____

Who?	Where?
Draw:	Draw:
Label:	Label:

What happened?	How did it end?
Draw:	Draw:
Label:	Label:

SUMMARY CUBE

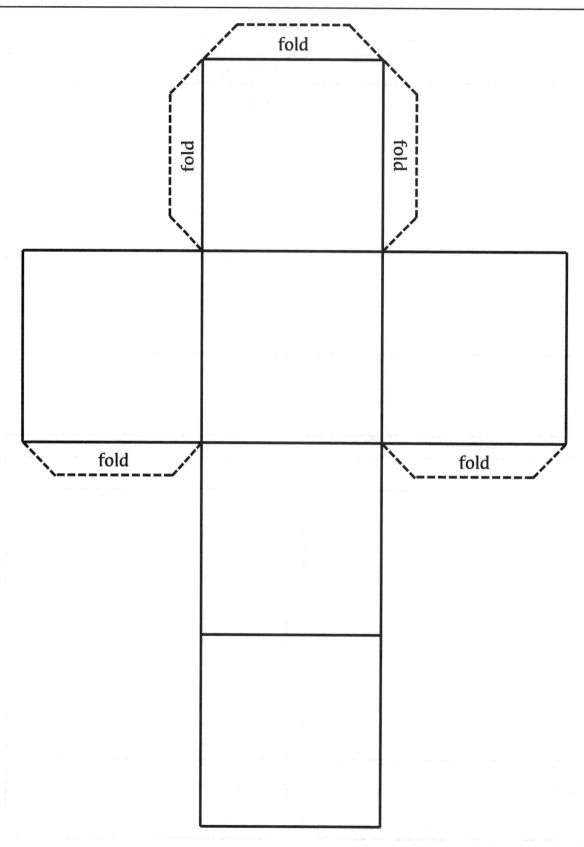

CONTRAST CHART

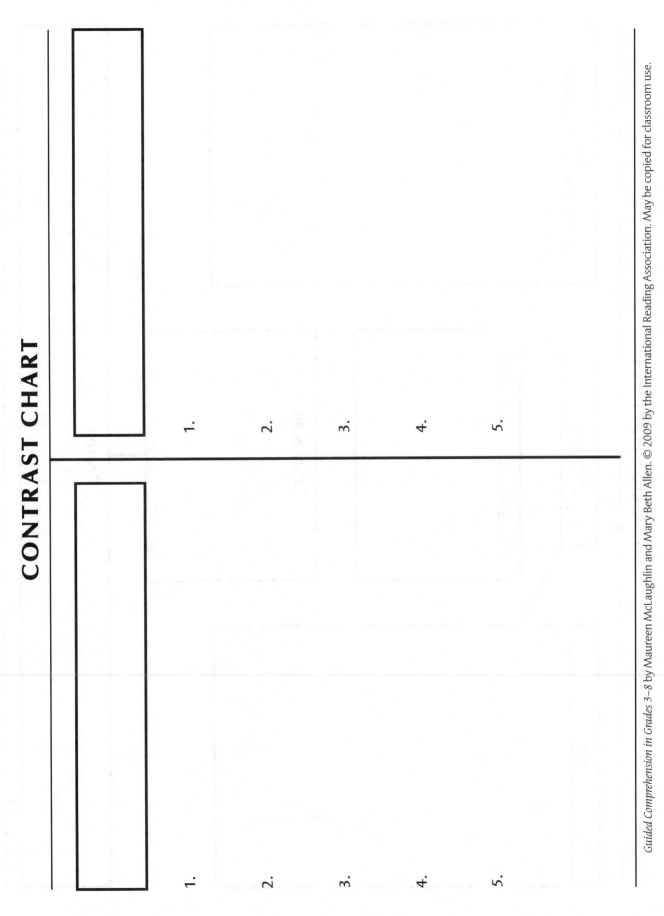

1.

2.

3.

4.

5.

1.

2.

3.

4.

5.

DISCUSSION WEB

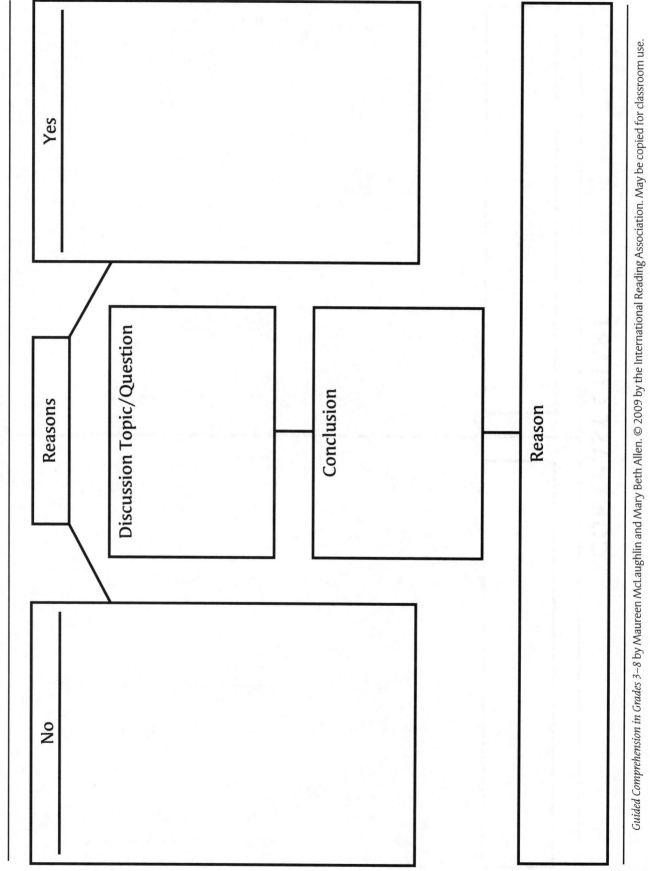

Yes

Reasons

No

Discussion Topic/Question

Conclusion

Reason

MIND AND ALTERNATIVE MIND PORTRAITS

Mind Portrait

Alternative Mind Portrait

Forms for Organizing and Managing Comprehension Centers and Routines

CENTER CHART FOR STUDENTS

Center: _____ Week: _____

Directions: If you used this center, sign your name and place a check mark underneath the day you visited.

Students	Monday	Tuesday	Wednesday	Thursday	Friday

CENTER REFLECTIONS

Name: _____ Date: _____

Center: _____

While I was working at this center, I was able to

_____

_____

_____

_____

I learned

_____

_____

_____

_____

The next time I plan to

_____

_____

_____

_____

_____

_____

CENTER RUBRIC

Center: _____

Directions: Think about what you did at the center today. Then use this rubric to describe
your performance.

	Excellent	Very Good	Satisfactory	Minimal
	Best effort Excellent thinking Great progress	Very good effort Significant thinking Considerable progress	Average effort Satisfactory thinking Acceptable progress	Poor effort Inadequate thinking Little progress
	4	3	2	1
My work is complete.	4	3	2	1
I followed the directions.	4	3	2	1
I made personal interpretations.	4	3	2	1
My presentation is appealing.	4	3	2	1
I made connections that are supported by the text.	4	3	2	1
I responded in multiple ways.	4	3	2	1

Comments:

_____

_____

_____

_____

_____

_____

_____

Name: _____   Date: _____

CENTER STUDENT SELF-ASSESSMENT

Name: _____   Date: _____

Center: _____

My goal was

_____

_____

_____

What I did well

_____

_____

_____

What I learned

_____

_____

_____

My new goal is

_____

_____

_____

_____

CHOOSE YOUR OWN PROJECT CHART

Choose one idea from each column to create the project you will complete to demonstrate your knowledge of the topic.

For example:

Verb	Topic/Theme	Products/Performance
	Desert	
Retell	characteristics	inquiry-based project
Explain	climate to survive	acrostic
Summarize	uses and benefits	fact/fiction book
Describe	environment	drawing
Construct	life span/process	diamante
Illustrate	protection	report
Show	extreme weather	newspaper article
Demonstrate		PowerPoint slide show presentation
Compare/Contrast		song
Classify		dramatic interpretation
Organize		collage
Predict		three-dimensional model
Imagine		self-authored or class authored book
Design		definition poem
Evaluate		biography/autobiography
Support		
Rate		

Example Project: Compare and contrast hurricanes and tornadoes, two types of extreme weather, using a PowerPoint slideshow.

- -

Verb	Topic/Theme	Products/Performance
	_____	
	Subtopics	
Retell	_____	acrostic
Explain		fact/fable book
Summarize	_____	drawing
Describe		diamante
Construct	_____	report
Illustrate		newspaper article
Show	_____	slide show presentation
Demonstrate		song
Compare	_____	dramatic interpretation
Classify		collage
Organize		three-dimensional model
Predict		
Imagine		_____
Design		
Evaluate		_____
Support		
Rate		

My Project: _____

Name: _____ Date: _____

CLASS CENTER CHART FOR TEACHERS

Centers					
Students					

DIRECTIONS FOR MAKING BOOKS

Slotted Book

STEP 1

Take at least two pieces of paper and hold them in a landscape (horizontal) position (Fig. 1). You can use more than two pages to create books with more than four pages.

STEP 2—MAKING THE SLOT

Separate one page from the pack of papers. Make sure the fold or SPINE is nice and flat. Measure 1 1/2 inches from the top of the spine and make a mark and the same at the bottom of the page of the spine.

Cut into the spine and carefully cut away the spine between the marks you have made. Only cut into the spine about 1/16 of an inch (Fig. 2). Open your page and you should see a SLOT (Fig. 3).

STEP 3—MAKING THE SLITS

Take the other page(s) and make sure the spine is nice and flat. Measure the same 1 1/2 inches from the top and bottom of the spine.

This time cut from the bottom of the page up to the mark to create a SLIT. Repeat the process at the top of the page. You should have a SLIT at the top and bottom of the page (Fig. 4).

STEP 4—SLIPPING THE BOOK TOGETHER

Open the slotted page. Take the other page(s) with slits and bend them in half horizontally. SLIP them through the slot until you have reached the center of the book. Carefully slip the slit and slot together and roll the pages open and fold it like a book.

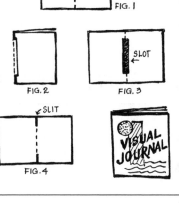

Dos à Dos Dialogue Journals

Dos à dos is a French expression meaning a couch or a carriage that holds two people sitting back to back. When two people sit back to back they see different things or they see the same thing from different points of view. This book is really two books in one (or three or more—you decide). There is room for each person's point of view or story. Dos à dos can be a wonderful way to structure a dialogue journal where you and another person write back and forth to each other. Each person has their own book and in turn responds to the others ideas, questions, and feelings. Turn them around and read each others response!

STEP 1

For a two part dos à dos take a piece of 11 x 17 paper and cut it lengthwise in half (5 1/2 inches). Take one strip and fold into three equal parts. It should look like a Z (Fig. 1).

STEP 2

Cut all the text pages so they are 8 x 5 1/2 inches. Fold them in half and divide them to create two booklets or signatures with equal pages.

STEP 3

Slip a signature into the first fold. The crease of the signature or booklet should be nested inside the crease of the cover. You can either staple the signature into the cover or sew the signature into the cover. The simplest way is to staple the booklet in by using a book arm stapler that lets you staple deep into the center of the signature.

STEP 4

Repeat step 3 for other signature nesting it in the other crease.

STEP 5

Fold the book back and forth so that you can open one signature from the front and one from the back.

STEP 6—DECORATE THE COVERS.

Consider these wild variations! As with any book, you can change the shape, size, and materials of this book. Make a dos à dos dialogue journal for three or four people (Fig. 2). Just make an extra long cover or paste together two of them. What an interesting conversation you could have!

Try different types of text pages. If you need some extra long pages, cut some text pages longer than the others, and make fold outs. Cut some pages taller than others and make fold downs. Add some pop-ups.

Basic Origami Book

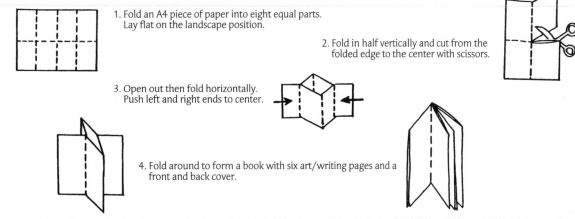

1. Fold an A4 piece of paper into eight equal parts. Lay flat on the landscape position.

2. Fold in half vertically and cut from the folded edge to the center with scissors.

3. Open out then fold horizontally. Push left and right ends to center.

4. Fold around to form a book with six art/writing pages and a front and back cover.

Source: Pinciotti, P. (2001). *Book arts: The creation of beautiful books.* East Stroudsburg, PA: East Stroudsburg University of Pennsylvania.

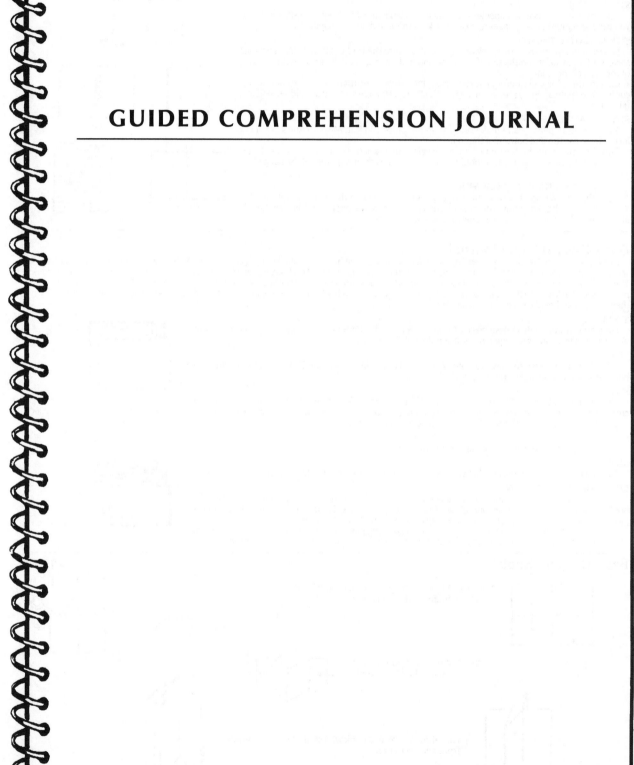

GUIDED COMPREHENSION JOURNAL

"IF I WERE IN CHARGE OF THE WORLD"

If I Were in Charge of _____

by _____

If I were in charge of_____ , I'd cancel

_____,

_____,

_____ , and also

_____.

If I were in charge of_____,

There'd be _____,

_____ , and

_____.

If I were in charge of _____,

You wouldn't have _____

You wouldn't have _____

You wouldn't have _____

Or _____

You wouldn't even have_____

If I were in charge of _____,

_____

_____

And a person _____

And _____

Would still be allowed to be in charge of the world.

Source: Adapted from Viorst, J. (1981). *If I were in charge of the world and other worries*. New York: Atheneum.

LITERATURE CIRCLE BOOKMARK

Literature Circle Bookmark

Name:_____

Date: _____

I will talk to my group about...

I will ask my group about...

My favorite part was ...

Other ideas...

Literature Circle Bookmark

Name:_____

Date: _____

I will talk to my group about...

I will ask my group about...

My favorite part was ...

Other ideas...

LITERATURE CIRCLE GROUP ASSESSMENT

Group Members

_____   _____

_____   _____

_____   _____

4 = Excellent   3 = Good   2= Fair   1 = Poor

   1. My group worked well together. _____

   2. My group used its time wisely. _____

   3. I worked well and completed all my jobs. _____

   4. I think my group deserves a _____

Student Comments:

Teacher Comments:

LITERATURE CIRCLE SELF-ASSESSMENT

Name: _____   Date: _____

Text: _____

1. How would you rate your participation in the discussion?

   just right   too much   too little   not at all

2. What did you do to prepare for the Literature Circle that was helpful?

   _____

   _____

   _____

3. What is something helpful that you contributed to the discussion?

   _____

   _____

   _____

4. What is something you learned in your Literature Circle?

   _____

   _____

   _____

5. How would you rate your group's discussion?

   lively   average   boring

6. How helpful was today's discussion?

   very helpful   somewhat helpful   not helpful

7. What worked well today? What will you do to improve next time?

   _____

   _____

   _____

   _____

Guided Comprehension in Grades 3–8 by Maureen McLaughlin and Mary Beth Allen.
© 2009 by the International Reading Association. May be copied for classroom use.

MAKING AND WRITING WORDS CENTER

How many words can you make from the word _____ ?

Two-letter words:

____ ____   ____ ____   ____ ____   ____ ____   ____ ____

Three-letter words:

____ ____ ____   ____ ____ ____   ____ ____ ____   ____ ____ ____

____ ____ ____   ____ ____ ____   ____ ____ ____   ____ ____ ____

____ ____ ____   ____ ____ ____   ____ ____ ____   ____ ____ ____

Four-letter words:

____ ____ ____ ____   ____ ____ ____ ____   ____ ____ ____ ____

____ ____ ____ ____   ____ ____ ____ ____   ____ ____ ____ ____

____ ____ ____ ____   ____ ____ ____ ____   ____ ____ ____ ____

Larger words:

_____   _____

_____   _____

Making and Writing Words

Directions: Use the vowels and consonants provided to make words based on the clues given by the teacher.

Vowels	Consonants

Directions: Listen carefully as your teacher or classmate provides clues to words that you will write in each box.

1	7	13
2	8	14
3	9	15
4	10	16
5	11	17
6	12	18

Source: Adapted from Rasinski, T.V. (1999). Making and writing words using letter patterns. *Reading Online* [Online]. Available: www.readingonline.org/articles/words/rasinski_index.html.

MANAGING STAGE TWO

OPTION 1: Participation Chart

Student	Session 1	Session 2

OPTION 2: Center Rotation Chart

Center *Group*	_____	_____	_____	_____
Blue	1	2	3	4
Green	2	3	4	1
Red	3	4	1	2
Yellow	4	1	2	3

MYSTERY PYRAMID

1. _____
   (one word—detective's name)

2. _____
   (two words—describe the detective)

3. _____
   (three words—describe the victim)

4. _____
   (four words—describe the crime/crime scene)

5. _____
   (five words—explain the motive)

6. _____
   (six words—clues that distract you from discovering the culprit)

7. _____
   (seven words—clues that help you discover the culprit)

8. _____
   (eight words—how the case was solved)

Guided Comprehension in Grades 3–8 by Maureen McLaughlin and Mary Beth Allen. © 2009 by the International Reading Association. May be copied for classroom use.

MYSTERY SUSPECT ORGANIZER

Name: _____   Date: _____

<u>Prediction</u>
(Who do you think the culprit is?)

_____

_____

_____

Suspect   Suspect   Suspect

_____   _____   _____

Clues: Clues: Clues:

_____   _____   _____

_____   _____   _____

_____   _____   _____

_____   _____   _____

_____   _____   _____

_____   _____   _____

<u>Conclusion</u>
(Who is the culprit? Why do you think so?)

_____

_____

_____

_____

_____

_____

_____

PATTERN BOOK ORGANIZER

Title:

Fortunately _____

Unfortunately _____

Fortunately _____

Unfortunately _____

Fortunately _____

Unfortunately _____

Fortunately _____

Unfortunately _____

Fortunately _____

Unfortunately _____

Fortunately _____

Unfortunately _____

Fortunately _____

Unfortunately _____

Fortunately _____

Unfortunately _____

Fortunately _____

Unfortunately _____

Source: Charlip, R. (1993). *Fortunately*. New York: Aladdin.

PATTERN BOOK ORGANIZER

Fact or Fable?

Fact or Fable

_____

_____

_____

Answer _____

Support

_____

_____

_____

_____

Fact or Fable

_____

_____

_____

Answer _____

Support

_____

_____

_____

_____

PATTERN BOOK ORGANIZER

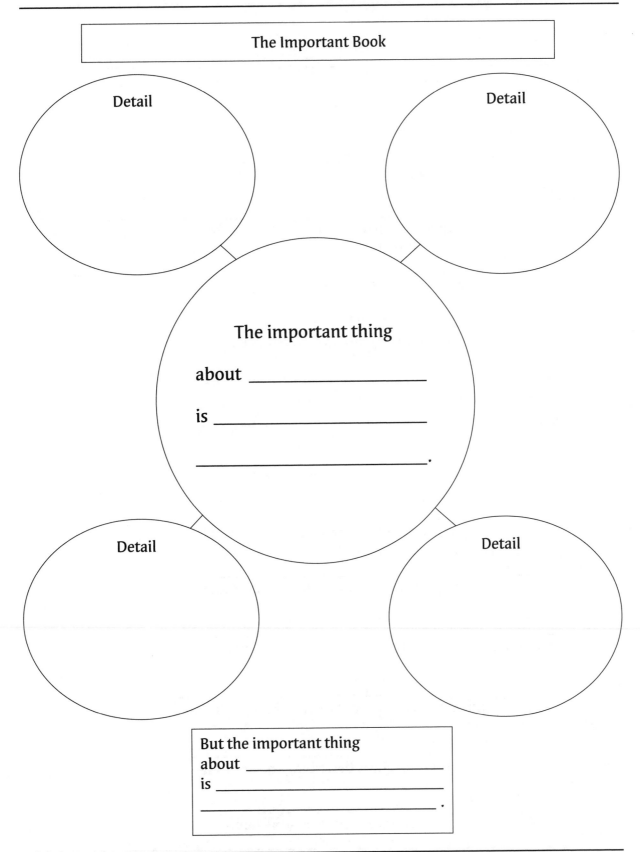

The Important Book

Detail

Detail

The important thing

about _____

is _____

_____ .

Detail

Detail

But the important thing
about _____
is _____
_____ .

POETRY FORMS

Cinquain

_____

one word—noun

_____   _____

two adjectives describing line one

_____   _____   _____

three -*ing* words telling actions of line 1

_____   _____   _____   _____

four word phrase describing a feeling related to line 1

_____

one word—synonym or reference to line 1

Diamante

_____

subject—one noun

_____   _____

two adjectives describing the subject

_____   _____   _____

three participles (-*ing*) telling about the subject

_____   _____   _____   _____

four nouns—first two relate to the subject; last two relate to the opposite

_____   _____   _____

three participles (-*ing*) telling about the opposite

_____   _____

two adjectives describing the opposite

_____

opposite of subject—one noun

POETRY FORMS

Bio-Poem

Line 1 — First name   _____

Line 2 — Four traits that describe #1   _____

Line 3 — Related to/sibling of   _____

Line 4 — Cares about/likes   _____

Line 5 — Who feels   _____

Line 6 — Who needs   _____

Line 7 — Who gives   _____

Line 8 — Who fears   _____

Line 9 — Who would like to see   _____

Line 10 — Resident of   _____

Line 11 — Last name   _____

Definition Poem

What is _____ ? (topic)

_____

Description of topic

_____

Description of topic

_____

Description of topic

_____

Description of topic

_____

Description of topic

_____

Description of topic

_____

Description of topic

That is _____ ! (topic)

QUESTIONING THE AUTHOR SELF-ASSESSMENT

Name: _____   Date: _____

Text: _____

1. How would you rate your participation in the discussion?

   just right   too much   too little   not at all

2. What did you figure out about the text from Questioning the Author? What new insights did you gain?

   _____

   _____

   _____

3. What message do you think the author was trying to convey?

   _____

   _____

   _____

4. What information was missing or discounted?

   _____

   _____

   _____

5. What is something you contributed to the discussion?

   _____

   _____

   _____

6. How would you rate your group's discussion?

   lively   average   boring

7. How helpful was today's discussion?

   very helpful   somewhat helpful   not helpful

8. What worked well today? What will you do to improve next time?

   _____

   _____

   _____

   _____

Guided Comprehension in Grades 3–8 by Maureen McLaughlin and Mary Beth Allen.
© 2009 by the International Reading Association. May be copied for classroom use.

RECIPROCAL TEACHING BOOKMARKS

Reciprocal Teaching Predicting Bookmark

Name: _____

Date: _____

Title: _____

Pages: _____

Make a prediction about what might happen next in the text.

My prediction is:

_____

_____

_____

_____

_____

I think this because:

_____

_____

_____

_____

_____

Prediction Prompts–

I think...   I predict...
I bet...   I anticipate...
I wonder...   I hypothesize...
I imagine...   Based on...I predict...
I suppose...

Reciprocal Teaching Questioning Bookmark

Name: _____

Date: _____

Title: _____

Pages: _____

Create questions that help to identify important information and connect prior knowledge with new ideas.

Questions:

1. _____

   _____

   _____

2. _____

   _____

   _____

3. _____

   _____

Question Prompts–

Who is...?   What if...?
Where...?   I wonder how...?
When...?   Which is better...? Why?
What...?   Why did...?
How...?   What do I think...?
Why is...?   Why?

RECIPROCAL TEACHING BOOKMARKS

Reciprocal Teaching Clarifying Bookmark

Name: _____

Date: _____

Title: _____

Pages: _____

Identify words or concepts that are difficult to understand. Share how you figured it out.

Word or concept:

_____

_____

_____

I figured it out by:

_____

_____

_____

Word or concept:

_____

_____

_____

I figured it out by:

_____

_____

_____

Clarifying Prompts—

I did not understand...
The confusing part was...
I need to know more about...
A difficult word/phrase is...

Reciprocal Teaching Summarizing Bookmark

Name: _____

Date: _____

Title: _____

Pages: _____

Identify the key ideas and summarize them.

Key ideas:

1. _____

_____

_____

2. _____

_____

_____

3. _____

_____

Summary:

_____

_____

_____

_____

_____

Summary Prompts—

The important ideas so far...
New facts I have learned...
The main character(s) is...
The problem is...
The important story events are...

Source: Allen, M.B. (2002). *Reciprocal teaching: A Guided Comprehension routine.* Paper presented at the 47th Annual Convention of the International Reading Association, San Francisco, CA..

RECIPROCAL TEACHING SELF-ASSESSMENT

Name: _____   Date: _____

Text: _____

1. How would you rate your participation in the discussion?

    just right   too much   too little   not at all

2. What did you figure out about the text from Reciprocal Teaching? What new insights did you gain?

    _____

    _____

    _____

3. What is the main message or theme of the text? What makes you think this?

    _____

    _____

    _____

4. How did the comprehension strategies you used help you read the text?

    _____

    _____

    _____

5. What is something you contributed to the discussion?

    _____

    _____

    _____

6. How would you rate your group's discussion?

    lively   average   boring

7. How helpful was today's discussion?

    very helpful   somewhat helpful   not helpful

8. What worked well today? What will you do to improve next time?

    _____

    _____

    _____

    _____

REQUIRED AND OPTIONAL CENTER FORM

Name: _____   Date: _____

Centers	Monday	Tuesday	Wednesday	Thursday	Friday
D					
D					
W					
W					
W					
W					
W	My Choice: _____				
W	My Choice: _____				

Mark the day with an *X* when you visit that center.
D = visit center daily; W = visit center weekly

WORD DETECTIVE—SEQUENTIAL ROUNDTABLE ORGANIZER

A	J	S
B	K	T
C	L	U
D	M	V
E	N	W
F	O	X
G	P	Y
H	Q	Z
I	R	

WRITE YOUR OWN MYSTERY

Draw, describe, or explain the crime scene.

Choose the detective, a suspect, or a victim and write four words to describe that character.

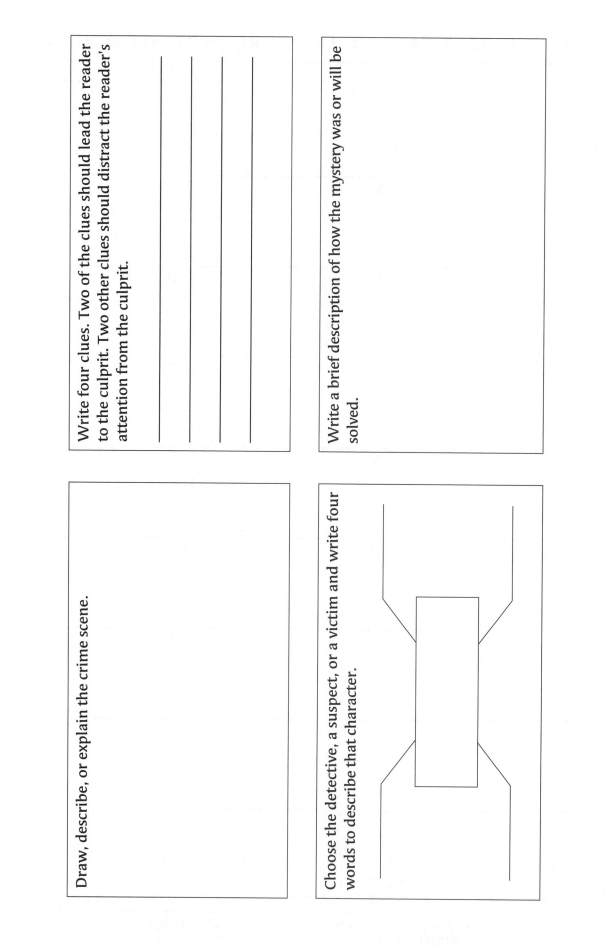

Write four clues. Two of the clues should lead the reader to the culprit. Two other clues should distract the reader's attention from the culprit.

_____

_____

_____

_____

Write a brief description of how the mystery was or will be solved.

101 Literature Response Prompts

Students may select the prompt to which they will respond. To accommodate personal strengths, offer students choices based on a variety of response modes—sketching, writing, dramatizing, etc.

Prompts That Focus on Writing

1. Write yourself into the story. Explain your reasoning.

2. Pretend that you are one of the characters and keep a journal as that person.

3. Use persuasive letter-writing techniques to write to the author to convince him or her to write a prequel or sequel.

4. Write newspaper articles appropriate for the time in which the novel took place.

5. What would happen next? Sketch the next chapter.

6. Write a letter of advice to the main character from your perspective.

7. Write a eulogy for one of the characters from the perspective of another character.

8. Rewrite the ending. Explain why you chose to end it the way you did.

9. Write a personal recommendation for the book for future readers.

10. Research the time period in which the novel takes place and choose an activity from the research center to report significant changes that have taken place over time.

11. Rewrite the story from another point of view and discuss how this changes the story.

12. Use a "Dear Abby" format to describe the problem or conflict in the story and assume the "Abby" role to write a response.

13. Write a letter to a character in the story relating the experiences of the character to experiences you have had.

14. Write a short story or poem addressing the theme of the novel.

15. Write the next chapter of the novel and publish it for the classroom library.

16. Assume the identity of the head of a publishing company and write a letter to the author and/or illustrator detailing why you have accepted or rejected the manuscript.

17. Explain how changing the setting would affect the story. (Example: If *To Kill a Mockingbird* had been set in New York, how would the story change?)

18. Create a Venn diagram to illustrate similarities and differences between the novel and its film version.

19. Create a storyboard of major elements in the novel.

20. Create a chapter chart, and record information about characters, plot, theme, and symbolism.

21. Rewrite the novel (or a chapter) in a different genre. (Example: Take a story and rewrite it into a play. Organize a group to assume roles such as director, program designer, costume designer, actors, etc.)

22. Imagine that you are one of the characters and a poem or note that you wrote about another character fell out of your pocket. What would it say?

23. Write a persuasive essay to convince someone why the book should or should not be read. Be specific when supporting your argument.

24. Write a letter to your friend, your parents, or your teacher to tell them about the book.

25. Compare or contrast this novel with others you have read or viewed from the same time period. What novel-related issues do you think tie into current events?

26. Write and perform a theme song for the book.

27. Compare or contrast segments of the film or video with various episodes of the novel.

28. E-mail the author and/or visit the author's website. Summarize what you learned in a Press Conference (see Chapter 3).

Prompts That Focus on Researching and Creating Projects

1. Create a museum exhibit for the novel as a whole-group or small-group project. (Example: Research clothing, music, sports, or transportation of the time in which the book was written.)

2. Create an illustrated timeline for the story. Be creative in your design.

3. Design a creative response to the novel. (Example: a dramatization, song, painting, or project)

4. Create a memorabilia bag or book report in a bag (a collection of concrete items that represent various facets of the story).

5. Create a Readers Theatre for a chapter of the book.

6. Create a "wanted" poster for a character in the book.

7. Create a comic strip based on a scene or chapter from the book.

8. Complete "I Prompts" based on the story. (Example: I think.... I feel.... I was surprised.... I do not understand....) Or, complete character prompts based on the novel. (Example: In *To Kill a Mockingbird*, Scout thinks.... Scout feels....)

9. Create a travel brochure for the setting of the story.

10. Create a book jacket to use in a book sell—a commercial to convince others to read the book. It may be as simple as introducing the book and telling part of the story without revealing the ending, or as elaborate as dressing up as a character and acting out part of the story.

11. Create an artistic rendering of a scene in the story and explain why you chose that scene.

12. Create audiotapes of excerpts from novels, short stories, plays, or poetry and include your critique of the work.

13. Decorate a section of the classroom in the time period of the book you are reading.

14. Create a scrapbook from the perspective of one of the characters in the novel. Explain why the artifacts are important to that character.

15. Create an alphabet quilt based on the novel.

16. Create a webpage about the book.

17. Create a cookbook or a menu of the favorite foods of characters in the book.

18. Create a time capsule from the perspective of one of the characters in the novel. Describe the significance of items to be included. Write a newspaper article about opening the time capsule in present day.

19. Create a children's book—narrative or alphabet—telling the essential story of the novel.

20. Create a newspaper based on the place and time of the book.

21. Create advertisements—audio, video, print—depicting characters or events in the book to persuade others to read the novel. (Examples: photography, paint, collage)

22. Videotape a "trailer" (film clip for advertising purposes) for the novel as it is being released as a film.

23. Develop background music for a particular scene or chapter in a novel. Explain how the music you chose relates to that section of the book.

24. Develop and market a product that would solve the major conflict in the novel.

25. Create a video or dramatization demonstrating a conflict between two characters and a resolution that could be achieved if more effective communication skills were used. Show the conflict segment to the class and follow this with discussion. Then show the resolution segment that features the more effective communication and follow this with discussion.

26. Use a memorable quote from the novel to create a picture book, repeated phrase poem, or other project.

27. Research the author's life and share what you learn through a creative presentation.

28. Research the historical or geographical elements of a book and use PowerPoint to present a descriptive timeline or map.

29. Create a transmediation. Change the content of the book into a poem, song lyrics, or picture book.

30. Invite a guest speaker from the community to visit your class to share his or her expertise about novel-related topics (adventure, survival, war, etc.).

Prompts That Involve Talk Shows or Game Shows

1. If a character were a guest on a talk show that you were hosting, what are four questions you would ask? Use your knowledge of the character and the novel to predict and support the character's responses. Choose your mode of response: audio, video, dramatization.

2. Create a game or game show that uses the literary elements (characters, setting, etc.) of the novel as its premise.

3. Formulate questions for *Jeopardy!*, *Wheel of Fortune*, or *Who Wants to Be a Millionaire?* based on the novel.

4. Create a game show atmosphere by developing questions related to the novel. Fold the questions and place them in a container. Have other students participate in the game show by choosing a question and responding to it.

Prompts That Focus on Characters

1. If you (from the perspective of another character) could have said one thing to the main character, what would it have been? At what point in the story would you have said it? How do you think it would have influenced the outcome of the story?

2. How do you think it would change the story if the character was a different gender? Support your thinking with examples from the story and your experience. (Example: How would *The View From Saturday* have changed if all four members of the group had been girls? Boys?)

3. If you could add or remove a character from the story, explain who it would be. Explain why you made this choice and how it would affect the story.

4. Select the character you admire the most and explain why.

5. Explain which character in the book you would trust or not trust. Support your thinking with examples from the text.

6. Become a particular character and deliver a monologue. Explain your choice.

7. Choose a character, note character traits from the text, and describe a gift you think the character would appreciate receiving. Make connections between your choice and the text.

8. Have a character from one book solve a problem or offer insights to a character in another book.

9. Develop character traits for major characters in a novel and then create a new story by placing the characters in a contemporary setting.

10. Choose a theme from a novel you have read and use it as the basis for writing a scene that includes a character from a young adult novel and a character from a classic novel.

11. Combine characters from various books and situate them in a new story.

12. Choose a character from the novel and describe how he or she changed as a result of the story. Predict what you think this character's next life experience will be.

13. Design a postcard illustrating your favorite scene and write the postcard to a character either from yourself or another character.

14. Create a short survey (four or five questions) about the characters and/or their actions. Survey class members about their opinions. Report your findings and discuss them with the class.

15. Write to the author as a character in the novel and question aspects of story and character development. (Example: In *To Kill a Mockingbird*, take on the identity of Tom Robinson and ask Harper Lee why she didn't have the jury acquit him instead of finding him guilty.) Another student who has read the same novel may reply as the author.

16. Create an acrostic poem about a character. Then create an artistic interpretation of the acrostic. (Example: Design a mobile made of the letters of the name and write the descriptors on the letters.)

17. Imagine that you are a character in the story. Use that person's "voice" to explain your role in the story (orally or in diary entry format).

18. Explain why you or one of your friends would be especially good at playing a particular character in the movie version of the book.

19. Create a character collage of pictures and words by cutting out faces that represent the characters and words to describe them.

20. Explain what you think would happen in a sequel to the novel that takes place 20 years after the original story. (Example: Include where you think the main characters will be located, what they will be doing, what their accomplishments have been, what joys and tragedies they have experienced, and what their future goals are.)

21. Create a dialogue journal between two characters.

22. Create a mural (wall-sized) character map.

23. Visualize and sketch a character from the story. Write a paragraph describing the character.

24. Create an emotion map indicating high and low points in the character's life. Support your thinking with examples from the story.

25. Use a Venn diagram to compare or contrast a character in the book and you. (Example: Identify the character you like the least in the novel. Use a Venn diagram to compare or contrast yourself with this character. Which traits, especially undesirable ones, do you share? What advice would you offer to eliminate such undesirable traits?)

26. Show how two minor characters felt and reacted to each other in the book. Explain how you think these characters contribute to the overall story.

27. Choose another novel in which you think a character from the book you are reading could play. Explain which role the character would play and why you think he or she would be effective in this role.

28. Create a two-sided mask showing a character at the beginning of the book and at the conclusion. Explain why you think the character changed.

29. Choose a character from the text and create a "MySpace" type of page for him or her.

30. Create a resume for a character based on his or her traits, experiences, and goals.

31. Create a job position and explain why a particular character would be well qualified for it.

32. Take on the identity of a character and orally share his or her critique of the story.

Prompts That Require Assuming the Identity of the Author

1. Explain why you wrote the book. Reflect on what you have written. What might you do differently now? Consider how author style impacts the reader.

2. If you could change one event in the story, what would it be? Explain your reasoning. What effect would this have on the story as a whole?

3. Explain your thoughts about having your novel turned into a movie. If you respond positively, explain whom you would cast to play the major characters.

4. Explain how you could change your writing to accommodate a different audience. (Example: If you were sharing this story with a primary class, how would you do it?)

5. Explain why you chose the title for the book. Offer an alternative title that you think would have also worked well.

6. Extend the study of your novel by teaching a narrative element literary device. (Example: Use traditional fairy tales versus transformational fairy tales to illustrate point of view, or use *The View From Saturday* to teach similes.)

7. Tell about something you learned, realized, or felt while you were writing the book that influenced your thinking.

Informal Assessments

Admit Slip

What I already know about this topic:

_____

_____

_____

_____

Admit Slip

One question I have about this topic:

_____

_____

_____

_____

ATTITUDE SURVEY 1

1. I think reading is _____

   because_____

   _____.

2. I think I am a _____ reader because _____

   _____

   _____.

3. I think _____ is a good reader because

   _____

   _____.

4. I think writing is _____

   because_____

   _____.

5. I think I am a _____ writer because _____

   _____

   _____.

6. I think _____ is a good writer because

   _____

   _____.

Name: _____ Date: _____

ATTITUDE SURVEY 2

Directions: Please place a check under the category that best describes your response.

SA = Strongly Agree
A = Agree
D = Disagree
SD = Strongly Disagree

	SA	A	D	SD
1. I read in my free time.	_____	_____	_____	_____
2. I like to receive books as gifts.	_____	_____	_____	_____
3. I like to choose what I read.	_____	_____	_____	_____
4. Reading is a rainy-day activity I enjoy.	_____	_____	_____	_____
5. I would rather read than watch television.	_____	_____	_____	_____
6. I keep a journal.	_____	_____	_____	_____
7. I like to write to my friends.	_____	_____	_____	_____
8. I like to write in school.	_____	_____	_____	_____
9. I use my computer to write.	_____	_____	_____	_____
10. I often revise my writing to make it better.	_____	_____	_____	_____

Name: _____ Date: _____

Guided Comprehension in Grades 3–8 by Maureen McLaughlin and Mary Beth Allen.

GUIDED COMPREHENSION PROFILE SUMMARY SHEET

Name: _____ Grade: _____ School Year:_____

Summary of Background Information:

Interests:

Reader Perceptions (September):

Reader Perceptions (June):

Writer Perceptions (September):

Writer Perceptions (June):

Reading Levels:	September	January	June
Independent			
Guided			
Strategy Use:			
Previewing			
Self-Questioning			
Making Connections			
Visualizing			
Knowing How Words Work			
Monitoring			
Summarizing			
Evaluating			

Not Observed (NO) – Student does not use the strategy.
Emerging (E) – Student attempts to use the strategy.
Developing (D) – Student is using the strategy on some occasions.
Consistent (C) – Student effectively uses the strategy to make meaning from text.

Comments:

INTEREST INVENTORY

1. What was your favorite subject last year? What do you think it will be this year? Why?

   _____

   _____

2. What is your favorite book? Why do you like it?

   _____

   _____

3. Do you have a library card? How often do you visit the library?

   _____

   _____

4. If someone were giving you a book as a gift, what would you want the book to be about?

   _____

   _____

5. What is a dream or wish you have?

   _____

6. What do you like to do after school?

   _____

   _____

7. If you had a day off from school, how would you spend the day?

   _____

   _____

8. If someone wanted to give you a magazine subscription for a gift, what magazine would you choose? Why?

   _____

   _____

9. If you won a contest and your grand prize was to meet and get to know any famous person in the world today, whom would you choose? What would you like to talk about?

   _____

10. If you could go into a bookstore and get any three books free, what kinds of books would you choose? _____

    _____

Name: _____ Date: _____

LITERACY HISTORY PROMPTS

The following are not questions to be answered, but rather ideas to prompt students' thinking as they are creating their literacy histories. Depending on the grade level, students may reflect on the entire list or the teacher may provide selected prompts.

1. What are your earliest memories of reading and writing?
2. Before you were able to read, did you pretend to read books? Can you remember the first time you read a book?
3. Do you read and/or write with your siblings or friends?
4. Can you recall your early writing attempts (scribbling, labeling drawings, etc.)?
5. Is a newspaper delivered to your home? Do you recall seeing others read the newspaper? Do you read the newspaper?
6. Do you subscribe to magazines? Do your parents/siblings have magazine subscriptions?
7. Do your parents belong to a book club? Do they maintain a personal library? Do they read for pleasure?
8. Do you receive or send mail (e.g., birthday cards, thank-you notes, letters)?
9. Can you detail your first memories of reading and/or writing instruction? Materials used? Methods of teaching? Content?
10. Can you recall reading for pleasure in elementary school?
11. Can you remember writing for pleasure in elementary school?
12. Can you recall the first book you chose to read in elementary school?
13. Can you recall your first writing assignment in elementary school?
14. Did you write a report in elementary school? What do you remember about this experience?
15. Do you remember the purposes for your reading and writing in elementary school? Do you recall any particular type of instruction you received? Can you describe any instructional materials that were used?
16. Can you recall the first book you loved (couldn't put down)?
17. Do you feel that you've ever read a book that has made a difference in your life?
18. Can you recall sharing books with friends?
19. Did you read a certain type of book (i.e., mysteries, biographies) at a particular age? Why do you think you made such choices?
20. When did you first visit a bookstore? What was it like?
21. What is your all-time favorite book?
22. Have you ever seen a book you've read turned into a film? Explain which you preferred.
23. What contributions have your reading and writing abilities made to your life?
24. Are you a reader now? What are you currently reading?
25. Are you a writer now? What are you currently writing?

Source: Adapted from McLaughlin, M., & Vogt, M.E. (1996). *Portfolios in teacher education*. Newark, DE: International Reading Association.

METACOGNITIVE READING AWARENESS INVENTORY

There's more than one way to cope when you run into difficulties in your reading. Which ways are best? Under each question here, put a checkmark beside all the responses you think are effective.

1. What do you do if you encounter a word and you don't know what it means?
   a. Use the words around it to figure it out.
   b. Use an outside source, such as a dictionary or expert.
   c. Temporarily ignore it and wait for clarification.
   d. Sound it out.

2. What do you do if you don't know what an entire sentence means?
   a. Read it again.
   b. Sound out all the difficult words.
   c. Think about the other sentences in the paragraph.
   d. Disregard it completely.

3. If you are reading science or social studies material, what would you do to remember the important information you've read?
   a. Skip parts you don't understand.
   b. Ask yourself questions about the important ideas.
   c. Realize you need to remember one point rather than another.
   d. Relate it to something you already know.

4. Before you start to read, what kind of plans do you make to help you read better?
   a. No specific plan is needed; just start reading toward completion of the assignment.
   b. Think about what you know about the subject.
   c. Think about why you are reading.
   d. Make sure the entire reading can be finished in as short a period of time as possible.

5. Why would you go back and read an entire passage over again?
   a. You didn't understand it.
   b. To clarify a specific or supporting idea.
   c. It seemed important to remember.
   d. To underline or summarize for study.

Source: Miholic, V. (1994). An inventory to pique students' metacognitive awareness of reading strategies. *The Journal of Reading, 38*, 84–86.

(continued)

METACOGNITIVE READING AWARENESS INVENTORY

(continued)

6. Knowing that you don't understand a particular sentence while reading involves understanding that
   a. the reader may not have developed adequate links or associations for new words or concepts introduced in the sentence.
   b. the writer may not have conveyed the ideas clearly.
   c. two sentences may purposely contradict each other.
   d. finding meaning for the sentence needlessly slows down the reader.

7. As you read a textbook, which of these do you do?
   a. Adjust your pace depending on the difficulty of the material.
   b. Generally, read at a constant, steady pace.
   c. Skip the parts you don't understand.
   d. Continually make predictions about what you are reading.

8. While you read, which of these are important?
   a. Know when you know and when you don't know key ideas.
   b. Know what it is that you know in relation to what is being read.
   c. Know that confusing text is common and usually can be ignored.
   d. Know that different strategies can be used to aid understanding.

9. When you come across a part of the text that is confusing, what do you do?
   a. Keep on reading until the text is clarified.
   b. Read ahead and then look back if the text is still unclear.
   c. Skip those sections completely; they are usually not important.
   d. Check to see if the ideas expressed are consistent with one another.

10. Which sentences are the most important in the chapter?
    a. Almost all of the sentences are important; otherwise, they wouldn't be there.
    b. The sentences that contain the important details or facts.
    c. The sentences that are directly related to the main idea.
    d. The ones that contain the most details.

Source: Miholic, V. (1994). An inventory to pique students' metacognitive awareness of reading strategies. *The Journal of Reading, 38*, 84–86.

(continued)

METACOGNITIVE READING AWARENESS INVENTORY

(continued)

DIRECTIONS FOR SCORING

Part One: Responses that indicate metacognitive reading awareness.

       1. a, b, c

       2. a, c

       3. b, c, d

       4. b, c

       5. a, c, d

       6. a, b, c

       7. a, d

       8. a, b, d

       9. a, b, d

     10. b, c

Part Two: Insights about the student's metacognitive reading awareness:

METACOMPREHENSION STRATEGY INDEX

Directions: Think about what kinds of things you can do to understand a story better before, during, and after you read it. Read each of the lists of four statements and decide which one of them would help *you* the most. *There are no right answers.* It is just what *you* think would help the most. Circle the letter of the statement you choose.

I. **In each set of four, choose the one statement which tells a good thing to do to help you understand a story better *before* you read it.**

1. Before I begin reading, it's a good idea to
    A. See how many pages are in the story.
    B. Look up all of the big words in the dictionary.
    C. Make some guesses about what I think will happen in the story.
    D. Think about what has happened so far in the story.

2. Before I begin reading, it's a good idea to
    A. Look at the pictures to see what the story is about.
    B. Decide how long it will take me to read the story.
    C. Sound out the words I don't know.
    D. Check to see if the story is making sense.

3. Before I begin reading, it's a good idea to
    A. Ask someone to read the story to me.
    B. Read the title to see what the story is about.
    C. Check to see if most of the words have long or short vowels in them.
    D. Check to see if the pictures are in order and make sense.

4. Before I begin reading, it's a good idea to
    A. Check to see that no pages are missing.
    B. Make a list of words I'm not sure about.
    C. Use the title and pictures to help me make guesses about what will happen in the story.
    D. Read the last sentence so I will know how the story ends.

5. Before I begin reading, it's a good idea to
    A. Decide on why I am going to read the story.
    B. Use the difficult words to help me make guesses about what will happen in the story.
    C. Reread some parts to see if I can figure out what is happening if things aren't making sense.
    D. Ask for help with the difficult words.

6. Before I begin reading, it's a good idea to
    A. Retell all of the main points that have happened so far.
    B. Ask myself questions that I would like to have answered in the story.
    C. Think about the meanings of the words which have more than one meaning.
    D. Look through the story to find all of the words with three or more syllables.

7. Before I begin reading, it's a good idea to
    A. Check to see if I have read this story before.
    B. Use my questions and guesses as a reason for reading the story.
    C. Make sure I can pronounce all of the words before I start.
    D. Think of a better title for the story.

8. Before I begin reading, it's a good idea to
    A. Think of what I already know about the things I see in the pictures.
    B. See how many pages are in the story.
    C. Choose the best part of the story to read again.
    D. Read the story aloud to someone.

Source: Schmitt, M.C. (1990). A questionnaire to measure children's awareness of strategic reading processes. *The Reading Teacher, 43*, 454–461.

(continued)

9. Before I begin reading, it's a good idea to
   A. Practice reading the story aloud.
   B. Retell all of the main points to make sure I can remember the story.
   C. Think of what the people in the story might be like.
   D. Decide if I have enough time to read the story.

10. Before I begin reading, it's a good idea to
   A. Check to see if I am understanding the story so far.
   B. Check to see if the words have more than one meaning.
   C. Think about where the story might be taking place.
   D. List all of the important details.

II. In each set of four, choose the one statement which tells a good thing to do to help you understand a story better *while* you are reading it.

11. While I'm reading, it's a good idea to
   A. Read the story very slowly so that I will not miss any important parts.
   B. Read the title to see what the story is about.
   C. Check to see if the pictures have anything missing.
   D. Check to see if the story is making sense by seeing if I can tell what's happened so far.

12. While I'm reading, it's a good idea to
   A. Stop to retell the main points to see if I am understanding what has happened so far.
   B. Read the story quickly so that I can find out what happened.
   C. Read only the beginning and the end of the story to find out what it is about.
   D. Skip the parts that are too difficult for me.

13. While I'm reading, it's a good idea to
   A. Look all of the big words up in the dictionary.
   B. Put the book away and find another one if things aren't making sense.
   C. Keep thinking about the title and the pictures to help me decide what is going to happen next.
   D. Keep track of how many pages I have left to read.

14. While I'm reading, it's a good idea to
   A. Keep track of how long it is taking me to read the story.
   B. Check to see if I can answer any of the questions I asked before I started reading.
   C. Read the title to see what the story is going to be about.
   D. Add the missing details to the pictures.

15. While I'm reading, it's a good idea to
   A. Have someone read the story aloud to me.
   B. Keep track of how many pages I have read.
   C. List the story's main character.
   D. Check to see if my guesses are right or wrong.

16. While I'm reading, it's a good idea to
   A. Check to see that the characters are real.
   B. Make a lot of guesses about what is going to happen next.
   C. Not look at the pictures because they might confuse me.
   D. Read the story aloud to someone.

17. While I'm reading, it's a good idea to
   A. Try to answer the questions I asked myself.
   B. Try not to confuse what I already know with what I'm reading about.
   C. Read the story silently.
   D. Check to see if I am saying the new vocabulary words correctly.

Source: Schmitt, M.C. (1990). A questionnaire to measure children's awareness of strategic reading processes. *The Reading Teacher, 43*, 454–461.

(continued)

18. While I'm reading, it's a good idea to
    A. Try to see if my guesses are going to be right or wrong.
    B. Reread to be sure I haven't missed any of the words.
    C. Decide on why I am reading the story.
    D. List what happened first, second, third, and so on.

19. While I'm reading, it's a good idea to
    A. See if I can recognize the new vocabulary words.
    B. Be careful not to skip any parts of the story.
    C. Check to see how many of the words I already know.
    D. Keep thinking of what I already know about the things and ideas in the story to help me decide what is going to happen.

20. While I'm reading, it's a good idea to
    A. Reread some parts or read ahead to see if I can figure out what is happening if things aren't making sense.
    B. Take my time reading so that I can be sure I understand what is happening.
    C. Change the ending so that it makes sense.
    D. Check to see if there are enough pictures to help make the story ideas clear.

III. In each set of four, choose the one statement which tells a good thing to do to help you understand a story better *after* you have read it.

21. After I've read a story it's a good idea to
    A. Count how many pages I read with no mistakes.
    B. Check to see if there were enough pictures to go with the story to make it interesting.
    C. Check to see if I met my purpose for reading the story.
    D. Underline the causes and effects.

22. After I've read a story it's a good idea to
    A. Underline the main idea.
    B. Retell the main points of the whole story so that I can check to see if I understood it.
    C. Read the story again to be sure I said all of the words right.
    D. Practice reading the story aloud.

23. After I've read a story it's a good idea to
    A. Read the title and look over the story to see what it is about.
    B. Check to see if I skipped any of the vocabulary words.
    C. Think about what made me make good or bad predictions.
    D. Make a guess about what will happen next in the story.

24. After I've read a story it's a good idea to
    A. Look up all of the big words in the dictionary.
    B. Read the best parts aloud.
    C. Have someone read the story aloud to me.
    D. Think about how the story was like things I already knew about before I started reading.

25. After I've read a story it's a good idea to
    A. Think about how I would have acted if I were the main character in the story.
    B. Practice reading the story silently for practice of good reading.
    C. Look over the story title and pictures to see what will happen.
    D. Make a list of the things I understood the most.

Source: Schmitt, M.C. (1990). A questionnaire to measure children's awareness of strategic reading processes. *The Reading Teacher, 43*, 454–461.

(*continued*)

METACOMPREHENSION STRATEGY INDEX (continued)

DIRECTIONS FOR SCORING

Part One: Responses that indicate metacomprehension strategy awareness.

I Before Reading:	II During Reading:	III After Reading:
1. C	11. D	21. C
2. A	12. A	22. B
3. B	13. C	23. C
4. C	14. B	24. D
5. A	15. D	25. A
6. B	16. B	
7. B	17. A	
8. A	18. A	
9. C	19. D	
10. C	20. A	

Part Two: Insights about the student's metacomprehension strategy use:

MOTIVATION TO READ PROFILE
CONVERSATIONAL INTERVIEW

Name: _____ Date:_____

A. Emphasis: Narrative text

Suggested prompt (designed to engage student in a natural conversation): I have been reading a good book...I was talking with...about it last night. I enjoy talking about good stories and books that I've been reading. Today I'd like to hear about what you have been reading.

1. Tell me about the most interesting story or book you have read this week (or even last week). Take a few minutes to think about it. (Wait time.) Now, tell me about the book or story.

Probes: What else can you tell me? Is there anything else?_____

_____

_____

_____

_____

2. How did you know or find out about this story? _____

_____

_____

☐ assigned   ☐ in school

☐ chosen   ☐ out of school

3. Why was this story interesting to you? _____

_____

_____

_____

_____

Source: Gambrell, L.B., Palmer, B.M., Codling, R.M., & Mazzoni, S.A. (1996). Assessing motivation to read. *The Reading Teacher, 49,* 518–533.

(continued)

B. Emphasis: Informational text

Suggested prompt (designed to engage student in a natural conversation): Often we read to find out about something or to learn about something. We read for information. For example, I remember a student of mine...who read a lot of books about...to find out as much as he/she could about.... Now, I'd like to hear about some of the informational reading you have been doing.

1. Think about something important that you learned recently, not from your teacher and not from television, but from a book or some other reading material. What did you read about? (Wait time.) Tell me about what you learned.

Probes: What else could you tell me? Is there anything else? _____

_____

_____

_____

_____

2. How did you know or find out about this book/article?_____

_____

_____

☐ assigned ☐ in school

☐ chosen ☐ out of school

3. Why was this book (or article) important to you?_____

_____

_____

_____

_____

Source: Gambrell, L.B., Palmer, B.M., Codling, R.M., & Mazzoni, S.A. (1996). Assessing motivation to read. *The Reading Teacher, 49,* 518–533.

(continued)

MOTIVATION TO READ PROFILE
CONVERSATIONAL INTERVIEW (continued)

C. Emphasis: General reading

1. Did you read anything at home yesterday? _____ What?

_____

_____

2. Do you have any books at school (in your desk/storage area/locker/book bag) today that you are reading? _____ Tell me about them.

_____

_____

3. Tell me about your favorite author.

_____

_____

4. What do you think you have to learn to be a better reader?

_____

_____

5. Do you know about any books right now that you'd like to read? Tell me about them.

_____

_____

6. How did you find out about these books?

_____

_____

7. What are some things that get you really excited about reading books?

_____

_____

8. Tell me about...

_____

_____

9. Who gets you really interested and excited about reading books?

_____

_____

10. Tell me more about what they do.

_____

_____

_____

Source: Gambrell, L.B., Palmer, B.M., Codling, R.M., & Mazzoni, S.A. (1996). Assessing motivation to read. *The Reading Teacher, 49*, 518–533.

LITERATURE CIRCLE OBSERVATION

Directions: Place a check if the behavior is observed.
Observation:

1. Student is prepared for the Literature Circle. _____

2. Student is focused on the group task. _____

3. Student engages in discussion. _____

   Talk focuses on the content of the book. _____

   Talk focuses on the reading process. _____

   Talk focuses on personal connections. _____

   Talk focuses on the group process. _____

4. Student is competent in his or her discussion role. _____

5. Student's contributions demonstrate
   depth of understanding. _____

6. Student respects ideas of other group members. _____

Student's self-evaluation indicates _____

_____

_____

_____

_____

Notes: _____

_____

_____

_____

_____

Name: _____ Date: _____

QUESTIONING THE AUTHOR (QtA) OBSERVATION

Directions: Place a check if the behavior is observed.
Observation:

1. Student is prepared for Questioning the Author. _____

2. Student is focused on the group task. _____

3. Student is actively engaged in QtA. _____

4. Student uses a reviser's eye. _____

5. Student generates meaningful queries. _____

6. Student contributes meaningful responses. _____

7. Student draws meaningful conclusions. _____

8. Student is a competent participant in QtA. _____

9. Student's contributions demonstrate depth of understanding. _____

10. Student respects ideas of other group members. _____

Student's self-evaluation indicates _____

_____

_____

_____

_____

_____

Notes: _____

_____

_____

_____

_____

_____

Name: _____ Date: _____

RECIPROCAL TEACHING OBSERVATION

Directions: Place a check if the behavior is observed.
Observation:

1. Student is prepared for Reciprocal Teaching. _____

2. Student is focused on the group task. _____

3. Student is actively engaged in Reciprocal Teaching. _____

4. Student successfully engages in prediction. _____

5. Student successfully generates meaningful questions. _____

6. Student successfully clarifies meaning. _____

7. Student successfully summarizes text. _____

8. Student uses strategy prompts. _____

9. Student's contributions demonstrate depth of understanding. _____

10. Student respects ideas of other group members. _____

Student's self-evaluation indicates _____

_____

_____

_____

_____

Notes: _____

_____

_____

_____

_____

Name: _____ Date: _____

READER SELF-PERCEPTION SCALE

Listed below are statements about reading. Please read each statement carefully. Then circle the letters that show how much you agree or disagree with the statement. Use the following scale:

SA = Strongly Agree   A = Agree   U = Undecided   D = Disagree   SD = Strongly Disagree

Example: **I think pizza with pepperoni is the best.**　　　　　SA　　A　　U　　D　　SD

If you are *really positive* that pepperoni pizza is best, circle SA (Strongly Agree).

If you *think* that it is good but maybe not great, circle A (Agree).

If you *can't decide* whether or not it is best, circle U (Undecided).

If you *think* that pepperoni pizza is not all that good, circle D (Disagree).

If you are *really positive* that pepperoni pizza is not very good, circle SD (Strongly Disagree).

		SA	A	U	D	SD
	1. I think I am a good reader.	SA	A	U	D	SD
[SF]	2. I can tell that my teacher likes to listen to me read.	SA	A	U	D	SD
[SF]	3. My teacher thinks that my reading is fine.	SA	A	U	D	SD
[OC]	4. I read faster than other kids.	SA	A	U	D	SD
[PS]	5. I like to read aloud.	SA	A	U	D	SD
[OC]	6. When I read, I can figure out words better than other kids.	SA	A	U	D	SD
[SF]	7. My classmates like to listen to me read.	SA	A	U	D	SD
[PS]	8. I feel good inside when I read.	SA	A	U	D	SD
[SF]	9. My classmates think that I read pretty well.	SA	A	U	D	SD
[PR]	10. When I read, I don't have to try as hard as I used to.	SA	A	U	D	SD
[OC]	11. I seem to know more words than other kids when I read.	SA	A	U	D	SD
[SF]	12. People in my family think I am a good reader.	SA	A	U	D	SD
[PR]	13. I am getting better at reading.	SA	A	U	D	SD
[OC]	14. I understand what I read as well as other kids do.	SA	A	U	D	SD
[PR]	15. When I read, I need less help than I used to.	SA	A	U	D	SD
[PS]	16. Reading makes me feel happy inside.	SA	A	U	D	SD
[SF]	17. My teacher thinks I am a good reader.	SA	A	U	D	SD
[PR]	18. Reading is easier for me than it used to be.	SA	A	U	D	SD
[PR]	19. I read faster than I could before.	SA	A	U	D	SD
[OC]	20. I read better than other kids in my class.	SA	A	U	D	SD
[PS]	21. I feel calm when I read.	SA	A	U	D	SD
[OC]	22. I read more than other kids.	SA	A	U	D	SD
[PR]	23. I understand what I read better than I could before.	SA	A	U	D	SD
[PR]	24. I can figure out words better than I could before.	SA	A	U	D	SD
[PS]	25. I feel comfortable when I read.	SA	A	U	D	SD
[PS]	26. I think reading is relaxing.	SA	A	U	D	SD
[PR]	27. I read better now than I could before.	SA	A	U	D	SD
[PR]	28. When I read, I recognize more words than I used to.	SA	A	U	D	SD
[PS]	29. Reading makes me feel good.	SA	A	U	D	SD
[SF]	30. Other kids think I'm a good reader.	SA	A	U	D	SD
[SF]	31. People in my family think I read pretty well.	SA	A	U	D	SD
[PS]	32. I enjoy reading.	SA	A	U	D	SD
[SF]	33. People in my family like to listen to me read.	SA	A	U	D	SD

Source: Henk, W.A., & Melnick, S.A. (1995). The Reader Self-Perception Scale (RSPS): A new tool for measuring how children feel about themselves as readers. *The Reading Teacher, 48,* 470–482.

(continued)

READER SELF-PERCEPTION SCALE (continued)

DIRECTIONS FOR ADMINISTRATION, SCORING, AND INTERPRETATION

The Reader Self-Perception Scale (RSPS) is intended to provide an assessment of how children feel about themselves as readers. The scale consists of 33 items that assess self-perceptions along four dimensions of self-efficacy (Progress, Observational Comparison, Social Feedback, and Physiological States). Children are asked to indicate how strongly they agree or disagree with each statement on a 5-point scale (5 = Strongly Agree, 1 = Strongly Disagree). The information gained from this scale can be used to devise ways to enhance children's self-esteem in reading and, ideally, to increase their motivation to read. The following directions explain specifically what you are to do.

Administration

For the results to be of any use, the children must: (a) understand exactly what they are to do, (b) have sufficient time to complete all items, and (c) respond honestly and thoughtfully. Briefly explain to the children that they are being asked to complete a questionnaire about reading. Emphasize that this is not a *test* and that there are no *right* answers. Tell them that they should be as honest as possible because their responses will be confidential. Ask the children to fill in their names, grade levels, and classrooms as appropriate. Read the directions aloud and work through the example with the students as a group. Discuss the response options and make sure that all children understand the rating scale before moving on. It is important that children know that they may raise their hands to ask questions about any words or ideas they do not understand.

The children should then read each item and circle their response for the item. They should work at their own pace. Remind the children that they should be sure to respond to all items. When all items are completed, the children should stop, put their pencils down, and wait for further instructions. Care should be taken that children who work more slowly are not disturbed by children who have already finished.

Scoring

To score the RSPS, enter the following point values for each response on the RSPS scoring sheet (Strongly Agree = 5, Agree = 4, Undecided = 3, Disagree = 2, Strongly Disagree = 1) for each item number under the appropriate scale. Sum each column to obtain a raw score for each of the four specific scales.

Interpretation

Each scale is interpreted in relation to its total possible score. For example, because the RSPS uses a 5-point scale and the Progress scale consists of 9 items, the highest total score for Progress is 45 ($9 \times 5 = 45$). Therefore, a score that would fall approximately in the middle of the range (22–23) would indicate a child's somewhat indifferent perception of her or himself as a reader with respect to Progress. Note that each scale has a different possible total raw score (Progress = 45, Observational Comparison = 30, Social Feedback = 45, and Physiological States = 40) and should be interpreted accordingly.

Source: Henk, W.A., & Melnick, S.A. (1995). The Reader Self-Perception Scale (RSPS): A new tool for measuring how children feel about themselves as readers. *The Reading Teacher, 48*, 470–482.

(continued)

READER SELF-PERCEPTION SCALE (continued)

SCORING SHEET

Student name _____

Teacher _____

Grade_____ Date _____

Scoring key: 5 = Strongly Agree (SA)
                     4 = Agree (A)
                     3 = Undecided (U)
                     2 = Disagree (D)
                     1 = Strongly Disagree (SD)

Scales

General Perception	Progress	Observational Comparison	Social Feedback	Physiological States
1. ____	10. ____	4. ____	2. ____	5. ____
	13. ____	6. ____	3. ____	8. ____
	15. ____	11. ____	7. ____	16. ____
	18. ____	14. ____	9. ____	21. ____
	19. ____	20. ____	12. ____	25. ____
	23. ____	22. ____	17. ____	26. ____
	24. ____		30. ____	29. ____
	27. ____		31. ____	32. ____
	28. ____		33. ____	
Raw score	____ of 45	____ of 30	____ of 45	____of 40
Score interpretation				
High	44+	26+	38+	37+
Average	39	21	33	31
Low	34	16	27	25

Source: Henk, W.A., & Melnick, S.A. (1995). The Reader Self-Perception Scale (RSPS): A new tool for measuring how children feel about themselves as readers. *The Reading Teacher, 48*, 470–482.

REFLECTION AND GOAL SETTING

Today my goal was

What I did

What I learned

Questions I have

When I reflect on how well I achieved my goal, I think

Tomorrow my goal will be

Name: _____ Date: _____

STUDENT SELF-REFLECTION AND GOAL SETTING

Hobby or Special Interest

This activity is designed to help you reflect on one of your hobbies or special interests. Remember that self-reflection involves thinking about what you did, how well you did it, and what you can do to make it better next time. To begin your reflection, focus on your hobby or special interest. Then think about the last time you did it. How well did it go? What is one thing you can do to improve it next time? What is your new goal?

My hobby or special interest is

Something I learned to do in my hobby or special interest is

The last time I did it

One thing I can do to improve it next time is

My new goal for my hobby or special interest is

Source: Adapted from McLaughlin, M. (1995). *Performance assessment: A practical guide to implementation*. Boston: Houghton Mifflin.

STUDENT SELF-REFLECTION AND GOAL SETTING IN GUIDED COMPREHENSION

This activity is designed to help you create a self-reflection about your reading. Remember that self-reflection involves thinking about what you did, how well you did it, and what you can do to make it better next time. To begin your reflection focus on something you have learned during Guided Comprehension. Then think about the last time you did it. How well did it go? What is one thing you can do to improve it next time? What is your new goal?

What I read

What I learned

The last time I did it

One thing I can do to improve it next time is

My new goal is

SPECIAL QUESTION FROM YOUR TEACHER: What can I do to help you reach your new goal?

Source: Adapted from McLaughlin, M. (1995). *Performance assessment: A practical guide to implementation*. Boston: Houghton Mifflin.

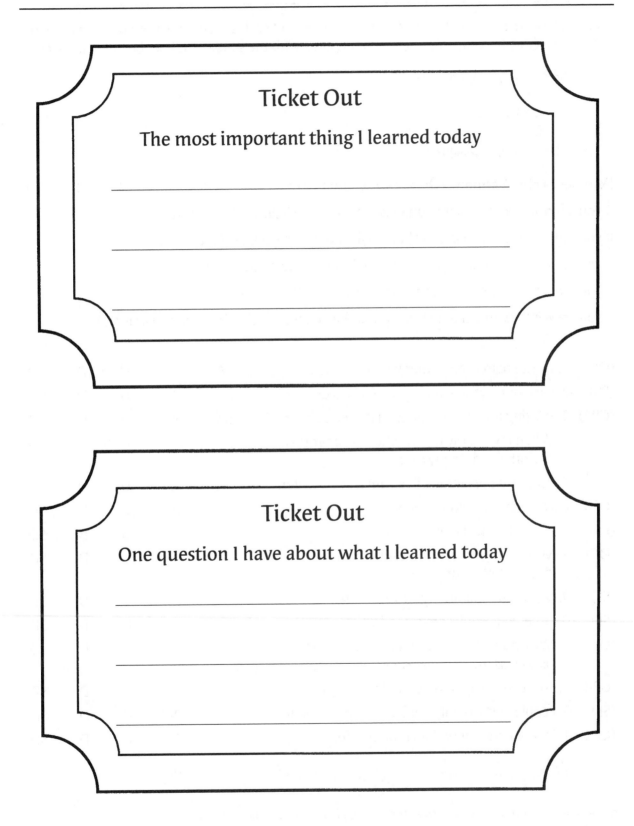

Ticket Out

The most important thing I learned today

_____

_____

_____

Ticket Out

One question I have about what I learned today

_____

_____

_____

WRITER SELF-PERCEPTION SCALE

Listed below are statements about writing. Please read each statement carefully. Then circle the letters that show how much you agree or disagree with the statement. Use the following scale:

SA = Strongly Agree
A = Agree
U = Undecided
D = Disagree
SD = Strongly Disagree

Example: **I think Batman is the greatest super hero.**　　SA　　A　　U　　D　　SD

If you are *really positive* that Batman is the greatest, circle SA (Strongly Agree).

If you *think* that Batman is good but maybe not great, circle A (Agree).

If you *can't decide* whether or not Batman is the greatest, circle U (Undecided).

If you *think* that Batman is not all that great, circle D (Disagree).

If you are *really positive* that Batman is not the greatest, circle SD (Strongly Disagree).

(OC)	1. I write better than other kids in my class.	SA	A	U	D	SD
(PS)	2. I like how writing makes me feel inside.	SA	A	U	D	SD
(GPR)	3. Writing is easier for me than it used to be.	SA	A	U	D	SD
(OC)	4. When I write, my organization is better than the other kids in my class.	SA	A	U	D	SD
(SF)	5. People in my family think I am a good writer.	SA	A	U	D	SD
(GPR)	6. I am getting better at writing.	SA	A	U	D	SD
(PS)	7. When I write, I feel calm.	SA	A	U	D	SD
(OC)	8. My writing is more interesting than my classmates' writing.	SA	A	U	D	SD
(SF)	9. My teacher thinks my writing is fine.	SA	A	U	D	SD
(SF)	10. Other kids think I am a good writer.	SA	A	U	D	SD
(OC)	11. My sentences and paragraphs fit together as well as my classmates' sentences and paragraphs.	SA	A	U	D	SD
(GPR)	12. I need less help to write well than I used to.	SA	A	U	D	SD
(SF)	13. People in my family think I write pretty well.	SA	A	U	D	SD
(GPR)	14. I write better now than I could before.	SA	A	U	D	SD

Source: Bottomley, D.M., Henk, W.A., & Melnick, S.A. (1997/1998). Assessing children's views about themselves as writers using the Writer Self-Perception Scale. *The Reading Teacher, 51,* 286–296.

(continued)

WRITER SELF-PERCEPTION SCALE (continued)

(GEN)15. I think I am a good writer.	SA	A	U	D	SD
(OC) 16. I put my sentences in a better order than the other kids.	SA	A	U	D	SD
(GPR)17. My writing has improved.	SA	A	U	D	SD
(GPR)18. My writing is better than before.	SA	A	U	D	SD
(GPR)19. It's easier to write well now than it used to be.	SA	A	U	D	SD
(GPR)20. The organization of my writing has really improved.	SA	A	U	D	SD
(OC) 21. The sentences I use in my writing stick to the topic more than the ones the other kids use.	SA	A	U	D	SD
(SPR) 22. The words I use in my writing are better than the ones I used before.	SA	A	U	D	SD
(OC) 23. I write more often than other kids.	SA	A	U	D	SD
(PS) 24. I am relaxed when I write.	SA	A	U	D	SD
(SPR) 25. My descriptions are more interesting than before.	SA	A	U	D	SD
(OC) 26. The words I use in my writing are better than the ones other kids use.	SA	A	U	D	SD
(PS) 27. I feel comfortable when I write.	SA	A	U	D	SD
(SF) 28. My teacher thinks I am a good writer.	SA	A	U	D	SD
(SPR) 29. My sentences stick to the topic better now.	SA	A	U	D	SD
(OC) 30. My writing seems to be more clear than my classmates' writing.	SA	A	U	D	SD
(SPR) 31. When I write, the sentences and paragraphs fit together better than they used to.	SA	A	U	D	SD
(PS) 32. Writing makes me feel good.	SA	A	U	D	SD
(SF) 33. I can tell that my teacher thinks my writing is fine.	SA	A	U	D	SD
(SPR) 34. The order of my sentences makes better sense now.	SA	A	U	D	SD
(PS) 35. I enjoy writing.	SA	A	U	D	SD
(SPR) 36. My writing is more clear than it used to be.	SA	A	U	D	SD
(SF) 37. My classmates would say I write well.	SA	A	U	D	SD
(SPR) 38. I choose the words I use in my writing more carefully now.	SA	A	U	D	SD

Source: Bottomley, D.M., Henk, W.A., & Melnick, S.A. (1997/1998). Assessing children's views about themselves as writers using the Writer Self-Perception Scale. *The Reading Teacher, 51,* 286–296.

(continued)

WRITER SELF-PERCEPTION SCALE (continued)

DIRECTIONS FOR ADMINISTRATION, SCORING, AND INTERPRETATION

The Writer Self-Perception Scale (WSPS) provides an estimate of how children feel about themselves as writers. The scale consists of 38 items that assess self-perception along five dimensions of self-efficacy (General Progress, Specific Progress, Observational Comparison, Social Feedback, and Physiological States). Children are asked to indicate how strongly they agree or disagree with each statement using a 5-point scale ranging from Strongly Agree (5) to Strongly Disagree (1). The information yielded by this scale can be used to devise ways of enhancing children's self-esteem in writing and, ideally, to increase their motivation for writing. The following directions explain specifically what you are to do.

Administration

To ensure useful results, the children must (a) understand exactly what they are to do, (b) have sufficient time to complete all items, and (c) respond honestly and thoughtfully. Briefly explain to the children that they are being asked to complete a questionnaire about writing. Emphasize that this is not a test and that there are no right or wrong answers. Tell them that they should be as honest as possible because their responses will be confidential. Ask the children to fill in their names, grade levels, and classrooms as appropriate. Read the directions aloud and work through the example with the students as a group. Discuss the response options and make sure that all children understand the rating scale before moving on. The children should be instructed to raise their hands to ask questions about any words or ideas that are unfamiliar.

The children should then read each item and circle their response to the statement. They should work at their own pace. Remind the children that they should be sure to respond to all items. When all items are completed, the children should stop, put their pencils down, and wait for further instructions. Care should be taken that children who work more slowly are not disturbed by classmates who have already finished.

Scoring

To score the WSPS, enter the following point values for each response on the WSPS scoring sheet (Strongly Agree = 5, Agree = 4, Undecided = 3, Disagree = 2, Strongly Disagree = 1) for each item number under the appropriate scale. Sum each column to obtain a raw score for each of the five specific scales.

Interpretation

Each scale is interpreted in relation to its total possible score. For example, because the WSPS uses a 5-point scale and the General Progress scale consists of 8 items, the highest total score is 40 (8 × 5 = 40). Therefore, a score that would fall approximately at the average or mean score (35) would indicate that the child's perception of her- or himself as a writer falls in the average range with respect to General Progress. Note that each remaining scale has a different possible maximum raw score (Specific Progress = 35, Observational Comparison = 45, Social Feedback = 35, and Physiological States = 30) and should be interpreted accordingly using the high, average, and low designations on the scoring sheet.

Source: Bottomley, D.M., Henk, W.A., & Melnick, S.A. (1997/1998). Assessing children's views about themselves as writers using the Writer Self-Perception Scale. *The Reading Teacher, 51,* 286–296.

(continued)

WRITER SELF-PERCEPTION SCALE (continued)

SCORING SHEET

Student name _____

Teacher _____

Grade_____ Date _____

Scoring key: 5 = Strongly Agree (SA)
4 = Agree (A)
3 = Undecided (U)
2 = Disagree (D)
1 = Strongly Disagree (SD)

Scales

General Progress (GPR)	Specific Progress (SPR)	Observational Comparison (OC)	Social Feedback (SF)	Physiological States (PS)
3. _____	22. _____	1. _____	5. _____	2. _____
6. _____	25. _____	4. _____	9. _____	7. _____
12. _____	29. _____	8. _____	10. _____	24. _____
14. _____	31. _____	11. _____	13. _____	27. _____
17. _____	34. _____	16. _____	28. _____	32. _____
18. _____	36. _____	21. _____	33. _____	35. _____
19. _____	38. _____	23. _____	37. _____	
20. _____		26. _____		
		30. _____		

Raw score				
_____ of 40	_____ of 35	_____ of 45	_____ of 35	_____ of 30

Score interpretation	GPR	SPR	OC	SF	PS
High	39+	34+	37+	32+	28+
Average	35	29	30	27	22
Low	30	24	23	22	16

Source: Bottomley, D.M., Henk, W.A., & Melnick, S.A. (1997/1998). Assessing children's views about themselves as writers using the Writer Self-Perception Scale. *The Reading Teacher*, *51*, 286–296.

Leveled Book Resources

This appendix features resources for leveled books created by teachers, school districts, and publishers. Information is also provided about lexiles and readability graphs. It is important to remember that all levels are approximate and that students' abilities to read text are influenced by multiple factors, including background knowledge and interest.

Websites Maintained by Individual Teachers

Leveled Book Lists by Nancy Giansante

home.comcast.net/~ngiansante/

This site features many titles of books easily sorted by title, author, or grade level. The information provided includes title, author, Guided Reading level, and grade level. For example, when you click on grade 5, you get a listing of titles spanning Guided Reading levels S–W. These are the first 10 titles:

Title	Author	Guided Reading	Grade Level
Aldo (books)	Hurwitz, Johanna	S	4.50
Amelia Earhart: Challenging the Skies	Sloate, Susan	S	4.50
Amelia Earhart: Courage in the Sky	Kerby, Mona	S	4.50
Amelia Earhart: Flying for Adventure	Wade, Mary Dodson	S	4.50
Animals Do the Strangest Things	Hornblow, Leonora	S	4.50
Anne Frank	Epstein, Rachel	S	4.50
Awake and Dreaming	Pearson, Kit	S	4.50
Back to the Day Lincoln Was Shot!	Gormley, Beatrice	S	4.50
Back to the Titanic!	Gormley, Beatrice	S	4.50
Barefoot: Escape on the Underground Railroad	Edwards, Pamela Duncan	S	4.50

Websites Maintained by School Districts

Portland Public Schools, Portland, Oregon

www.pps.k12.or.us/instruction-c/literacy/leveled_books

On this site, you can type in a title, an author, or a grade level and a list of corresponding books is displayed. For example, if you type in 4 for the grade level, 72 titles are presented. These are the first 10 titles:

Title	Author	Reading Recovery Level	Grade Level
After the Goat Man	Byars, Betsy		4.7
All About Sam	Lowry, Lois		4.0
Animals Do the Strangest Things	Hornblow, Leonora		4.4
Arthur, For the Very First Time	MacLachlan, Patricia		4.0
Back Yard Angel	Delton, Judy		4.6
Bears' House, The	Sachs, Marilyn		4.0
Beezus and Ramona	Cleary, Beverly		4.5
Best Christmas Pageant Ever, The	Robinson, Barbara		4.0
Canada Geese Quilt, The	Kinsey-Warnock, Natalie		4.6
Case of the Elevator Duck, The	Berends, Polly Berrien		4.0

When you type in an individual title, you get the author and a grade level. For example, if you type in *Tuck Everlasting*, the following information is displayed:

Title	Author	Reading Recovery Level	Grade Level
Tuck Everlasting	Babbitt, Natalie		6.3

If you put Cleary in the author column, 21 titles with grade levels are presented, including the following:

Title	Author	Reading Recovery Level	Grade Level
Beezus and Ramona	Cleary, Beverly		4.5
Emily's Runaway Imagination	Cleary, Beverly		4.7
Fifteen	Cleary, Beverly		6.0
Growing-Up Feet, The	Cleary, Beverly	20	2.3
Henry and Beezus	Cleary, Beverly	34	3.7
Henry and Ribsy	Cleary, Beverly	27	3.0
Henry and the Clubhouse	Cleary, Beverly	32	3.5
Henry and the Paper Route	Cleary, Beverly		4.3
Mouse and the Motorcycle, The	Cleary, Beverly		5.6
Muggie Maggie	Cleary, Beverly		4.0

Beaverton School District Leveled Books Database

registration.beavton.k12.or.us/lbdb/

This site includes a large collection of titles classified by Guided Reading and Reading Recovery levels. You can search by title, publisher, author, keyword, or level. For example, if you want books that are at a T Guided Reading level, you would put T in that box, and a list of 285 books is displayed. Here are the first 10 titles of that list:

Title	Author
Remarkable Rocks	Ranger Rick
The Restless Earth	Ranger Rick
A World of Sound	Ranger Rick
A Wonder of Light	Ranger Rick
Abel's Island	Steig, William

(continued)

Title	Author
An Early Winter	Bauer, Marion Dane
Animal Dazzlers: The Role of Brilliant Colors in Nature	Collard, Sneed B. III
Arctic Investigations: Exploring the Frozen Ocean	Young, Karen Romano
Baby	MacLachlan, Patricia
A Ballad of the Civil War	Stolz, Mary

Leveled Materials Available From Publishers

Scholastic Teacher Book Wizard

bookwizard.scholastic.com/tbw/homePage.do

This is a site where you can enter titles and get an approximate level, you can enter levels and get a list of books at that level, or you can enter a title and get other books that are written at that approximate level. For example, if you enter the title *Twilight*, you get a list of books that have *twiligh*t in the title. If you are interested in the book by Stephenie Meyer, you would look at that one and find it has a grade-level equivalent of 5.6. Then you can put that same title in the Book Alike section, and it will provide titles in that genre or theme at similar levels. When you put in the title *Twilight* and click on the one by Stephenie Meyer, you get several pages of books that are similar. Finally, you can search by putting in a range of grade-equivalent levels and choosing type, topic, and genre. Then a list of books meeting those criteria is displayed.

Lexiles and Readability Graphs

The Lexile Framework for Reading

www.lexile.com/EntrancePageHtml.aspx?1

The Lexile Framework levels books according to sentence length and word frequency and assigns each book a lexile based on this information. The site defines *lexile* as "a unit of measurement used when determining the difficulty of text and the reading level of readers." The site has a large book database that is easy to use. Books can be searched by author or by title, and a lexile level is displayed. For example, if you search the title *A Wrinkle in Time* by Madeleine L'Engle, a 740L suggests that this title is in the fourth-grade level range.

The company recommends lexiles for grade 3 in the range of 500 (*The Magic School Bus Inside the Earth*) to 700 (*Bunnicula*). The range for grade 8 is approximately 1000L (*Black Beauty*) to 1100L (*Pride and Prejudice*). (For a chart describing the range of lexiles for each grade, see www.lexile.com/uploads/PDF%27s/LexileMapColor_4-4-07_11x17.pdf.)

Kathy Schrock's Guide for Educators—Fry's Readability Graph: Directions for Use

school.discoveryeducation.com/schrockguide/fry/fry.html

This site offers a clear description of how to analyze a text using Fry's Readability Graph. The Fry Graph uses sentence length and vocabulary complexity for determining levels of reading materials. Although this tool gives an estimate of level, it will give you some ideas about the ease or difficulty of a particular text.

Guided Comprehension Lesson Planning Forms

SAMPLE THEME-BASED PLAN FOR GUIDED COMPREHENSION

Goals and Connections to State Standards

Students will

Assessment

The following measures can be used for a variety of purposes, including diagnostic, formative, and summative assessment:

Comprehension Strategies	Teaching Ideas
1.	
2.	
3.	
4.	

Comprehension Centers

Students will apply the comprehension strategies and related teaching ideas in the following comprehension centers:

Text	Title	Theme	Level

Comprehension Routines

Students will apply the comprehension strategies and related teaching ideas in the following comprehension routines:

Technology Resources

GUIDED COMPREHENSION PLANNING FORM

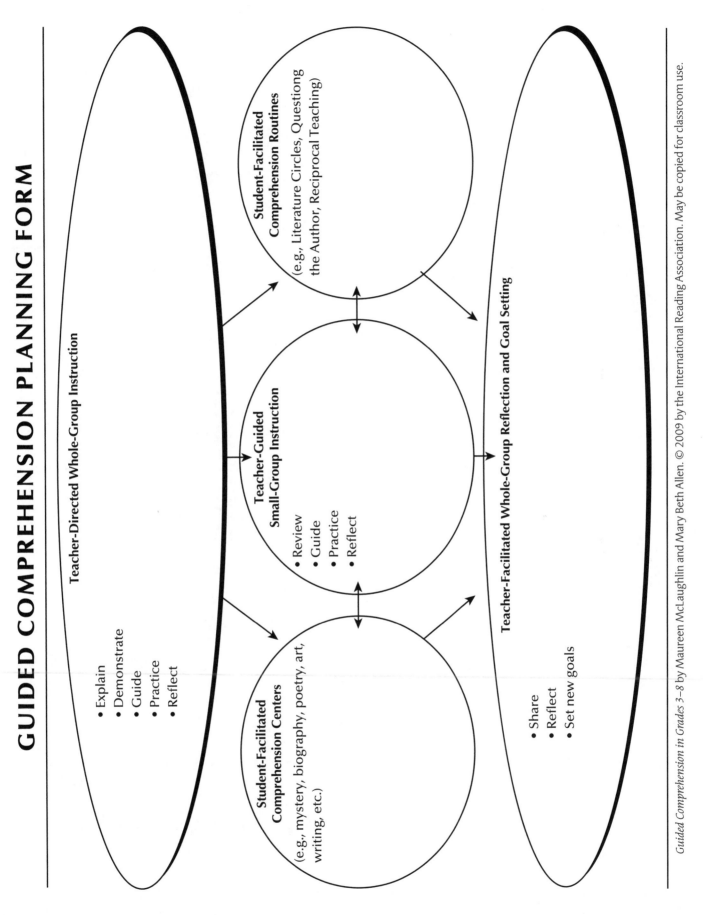

Teacher-Directed Whole-Group Instruction

- Explain
- Demonstrate
- Guide
- Practice
- Reflect

Student-Facilitated Comprehension Routines

(e.g, Literature Circles, Questiong the Author, Reciprocal Teaching)

Teacher-Guided Small-Group Instruction

- Review
- Guide
- Practice
- Reflect

Student-Facilitated Comprehension Centers

(e.g., mystery, biography, poetry, art, writing, etc.)

Teacher-Facilitated Whole-Group Reflection and Goal Setting

- Share
- Reflect
- Set new goals

REFERENCES

Allen, M.B. (2002, May). *Reciprocal teaching: A Guided Comprehension routine*. Paper presented at the 47th Annual Convention of the International Reading Association, San Francisco, CA.

Allen, M.B., & Mohr, K.A.J. (2008, May). *During reading: Where the action is for teaching comprehension*. Workshop presented at the 53rd Annual Convention of the International Reading Association, Atlanta, GA.

Almasi, J.F. (1996). A new view of discussion. In L.B. Gambrell & J.F. Almasi (Eds.), *Lively discussions! Fostering engaged reading* (pp. 2–24). Newark, DE: International Reading Association.

Alvermann, D. (1991). The discussion web: A graphic aid for learning across the curriculum. *The Reading Teacher, 45*, 92–99.

Alvermann, D.E., Phelps, S.F., & Ridgeway, V.G. (2007). *Content area reading and literacy: Succeeding in today's diverse classrooms* (5th ed.). Boston: Allyn & Bacon.

Anderson, R.C. (1994). Role of reader's schema in comprehension, learning, and memory. In R.B. Ruddell, M.R. Ruddell, & H. Singer (Eds.), *Theoretical models and processes of reading* (4th ed., pp. 469–482). Newark, DE: International Reading Association.

Anderson, R.C., & Pearson, P.D. (1984). A schema-theoretic view of basic processes in reading comprehension. In P.D. Pearson, R. Barr, M.L. Kamil, & P. Mosenthal (Eds.), *Handbook of reading research* (pp. 225–253). New York: Longman.

Au, K.H., & Raphael, T.E. (1998). Curriculum and teaching in literature-based programs. In T.E. Raphael & K.H. Au (Eds.), *Literature-based instruction: Reshaping the curriculum* (pp. 123–148). Norwood, MA: Christopher-Gordon.

Baker, L., Afflerbach, P., & Reinking, D. (1996). Developing engaged readers in school and home communities: An overview. In L. Baker, P. Afflerbach, & D. Reinking (Eds.), *Developing engaged readers in school and home communities* (pp. xiii–xxvii). Hillsdale, NJ: Erlbaum.

Baker, L., & Wigfield, A. (1999). Dimensions of children's motivation for reading and their relations to reading activity and reading achievement. *Reading Research Quarterly, 34*, 452–481.

Baumann, J.F., & Kame'enui, E.J. (1991). Research on vocabulary instruction: Ode to Voltaire. In J. Flood, J.M. Jensen, D. Lapp, & J.R. Squire (Eds.), *Handbook of research on teaching the English language arts* (pp. 604–632). New York: Macmillan.

Bean, T.W. (2000). Music in the content areas. In M. McLaughlin & M.E. Vogt (Eds.), *Creativity and innovation in content area teaching* (pp. 91–103). Norwood, MA: Christopher-Gordon.

Beaver, J., & Carter, M. (2009). *Developmental reading assessment 2 (DRA2): Grades 4–8*. Lebanon, IN: Pearson Education.

Beck, I.L., & McKeown, M.G. (1991). Conditions of vocabulary acquisition. In R. Barr, M.L. Kamil, P. Mosenthal, & P.D. Pearson (Eds.), *Handbook of reading research* (Vol. 2, pp. 789–814). White Plains, NY: Longman.

Beck, I.L., & McKeown, M.G. (2006). *Improving comprehension with Questioning the Author: A fresh and expanded view of a powerful approach*. New York: Scholastic.

Beck, I.L., McKeown, M.G., Hamilton, R.L., & Kucan, L. (1997). *Questioning the Author: An approach for enhancing student engagement with text*. Newark, DE: International Reading Association.

Berne, J.I., & Clark, K.F. (2008). Focusing literature discussion groups on comprehension strategies. *The Reading Teacher, 62*, 74–79.

Blachowicz, C.L. (1986). Making connections: Alternatives to the vocabulary notebook. *Journal of Reading, 29*, 643–649.

Blachowicz, C.L., Fisher, P., Ogle, D.M., & Watts-Taffe, S. (2006). Vocabulary: Questions from the classroom. *Reading Research Quarterly, 41*, 524–539.

Blachowicz, C.L., & Lee, J.J. (1991). Vocabulary development in the whole literacy classroom. *The Reading Teacher, 45*, 188–195.

Blanton, W.E., Pilonieta, P., & Wood, K.D. (2007). Promoting meaningful adolescent reading instruction through integrated literacy circles. In J. Lewis & G. Moorman (Eds.), *Adolescent literacy instruction: Policies and promising practices* (pp. 212–237). Newark, DE: International Reading Association.

Block, C.C., Schaller, J.L., Joy, J.A., & Gaine, P. (2002). Process-based comprehension instruction: Perspectives of four reading educators. In C.C. Block & M. Pressley (Eds.), *Comprehension instruction: Research-based best practices* (pp. 42–61). New York: Guilford.

Bogner, K., Raphael, L., & Pressley, M. (2002). How grade 1 teachers motivate literate activity by their students. *Scientific Studies of Reading, 6*(2), 135–165.

Bottomley, D.M., Henk, W.A., & Melnick, S.A. (1997/1998). Assessing children's views about themselves as writers using the Writer Self-Perception Scale. *The Reading Teacher, 51,* 286–296.

Brabham, E.G., & Villaume, S.K. (2000). Continuing conversations about literature circles. *The Reading Teacher, 54,* 278–281.

Brabham, E.G., & Villaume, S.K. (2002). Leveled text: The good news and the bad news. *The Reading Teacher, 55,* 438–441.

Brevig, L. (2006). Engaging in retrospective reflection. *The Reading Teacher, 59,* 522–530.

Brooks, J.G., & Brooks, M.G. (1993). *In search of understanding: The case for constructivist classrooms.* Alexandria, VA: Association for Supervision and Curriculum Development.

Brown, L.A. (1993). Story collages: Help for reluctant writers. *Learning, 22*(4), 22–25.

Buehl, D. (2001). *Classroom strategies for interactive learning* (2nd ed.). Newark, DE: International Reading Association.

Busching, B.A., & Slesinger, B.A. (1995). Authentic questions: What do they look like? Where do they lead? *Language Arts, 72,* 341–351.

Cambourne, B. (2002). Holistic, integrated approaches to reading and language arts instruction: The constructivist framework of an instructional theory. In A.E. Farstrup & S.J. Samuels (Eds.), *What research has to say about reading instruction* (3rd ed., pp. 25–47). Newark, DE: International Reading Association.

Ciardello, A.V. (1998). Did you ask a good question today? Alternative cognitive and metacognitive strategies. *Journal of Adolescent & Adult Literacy, 42,* 210–219.

Ciardiello, A.V. (2007). *Puzzle them first: Motivating adolescent readers with question-finding.* Newark, DE: International Reading Association.

Clay, M.M. (1991). Introducing a new storybook to young readers. *The Reading Teacher, 45,* 264–273.

Clemmons, J., Laase, L., Cooper, D., Areglado, N., & Dill, M. (1993). *Portfolios in the classroom: A teacher's sourcebook.* New York: Scholastic.

Cooper, J.D., & Kiger, N.D. (2001). *Literacy assessment: Helping teachers plan instruction.* Boston: Houghton Mifflin.

Cunningham, P. (1995). *Phonics they use: Words for reading and writing.* New York: HarperCollins.

Cunningham, P., & Allington, R. (1999). *Classrooms that work: They can all read and write* (2nd ed.). New York: Addison-Wesley.

Daniels, H. (1994). *Literature circles: Voice and choice in the student-centered classroom.* York, ME: Stenhouse.

Daniels, H. (2002). *Literature circles: Voice and choice in book clubs and reading groups* (2nd ed.). Portland, ME: Stenhouse.

Darling-Hammond, L.D., Ancess, J., & Falk, B. (1995). *Authentic assessment in action: Studies of schools and students at work.* New York: Teachers College Press.

Davey, B. (1983). Think-aloud—modeling the cognitive processes of reading comprehension. *Journal of Reading, 27,* 44–47.

Dewey, J. (1933). *How we think: A restatement of reflective thinking to the educative process.* Boston: D.C. Heath.

Dixon-Krauss, L. (1996). *Vygotsky in the classroom: Mediated literacy instruction and assessment.* White Plains, NY: Longman.

Douillard, K. (2002). Going past done: Creating time for reflection in the classroom. *Language Arts, 80*(2), 92–99.

Duffy, G.G., Roehler, L.R., Sivan, E., Rackliffe, G., Book, C., Meloth, M., et al. (1987). Effects of explaining the reasoning associated with using reading strategies. *Reading Research Quarterly, 22,* 347–368.

Duke, N. (2001, December). *A new generation of researchers looks at comprehension.* Paper presented at the 51st annual meeting of the National Reading Conference, San Antonio, TX.

Duke, N.K., & Pearson, P.D. (2002). Effective practices for developing reading comprehension. In A.E. Farstrup & S.J. Samuels (Eds.), *What research has to say about reading instruction* (3rd ed., pp. 205–242). Newark, DE: International Reading Association.

Durkin, D. (1978/1979). What classroom observations reveal about reading comprehension instruction. *Reading Research Quarterly, 14,* 481–533.

Dzaldov, B.S., & Peterson, S. (2005). Book leveling and readers. *The Reading Teacher, 59,* 222–229.

Fielding, L.G., & Pearson, P.D. (1994). Reading comprehension: What works. *Educational Leadership, 51*(5), 62–68.

Forman, E.A., & Cazden, C.B. (1994). Exploring Vygotskian perspectives in education: The cognitive value of peer interaction. In R.B. Ruddell, M.R. Ruddell, & H. Singer (Eds.), *Theoretical models and processes of reading* (4th ed., pp. 391–413). Newark, DE: International Reading Association.

Fountas, I.C., & Pinnell, G.S. (1996). *Guided reading: Good first teaching for all children*. Portsmouth, NH: Heinemann.

Fountas, I.C., & Pinnell, G.S. (2008). *Fountas and Pinnell benchmark assessment system: Grades 3–8*. Portsmouth, NH: Heinemann.

Fry, E. (1977). Fry's readability graph: Clarifications, validity, and extension to level 17. *Journal of Reading, 21*(3), 242–252.

Gambrell, L.B. (1996). Creating classroom cultures that foster reading motivation. *The Reading Teacher, 50*, 14–25.

Gambrell, L.B. (2001). *It's not either/or but more: Balancing narrative and informational text to improve reading comprehension*. Paper presented at the 46th Annual Convention of the International Reading Association, New Orleans, LA.

Gambrell, L.B. (2004). Shifts in the conversation: Teacher-led, peer-led, and computer-mediated discussions. *The Reading Teacher, 58*, 212–215.

Gambrell, L.B., Malloy, J.A., & Mazzoni, S.A. (2007). Evidence-based best practices for comprehensive literacy instruction. In L.B. Gambrell & L.M. Morrow (Eds.), *Best practices in literacy instruction* (3rd ed., pp. 11–29). New York: Guilford.

Gambrell, L.B., Palmer, B.M., Codling, R.M., & Mazzoni, S.A. (1996). Assessing motivation to read. *The Reading Teacher, 49*, 518–533.

Gaskins, I.W., Ehri, L.C., Cress, C., O'Hara, C., & Donnelly, K. (1996). Procedures for word learning: Making discoveries about words. *The Reading Teacher, 50*, 2–18.

Gibson, V., & Hasbrouck, J. (2008). *Differentiated instruction: Grouping for success*. New York: McGraw-Hill.

Gilles, C. (1998). Collaborative literacy strategies: "We don't need a circle to have a group. In K.G. Short & K.M. Pierce (Eds.), *Talking about books: Literature discussion groups in K–8 classrooms* (pp. 55–68). Portsmouth, NH: Heinemann.

Goldman, S.R., & Rakestraw, J.A. (2000). Structural aspects of constructing meaning from text. In M.L. Kamil, P.D. Pearson, & R. Barr (Eds.), *Handbook of reading research* (Vol. 3, pp. 311–335). Mahwah, NJ: Erlbaum.

Goodman, Y.M. (1997). Reading diagnosis—Qualitative or quantitiative? *The Reading Teacher, 50*, 534–538.

Goodman, Y.M., Watson, D.J., & Burke, C. (1987). *Reading miscue inventory*. Katonah, NY: Richard C. Owen.

Graves, M.F., & Watts-Taffe, S.M. (2002). The place of word consciousness in a research-based vocabulary program. In A.E. Farstrup & S.J. Samuels (Eds.), *What research has to say about reading instruction* (3rd ed., pp. 140–165). Newark, DE: International Reading Association.

Guthrie, J.T., & Alvermann, D. (Eds.). (1999). *Engaged reading: Processes, practices, and policy implications*. New York: Teachers College Press.

Guthrie, J.T., & Wigfield, A. (Eds.). (1997). *Reading engagement: Motivating readers through integrated instruction*. Newark, DE: International Reading Association.

Guthrie, J.T., Wigfield, A., Humenick, N.M., Perencevich, K.C., Taboada, A., & Barbosa, P. (2006). Influences of stimulating tasks on reading motivation and comprehension. *The Journal of Educational Research, 99*(4), 232–246.

Haggard, M.R. (1986). The vocabulary self-collection strategy: Using student interest and world knowledge to enhance vocabulary growth. *Journal of Reading, 29*, 634–642.

Hansen, J. (1998). *When learners evaluate*. Portsmouth, NH: Heinemann.

Harris, T.L., & Hodges, R.E. (Eds.). (1995). *The literacy dictionary: The vocabulary of reading and writing*. Newark, DE: International Reading Association.

Harvey, S., & Goudvis, A. (2000). *Strategies that work: Teaching comprehension to enhance understanding*. York, ME: Stenhouse.

Henk, W.A., & Melnick, S.A. (1995). The Reader Self-Perception Scale (RSPS): A new tool for measuring how children feel about themselves as readers. *The Reading Teacher, 48*, 470–482.

Hiebert, E.H. (1994). Becoming literate through authentic tasks: Evidence and adaptations. In R.B. Ruddell, M.R. Ruddell, & H. Singer (Eds.), *Theoretical models and processes of reading* (pp. 391–413). Newark, DE: International Reading Association.

Hiebert, E.H. (2006). Becoming fluent: Repeated reading with scaffolded texts. In S.J. Samuels & A.E. Farstrup (Eds.), *What research has to say about fluency instruction* (pp. 204–226). Newark, DE: International Reading Association.

Hiebert, E.H., Pearson, P.D., Taylor, B.M., Richardson, V., & Paris, S.G. (1998). *Every child a reader.* Ann Arbor, MI: Center for the Improvement of Early Reading Achievement (CIERA).

Hill, B.C., Ruptic, C.A., & Norwick, L. (1998). *Classroom based assessment.* Norwood, MA: Christopher-Gordon.

Holmes, K., Powell, S., Holmes, S., & Witt, E. (2007). Readers and book characters: Does race matter? *The Journal of Educational Research, 100*(5), 276–282.

Hoyt, L., & Ames, C. (1997). Letting the learner lead the way. *Primary Voices, 5,* 16–29.

Hunt, L.C. (1996/1997). The effect of self-selection, interest, and motivation upon independent, instructional, and frustration levels. *The Reading Teacher, 50,* 278–282.

International Reading Association. (1999). *Using multiple methods of beginning reading instruction: A position statement of the International Reading Association.* Newark, DE: Author.

International Reading Association. (2000). *Excellent reading teachers: A position statement of the International Reading Association.* Newark, DE: Author.

Johnson, D.D., & Pearson, P.D. (1984). *Teaching reading vocabulary* (2nd ed.). New York: Holt, Rinehart and Winston.

Keene, E.O., & Zimmermann, S. (2007). *Mosaic of thought: Teaching comprehension in a reader's workshop* (2nd ed.). Portsmouth, NH: Heinemann.

Ketch, A. (2005). Conversation: The comprehension connection. *The Reading Teacher, 59,* 8–13.

Kucan, L., & Beck, I.L. (2003). Inviting students to talk about expository texts: A comparison of two discourse environments and their effects on comprehension. *Reading Research and Instruction, 42,* 1–29.

Langer, J. (1981). From theory to practice: A prereading plan. *Journal of Reading, 25,* 152–156.

Lasear, D. (1991). *Seven ways of teaching: The artistry of teaching with multiple intelligences.* Palatine, IL: Skylight.

Leslie, L., & Caldwell, J.S. (2005). *Qualitative reading inventory—4* (4th ed.). Boston: Allyn & Bacon.

Lewin, L. (1998). *Great performances: Creating classroom-based assessment tasks.* Alexandria, VA: Association for Supervision and Curriculum Development.

Lipson, M.Y. (2001). *A fresh look at comprehension.* Paper presented at the Reading/Language Arts Symposium, Chicago, IL.

Lipson, M.Y., & Wixson, K.K. (2009). *Assessment and instruction of reading and writing difficulties: An interactive approach* (4th ed.). Boston: Allyn & Bacon.

Macon, J.M. (1991). *Literature response.* Paper presented at the Annual Literacy Workshop, Anaheim, CA.

Maring, G., Furman, G., & Blum-Anderson, J. (1985). Five cooperative learning strategies for mainstreamed youngsters in content area classrooms. *The Reading Teacher, 39,* 310–313.

McGinley, W., & Denner, P. (1987). Story impressions: A prereading/prewriting activity. *Journal of Reading, 31,* 248–253.

McKeown, M.G., Beck, I.L., & Worthy, M.J. (1993). Grappling with text ideas: Questioning the author. *The Reading Teacher, 46,* 560–566.

McLaughlin, E.M. (1987). QuIP: A writing strategy to improve comprehension of expository structure. *The Reading Teacher, 40,* 650–654.

McLaughlin, M. (1995). *Performance assessment: A practical guide to implementation.* Boston: Houghton Mifflin.

McLaughlin, M. (2000). Inquiry: Key to critical and creative thinking in the content areas. In M. McLaughlin & M.E. Vogt (Eds.), *Creativity and innovation in content area teaching* (pp. 31–54). Norwood, MA: Christopher-Gordon.

McLaughlin, M. (2002). Dynamic assessment. In B. Guzzetti (Ed.), *Literacy in America: An encyclopedia of history, theory, and practice.* Santa Barbara, CA: ABC-CLIO.

McLaughlin, M. (2010). *Content area reading: Teaching and learning in an age of multiple literacies.* Boston: Allyn & Bacon.

McLaughlin, M., & Allen, M.B. (2002). *Guided Comprehension: A teaching model for grades 3–8.* Newark, DE: International Reading Association.

McLaughlin, M., & Vogt, M.E. (1996). *Portfolios in teacher education.* Newark, DE: International Reading Association.

McTighe, J., & Lyman, F.T. (1988). Cueing thinking in the classroom: The promise of theory-embedded tools. *Educational Leadership, 45*(7), 18–24.

Miholic, V. (1994). An inventory to pique students' metacognitive awareness of reading strategies. *Journal of Reading, 38,* 84–86.

Minick, N. (1987). Implications of Vygotsky's theories for dynamic assessment. In Lidz, C.S. (Ed.), *Dynamic assessment: An interactional approach for evaluating learning potential* (pp. 116–140). New York: Guilford.

Morrow, L.M. (1985). Retelling stories: A strategy for improving children's comprehension, concept of story, and oral language complexity. *The Elementary School Journal, 85*(5), 647–661.

Mowery, S. (1995). *Reading and writing comprehension strategies*. Harrisburg, PA: Instructional Support Teams Publications.

National Commission on Teaching and America's Future. (1997). *Doing what matters most: Investing in quality teaching* [Online]. Available: www.tc.columbia.edu/-teachingcomm.

National Institute of Child Health and Human Development. (2000). *Report of the National Reading Panel. Teaching children to read: An evidence-based assessment of the scientific research literature on reading and its implications for reading instruction (NIH Publication No. 00–4769)*. Washington, DC: U.S. Government Printing Office.

Newmann, F.M., & Wehlage, G.G. (1993). Five standards for authentic instruction. *Educational Leadership, 50*, 8–12.

Noe, K.L., & Johnson, N.J. (1999). *Getting started with literature circles*. Norwood, MA: Christopher-Gordon.

Ogle, D. (1986). K-W-L: A teaching model that develops active reading of expository text. *The Reading Teacher, 39*, 564–570.

Ogle, D. (2000). Making it visual: A picture is worth a thousand words. In M. McLaughlin & M.E. Vogt (Eds.), *Creativity and innovation in content area teaching* (pp. 55–71). Norwood, MA: Christopher-Gordon.

Palincsar, A.S., & Brown, A.L. (1984). Reciprocal teaching of comprehension-fostering and monitoring activities. *Cognition and Instruction, 1*, 117–175.

Palincsar, A.S., & Brown, A.L. (1986). Interactive teaching to promote independent learning from text. *The Reading Teacher, 39*, 771–777.

Pearson, P.D. (2001). *Comprehension strategy instruction: An idea whose time has come again*. Paper presented at the annual meeting of the Colorado Council of the International Reading Association, Denver, CO.

Pennsylvania Department of Education. (1998). *Reading rubric for student use* [Online]. Available: www.pde.psu.edu/connections.

Peterson, R., & Eeds, M. (1990). *Grand conversations: Literature groups in action*. New York: Scholastic.

Pinciotti, P. (2001). *Book arts: The creation of beautiful books*. East Stroudsburg: East Stroudsburg University of Pennsylvania.

Pitcher, B., & Fang, Z. (2007). Can we trust levelled texts? An examination of their reliability and quality from a linguistic perspective. *Literacy, 41*(1), 43–51.

Pressley, M. (2000). What should comprehension instruction be the instruction of? In M.L. Kamil, P.B. Mosenthal, P.D. Pearson, & R. Barr (Eds.), *Handbook of reading research* (Vol. 3, pp. 545–561). Mahwah, NJ: Erlbaum.

Pressley, M. (2006, April). *What the future of reading research could be*. Paper presented at the International Reading Association Reading Research Conference, Chicago, Illinois.

Raphael, T. (1986). Teaching children Question–Answer Relationships, revisited. *The Reading Teacher, 39*, 516–522.

Raphael, T.E., Highfield, K., & Au, K.H. (2006). *QAR now: A powerful and practical framework that develops comprehension and higher-level thinking in all students*. New York: Scholastic.

Rasinski, T.V. (1999). Making and writing words using letter patterns. *Reading Online* [Online]. Available: www.readingonline.org/articles/words/rasinski_index.html.

Rasinski, T.V. (2003). *The fluent reader: Oral reading strategies for building word recognition, fluency, and comprehension*. New York: Scholastic.

Readence, J.E., Bean, T.W., & Baldwin, R. (2000). *Content area reading: An integrated approach* (7th ed.). Dubuque, IA: Kendall Hunt.

Richard-Amato, P.A. (1988). *Making it happen: Interaction in the second language classroom*. New York: Longman.

Roehler, L.R., & Duffy, G.G. (1984). Direct explanation of comprehension processes. In G.G. Duffy, L.R. Roehler, & J. Mason (Eds.), *Comprehension instruction: Perspectives and suggestions* (pp. 265–280). New York: Longman.

Rog, L.J., & Burton, W. (2001/2002). Matching texts and readers: Leveling early reading materials for assessment and instruction. *The Reading Teacher, 55*(4), 348–356.

Rosenblatt, L.M. (1978). *The reader, the text, and the poem: The transactional theory of the literary work*. Carbondale: Southern Illinois University Press.

Rosenblatt, L.M. (2002, December). *A pragmatist theoretician looks at research: Implications and questions calling for answers*. Paper presented at the 52nd annual meeting of the National Reading Conference, Miami, FL.

Ruddell, R.B. (1995). Those influential literacy teachers: Meaning negotiators and motivation builders. *The Reading Teacher, 48,* 454–463.

Ruddell, R.B. (2004). Researching the influential literacy teacher: Characteristics, beliefs, strategies, and new research directions. In R.B. Ruddell & N.J. Unrau (Eds.), *Theoretical models and processes of reading* (5th ed., pp. 979–997). Newark, DE: International Reading Association.

Samway, K.D., & Wang, G. (1996). *Literature study circles in a multicultural classroom.* York, ME: Stenhouse.

Schmitt, M.C. (1990). A questionnaire to measure children's awareness of strategic reading processes. *The Reading Teacher, 43,* 454–461.

Schon, D. (1987). *Educating the reflective practitioner.* San Francisco: Jossey-Bass.

Schwartz, R., & Raphael, T. (1985). Concept of definition: A key to improving students' vocabulary. *The Reading Teacher, 39,* 198–205.

Short, K.G., & Burke, C. (1996). Examining our beliefs and practices through inquiry. *Language Arts, 73,* 97–103.

Short, K.G., Harste, J.C., & Burke, C. (1996). *Creating classrooms for authors and inquirers.* Portsmouth, NH: Heinemann.

Sippola, A.E. (1995). K-W-L-S. *The Reading Teacher, 48,* 542–543.

Smith, F. (2005). *Reading without nonsense* (4th ed.). New York: Teachers College Press.

Snow, C.E., Burns, M.S., & Griffin P.G. (Eds.). (1998). *Preventing reading difficulties in young children.* Washington, DC: National Academy Press.

Stahl, S., & Kapinus, B. (1991). Possible sentences: Predicting word meaning to teach content area vocabulary. *The Reading Teacher, 45,* 36–43.

Stauffer, R. (1975). *Directing the reading-thinking process.* New York: Harper & Row.

Stien, D., & Beed, P.L. (2004). Bridging the gap between fiction and nonfiction in the literature circle setting. *The Reading Teacher, 57,* 512–518.

Szymusiak, K., & Sibberson, F. (2001). *Beyond leveled books: Supporting transitional readers in grades 2–5.* Portland, ME: Stenhouse.

Tierney, R.J. (1998). Literacy assessment reform: Shifting beliefs, principled possibilities and emerging practices. *The Reading Teacher, 51,* 374–390.

Tierney, R.J., & Pearson, P.D. (1994). A revisionist perspective on learning to learn from text: A framework for improving classroom practice. In R.B. Ruddell, M.R. Ruddell, & H. Singer (Eds.), *Theoretical models and processes of reading* (4th ed., pp. 514–519). Newark, DE: International Reading Association.

Tomlinson, C.A. (1999). *The differentiated classroom: Responding to the needs of all learners.* Alexandria, VA: Association for Supervision and Curriculum Development.

Tompkins, G.E. (2006). *Literacy for the 21st century: A balanced approach* (4th ed.). Upper Saddle River, NJ: Prentice Hall.

Tyner, B., & Green, S.E. (2005). *Small-group reading instruction: A differentiated teaching model for intermediate readers, grades 3–8.* Newark, DE: International Reading Association.

Vacca, R.T., & Vacca, J.L. (2008). *Content area reading: Literacy and learning across the curriculum* (9th ed.). Boston: Allyn & Bacon.

Vaughn, J., & Estes, T. (1986). *Reading and reasoning beyond the primary grades.* Boston: Allyn & Bacon.

Vogt, M.E. (2000). Active learning: Dramatic play in the content areas. In M. McLaughlin & M.E. Vogt (Eds.), *Creativity and innovation in content area teaching* (pp. 55–71). Norwood, MA: Christopher-Gordon.

Vygotsky, L.S. (1978). In M. Cole, V. John-Steiner, S. Scribner, & E. Souberman (Eds.), *Mind in society: The development of higher psychological processes.* Cambridge, MA: Harvard University Press. (Original work published 1934)

Waldo, B. (1991). Story pyramid. In J.M. Macon, D. Bewell, & M.E. Vogt (Eds.), *Responses to literature: Grades K–8* (pp. 23–24). Newark, DE: International Reading Association.

Weaver, B.M. (2000). *Leveling books K–6: Matching readers to text.* Newark, DE: International Reading Association.

Wigfield, A., & Guthrie, J.T. (1997). Relations of children's motivation for reading to the amount and breadth of their reading. *Journal of Educational Psychology, 89*(3), 420–432.

Wiggins, G., & McTighe, J. (2008). Put understanding first. *Educational Leadership, 65*(8), 36–41.

Wood, K. (1984). Probable passages: A writing strategy. *The Reading Teacher, 37,* 496–499.

Literature Cited

Adams, S. (2007). *World War II.* New York: Dorling Kindersley.

Adler, D.A. (1994). *A picture book of Jackie Robinson.* New York: Holiday House.

Adler, D.A. (2003). *Mama played baseball.* San Diego, CA: Gulliver.

Allen, T.B. (2001). *Remember Pearl Harbor: American and Japanese survivors tell their stories.* Washington, DC: National Geographic Society.

Andreae, G., & Parker-Rees, G. (2001). *Giraffes can't dance.* New York: Scholastic.

Angelou, M. (1986). *All God's children need traveling shoes.* New York: Random House.

Angelou, M. (1993). *Life doesn't frighten me.* New York: Stewart, Tabori & Chang.

Bader, B., & Harrison, N. (2008). *Who was Martin Luther King, Jr.?* New York: Grosset & Dunlap.

Bartoletti, S.C. (1996). *Growing up in coal country.* Boston: Houghton Mifflin.

Base, G. (1996). *Animalia.* New York: Penguin.

Battle-Lavert, G. (2003). *Papa's mark.* New York: Holiday House.

Berger, M., & Berger, G. (2000a). *Do penguins get frostbite? Questions and answers about polar animals.* New York: Scholastic.

Berger, M., & Berger, G. (2000b). *Do tornadoes really twist? Questions and answers about tornadoes and hurricanes.* New York: Scholastic.

Bobrick, B. (2004). *Fight for freedom: The American Revolutionary War.* New York: Atheneum.

Bolden, T. (2007). *M.L.K.: Journey of a king.* New York: Abrams.

Bramwell, M. (2001). *Ocean watch: Protecting our planet.* London: DK Books.

Bray, R.L. (1995). *Martin Luther King.* New York: Greenwillow.

Bright, M. (2002). *The encyclopedia of awesome oceans.* Brookfield, CT: Copper Beech.

Brown, D. (2004). *Odd boy out: Young Albert Einstein.* Boston: Houghton Mifflin.

Brown, M.W. (1990). *The important book.* New York: Harper & Row.

Buehner, C. (2004). *Superdog: The heart of a hero.* New York: HarperCollins.

Bunting, E. (1998). *So far from the sea.* New York: Clarion.

Burns, L.G. (2007). *Tracking trash: Flotsam, jetsam, and the science of ocean motion.* Boston: Houghton Mifflin.

Charlip, R. (1993). *Fortunately.* New York: Aladdin.

Choldenko, G. (2004). *Al Capone does my shirts.* New York: Putnam.

Clements, A. (1996). *Frindle.* New York: Simon & Schuster.

Cole, M. (2002). *Elephants.* New York: Thomson Gale.

Cronin, D. (2005). *Diary of a spider.* New York: Joanna Cotler.

DiCamillo, K. (2006). *The miraculous journey of Edward Tulane.* Cambridge, MA: Candlewick.

Douglass, F. (2004). *Narrative of the life of Frederick Douglass.* Clayton, DE: Prestwick House.

DuPrau, J. (2003). *The city of Ember.* New York: Yearling.

Engle, M. (2006). *The poet slave of Cuba: A biography of Juan Francisco Manzano.* New York: Henry Holt.

Fleischman, P. (1988). *Joyful noise: Poems for two voices.* New York: Harper & Row.

Fleischman, P. (2000). *Big talk: Poems for four voices.* Cambridge, MA: Candlewick.

Fosberry, J. (2008). *My name is not Isabella.* Union City, CA: Monkey Barrel Press.

French, V. (1998). *Whale journey.* New York: Zero to Ten Limited.

George, J.C. (2003). *Julie of the wolves.* New York: HarperCollins.

Gibbons, G. (2002). *Polar bears.* New York: Scholastic.

Giovanni, N. (2005). *Rosa.* New York: Henry Holt.

Grey, C. (2006). *Leonardo's shadow: Or, my astonishing life as Leonardo da Vinci's servant.* New York: Atheneum.

Grimes, N. (2002). *Talkin' about Bessie: The story of aviator Elizabeth Coleman.* New York: Orchard.

Howard, E.F. (2001). *Aunt Flossie's hats (and crab cakes later).* New York: Clarion.

Hughes, L. (1995). *The collected poems of Langston Hughes.* New York: Vintage.

Joel, B. (2005). *New York state of mind.* New York: Scholastic.

Judge, L. (2007). *One thousand tracings: Healing the wounds of World War II.* New York: Hyperion.

Kazlowski, S. (2008). *The last polar bear: Facing the truth of a warming world.* Seattle, WA: Mountaineers.

Kelley, T. (2002). *Pablo Picasso: Breaking all the rules.* New York: Grosset & Dunlap.

Kostecki-Shaw, J.S. (2008). *My travelin' eye.* New York: Henry Holt.

Krull, K. (2008). *Hillary Rodham Clinton: Dreams taking flight.* New York: Simon & Schuster.

L'Engle, M. (1962). *A wrinkle in time*. New York: Farrar, Straus and Giroux.

Law, I. (2008). *Savvy*. New York: Dial.

Leeds, C. (2007). *The silver cup*. New York: Penguin.

Levitt, P. (1990). *The weighty word book*. Boulder, CO: Manuscripts Ltd.

Lewis, C.S. (1951). *Prince Caspian*. New York: HarperTrophy.

Lewis, C.S. (2005). *The lion, the witch and the wardrobe*. New York: HarperCollins.

Lisandrelli, E.S. (1996). *Maya Angelou: More than a poet*. Springfield, NJ: Enslow.

Lubar, D. (2005). *Sleeping freshmen never lie*. New York: Dutton.

McPherson, J.M. (2002). *Fields of fury: The American Civil War*. New York: Atheneum.

Meyer, S. (2006). *Twilight*. New York: Little, Brown.

Murphy, C., & Haigh, J.G. (1999). *Children of the gold rush*. Boulder, CO: Roberts Rinehart.

Murray, S. (2005). *Vietnam War*. New York: Dorling Kindersley.

Noble, T.H. (2006). *The last brother: A Civil War tale*. Chelsea, MI: Sleeping Bear.

Old, W.C. (2000). *The Wright brothers: Inventors of the airplane*. Berkeley Heights, NJ: Enslow.

Osborne, M.P. (1998). *Polar bears past bedtime (Magic Tree House, no. 12)*. New York: Random House.

Osborne, M.P. (2002). *Good morning, gorillas (Magic Tree House, no. 26)*. New York: Random House.

Osborne, M.P., & Boyce, N.P. (2007). *Polar bears and the Arctic (Magic Tree House Research Guide, no. 16)*. New York: Random House.

Patterson, J. (2005). *Maximum ride: The angel experiment*. New York: Little, Brown.

Paulsen, G. (1987). *Hatchet*. New York: Simon & Schuster.

Paulsen, G. (1995). *The gorgon slayer*. New York: Dell.

Paulsen, G. (1996). *The seventh crystal*. New York: Dell.

Perlman, J. (1992). *Cinderella Penguin: Or, the little glass flipper*. New York: Viking.

Pilkey, D. (2004). *Dog breath: The horrible trouble with Hally Tosis*. New York: Scholastic.

Polacco, P. (1987). *Meteor!* New York: Philomel.

Polacco, P. (2007). *The lemonade club*. New York: Philomel.

Prelutsky, J. (1996). *A pizza the size of the sun*. New York: Greenwillow.

Rappaport, D. (2001). *Martin's big words: The life of Dr. Martin Luther King, Jr.* New York: Hyperion.

Relf, P. (2000). *A dinosaur named Sue: The story of the colossal fossil*. New York: Scholastic.

Robinson, S. (2006). Safe at home. New York: Scholastic.

Rosing, N. (2006). *The world of the polar bear*. Richmond Hill, ON: Firefly.

Rowling, J.K. (2007). *Harry Potter and the deathly hallows*. New York: Scholastic.

Shetterly, R. (2005). *Americans who tell the truth*. New York: Dutton.

Silverstein, S. (1974). *Where the sidewalk ends*. New York: HarperCollins.

Simon, S. (1979). *Animal fact/animal fable*. New York: Crown.

Simon, S. (1988). *Volcanoes*. New York: Mulberry.

Simon, S. (1991). *Earthquakes*. New York: Scholastic.

Simon, S. (2009). *Wolves*. New York: Collins.

Sonnenblick, J. (2007). *Zen and the art of faking it*. New York: Scholastic.

Spinelli, J. (1998). *Knots in my yo-yo string*. New York: Random House.

Steele, P. (1998). *The best book of mummies*. New York: Kingfisher.

Stevenson, H. (2003). *Looking at liberty*. New York: Katherine Tegen.

Taylor, B. (1992). *Rain forest*. New York: Dorling Kindersley.

Towle, W. (1993). *The real McCoy: The life of an African-American inventor*. New York: Scholastic.

Van Allsburg, C. (1984). *The mysteries of Harris Burdick*. Boston: Houghton.

Van Allsburg, C. (1990). *Just a dream*. Boston: Houghton Mifflin.

Van Allsburg, C. (2002). *Zathura*. Boston: Houghton Mifflin.

Viorst, J. (1981). *If I were in charge of the world and other worries*. New York: Atheneum.

Volavkova, H. (1993). *I never saw another butterfly: Children's drawings and poems from Terezin Concentration Camp 1942–1944*. New York: Schocken.

Walker, A. (2007). *Why war is never a good idea*. New York: HarperCollins.

Weisner, D. (1997). *Tuesday*. New York: Clarion.

Weisner, D. (1999). *Sector 7*. New York: Clarion.

Weisner, D. (2006). *Flotsam*. New York: Clarion.

Wells, R.E. (2008). *Polar bear, why is your world melting?* Morton Grove, IL: Albert Whitman.

Wise, B. (2007). *Louis Sockalexis: Native American baseball pioneer.* New York: Lee & Low.

Woodruff, E. (1992). *The summer I shrank my grandmother.* New York: Scholastic.

Woodruff, E. (1994). *The magnificent mummy maker.* New York: Scholastic.

Ziefert, H. (2001). *Murphy meets the treadmill.* Boston: Houghton Mifflin/Walter Lorraine.

Note. Page numbers followed by *f* indicate figures.

A

B

H

I